International Aspects
of Fiscal Policies

A National Bureau
of Economic Research
Conference Report

International Aspects of Fiscal Policies

Edited by   Jacob A. Frenkel

The University of Chicago Press

Chicago and London

Jacob A. Frenkel is the David Rockefeller Professor of
International Economics at the University of Chicago, Economic
Counsellor and Director of Research at the International Monetary
Fund, and a research associate of the National Bureau of Economic
Research.

The University of Chicago Press, Chicago 60637
The University of Chicago Press, Ltd., London
© 1988 by the National Bureau of Economic Research
All rights reserved. Published 1988
Printed in the United States of America
97 96 95 94 93 92 91 90 89 88   5 4 3 2 1

Library of Congress Cataloging-in-Publication Data

International aspects of fiscal policies / edited by Jacob A. Frenkel.
    p.   cm. — (A National Bureau of Economic Research conference
report)
  Bibliography: p.
  Includes indexes.
  ISBN 0-226-26251-0
  1. Fiscal policy.   2. International economic relations.
I. Frenkel, Jacob A.   II. Series: Conference report (National Bureau
of Economic Research)
HJ141.I58 1988
332′.042—dc19   87-25549
                                                                  CIP

Contents

Preface

This volume consists of papers and comments presented at a conference on International Aspects of Fiscal Policies held at the Royal Sonesta Hotel in Cambridge, Massachusetts, on December 13–14, 1985. It was sponsored and supported by the National Bureau of Economic Research as part of its research program on international studies.

The "call for papers" for the conference specified the range of topics and scope of coverage as follows:

The conference will be broad enough to accommodate a wide variety of issues relating in one way or another to international macroeconomics. Appropriate for the conference are papers dealing with the following topics: the international effects and transmission of government spending and budget deficits; fiscal policies in intertemporal macroeconomic models; the interaction between fiscal policy, the current and the capital account; fiscal policies and capital formation; the interaction between fiscal and monetary policies in an open economy; fiscal policy, exchange rates and interest rates; the role and effectiveness of fiscal policies under alternative exchange-rate regimes; fiscal policies and international capital movements; the effects of fiscal policies in industrial countries on capital flows to developing countries; fiscal policies and the international debt problem; fiscal policies and international capital markets; the role of fiscal policies in economic stabilization and liberalization programs; the interaction between fiscal policies and commercial policies; fiscal policies, structural adjustment and international competitiveness; labor-market institutions, indexation and fiscal policies; fiscal policies and exchange-rate policies; the international consistency of fiscal policies and the role of coordination. Other possible topics that can be interpreted as related to international macroeconomics will be considered. Priority will be given to empirically oriented research, but submission of theoretical papers on these topics is also welcome.

Papers will be selected on the basis of abstracts of about 500 words or, when possible, complete papers. Preference will be given to papers by younger members of the profession. Any research that will not have been published at the time of the conference may be submitted.

This call for papers was met with considerable interest. The number of submissions of papers and abstracts has been very large. In making the final selection, I have attempted to provide a representative sample of the range of research topics and of the scope of techniques used in carrying out such research. Each paper was assigned to two formal discussants whose comments are also included in this volume. As usual, the opinions expressed in this volume are those of the individual authors and discussants and do not necessarily reflect the views of the National Bureau of Economic Research.

Jacob A. Frenkel

1 An Introduction to International Aspects of Fiscal Policies

Jacob A. Frenkel

This introduction provides a reader's guide to the book. It contains a summary of each chapter and an outline of the discussants' comments.

In chapter 2, Malcolm D. Knight and Paul R. Masson apply an investment-savings framework to the analysis of the effects of fiscal changes in the United States, the Federal Republic of Germany, and Japan. They start the analysis by noting that the sharp rise in the U.S. budget deficit from 1981 to 1985, and the contemporaneous moves to fiscal restraint in Germany and Japan, constitute an important shift in the pattern of fiscal positions among the largest industrial economies. During this same period, the international economy has been characterized by three "stylized facts": the persistently high level of real interest rates in international financial markets; the sharp rise in the current account deficit of the United States and the increased surpluses of Germany and Japan; and the sustained appreciation in the real effective exchange rate of the U.S. dollar. Knight and Masson examine the extent to which the three major developments that characterize the international economy over the years 1981–85 may be related to these fiscal shifts.

Their analysis emphasizes the basic point that the fiscal changes of recent years constitute major disturbances to net saving and investment flows. Thus, following the work of Laursen and Metzler, Sachs and Wyplosz, and Frenkel and Razin, they model the overall current account in terms of intertemporal decisions regarding private saving and investment and the government fiscal deficit. Specifically, they

Jacob A. Frenkel is the David Rockefeller Professor of International Economics at the University of Chicago, Economic Counsellor and Director of Research at the International Monetary Fund, and a research associate of the National Bureau of Economic Research.

1

show that, if "full Ricardian equivalence" of government debt and taxes does not hold, then the three stylized facts referred to above are yielded by a simple neoclassical model in which two large countries borrow and lend in an integrated world capital market. The reason for this result is readily discernible. Unless changes in the stock of government debt leave private wealth unaltered, an autonomous increase in, for example, the U.S. fiscal deficit means that the United States must use more (or provide less) of the flow of net savings vis-à-vis the rest of the world, so that the world interest rate has to rise. In order for the increased flow of foreign savings to enter through the capital account, the U.S. current account must be pushed into deficit via an appreciation of the real exchange rate and a loss of international competitiveness.

Given these implications of simple neoclassical theory, several interesting empirical questions arise: Is "Ricardian equivalence" consistent with the data for major countries? If not, what fraction of the overall movements in real interest rates and exchange rates can we attribute to changes in fiscal policy as opposed to other factors? To address these questions, Knight and Masson specify and estimate an empirical model, based on simple theory, in which the determinants of both stocks of private sector assets and flows of private saving are specified so as to allow any proportion of government debt to be viewed by the private sector as part of its net wealth. Parameter estimates obtained from annual data over the period 1961–83 for the United States, Germany, and Japan suggest that, although *full* Ricardian equivalence does not hold, a substantial fraction—perhaps nearly half–of any increase in public sector saving is likely to be offset by induced declines in private saving at unchanged real interest rates.

Simulation experiments with the model are used to analyze several important policy issues. First, what is the effect of an autonomous reduction of the fiscal deficit in each of the three largest industrial countries separately? If the results for the United States are taken as an example, the simulations suggest that a permanent reduction in the fiscal deficit of 1% of U.S. capacity output produces a large decline (nearly 3 percentage points) in U.S. (and world) real interest rates and that this effect will appear quite quickly after the fiscal change is implemented. The simulations also suggest that such a fiscal change would lead to a large initial depreciation in the U.S. dollar, but its real value could be either above or below the preshock level in the long run, depending (among other things) on the degree to which the private sector regards changes in the stock of domestic government debt as part of its net wealth and on the interest responsiveness of private saving and investment. Thus the model suggests that fiscal shifts may cause the real exchange rate initially to "overshoot" the value that would be sustainable in the longer run.

It is, of course, quite clear that changes in the pattern of fiscal positions, taken in isolation, can provide only part of the explanation for the movements in real interest rates, exchange rates, and current account positions of the largest industrial economies over the period 1981–85. Relative shifts in the degree of monetary restraint were obviously important, particularly at the beginning and end of this period; cyclical effects were certainly a factor, especially in 1984, when U.S. output growth was unexpectedly rapid. These monetary and cyclical factors have intentionally been excluded from this model. Thus the question arises whether the neoclassical effects of fiscal shifts that are emphasized by the analysis account for a large proportion of the changes that actually took place or whether other factors have been predominant. The second set of simulation experiments assesses the extent to which the pattern of fiscal shifts that has been observed among the largest industrial economies since 1981 helps to explain the direction and magnitude of the net movements in interest rates and exchange rates during this period.

The simulation results suggest that, excluding cyclical and monetary effects, fiscal changes like those that occurred during the period 1981–85 might have increased world real interest rates by nearly 4 percentage points relative to what they would otherwise have been, and the U.S. dollar is also simulated to increase substantially. While fiscal shifts appear to be quite important quantitatively in the net changes in interest rates, exchange rates, and current accounts, they do not help to explain their timing. Like other models that focus on fiscal effects, the model analyzed by Knight and Masson suggests that the fiscal changes occurring from 1981 onward, if correctly anticipated, should have induced a large initial appreciation of the U.S. dollar followed by a subsequent depreciation, whereas its value rose nearly continuously from 1980 to early 1985. Part of the explanation for this difference in timing may be shifts in the degree of monetary restraint and cyclical effects that are excluded from the analysis. It may also be that the extent of the increase in the U.S. fiscal deficit during the first years of the period was consistently underestimated by market participants, leading to repeated fiscal "surprises."

In discussing Knight and Masson's paper, Olivier Blanchard and Rudiger Dornbusch address the theoretical as well as the empirical issues. Both discussants elaborate and clarify the channels of the international transmission mechanism highlighting the critical role that interest rates play in intertemporal modeling of the open economy. In this context a special emphasis should be given to the distinction between short run and long run and between transitory and permanent policies. In commenting on the empirical applications, the discussants focused on the authors' specification of the saving and the investment functions that are central to the forward-looking character of the model.

4 Jacob A. Frenkel

In the third chapter Warwick J. McKibbin and Jeffrey D. Sachs analyze the question of coordination of monetary and fiscal policies in the Organization for Economic Cooperation and Development (OECD). They note that discontent with the functioning of the world monetary system has led to many proposals for international monetary reform. These proposals range from enhanced consultations under the current regime of floating exchange rates to a regime of fixed exchange rates, as proposed by Ronald McKinnon. The authors examine the implications of several alternative monetary arrangements for fiscal policy in the world economy. In particular they focus upon two issues, first, the effects of alternative monetary arrangements on the international transmission of fiscal policy, and second, the implications of the alternative regimes for strategic aspects of fiscal policymaking.

They consider four alternative monetary regimes. The first is a floating exchange rate regime in which countries independently choose monetary and fiscal policies. The second is a dollar standard in which non-U.S. countries intervene in their domestic money markets to maintain a fixed exchange rate pegged to the U.S. dollar. The third regime is that proposed by Ronald McKinnon, in which each country intervenes in its domestic money market to maintain a fixed exchange rate with the additional constraint that the weighted sum of the money stocks remains fixed. In the fourth regime they again assume a fixed exchange rate but with the weighted sum of world money stocks no longer fixed but determined cooperatively by the countries.

McKibbin and Sachs use a static Mundell-Fleming model to derive multipliers for the international transmission of fiscal policy under each regime. They find that under a fixed exchange rate, fiscal policy can be negatively transmitted. To quantify the channels of transmission the authors use the McKibbin-Sachs Global (MSG) model, which is a general equilibrium macroeconomic simulation model of the world economy. They find that under a flexible exchange rate a fiscal expansion in one country raises output in the rest of the world, raises world interest rates, and appreciates the currency of the expanding country. Under a dollar standard, however, a fiscal expansion in the U.S. is negatively transmitted to the other regions because of an endogenous contraction of monetary policy in these regions that is necessary to stabilize their currencies. A fiscal expansion outside the United States, on the other hand, is positively transmitted to the United States since under a dollar standard the U.S. has no obligation to contract its money supply. The McKinnon regime removes this asymmetry, so that a fiscal expansion in each region is negatively transmitted to the other regions.

The second part of the chapter deals with the strategic implications of fiscal policy under the alternative monetary regimes. Again the authors use the static Mundell-Fleming model to illustrate the key issues involved. In the case of an inflation shock under a floating exchange rate, they show that each country attempts to appreciate its currency in order to reduce domestic inflation. In the symmetric Nash equilibrium, the result is no change in any exchange rate, but an inefficiently low level of output and high fiscal deficits in all countries. By imposing a fixed exchange rate (assuming symmetry of countries and shocks and an optimally chosen world money stock), McKibbin and Sachs illustrate a case where the monetary regime removes the inefficiency of policymaking, even when fiscal policies are still chosen noncooperatively.

Techniques of dynamic game theory are then applied to the MSG model in an attempt to consider the issues in a more general framework. The authors first calculate a set of cooperative policy rules under flexible exchange rates as well as rules where each country chooses its fiscal policy noncooperatively under each of the alternative regimes. They then consider the short-run response to a global inflationary shock and find that the McKinnon rule leads to an outcome close to the cooperative equilibria.

In an attempt to measure the average operating characteristics of each of the regimes when governments are choosing fiscal policy strategically, McKibbin and Sachs add stochastic shocks to the behavioral equations for aggregate demand, prices, and money in the United States and the rest of the OECD. They next calculate the stochastic steady state variances of various macroeconomic targets (e.g., output, inflation, current account) assuming that shocks are independently distributed. In this case the McKinnon rule performs poorly (in terms of higher variance of target variables) relative to the noncooperative floating regime and relative to the cooperative regime. In the cooperative regime the policy response is a form of managed exchange rates. Finally, the authors consider a case in which money velocity shocks are negatively correlated across countries. In this case, the McKinnon rule performs extremely well.

As is generally the case in the discussion of exchange regimes, McKibbon and Sachs find that the choice of the monetary system is crucially dependent upon the source and nature of the shocks hitting the world economy. In this chapter they show that the monetary regime also has important implications for the transmission of fiscal policy in the world economy and for the nature of the strategic games played by fiscal authorities. However, fixed exchange rates do not necessarily eliminate the inefficient equilibria that can occur when fiscal authorities behave noncooperatively.

In his comments on the McKibbin and Sachs chapter, William H. Branson provides a guide to the MSG model and helps to place the McKibbin-Sachs paper within the broader body of research on coordination of macroeconomic policies. He notes that the research strategy followed by McKibbin and Sachs is a simulation study that takes the empirical parameters and the institutional framework as given. Branson suggests that a useful extension would lead to the understanding of the design of institutions and regimes that offer policymakers the incentives to coordinate.

Commenting on the same paper, Robert P. Flood starts by listing some caveats concerning the simulation exercise. He then proceeds to discuss the rationale underlying the specification of the loss function used by the authors, and finally he raises some methodological issues concerning the use of the model for policy evaluation.

In the fourth chapter Willem H. Buiter uses a small analytical two-region model (the United States and the rest of the industrial world) to analyze three issues concerning international economic interdependence and macroeconomic policy coordination that have been central to recent academic and official discussions. The formal model is the two-country Mundell-Dornbusch model, with a floating exchange rate, perfect international capital mobility, rational expectations in the foreign exchange market, and sluggish adjustment of gross domestic product (GDP) deflators in the short run. The long-run properties of the model are classical: Output is at its exogenously determined capacity level; a country's inflation rate equals the proportional rate of growth of its money stock; and real competitiveness is independent of monetary policy. Expansionary fiscal policy at home and contractionary fiscal policy abroad cause a long-run real exchange rate appreciation, as do adverse shocks to domestic capacity output and positive shocks to foreign capacity output. Expansionary fiscal policy in either region and negative shocks to capacity output in either region will raise the real interest rate equally in both regions.

Most of Buiter's analysis is conducted on the assumption that the two regions have identical structures, which permits considerable simplification in the algebraic analysis and allows for a very transparent graphical description of the adjustment dynamics.

The three policy issues raised are: (1) What should be the monetary and/or fiscal response in the rest of the industrial world to a tightening of U.S. fiscal policy and what should be the U.S. monetary response? (2) What should be the monetary and/or fiscal response in the United States and in the rest of the industrial world to a "collapse of the U.S. dollar"? The paper emphasizes the importance of determining the causes of such a "hard landing" for the U.S. dollar, as the appropriate policy responses are very sensitive to this. (3) What should be the macroeconomic policy response both in the United States and in the rest of the industrial world to a disappointing real growth performance? Again the correct identification of the reason(s) for this disappointing performance is shown to be crucial.

A unilateral U.S. fiscal contraction is shown to cause a temporary slowdown of world economic activity as well as a sudden drop in the nominal and real value of the dollar. Merely preventing the nominal exchange rate from adjusting through nonsterilized foreign exchange market intervention does not reduce the magnitude of the global recession or alter the real long-run adjustment that takes place in response to the U.S. fiscal contraction. It would redistribute the unchanged global unemployment and excess capacity burden toward the United States and away from the rest of the industrial world. If the United States (but not the rest of the industrial world) sterilized its foreign exchange losses when fixing the nominal exchange rate, the effect on global and regional economic activity is ambiguous, as there now are two policy changes (contractionary U.S. fiscal policy and expansionary U.S. monetary policy) working in opposite directions. The long-run effects of these policy changes are independent of the monetary policy and the exchange rate regime. In the long run, a U.S. fiscal contraction lowers real interest rates at home and abroad and improves U.S. competitiveness.

A compensating fiscal expansion in the rest of the industrial world would permit the desired traverse to a better level of U.S. competitiveness without a global slump, but it would be inconsistent with a reduction in the global real interest rate. A combined expansionary monetary policy move in both regions can help achieve the desired improvement in U.S. competitiveness and reduction in the world real interest rate at full employment. These monetary stimuli could but need not be permanent increases in the rate of money growth. Once-off credible open market purchases raising the levels of the nominal money stocks suffice.

Buiter argues that if a sudden drop in the dollar reflects the bursting of a speculative bubble, there are no obvious monetary and fiscal policy implications. Collapses reflecting perceived changes in fundamentals do in general call for stabilization policy responses. A "direct currency substitution" shift in liquidity preference out of the dollar calls for open market sales in the United States and open market purchases in the rest of the industrial world. The adverse consequences of the emergence of a real risk premium on the return from foreign investment in the United States can be neutralized by raising the rate of taxation by the United States on interest income from abroad or by appropriate monetary and/or fiscal responses.

If a slowdown in global economic activity reflects an adverse global aggregate supply shock, demand-reducing measures are called for in both countries to avoid stagflationary consequences. If deficient private effective demand is the culprit, appropriate fiscal and/or monetary stimuli are called for.

In the final section of the chapter Buiter discusses and qualifies the activist policy conclusions derived from the formal analysis. The alleged "ineffectiveness" of anticipated (and/or correctly perceived) monetary and fiscal policy is not an obstacle, as it occurs only in a very restricted and implausible set of models. Uncertainty about the nature of the true model greatly complicates optimal policy design but does not affect the superiority, in principle, of contingent (or feedback) policy rules. Credibility problems (the reversibility of expansionary "temporary fiscal stimuli"; the ability to commit the monetary authority to a policy of not attempting to use inflationary surprises to stimulate output or amortize non-index-linked government debt in real terms) are potentially serious but have political and institutional solutions.

Commenting on Buiter's analysis, Maurice Obstfeld questions the assumptions that policymakers know precisely the nature of disturbances and that the effects of policy actions are readily predictable. Obstfeld notes that uncertainties about the nature of shocks and the effects of policies preclude sophisticated fine tuning and yield instead simple policy rules. In this regard he compares the consequences of purely floating exchange rates and fixed exchange rates, highlighting considerations of risk sharing.

Stephen J. Turnovsky's comments on Buiter's analysis deal with the specification of the model, the effects of anticipated future shocks, and strategic aspects of the analysis. Turnovsky concludes his comments by advocating the use of an alternative optimizing model. The latter extension is especially important since, as Turnovsky notes, the replacement of the postulated model by an optimizing model provides the basis for an analysis of the welfare implications of policies.

In the fifth chapter David Backus, Michael Devereux, and Douglas Purvis provide a positive theory of fiscal policy in open economies. They first note that when consumers have infinite horizons, the timing of taxes has, to a first approximation, no effect on the allocation of resources. The question arises: Why do governments appear consistently to set taxes so that both tax rates and tax revenues vary directly with current income? In answering this question, the authors argue that consumers with finite lives (and no bequest motive) provide an incentive for governments to redistribute income over time in order to smooth utility across generations. This argument for income-smoothing, made in the context of an overlapping-generations economy, has a number of implications for the dynamics of aggregate time series.

First, the government in a small, open, pure-exchange economy can exploit its access to long-term capital markets to smooth fluctuations in private agents' income streams. In this case government deficits coincide exactly with balance of trade deficits.

Second, when goods are storable, they provide an alternative method for smoothing income. In an open economy, however, consumption and investment decisions are separable; the exact identity between government deficits and trade deficits is broken, although they remain correlated.

Third, in a world composed of many economies there are no policy conflicts if all countries are small in the sense of being price-takers. The equilibrium that results when each country smooths its own income stream is efficient from a global viewpoint.

Finally, the theory implies that tests of the Ricardian equivalence theorem based on aggregate time series have no power: if the government redistributes income optimally, aggregate consumption behaves as if it were chosen by a single, infinitely-lived household.

In commenting on the Backus, Devereux, and Purvis paper, Stanley Fischer provides an intuitive explanation of the results and discusses their relevance to "real world" fiscal policy. He notes that in general the correlations among endogenous variables depend upon the underlying shocks. In this regard, Fischer points out that the analysis in the paper is especially applicable to situations in which the disturbance is a transitory productivity shock.

Commenting on the same paper, Kenneth Rogoff discusses some extensions and elaborations of the analysis. He points out that there are many plausible reasons why the Ricardian equivalence may not hold: finite lives, tax distortions, imperfect capital markets, uncertain fertility, and the like. Although many different reasons may imply that the timing of taxes "matters," they do not imply the same positive or normative conclusions. Rogoff notes that it would be worthwhile to examine the sensitivity of the main results of the paper to alternative assumptions underlying the departure from the Ricardian equivalence.

In the sixth chapter Alan C. Stockman analyzes the effects of fiscal policies in an open economy when international financial markets are well enough developed that consumers can use them to hedge against the risk of adverse changes in future government policies. When consumers choose portfolio allocations to combine risk and return in an optimal fashion, they can be interpreted as hedging against risks due to underlying disturbances to the economy. In equilibrium, both portfolio allocations and the returns on financial assets reflect these underlying disturbances.

Stockman notes that disturbances to the economy may come not only from nature (as shocks to production, population, or tastes), but also from government policies. (Alternatively, changes in government policies may be treated as endogenous responses to underlying disturbances from nature.) Optimal portfolio diversification entails hedging risk due to possible future changes in policies. Some examples of this phenomenon are common: consumers may hold real assets (such as housing) as a hedge against inflation (monetary policy), or firms engaged in international trade may hedge their assets against the prospects of exchange controls by diversifying across countries and holding less in assets with a greater risk of being controlled. Similarly, equity prices (such as prices of oil company stocks) theoretically reflect risks of changes in the corporation income tax, investment tax credits, or other taxes (such as fees on imported oil).

The effects of actual changes in government policies depend on the assets that were available to consumers and firms when their portfolio choices were made and on their expectations about the probabilities of various changes in policies. Stockman's paper, which assumes that people have rational expectations, examines the effects of fiscal policies in an open economy when there are complete international financial markets and contrasts the results with the effects of the same policies when international financial markets are more limited. These thought experiments are helpful in evaluating the impact of the rapid development of domestic and international financial markets currently taking place. The effects of government policies may be quite different in the emerging world of sophisticated asset markets than in past situations with more limited opportunities for trade in financial assets.

The first example in Stockman's paper involves a change in government spending in a large open economy (part of a two-country world) with two goods. Government expenditure is assumed to be productive in reducing real transaction costs associated with consuming the good that is exported by the domestic country, and lump-sum taxes are varied to maintain a balanced budget. Results are obtained in the neighborhood of the socially optimal level of government spending. The analysis shows that, in the absence of any international financial markets, changes in domestic government spending have indeterminate effects on international trade and domestic consumption of the importables. But the indeterminacies vanish in the presence of complete international financial markets, and the effects of a change in government spending on domestic imports may be reversed.

The second example concerns the effects of temporary changes in distortionary taxes in a simple two-period model with two countries. The domestic government is assumed to vary spending (on a public good that enters utility in an additively separable way) with changes in revenue from a tax on domestic consumption. In contrast to the results obtained when there are only limited international financial markets, a temporary increase in the consumption tax in the presence of complete asset markets reduces current domestic consumption but leaves all future prices and quantities unchanged. Complete financial markets, therefore, alter the dynamic responses of the domestic and foreign economies to changes in domestic fiscal policy. In addition, complete financial markets remove indeterminacies regarding the effect of higher domestic taxes on foreign production: domestic and foreign production move in the same direction in response to a change in domestic taxes.

The third example concerns the international effects of changes in government budget deficits brought about by changes in lump-sum taxes, in a model without Ricardian equivalence. The paper adds complete international financial markets to a two-country model of the world economy and studies the international effects of changes in deficits. When international financial markets are very limited, a deficit raises domestic wealth and aggregate demand but may reduce foreign wealth and demand. In contrast, domestic and foreign wealth must initially change in the same direction when there are complete international financial markets. In the long run, however, the results are independent of the menu of assets that may be traded.

Stockman concludes the analysis by noting that complete international financial markets alter the international effects of fiscal policies because they eliminate all income-redistribution effects of those policies. Only substitution effects and aggregate (world) wealth effects remain. Any models of fiscal policy in which income redistribution and the subsequent dynamics of asset accumulation play a major role are sensitive, therefore, to assumptions about international financial markets. The considerations in this chapter should grow in empirical relevance as international financial markets continue to develop in breadth and sophistication.

In his comments on Stockman's paper, Andrew B. Abel analyzes a simplified version of one of Stockman's models to illustrate the conditions under which international financial markets permit sharing of country-specific risk. Abel proceeds by analyzing the implications of regime changes. In this regard he illustrates Stockman's observation that the effectiveness of fiscal policy depends on the degree of availability of insurance against various changes in policy and/or policy regimes. Abel concludes his comments with an analysis of optimal domestic fiscal policies in the absence of international financial markets.

Commenting on the same paper, Patrick J. Kehoe expands on two main themes, stimulated by Stockman's paper. He explores the implications of deterministic and stochastic models for comparative-statics analysis, and he analyzes the implications of market completeness for stochastic comparative statics.

In the seventh chapter, Linda S. Kole examines the issue of international interdependencies in the context of fiscal policies. Her analysis investigates the effects of a large nation's fiscal expansion on the real exchange rate, real interest rates, and the balance of payments. Within a two-country macroeconomic model, the initial impact, dynamic adjustment path, and long-run changes associated with an increase in government spending are analyzed. It is shown that the dynamic and steady state effects of expansionary fiscal policy can be dramatically different if one relaxes the assumption that the expanding country is small relative to international capital markets. Two crucial factors in determining the economic responses to fiscal policy are shown to be the size of initial cross-country bond holdings and the degree of substitutability between domestic and foreign assets.

Kole notes that most economic analyses of fiscal policy have assumed that the country undergoing an expansion is small in the sense that it faces infinitely elastic demand for its goods and assets. In this setting, if international assets are close substitutes, a balanced budget increase in government spending causes an initial appreciation, followed by gradual depreciation and decumulation of net foreign assets through a current account deficit caused primarily by a decline in the domestic trade balance. But, if the country embarking on a balanced budget or bond-financed fiscal expansion is large enough on world capital markets to affect world interest rates, then different results may obtain. With a sufficiently large degree of international capital market integration or imperfect asset substitutability, initial appreciation may be followed by further appreciation, along with accumulation of net foreign assets mainly through persistent service account surpluses. This type of dynamic adjustment is applicable to large countries such as the United States, where the trade balance deficits resulting from a fiscal expansion may be outweighed by service account surpluses because of the associated increase in world interest rates over the short or medium run.

Using a two-country model, Kole shows that the dynamic paths of the real exchange rate and the stock of net foreign assets between the time of anticipation and occurrence of a fiscal expansion depend crucially on the degree of international asset substitutability and the size of the expanding nation relative to world capital markets. The model is also used to compare the effects of tax vs. bond finance of an increase in government spending. Simulations are performed to illustrate the different dynamic and long-run effects associated with these two financing schemes.

The chapter briefly considers the U.S. experience with large bond-financed deficits and steady real appreciation in light of the above theoretical framework. Kole notes that, given the size of the U.S. fiscal expansion, it is not particularly surprising that we have witnessed real appreciation, high real interest rates, and unprecedented current account deficits. What the author finds difficult to explain, however, is the precise magnitude of the changes and the pattern of events that occurred, especially the experience of steady appreciation along with a massive decumulation of net foreign assets that occurred from mid-1982 to the beginning of 1985. As a result, Kole concludes that other factors in addition to fiscal policy must have played a role in yielding the high world real interest rates, the strength of the dollar, and the deterioration of the U.S. external position.

Commenting on Kole's paper, Robert J. Hodrick extends the model by incorporating the monetary sector and reexamines some of the simplifying assumptions. Among the considerations advanced by Hodrick's analysis are: the role of stochastic elements, the role of sticky prices, the role of investment, capital accumulation, and the real business cycle, and the role of the Ricardian equivalence.

In commenting on the same paper, Alessandro Penati remarks on some of the properties of the consumption function used by Kole and on the wealth effects induced by exchange rate changes. He expresses skepticism about the suitability of traditional portfolio models for the analysis of the evolution of the U.S. current account and the real exchange rate during the first half of the 1980s.

In the eighth chapter, Sweder van Wijnbergen provides an empirical analysis of the interrelations among fiscal policies, trade intervention and world interest rates. He develops a general equilibrium model designed to discuss the global effects on intertemporal and intratemporal trade of various fiscal policy measures and interventions in commodity trade.

The theoretical structure suggests two tests of debt neutrality, both of which, when applied to OECD data, reject the debt neutrality hypothesis. These two tests are then incorporated in an empirical version of the theoretical model. The empirical global model has a tightly focused structure, designed around questions concerning the impact of fiscal policy measures and interventions in commodity trade on intertemporal and intratemporal trade patterns and relative prices. The global general equilibrium structure is a distinguishing feature of the model, with the real interest rate and the structure of the terms of trade resulting from global current account balance and various commodity market–clearing conditions. Another feature that sets this model apart from many other empirical macromodels is its explicit incorporation of aggregate supply considerations. At the core of the industrial countries bloc, finally, is an explicit analysis of the interaction between private and public savings.

In the applied part of the paper van Wijnbergen first presents data demonstrating that government revenues net of social security outlays have remained remarkably constant as a share of national income from 1965 right up to 1984. On the basis of this observation he believes the fiscal policy debate has focused too much on tax cuts and not enough on deficit-financed increase in government expenditure. The author then assesses the effect of this deficit-financed increase in real government expenditure on real interest rates by running a simulation with the empirical model presented earlier under the assumption of a halving of that increase in government expenditure.

The results show, first of all, that fiscal policy explains only a negligible fraction of the rapid increase in real interest rates between 1979 and 1982. But since 1982 almost all of the increase in real interest rates can be ascribed to the pressure on world savings exerted by increased fiscal expenditure and the fact that that increase was deficit-financed.

In the last section van Wijnbergen discusses various trade interventions designed to reduce fiscal deficits. He points out, and documents empirically through simulation runs, the importance of interactions between intertemporal and intratemporal trade. A tariff directed against Less Developed Countries' (LDC) exports (along the line of proposals under discussion in the U.S. Congress) is shown to cause significant deterioration in the LDC terms of trade. This in turn leads to a significant ex ante deterioration of the LDC's current account without an offsetting ex ante improvement in the OECD current account. The net result is an increase in the world interest rate to restore global current account balance, a possibility pointed out in the theoretical section. The simulation exercise demonstrates the empirical importance of this mechanism: after imposition of a 10% tariff against LDC exports, real interest rates rise a full 2 percentage points initially. They are still half a percentage point higher after five years. Protectionism directed against LDCs, therefore, not only shifts their intratemporal terms of trade unfavorably but also causes a deterioration of their intertemporal terms of trade.

In discussing van Wijnbergen's paper, Guillermo A. Calvo notes that the author assumes that taxes were transitory. Calvo claims that if a current tax cut induces expectations of a future cut in government spending then current consumption would depend positively on fiscal deficits. Accordingly, Calvo questions the robustness of the procedure employed in testing the Ricardian equivalence. In addition he indicates the desirability of a detailed theoretical specification of the assumptions regarding capital mobility and the type of assets available to portfolio holders.

Commenting on the same paper, John T. Cuddington proposes that a more refined aggregation of countries would reveal insightful effects of intra-OECD differences. He then raises several measurement issues related to "inflation-adjusted" deficit, "full employment" deficit, and the treatment of transfer payments. Cuddington believes that while the paper explains why real interest rates stayed high in the early 1980s, it does not provide an explanation of why these rates rose in the first place. For this he believes that one needs to recognize the role played by monetary policy.

In the ninth chapter, Kent P. Kimbrough provides an analysis of optimal tax policy for balance of payments objectives. He notes that much work has been done in international economics on the proper role of tax policy in open economies. One major strand of this literature deals with the optimal use of taxes to offset distortions and to achieve noneconomic objectives. The main policy prescription emerging from this literature is that in both instances the optimal policy requires directly influencing the relevant marginal rate of substitution or marginal rate of transformation. The literature on the optimum structure of taxation for attaining noneconomic objectives has focused exclusively on microeconomic goals such as a target level of output in a certain sector of the economy or target levels for imports and exports. Yet, many practical policy questions concern the use of tax policy for attaining various macroeconomic objectives. For example, the most pervasive and persistent argument for tariffs and other impediments to international trade in goods and assets is that such policies are useful devices for coping with balance of payments or trade balance difficulties. The recent large U.S. trade balance deficits and the policies suggested to remedy them attest to the fact that such protectionist sentiments are alive and well today.

With this background Kimbrough examines, from the perspective of the literature on noneconomic objectives, the optimal tax policies for achieving various balance-of-payments–related objectives. The aim is to provide a general welfare theoretic framework for studying optimal policies concerning balance of payments and other international finance–related objectives. Kimbrough considers a general equilibrium model of a monetary economy, and uses the cash-in-advance, exchange economy setup extended to a two-good, production economy. The resulting framework is used to characterize the optimal tax structure for four balance-of-payments–related objectives: a trade balance target, a wealth target, an international reserve target, and a balance of payments target.

The optimal tax policies for attaining trade balance and wealth targets are quite similar, the latter being the stock accumulated through the flows associated with the former. A key feature of the optimal tax structures for these goals is that within-period consumption and production decisions are left undistorted (i.e., marginal rates of substitution and transformation between goods at a point in time are set equal to the world relative price). In both instances the objective is optimally achieved by levying a tax on international borrowing. The intuition here is straightforward: trade balance targets and wealth targets can both be attained by an appropriate shifting of intertemporal consumption patterns. It is therefore optimal to put into place a tax structure that strikes directly at intertemporal relative prices while leaving within-period relative prices undistorted. This rules out traditional import substitution and export promotion strategies, both of which drive a wedge between domestic and world within-period relative prices, as part of the optimal tax package for achieving trade balance and wealth targets. The main difference between the optimal policies for trade balance and wealth targets is shown to be the time profile of taxes on international borrowing. Generally speaking, a sequence of trade balance targets calls for a tax on international borrowing that varies over time while a wealth target calls for a tax on international borrowing that is constant across periods. Kimbrough also points out that, as an empirical matter, from the viewpoint of the permanent income hypothesis, the enactment of such policies will result in consumption exhibiting what appears to be excess sensitivity to current income.

The optimal policies for the other two objectives that are studied by Kimbrough, an international reserve target and a balance of payments target, also have much in common with one another. In both instances the first-best policy is to devalue or cut back on domestic credit creation. This follows from the fact that, as a consequence of Ricardian equivalence, exchange rate management policies have no real effects. Hence undertaking such policies does not reduce welfare from its distortion-free level. Kimbrough notes that despite advice along these lines from economists, countries experiencing balance of payments difficulties often resort to tariffs, export subsidies, and other trade interventions. A practical question then concerns the optimal tax policy, i.e., the second-best policy, for achieving an international reserve target or a balance of payments target. With money holdings being motivated by the cash-in-advance constraint, the demand for money, whose intertemporal behavior is fundamental for the balance of payments, is simply the value of domestic output at consumer prices. Hence the optimal tax policy for building up international reserves through an improved balance of payments calls, when starting from an initial steady-state equilibrium, for a set of consumption taxes and production subsidies to increase the demand for money. Therefore, unlike the optimal policies for trade balance and wealth targets, those for international reserve and balance of payments objectives can be structured to include tariffs, export subsidies, or equivalent trade interventions that introduce a wedge between domestic and world within-period relative prices. Additionally, the optimal tax structure also calls for a supporting set of subsidies to international borrowing so as to shift consumption toward those periods when it is taxed most heavily and thereby minimize the associated welfare loss.

In commenting on Kimbrough's paper, Joshua Aizenman extends the analytical framework by allowing for departures from Ricardian assumptions. He discusses Kimbrough's methodology as well as the specification of the cash-in-advance formulation underlying the monetary sector. Aizenman casts Kimbrough's analysis in terms of the traditional analysis of commercial policies; he examines the implications of limited access to capital markets and allows for the possibilities of cost of tax collection and revenue targets.

In commenting on the same paper, Robert G. Murphy focuses on the implications of the monetary mechanisms underlying Kimbrough's analysis and identifies the circumstances under which the main results are robust with respect to alternative specifications of the monetary sector. In this regard he notes that the choice of optimal policies aimed at the overall balance-of-payments target depends critically on the specification of the monetary mechanism.

The tenth chapter, by Lawrence H. Summers, concludes the volume. This chapter focuses on tax policy and international competitiveness. The author notes that international considerations are coming to play an increasingly important role in U.S. tax policy debates. Policy discussions of tax provisions bearing on foreign investment in the United States and American investment abroad have long focused on the competitiveness question. He notes that recently general reductions in taxes on business investment have been advocated on the grounds that they will increase American competitiveness. Excessive tax burdens are frequently blamed for the poor international performance of some American industries. Indeed the President's Commission on International Competitiveness recently urged business tax relief as a major element in strategy directed at improving the trade position of the United States. Tax increases to reduce looming budget deficits are often defended on the grounds that they will reduce trade deficits.

Against this background Summers provides an analysis of the impact of tax policy on international competitiveness, stressing the crucial role of capital mobility in determining the impact of tax reforms on an economy's trading goods sector. He begins by examining theoretically the relationship between tax changes and competitiveness under the assumption of perfect international capital mobility. This common assumption of free international capital mobility leads to striking conclusions regarding the short-run impact of tax policies. Tax measures that stimulate investment but do not affect savings will inevitably lead to declines in international competitiveness as long as capital is freely mobile internationally. Measures that promote investment attract funds from abroad, leading to appreciation in the real exchange rate and a reduction in the competitiveness of domestic industry. The accounting identity holding that the current account equals the difference between national savings and national investment insures that increases in investment *ceteris paribus* will be associated with decreases in the trade balance. Conversely, tax policies that promote savings and do not have a direct impact on investment will improve trade performance.

According to Summers, these results challenge the commonly expressed view that reductions in tax burdens on business will improve competitiveness by enabling business to undertake more productivity-enhancing investments. They also raise an interesting question in political economy. Why do firms in the trading goods sector, whose competitiveness will be hurt by the capital inflows associated with investment incentives, lobby in favor of them? Consideration of this question leads naturally to an examination of the premise of free international capital mobility, which underlies the arguments in the previous paragraph. If capital is not internationally mobile, stimulus to investment will not lead to capital inflows and therefore will not be associated with trade balance deterioration. While there certainly is a large pool of internationally mobile capital, Martin Feldstein has pointed to an important puzzle raised by the hypothesis of international capital mobility. This hypothesis predicts that there should be no systematic relationship between domestic saving and investment rates so that the capital can flow freely. Yet looking across the OECD nations, there is in fact a very strong positive correlation between savings and investment rates. Over a long period of time, cumulative current account deficits or surpluses are quite small despite large variations in domestic savings rates. On a very consistent basis, high savings countries are also high investment countries while low savings countries like the United States have relatively low rates of investment.

The high correlation between domestic savings and investment rates raises difficult issues of interpretation. It can be argued that the high correlation suggests that it is likely to be impossible for tax policies to change domestic savings or investment in isolation without affecting the other quantity. Alternatively, some argue that the high correlation between domestic savings and investment rates is spurious, reflecting the impact of third factors. Yet another possibility is that capital is freely mobile across international borders but that nations consistently pursue policies which drive capital, saving, and investment into balance. These hypotheses have very different implications for international tax policies. Summers assesses the evidence on each of them and concludes that the maintained external balance hypothesis holding that national savings and investment rates are highly correlated because of policy actions by countries probably is the most important empirically.

This finding raises important questions. Given that policies to limit net capital mobility are frequently pursued, how should the effects of tax policy reforms which affect savings or investment be evaluated? Summers notes that if no other policy measures are undertaken, their effects should be analyzed under the assumption that capital is perfectly normal. Historical record suggests that current account imbalances are likely to be offset by other policy actions. Is this use of obvious relevance to the current American situation of business tax reductions, a period that has stimulated a significant amount of capital formation and drawn capital in from abroad in large quantity, but where the trade deficit is largely seen as the major problem?

In commenting on Summers's paper, Jeffrey A. Frankel reviews the statistical facts concerning the correlations between national savings and investment and comments on some of the econometric procedures adopted by Summers. He then makes the central point that such correlations do not provide useful information concerning the degree of international capital mobility. The latter should be analyzed by international comparisons among expected real rates of return.

Commenting on the same paper, Roger H. Gordon proposes an alternative model that predicts a close association between savings and investment even in the absence of government restrictions on capital mobility. Moreover, in Gordon's framework such restrictions are desirable on welfare grounds.

2   Fiscal Policies, Net Saving, and Real Exchange Rates: The United States, the Federal Republic of Germany, and Japan

Malcolm D. Knight and Paul R. Masson

2.1 Introduction

In recent years, substantial changes in the pattern of fiscal positions of major industrial countries have occurred. From 1981 to 1985, for example, the fiscal deficit of the U.S. federal government is estimated to have risen by 2.8% of the U.S. GNP, while the deficits of central governments in the Federal Republic of Germany and Japan, both of which have implemented medium-term fiscal restraint programs, declined by about 0.6% of their GNPs. A better measure of the underlying stance of policy, the fiscal impulse as a percent of GNP cumulated over the years 1981–85, shows a shift in the United States toward expansion by 3% and contractionary shifts of 1.9% in the Federal Republic of Germany and 0.8% in Japan (International Monetary Fund 1985, Appendix table 15). It is widely acknowledged that this pattern of fiscal shifts is at least one of the factors responsible for three important developments that have characterized the first five years of the present decade: the persistently high level of real interest rates in international financial markets, the rising current-account deficit of the United States and the surpluses of Japan and Germany, and the sustained appreciation in the real effective exchange rate of the U.S. dollar.

Malcolm D. Knight is Chief of the External Adjustment Division, Research Department, International Monetary Fund. This paper was completed while he was an academic visitor at the Centre for Labour Economics, London School of Economics and Political Science, in 1985–86. Paul R. Masson is a senior economist in the Research Department, International Monetary Fund.

The views expressed here are those of the authors and do not necessarily represent those of the International Monetary Fund. We are grateful to Charles Adams, Olivier Blanchard, James Boughton, Rudiger Dornbusch, Jeffrey Frankel, Charles Goodhart, and several conference participants for helpful comments; and to David Hicks for research assistance.

The purpose of this paper is to describe a very simple model that is consistent with all three of these stylized facts and to specify and estimate a somewhat more sophisticated dynamic version of the model for the United States, the Federal Republic of Germany, Japan, and a highly aggregated rest-of-the-world sector. Simulation experiments are performed with the empirical model to see the effects of shifts in fiscal policy in major industrial countries on world interest rates and on the pattern of real exchange rates and current-account balances that evolves among them after the initial policy shock.

In order to isolate the medium-term patterns that are our major interest, we abstract from the portfolio allocation decisions regarding stocks of domestic and foreign assets (Kouri and Porter 1974; Dornbusch 1975; Girton and Henderson 1977; Branson, Halttunen, and Masson 1977) and concentrate instead on the intertemporal decisions that determine flows of domestic saving and capital accumulation. Of course, in a fully articulated macromodel the determinants of both portfolio allocation and saving-investment decisions would be derived consistently from a general maximizing framework. But we emphasize the intertemporal aspect because its role in the determination of exchange rates has received less attention in the literature and because, *prima facie,* the fiscal changes referred to above are likely to have resulted in major disturbances to national saving and investment flows. Obviously, a model which concentrates on the underlying determinants of saving and investment in the largest industrial economies is unlikely to provide much insight into the causes of day-to-day or month-to-month fluctuations in market exchange rates. Nor does it indicate the effects of changes in fiscal policy in smaller countries. Nevertheless, such a model may serve to highlight how shifts in fiscal policy in the largest industrial economies influence private saving and investment behavior both at home and abroad, leading to changes in the level of world interest rates and in the pattern of real exchange rates and current-account positions that is sustainable over the medium term.

The analysis of current account and exchange rate movements in terms of saving and investment behavior has a long history in the literature, extending back to the classic work of Laursen and Metzler (1950).[1] Mundell (1963) discussed these interrelations in some detail, but his analysis was limited by the Keynesian assumption that saving responded only to movements in current income. More recently, following the supply shocks of the 1970s, a number of writers (e.g., Dornbusch and Fischer 1980, Sachs 1981) have emphasized the role of saving and investment decisions, and intertemporal choice generally, in determining the current-account positions that are sustainable over the medium term for industrial countries that can borrow or lend freely in an efficient world capital market. Svensson and Razin (1983) develop models based on a rigorous analysis of intertemporal behavior, and Sachs and Wyplosz (1984) study the effects of fiscal policy in a model that takes account of wealth accumulation and forward-looking expectations, but both of these analyses are restricted to the case of a small country facing a given world interest rate. Finally, Frenkel and Razin (1984, 1985a, 1985b) have integrated intertemporal decisions, fiscal policy, interest rates, and terms-of-trade effects in a two-country framework that yields a large number of useful insights. The empirical model described later in this paper is in the spirit of these recent contributions.

The rest of this paper is organized as follows. Section 2.2 presents a highly simplified theoretical model that illustrates how a change in fiscal policy in a large country can shift the world level of real interest rates and—via its impact on private saving and investment decisions— alter the pattern of current accounts and real exchange rates. In section 2.3 we specify and estimate a more realistic dynamic model for three major industrial countries. In this model, real exchange rates and interest rates are determined implicitly by conditions of market clearing. The model also allows for country-specific interest rates, cyclical effects, and the possible neutrality of government debt. In section 2.4 the model is closed to yield the full simultaneous system and the policy simulations are discussed. Section 2.5 provides a brief summary of the conclusions.

2.2   A Simple Model of Government Deficits, the Current-Account Balance, and the Real Exchange Rate

The starting point of our analysis is the proposition that if there is a disturbance in the domestic saving-investment balance of a large industrial country that maintains a floating exchange rate, the equilibrating mechanism will alter the international allocation of net saving.[2] For example, unless an autonomous rise in a country's fiscal deficit leads to a corresponding increase in private saving, that country will have to rely more heavily on saving from abroad (or on a reduction in the amount of domestic saving provided to the rest of the world). In order for the increased saving from abroad to enter through the capital account, the current account must be pushed into deficit. The mechanism by which the current-account deficit arises involves an appreciation of the real effective exchange rate and a loss of international competitiveness. Only in this way can the international capital transfer necessitated by the disturbance in the saving-investment balance be "effected."

This relation between the real exchange rate, the current account, and the capital account has been widely discussed in recent years. For example, Henry C. Wallich (1983) observed:

In the United States . . . we do not have a current-account deficit because we need or even want it. We have a current-account deficit mainly because we have a budget deficit. The mechanism by which the budget deficit causes the current-account deficit is straightforward. The budget deficit raises interest rates. Higher interest rates, relative to foreign rates, cause a demand for dollar assets. The demand for dollar assets drives up the dollar exchange rate. The high dollar exchange rate causes the current-account deficit. Put differently, we do not have a capital inflow because we have a current-account deficit. The causal sequence runs the other way. We have a current-account deficit because we have a capital inflow.

The purpose of this section is to derive a simple heuristic model where shifts in saving and investment, including government saving, produce the phenomenon that Wallich and others have described. For this purpose, it is convenient to use a model that does not depend on an elaborate specification of the effects of fiscal policy on the level of real income[3] and that avoids the complex issue of the effect of international interest rate differentials on exchange rates and capital flows. In addition, we assume flexibility of goods prices, so that we can ignore the effects of changes in the level of the money supply on real magnitudes. The next section, however, presents an empirical model that addresses some of these complications and is dynamic in the sense that it accounts for accumulations of asset stocks and their feedback onto saving and investment flows.

Consider a model of saving and investment behavior in a world of two large countries: the home country and the rest of the world, *ROW* (variables followed by an asterisk). All variables, including the exchange rate and the interest rate, are defined in real terms, taking the price of domestic output as the numeraire. Flow variables, such as saving, investment and fiscal deficits, are all defined as ratios of each country's level of capacity output. The notation of the model is:

ϵ The exchange rate (relative price of *ROW* output in terms of home-country output)

R The world real interest rate

S, S^* Flows of private sector saving in the home country and the rest of the world, respectively

I, I^* Private sector fixed capital formation in the home country and the rest of the world

N, N^* The current-account balance of the home country and the rest of the world, (surplus $= +$)

D, D^* Public sector fiscal deficit in the home country and the rest of the world

For any function $F(x)$, $F_x = \dfrac{\partial F}{\partial x}$

Both private investment and government fiscal deficits are financed by the issue of one-period bonds, and all bonds are viewed as perfect substitutes by private savers. To further simplify the analysis of this section, we assume that market participants expect that the current real exchange rate will persist in the future.[4] These assumptions ensure that there is a fully integrated world credit market with a single real interest rate, R.[5]

Ex ante saving and investment, expressed as ratios of capacity output, are both assumed to depend on the real interest rate. Because of adjustment costs, real private net investment exhibits lagged adjustment to an optimal capital stock, which in turn depends on the user cost of capital (Gould 1968). Saving is taken here to result from individuals' intertemporal optimization of the utility from consumption (Mussa 1976). For a given rate of time preference and expected future wage income, higher real interest rates will decrease consumption. A rise in the real interest rate, however, may either raise or lower real private saving, since current income is increased for households holding positive net claims. Hence the sign of the partial derivative of saving with respect to R is ambiguous. We impose the weaker restriction that if intended saving declines when the interest rate rises, it falls by less than intended investment.

A crucial question for the analysis of fiscal policy is the extent to which the government bonds issued to finance a fiscal deficit are viewed by the private sector as part of its net wealth. The Ricardo-Barro debt neutrality hypothesis asserts that if individuals and firms anticipate that the government will raise taxes in the future to finance the debt service on the bonds, and that they or their descendants will have to pay those taxes eventually, then there may be little or no difference between financing government spending through tax increases or bond issues (Barro 1974; Carmichael 1982). In the extreme case where individuals are fully rational, can borrow and lend in perfect capital markets, and value their descendants' consumption as highly as their own, bonds issued by the home government are not properly treated as a component of the private sector's net wealth, which will consist only of the capital stock and net claims on foreign residents. In this case a rise in the fiscal deficit (i.e., an increase in public sector dissaving) would be exactly offset by a higher flow of saving by the private sector. Holdings of bonds issued by foreign governments would still be part of wealth because the taxes to service them are levied on foreign residents.[6]

Most economists would now concede that changes in public sector saving are likely to be at least partially offset by alterations in private saving behavior. There are, however, a number of reasons for expecting that, in practice, households would not make a full offset of any change in their holdings of bonds to take account of future taxes: they may think that they can avoid these taxes, they may not value their descendants' welfare equally with their own, and they certainly face significant capital market imperfections (see Buiter and Tobin 1979 for a more complete discussion).

One way of modeling the lack of full offset is to stipulate that the private sector has a higher discount rate than the borrowing government; for instance, a fixed probability of death p will cause the private sector's discount rate to be higher than the government's by that amount (Blanchard 1985). In Blanchard's model, private consumption depends on the sum of financial wealth and the discounted present value (using discount rate $r + p$) of future wage income net of taxes. The government, on the other hand, faces an intertemporal budget constraint in which future taxes are discounted at rate r: given a path for government spending, higher initial levels of government debt must be offset by higher future taxes, discounted at rate r. This budget constraint can be used to calculate a *net* financial wealth variable, which deducts from private sector holdings of government bonds the discounted value of future taxes relevant to households alive today. If taxes and real interest rates are expected to remain constant in the future, then the proportion of government bond holdings that is considered net wealth by the private sector will be unity minus the ratio of the government discount rate to the private sector's. We will call this proportion ϕ; it should lie between zero and unit.[7] A value of $\phi < 1$ implies that the private sector only treats a corresponding fraction of its acquisition of government debt as an increment to its net worth, with the rest reflecting the present discounted value of future tax liabilities.

Measured private saving equals the private sector's total net asset accumulation, including its acquisition of government debt. Thus, total private saving S equals the change in private net wealth plus $(1 - \phi)$ times the government deficit D (i.e., the increase in the outstanding stock of government debt):

$$(1) \qquad S = S(R) + (1 - \phi)D$$

where $S(R)$ is the (interest-sensitive) component of saving that the private sector undertakes in order to accumulate wealth, and $(1 - \phi)D$ is the component reflecting the private sector's response to public sector dissaving.

It is assumed that since net exports of goods and services N (the current-account surplus) respond to the price of the home good relative to the foreign good, the home country's current account tends toward deficit when its currency appreciates in real terms (ϵ falls) and vice versa when the home currency depreciates. The response of the current account balance to the real exchange rate embodies expenditure switching by both home and foreign consumers: a rise in the relative price of domestic output leads to lower demand for home goods by both foreigners and domestic residents.[8]

Macroeconomic equilibrium in the home country occurs when *ex ante* private saving minus private domestic investment and the government's fiscal deficit equal the current-account surplus:

(2) $$S - I(R) - D = N(\epsilon).$$

Substituting (1) into (2) yields the following modification of the equilibrium condition:[9]

(3) $$S(R) - I(R) - \phi D = N(\epsilon).$$

The restrictions on the partial derivatives of the behavioral functions of equation (3) are:

$$N_\epsilon > 0 \quad I_R < 0 \quad (S_R - I_R) > 0 \quad 1 \geq \phi \geq 0.$$

An analogous saving-investment equilibrium holds for the rest of the world:

(4) $$S^*(R) - I^*(R) - \phi^* D^* = N^*(\epsilon)$$

with the restrictions

$$I_R^* < 0 \quad (S_R^* - I_R^*) > 0 \quad 1 \geq \phi^* \geq 0.$$

Equations (1) and (2) clearly do not constitute two independent conditions for macroeconomic equilibrium. This is because, in a two-country world, the home country's current-account surplus must equal the deficit of the rest of the world, so that

(5) $$N^*(\epsilon) = -N(\epsilon).$$

This identity serves to emphasize the fact, already noted above, that the partial derivative N_ϵ subsumes the responses of *both* home-country and rest-of-the-world residents to changes in international competitiveness. Finally, assuming a 'pure' float, real private capital transfers from the rest of the world to the home country (i.e., the use of foreign savings by the home country) must always equal N^*.

The simple model (3)–(5) determines three endogenous variables: the world real interest rate, R; the real exchange rate, ϵ; and the current account balance, $N = -N^*$, prevailing between the home country and the rest of the world. The only exogenous variables are the public sector fiscal deficits at home and abroad, D and D^*.

The total differential of the system (3)–(5) is:

(6) $$\begin{bmatrix} (S_R - I_R) & -N_\epsilon \\ (S_R^* - I_R^*) & N_\epsilon \end{bmatrix} \begin{bmatrix} dR \\ d\epsilon \end{bmatrix} = \begin{bmatrix} \phi dD \\ \phi^* dD^* \end{bmatrix}.$$

The determinant of the coefficient matrix, Λ, is

(7) $$\Lambda = N_\epsilon(S_R - I_R) + N_\epsilon(S_R^* - I_R^*)$$

which, given our assumptions about the partial derivatives, is unambiguously positive.

Suppose that, starting from a balanced current-account position, the government of either the home country or the foreign country increases its fiscal deficit by some amount dD. The system (6) gives the following effects on the endogenous variables:

$$
(8) \quad \frac{dR}{dD} = \frac{\phi N_\epsilon}{\Lambda} > 0 \qquad\qquad \frac{dR}{dD^*} = \frac{\phi^* N_\epsilon}{\Lambda} > 0
$$

$$
\frac{d\epsilon}{dD} = \frac{\phi(I_R^* - S_R^*)}{\Lambda} < 0 \qquad\qquad \frac{d\epsilon}{dD^*} = \frac{\phi^*(S_R - I_R)}{\Lambda} > 0
$$

$$
\frac{dN}{dD} = \frac{\phi N_\epsilon(I_R^* - S_R^*)}{\Lambda} < 0 \qquad\qquad \frac{dN}{dD^*} = \frac{\phi^* N_\epsilon(S_R - I_R)}{\Lambda} > 0
$$

Assuming that the private sector treats some fraction ($\phi > 0$) of domestic government bonds as a component of its net worth, an increase in the home country's fiscal deficit, dD, will raise the world interest rate, cause the domestic currency to appreciate in real terms, and induce a deterioration of the home country's current-account balance, financed by a transfer of capital from the rest of the world. These results have a simple intuitive rationale. When an increase in the home country's public sector budget deficit disturbs the domestic saving-investment balance, the excess demand for saving must be financed by an inflow of capital from the rest of the world. In order for this capital transfer to be affected, the home country's current account must move into deficit, and this movement is accomplished by a real appreciation of the domestic currency in the foreign exchange market. However, other things equal an increase in public sector dissaving by the home country creates an imbalance between global saving and investment, necessitating a rise in the *world* real interest rate to restore equilibrium.[10]

Analogous results hold for the case of an increase of the public sector fiscal deficit, dD^*, in the rest of the world: provided $\phi^* > 0$, a more expansionary fiscal policy in the rest of the world will also raise the world interest rate but will cause the home currency to depreciate and induce a current-account movement in the opposite direction to that referred to above.[11]

It should be reiterated, however, that these results hold for fiscal shifts in each country only if the relevant value of $\phi \neq 0$, implying that full Ricardian equivalence does not hold. In general, the value of ϕ depends, among other things, on the life expectancies of households (Blanchard 1985) and on private sector expectations about the specific types of future tax and spending measures that the government will introduce in order to achieve its desired stance of fiscal policy. Thus the values of φ may differ significantly, not only across countries but over time, as views change about likely future fiscal policies.

The implications of the preceding analysis for the world real interest rate and the real exchange rate between the two countries are illustrated in figure 2.1. In the figure, the vertical axis is the real price of the currency of the rest of the world in terms of home currency, while the horizontal axis is the world real interest rate. The *SI* curve is the locus of combinations of the interest rate and the real exchange rate which, for given public sector fiscal positions, equates the *ex ante* home-country private saving and investment balance with the *ex ante* current-account balance. This curve slopes upward on our assumption that a rise in the interest rate causes desired investment to fall relative to intended saving, leading to an improvement in the home country's current-account balance in real terms. Such an improvement requires a depreciation of the home currency (a rise in ε) to equate the *ex ante* current-account balance to the new desired pattern of saving and investment. For analogous reasons, the rest-of-the-world's saving-investment balance curve, *SI**, slopes downward in ε–R space.

The nature of the interest rate and exchange rate movements that result from an autonomous shift in one country's fiscal position will obviously depend on the responsiveness of the real interest rate and exchange rate to a disturbance in the world market for saving, or to a disequilibrium in the world goods market. Figure 2.1 illustrates the effect of an expansionary fiscal policy in the home country. An increase in the home country fiscal deficit must shift the *SI* curve to the right: at a given exchange rate and current account the increased demand for private saving can only be brought about through a rise in the real

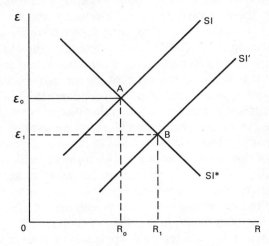

Fig. 2.1   Equilibrium real interest rate and real exchange rate

interest rate which "crowds out" private investment relative to desired saving. The new equilibrium, B, will involve a real appreciation of the home currency and a higher world interest rate. Not described is the nature of the path to equilibrium. If there is lagged adjustment of trade flows to real exchange rates, or if saving and investment flows embody gradual movements toward desired stocks of wealth and physical capital, respectively, then the dynamic adjustment path of the real interest rate to R_1 and the real exchange rate to ϵ_1 in response to a fiscal policy change are likely to be quite complex. The issue of the path of adjustment after a fiscal shock is clearly an important empirical question, and it will be considered at greater length in section 2.4.

2.3 An Empirical Model for the United States, the Federal Republic of Germany, and Japan

The model described in the preceding section is too simple to capture such real-world complications as cyclical variations (which tend to cause common movements in the historical data), or the accumulation of real and financial assets resulting from flows of net saving, investment, and payments to foreigners. A more fully specified model would also ensure that in the steady state asset supplies and demands are equilibrated and that each outstanding stock settles down to some proportion of output. Finally, to be useful as an explanation of recent developments in exchange rates and current-account balances the model should be extended to a multi-country context. In this section we specify and estimate a model that takes account of these complexities.

The empirical model includes equations for private saving, private investment, and the non-oil merchandise exports and imports of the United States, the Federal Republic of Germany, and Japan. The rest of the world is captured in a rudimentary way through an aggregate function explaining total *ROW* saving minus investment. For each of the three countries there are equations linking fiscal deficits to the increase in outstanding government debt, net investment to the change in the real capital stock, and imports and exports—via an identity equating the current balance to net merchandise exports plus the balance on services—to the change in claims on foreigners. In addition, the model implicitly determines the level of the real effective exchange rate of each of the three countries as the rate that makes the supply of private saving, minus the demands for saving from net private domestic investment and the government deficit, equal to net exports. (The real effective exchange rate of the remaining countries as a group is thus residually determined, as are its net exports.) The model retains the assumption of a single integrated world capital market with perfect substitutability among the claims on capital in the three countries.

However, to the extent that the real bilateral value of the U.S. dollar is expected to depreciate (appreciate) in terms of the deutsche mark and the yen, real interest rates in Germany and Japan will be lower (higher) than the rate in the United States by an amount equal to the expected rate of dollar depreciation (appreciation).

2.3.1 Specification

We now set out the structural equations for each country in the model. In what follows, the subscript i is incremented over the list of countries (US, GE, JA) unless otherwise noted.

Our model is similar in spirit to that of Metzler (1951) in focusing on the interaction of saving and wealth. It also resembles a more recent theoretical model (Dornbusch 1975), though it ignores portfolio balance considerations treated there. We assume that private saving adjusts to close the gap between the private sector's desired wealth and its actual holdings at the beginning of each period. Desired wealth is a function of the domestic real interest rate and permanent income (here proxied by the current level of income). Consistently with the model of the preceding section (and also to avoid problems of heteroscedasticity and spurious correlations among trended variables) we deflate real private saving and real wealth in each country by a measure of capacity output (see Appendix for the sources of data). The income variable, which appears in the equation because it helps to explain target wealth, therefore has the form of a gap between actual and capacity output (see Artus 1977 for methodology).

Given the stringency of the assumptions (discussed in the preceding section) that are required in order for autonomous shifts in public sector saving to be fully offset by induced movements in private saving, we treat the validity of Ricardo-Barro debt neutrality as essentially an empirical hypothesis to be decided by the data. Thus our empirical model retains the assumption that the private sector's perceived net wealth may include any proportion ϕ of government debt, with ϕ to be dictated by the data.

The equation for private saving in each country, i, embodies the hypothesis that the change in private sector real wealth, as a proportion of capacity output, YC_i, is equal to a fraction of the gap between the private sector's end-of-period target real wealth, W_i^*, and lagged wealth,

$$\Delta(W_i/YC_i) = a_i[W_i^*/YC_i - W_i(-1)/YC_i(-1)] \text{ where } W_i^* = W_i^*(Y_i, R_i),$$

that is, target wealth is a function of domestic real income and the domestic real interest rate. Wealth is composed of some proportion, ϕ_i, of the real stock of government debt, B_i, plus the real net capital stock K_i, and real net claims on foreigners, F_i:[12]

$$W_i = \phi_i B_i + K_i + F_i.$$

In the empirical model we retain the assumption of section 2.2 that there is a single world capital market, but we no longer impose the assumption of static expectations of the real exchange rate. The real interest rate on (private and government) bonds valued in units of U.S. output is R_{US}. However, since the real value of the U.S. dollar can change in terms of the other two currencies over the holding period, real interest rates in Germany and Japan are given by:

$$R_i = R_{US} - ERDOT_i \qquad i = GE, JA$$

where $ERDOT_i$ is the market's anticipated rate of appreciation in the real exchange rate of currency i vis-à-vis the U.S. dollar.[13]

Saving data are calculated such that private saving equals the difference between after-tax disposable income and consumption—that is, the private sector's acquisition of assets including government debt. Thus, based on the arguments of section 2.2 above, we define private saving as the change in net wealth plus $(1 - \phi)$ times the real government deficit (*DEF,* equal to ΔB):

$$S_i = \Delta W_i + (1 - \phi_i)DEF_i.$$

This is the specification of the flow of private saving that is required for consistency with the equation that defines the stock of private sector wealth (above). It emphasizes that if households are rational, not all of private saving serves the purpose of acquiring net wealth; individuals increase their saving by some fraction $(1 - \phi)$ of the government deficit in order to accumulate the assets needed to pay future taxes that will be levied by the government to service the additional debt. Combining this identity with the wealth adjustment equation given above, we obtain

$$S_i/YC_i = a_i[W_i^*/YC_i - W_i(-1)/YC_i(-1)] + (1 - \phi_i)DEF_i/YC_i$$
$$+ (n_i/(1 + n_i))W_i(-1)/YC_i(-1)$$

where n is the growth rate of capacity output. After substituting for W and W^* and grouping terms, the equation that is to be estimated takes the form

$$(9) \quad S_i/YC_i = b0_i + b1_i R_i + b2_i GAP_i + b3_i[\phi_i B_i(-1) + K_i(-1)$$
$$+ F_i(-1)]/YC_i(-1) + (1 - \phi_i)DEF_i/YC_i$$

where $b3_i = (n_i/(1 + n_i) - a_i)$ and $b0_i$, $b1_i$, and $b2_i$ depend on the W^* function as well as the speed of adjustment a_i. *GAP* is defined as the ratio of actual to capacity output, minus unity: $GAP = Y/YC - 1$.

The current-account balance, which is the difference between total national saving $(S_i - DEF_i)$ and private investment, is given by:

$$CA_i = S_i - I_i - DEF_i.$$

Combining the three preceding equations it is clear that if Ricardian equivalence holds (Barro 1974), the $\phi = 0$ and private saving increases one-for-one with the government deficit, leaving (public plus private) net national saving unchanged. In this case the current-account balance would also be unaffected by changes in fiscal policy, provided, of course, that investment (considered below) was not directly affected. In the other polar case, $\phi = 1$, all of the increased government debt would be considered part of private net wealth, so that there would be no automatic increase in private saving to allow for future tax liabilities. Here the current-account balance would change by an amount that would depend on endogenous movements in interest rates and exchange rates. Of course, our model also admits of intermediate cases where $0 < \phi < 1$; in these cases full Ricardian equivalence would not hold, and there would be some direct, but incomplete, positive response of private saving to increases in government deficits.

The investment equation assumes lagged adjustment of the real (net) capital stock divided by capacity output, where the desired capital stock depends on expected output and the domestic real interest rate, and expected output is assumed to be equal to actual output:

$$\Delta(K_i/YC_i) = c_i[K_i^*/YC_i - K_i(-1)/YC_i(-1)]$$

where $K_i^* = K_i^*(Y_i, R_i)$. The equation has the familiar accelerator property: an increase in output, relative to capacity output, tends to increase investment. We assume that the K^* function is homogeneous in Y, and we write the investment equation in terms of the output gap. After grouping terms, the estimating equation takes the form:

(10) $I_i/YC_i = f0_i + f1_iR_i + f2_iGAP_i + f3_iK_i(-1)/YC_i(-1)$

where $f3_i = (n_i/(1 + n_i) - c_i)$.

The equations that determine flows of merchandise trade are modeled in a manner similar to those of the IMF's World Trade Model (see Spencer 1984 for the latest version of that model). Non-oil merchandise export volumes, XV, are assumed to depend on foreign demand, here proxied by the foreign output gap, $GAPF = YF/YCF - 1$, and on the real effective exchange rate, $REEX$ (defined as the ratio of normalized unit labor costs in the home country to those in foreign countries, so an increase in $REEX$ indicates a real appreciation). In addition, the ratio of exports to the home country's capacity output, YC, may vary with a time trend (T), for instance, as a result of a gradual expansion of trade flows, relative to output, over the post–World War II period. Non-oil merchandise import volumes, MV, are assumed to depend on the country's output gap and its real effective exchange rate and again may exhibit a time trend when divided by capacity output. In addition, we allow for slow adjustment of volumes to activity and exchange rate changes. The estimating equations take the form:

(11) $XV_i/YC_i = g0_i + g1_iT + g2_iGAPF_i + g3_iREEX_i$
$$+ g4_iXV_i(-1)/YC_i(-1);$$

(12) $MV_i/YC_i = h0_i + h1_iT + h2_iGAP_i + h3_iREEX_i$
$$+ h4_iMV_i(-1)/YC_i(-1).$$

Finally, we also include in the model an equation explaining the aggregate saving (minus investment) of the rest of the world. In the absence of data on the fiscal positions and wealth stocks of those countries, we simply make this net saving variable (also equal to the current-account position of the rest of the world, $CAROW$) a function of their real interest rate ($RROW$), proxied by an average of rates prevailing in the United States, Germany, and Japan:

(13) $$CAROW/YCROW = k_0 + k_1 RROW$$

Equations (9)–(13) above constitute the model that is to be estimated. Data sources are described in the Appendix, but some explanation here is warranted. The basic data for saving, investment, and current-account flows are at an annual frequency and come from the national accounts of the country concerned. Data on asset stocks are cumulated from these flow data using whatever information is available concerning a benchmark stock figure. The capital stock is just the cumulation of the flow of net private real investment. As for the real value of government debt, a correction has been made to national accounts fiscal deficits for the portion of nominal interest payments that corresponds to compensation for inflation (see Jump 1980). The calculation was performed in the following fashion: nominal deficits were cumulated from a benchmark stock for government debt, and this series was deflated by the GDP deflator to get the real debt stock. The adjusted real deficit was defined as the first difference of this stock. A similar correction could be made to the published current-account balance (Sachs 1981), but it is clear that flows of investment income do not correspond solely to payments of interest on financial assets fixed in nominal terms. Also included are dividends on shares and earnings from foreign investment. In the absence of detailed data on the nature of the claims acquired, we assumed that all claims on foreigners correspond to real claims, and no correction was made to the current account. Real net claims on foreigners were simply calculated as the sum of past real current-account surpluses. Finally, real net private sector saving was calculated residually, in order to make it consistent with the other flow data, as the sum of the real current balance, real net private investment, and the corrected real government deficit. It thus embodies a partial correction for inflation, to the extent that assets acquired take the form of claims on government.

2.3.2 Estimation

The equations for each country were estimated over the longest time period for which annual data were available, in most cases from 1961 to 1983. The equations were estimated in blocks using nonlinear three-stage least squares. Since real interest rates, real exchange rates, and output gaps are endogenous to the full model, they were not treated as being predetermined in each block; instruments used included the lagged asset stocks, government deficits, and capacity output. Saving and investment equations were estimated jointly for the three countries, along with the net saving function for the rest of the world. Estimates are presented in table 2.1. Import and export equations were also estimated jointly for the three countries; results are reported in table 2.2. Joint estimation by blocks allowed appropriate restrictions, discussed below, to be imposed across equations. It also permitted efficiency gains by allowing for correlation among the shocks facing the same sectors in different countries. Joint estimation of all the equations together was not feasible owing to computer limitations.

In this preliminary analysis, two assumptions were employed in the estimation and simulation work. The saving equation for each country embodies a nonlinear restriction on the coefficients, since ϕ appears in both the definition of wealth and the coefficient applied to the budget deficit. We initially estimated ϕ separately for each country. In all three cases its value was significantly different from zero, indicating that full Ricardian equivalence (and thus debt neutrality) does not hold. Further, the unrestricted estimate yielded a lower value of ϕ for the United States (0.25) than for Germany and Japan (about 0.6).

Of course, one would expect ϕ to differ not only over time but across countries, because individual households form expectations about the specific types of tax and spending measures that their government is most likely to implement in altering its fiscal position. Each household can then form views about whether, for example, an expected reduction in public consumption is a close substitute for its own expenditure and whether it is likely to have to share the burden of future tax increases. Nevertheless, allowing ϕ to differ across countries produces some simulation results that do not have a very transparent explanation.[14] Thus our first simplification in this preliminary analysis was to constrain ϕ to have the same value in all three countries. This restriction was accepted by the data, on the basis of a likelihood ratio test, at the 2.5% level. The estimated common value of ϕ is significantly different from both zero and unity. The value of 0.43 yielded by our sample implies that neither Ricardo-Barro debt neutrality nor the full inclusion of government bonds in private net wealth is warranted on the basis of the data and is consistent with earlier estimates based on consumption

Table 2.1 **Coefficient Estimates for Investment and Saving Equations, Three-Stage Least Squares, 1966–83 (t-ratios in parentheses)**

Parameter (Associated Variable)		Saving Equations					
	b_0 (Constant)	b_1^a (R)	b_2 (GAP)	b_3 (W(−1))	ϕ^a (B,DEF)	R^2	S.E.E.
United States	.2181 (8.85)	−.0707 (1.68)	.257 (16.59)	−.0776 (6.00)	.4252 (10.32)	.629	.0076
Germany	.4274 (13.94)	−.0707 (1.68)	.157 (5.91)	−.1322 (10.40)	.4252 (10.32)	.806	.0071
Japan	.2678 (8.80)	−.0707 (1.68)	.202 (5.16)	−.0513 (3.67)	.4252 (10.32)	.153	.0127

		Investment Equations				
Parameter (Associated Variable)	f_0 (Constant)	f_1 (R)	f_2 (GAP)	f_3 (K(−1))	R^2	S.E.E.
United States	.2838 (8.41)	−.1713 (2.90)	.327 (15.84)	−.1208 (6.30)	.888	.0069
Germany	.4647 (4.58)	−.2155 (1.33)	.342 (4.94)	−.1477 (3.51)	.621	.0139
Japan	.4045 (10.97)	−.1233 (2.55)	.338 (9.09)	−.1174 (6.95)	.858	.0087

Rest-of-World Saving Minus Investment

Parameter (Associated Variable)	k_0 (Constant)	k_1 (RROW)			R^2	S.E.E.
	.00415 (9.77)	.0401 (3.06)			.249	.0014

System log likelihood: 412.6   System R^2: .969   Weighted S.E.E.: .0102

Note: For the form of the investment and saving equations, see equations (9), (10), and (13) in the text, respectively. All variables are expressed as decimal fractions or as ratios to capacity output.

[a]Constrained to the same value for all three countries.

Table 2.2 Coefficient Estimates for Export and Import Volume Equations, Three-Stage Least Squares, 1961–83 (t-ratios in parentheses)

Export Volume Equations

Parameter (Associated Variable)	g_0 (Constant)	g_1 (T)	g_2 (GAPF)	g_3 (REEX)	g_4 (XV(−1))	R^2	S.E.E.
United States	.0825 (8.67)	.00055 (2.99)	.150 (6.36)	−.03548 (7.59)	.3988 (4.35)	.974	.0025
Germany	.0227 (1.39)	.00097 (1.25)	.206 (4.86)	−.00535 [a]	.9086 (8.04)	.959	.0079
Japan	.0663 (5.28)	.00258 (4.89)	−.012 (.42)	−.05200 (4.35)	.4797 (11.62)	.971	.0047

Import Volume Equations

Parameter (Associated Variable)	h_0 (Constant)	h_1 (T)	h_2 (GAP)	h_3 (REEX)	h_4 (MV(−1))	R^2	S.E.E.
United States	.0021 (.20)	.00144 (4.49)	.058 (3.98)	.01015 (1.76)	.3940 (3.23)	.904	.0040
Germany	−.0017 (2.52)	.00180 (4.13)	.137 (3.22)	.04867 [b]	.5840 (4.80)	.955	.0068
Japan	−.0278 (1.98)	.00106 (3.74)	.085 (4.60)	.05271 (3.70)	.3384 (3.12)	.826	.0057

System log likelihood: 520.9   System R^2: .989   Weighted S.E.E.: .0055

Note: For the form of the export and import volume equations, see equations (11) and (12) in the text, respectively. All variables are expressed as decimal fractions or as ratios to capacity output, except time T which is incremented by one each year, and the real effective exchange rate which is an index number, 1980 = 1.

[a]Constrained to equal the average of the export price elasticities cited for Germany in Helliwell-Padmore 1985, in the long run.

[b]Constrained to equal the average of the import price elasticities cited for Germany in Goldstein-Khan 1985, in the long run.

functions (see Kochin 1974; Tanner 1979; Buiter and Tobin 1979; and Seater 1982).

In view of the well-known difficulties of isolating a statistically robust effect of the real interest rate on saving, our second simplification was to constrain this coefficient to be the same for the three countries. Our estimate implies a small negative response of saving to an increase in the interest rate, suggesting that the income effect slightly outweighs the substitution effect.[15] The equations for net investment are similar in the three countries; in all cases, investment responds positively to the output gap and negatively to the real interest rate. Coefficient $f3$ implies a similar, rather slow, speed of adjustment to the desired capital stock in all three countries. The effect of the real interest rate on investment is larger than that on saving; consequently, saving minus investment in each of these countries responds positvely to the interest rate. Saving minus investment in the rest of the world also responds positively to an increase in the real interest rate, proxied here as a weighted average of real rates in the United States, Germany, and Japan.

The trade volume equations (for non-oil merchandise exports and imports relative to capacity output) depend on economic activity, the country's real exchange rate, and a time trend. Historically, exports and imports have increased as a proportion of output over time, owing to the secular effects of the postwar liberalization of trade and increased specialization to exploit comparative advantage. For the three largest industrial countries there is a positive and statistically significant trend effect on trade volumes over and above the increase in capacity output. There are also significant cyclical effects, as measured by foreign and domestic gap variables in export and import equations, respectively. Export volumes respond negatively and imports positively to an appreciation of the real effective exchange rate (an increase in *REEX*). However, data for Germany had difficulty capturing these effects and we imposed a long-run elasticity of exports equal to 0.28 (at sample means), which is an average of estimates for Germany presented in Helliwell and Padmore (1985), and a long-run elasticity of exports equal to 0.79, the average of estimates for German total exports (Goldstein and Khan 1985, 1079). For both exports and imports, lags in adjustment to relative price and activity changes seem to be present.

2.4 Simulated Effects of Shifts in Fiscal Policies

In order to gauge the effects of shifts in fiscal policies on the level of world interest rates and on the pattern of current accounts and real exchange rates, we must specify the equations that close the system; the complete model is presented in table 2.3. First, we include an

Table 2.3   **Equations of the Simulation Model**

For $i = US$, Germany (GE), and Japan (JA):

(1) $S_i/YC_i = b0_i + b1_iR_i + b2_iGAP_i + b3_iW_i(-1)/YC_i(-1)$
$+ (1 - \phi_i)DEF_i/YC_i$

(2) $I_i/YC_i = f0_i + f1_iR_i + f2_iGAP_i + f3_iK_i(-1)/YC_i(-1)$

(3) $W_i = \phi_iB_i + K_i + F_i$

(4) $XV_i/YC_i = g0_i + g1_iT + g2_iGAPF_i + g3_iREEX_i + g4_iXV_i(-1)/YC_i(-1)$

(5) $MV_i/YC_i = h0_i + h1_iT + h2_iGAP_i + h3_iREEX_i + h4_iMV_i(-1)/YC_i(-1)$

(6) $K_i = K_i(-1) + I_i$

(7) $CA_i = S_i - I_i - DEF_i = XV_i - MV_i + R_i F_i(-1) + RES_i$

(8) $B_i = B_i(-1) + DEF_i$

(9) $F_i = F_i(-1) + CA_i$

(10) $LN(YC_i) = j0_i + j1_iT LN(1 + n_i) + (1 - j1_i)LN(K_i)$

For $i = GE$ and JA:

(11) $R_i = RUS - ERDOT_i$

For the rest of the world (ROW):

(12) $CAROW/YCROW = k0 + k1 \cdot RROW$

(13) $RROW = w1 RUS + w2 RGE + w3 RJA$

(14) $CAROW = -(CAUS + CAGE/e80.GE + CAJA/e80.JA)$

---

identity that relates the current account balance to non-oil merchandise exports minus non-oil merchandise imports, plus investment income (which we proxy by the real interest rate multiplied by the stock of real net foreign assets), plus other net exports of goods and services (oil trade, other services and unilateral transfers). The model solves for the values of the endogenous variables that make this definition consistent with the other way of expressing the current balance; namely, private saving minus private investment minus the government fiscal deficit. This dual identity is given as equation (7) in table 2.3. Though the model is fully simultaneous, it is useful to think of the role of the real exchange rate as making these two definitions equal, given real interest rates and output gaps in each of the countries.

We also include a simple production function relationship (equation 10) between the capital stock and capacity output. We do not include the labor force explicitly, but rather include a trend term which captures both population growth and technical progress. On the basis of sample averages for the growth of the capital stock and output, we impose a plausible number for this growth rate, 3% per year, and make it common to all countries so that we can compare steady state solutions of the model. We also arbitrarily impose a common Cobb-Douglas production function (differing, however, by a scale factor), with a share of capital equal to one third.

In the theoretical model of section 2.2, the world rate of interest brings about equality of world saving and world investment; the distribution of saving and investment between countries helps determine the real exchange rate between their currencies. The equality of world saving and investment is equivalent to the condition that current-account balances sum to zero globally, and in the simulation model we add the equation, (equation 14 in table 2.3) that enforces this condition for the United States, Japan, Germany, and the remaining countries taken as a group. In the data this condition also holds, as we have calculated residually the rest-of-world current balance, expressed in real U.S. dollar terms; $e80 \cdot GE$ and $e80 \cdot JA$ are just base-period (1980) dollar-exchange rates of the deutsche mark and the yen.

The model is classical in that saving and investment determine real interest rates; monetary influences on real interest rates and real exchange rates are intentionally neglected. Furthermore, the Keynesian adjustment mechanism, whereby shifts in savings and investment bring about changes to aggregate output, is also ignored; in simulation, the *GAP* variable is taken as exogenous to the model. As already noted, under floating exchange rates perfect substitutability between domestic and foreign assets does not require that real interest rates be equal at home and abroad: the two real rates will differ by the expected rate of change of the real exchange rate, which we call *ERDOT*. The simulation model includes the equations that relate real interest rates in Germany and Japan to that in the United States and to the expected real appreciation or depreciation of the deutsche mark or the yen relative to the dollar. In the first simulations, reported in tables 2.4 to 2.7 below, these expected rates of change, $ERDOT_i$, are treated as exogenous.

Table 2.3 summarizes the equations of the full simulation model, including all identities; the coefficients used are those given in tables 2.1 and 2.2. To begin the simulations a baseline was created with residuals added back to the equations so that the model replicated historical data. For convenience, it was further assumed that from 1983 onward the values of variables were consistent with a steady state for the economy: in the baseline, ratios of real flows and stocks divided by capacity output are constant, as are real interest rates and real exchange rates. The baseline thus embodies the simplifying assumption that the secular growth in the relative importance of international trade comes to an end, so that there is no trend growth in exports and imports relative to capacity output.

Our first set of experiments assumes independent reductions of the fiscal deficit by one percent of real capacity output in each of the three countries separately, beginning in 1985. We calculate the effects of these

Table 2.4   **Simulation of a U.S. Fiscal Deficit Reduction Equal to 1 Percent of Capacity Output, Starting in 1985: Deviations from Baseline,** as percent of baseline capacity output

Year	U.S. Variables							
	S	I	CA	K	F	W	REEX[a]	R[b]
1985	−0.48	0.24	0.28	0.24	0.28	0.10	−5.57	−1.40
1986	−0.47	0.24	0.29	0.48	0.57	0.21	−3.30	−1.51
1987	−0.46	0.24	0.30	0.71	0.85	0.32	−3.26	−1.61
1988	−0.45	0.24	0.31	0.93	1.13	0.43	−3.22	−1.71
1989	−0.45	0.24	0.31	1.14	1.41	0.55	−3.18	−1.79
1990	−0.44	0.24	0.32	1.34	1.69	0.67	−3.14	−1.88
1991	−0.44	0.24	0.32	1.54	1.96	0.79	−3.10	−1.95
1995	−0.43	0.22	0.34	2.25	3.04	1.25	−2.92	−2.20
1999	−0.43	0.21	0.36	2.82	4.06	1.67	−2.72	−2.34
Long-run	−0.48	0.13	0.39	4.48	12.96	3.32	0.52	−2.72

Year	German Variables				Japanese Variables			
	S	I	K	W	S	I	K	W
1985	0.10	0.30	0.30	0.10	0.10	0.18	0.18	0.10
1986	0.11	0.30	0.60	0.21	0.11	0.18	0.35	0.21
1987	0.12	0.30	0.87	0.33	0.12	0.18	0.52	0.32
1988	0.13	0.29	1.14	0.45	0.13	0.18	0.68	0.44
1989	0.13	0.29	1.40	0.57	0.13	0.18	0.84	0.56
1990	0.14	0.28	1.63	0.69	0.14	0.18	0.99	0.68
1991	0.14	0.27	1.86	0.81	0.14	0.18	1.14	0.80
1995	0.14	0.25	2.65	1.27	0.15	0.17	1.69	1.28
1999	0.14	0.23	3.28	1.67	0.16	0.16	2.14	1.74
Long-run	0.09	0.15	4.87	2.87	0.12	0.11	3.54	3.89

[a]Percentage deviation from baseline.
[b]Deviation from baseline, in percentage points.

hypothetical changes on the steady state of the model, using a non-dynamic version of it, as well as the dynamic path of the endogenous variables. As detailed above, the dynamics of the model arise from lagged adjustment of the capital stock and of private net wealth to their desired levels, as well as the gradual accumulation of government debt owing to the (assumed exogenous) fiscal deficit. In addition, there is slow adjustment of trade flows and the gradual accumulation of net claims on, or liabilities to, foreigners.

Tables 2.4, 2.5, and 2.6 present separate simulation results for deficit reduction programs in the United States, Germany and Japan, respectively. Stock and flow variables are scaled by capacity output so that induced changes in them can be compared directly with the autonomous shock to the fiscal deficit and so that the simulation results are comparable across countries. It should be stressed here that it is the total deficit (inclusive of interest payments) that is being changed in these simulations; thus (unless $n_i = 0$) the model does not produce explosive growth in the ratio of the debt stock to capacity output, as would be the case if the primary deficit were increased autonomously and interest payments were allowed to grow without bound. Our experiments should therefore be viewed as changing the steady-state stock of bonds, with offsetting changes to taxes, so that the government's intertemporal budget constraint is satisfied. Figure 2.2 compares the paths of real exchange rates and real interest rates in the three simulations, and figure 2.3 plots the current-account balance and private investment, both as ratios to capacity output.

A permanent fiscal deficit reduction of 1% of capacity output in the United States produces a substantial decline in U.S. real interest rates, from 6.8% in our baseline to 4.1% in the new steady state, a fall of 2.7 percentage points (table 2.4). Since interest parity holds for real interest rates in the model and expected real exchange rate changes are assumed exogenous, foreign rates (not reported) also move by the same amount. Private saving declines by almost half of the reduction in government dissaving, mainly owing to the direct offset of $(1 - \phi)$ multiplied by

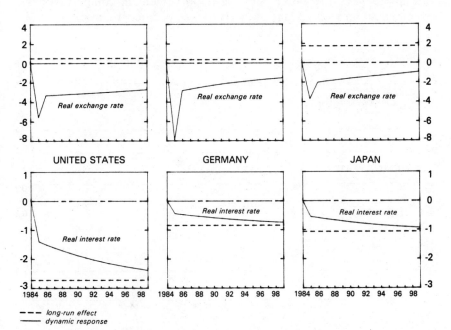

--- long-run effect
—— dynamic response

Fig. 2.2   Simulated changes in real exchange rates and real interest rates in response to a fiscal deficit reduction, starting in 1985, equal to one percent of capacity output in the country concerned

the fiscal deficit—equal to 0.57% of capacity output. The effect on saving changes over time in response to two contrary forces: as the interest rate declines, target wealth increases, raising saving, but as wealth accumulation proceeds the positive effect on saving diminishes. Investment rises strongly, both on impact and in the long run, but not by enough to offset the increase in national saving resulting from the lower fiscal deficit. Consequently, the current account improves by an amount that expands over time to about four-tenths of 1% of capacity output and the net foreign claim position of the United States eventually rises by 13% of capacity output. As a result, net wealth of the U.S. private sector increases, both in the short run and in the long run, despite a fall in the government debt component—only a fraction of which (0.43) is part of wealth.

The real effective exchange rate displays interesting dynamics (fig. 2.2). It depreciates substantially on impact—in the case of a U.S. deficit reduction, the real effective exchange rate of the dollar depreciates by almost 6%—as the increase in net national saving, to be consistent with a corresponding excess of exports over imports, requires an improvement in competitiveness of that amount. However, the real exchange rate appreciates thereafter, and the improvement in competitiveness becomes attenuated as lags in the response of import and export vol-

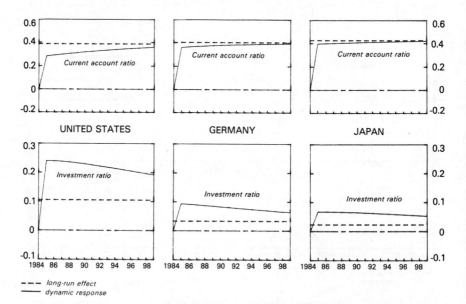

--- long-run effect
——— dynamic response

Fig. 2.3   Simulated changes in current balances and private investment as percentages of capacity output, in response to a fiscal deficit reduction, starting in 1985, equal to one percent of capacity output in the country concerned

umes work themselves out; in addition, as the U.S. accumulates claims on foreigners its investment income account also improves, requiring less of a surplus on merchandise trade. By showing that the steady-state change in the real exchange rate may actually be in a direction opposite to the impact effects given by the simple model of section 2.2, the simulation model illustrates the importance of taking into account the effects of alternative policies on the rates of wealth and capital accumulation. It also demonstrates that overshooting of real exchange rates can occur not only in response to monetary shocks in the presence of sticky prices as in Dornbusch (1976), but also as the result of real shocks when there is slow adjustment of trade flows, a point emphasized in theoretical work by Dornbusch and Fischer (1980) and Frenkel and Rodriguez (1982).

The U.S. deficit reduction has consequences for the rest of the world through changes in other countries' exchange rates and interest rates. The decline in the latter stimulates investment and increases the equilibrium capital stock in Germany and Japan (table 2.4). Private saving increases in both countries (though only slightly) and as a result the current-account balance (here equal to changes in saving minus investment, as the fiscal position has not changed) worsens in both countries in the short and medium run. The current balance of the rest of the world (not reported) also worsens as a result of the shock.

Given, among other assumptions, a common value of ϕ for the three countries, fiscal deficit reductions in Germany and Japan produce broadly similar patterns for the variables of interest (tables 2.5 and 2.6). However, effects on domestic (and world) interest rates are smaller in response to a fiscal deficit reduction equivalent to 1% of capacity output. In contrast, the current-account effects are considerably larger than for the United States, owing mainly to a smaller stimulus to private investment. It is also interesting to note that for Germany and Japan, as well as the United States, the long-run effect on the real exchange rate is the opposite of its short-run effect. In the long run the real exchange rate appreciates in response to a shift to fiscal restraint because the resulting increase in the net foreign claims position improves the services account sufficiently that it must be offset by an appreciation, in order for net foreign claims to settle down to a constant proportion of capacity output (or of wealth). It need not necessarily be the case, however, that appreciation is the long-run outcome. For a given positive net claim position, the services account will tend toward deficit as interest rates decline. Thus it is possible that the services balance will deteriorate and the real exchange rate depreciate in the long run. Obviously, the sign of this long-run effect is dependent on a number of parameters, including investment and saving elasticities, whether the country is a net creditor or debtor, and the "economic size" of the country (see Sachs and Wyplosz 1984).

Table 2.5   **Simulation of a German Fiscal Deficit Reduction Equal to One Percent of Capacity Output, Starting in 1985: Deviations from Baseline,** as percent of baseline capacity output

Year	German Variables							
	S	I	CA	K	F	W	$REEX$[a]	R[b]
1985	−0.54	0.09	0.36	0.09	0.36	0.03	−7.90	−0.43
1986	−0.54	0.09	0.37	0.18	0.72	0.07	−2.83	−0.47
1987	−0.54	0.09	0.37	0.27	1.07	0.10	−2.67	−0.50
1988	−0.54	0.09	0.37	0.35	1.41	0.14	−2.53	−0.53
1989	−0.53	0.09	0.38	0.43	1.74	0.18	−2.40	−0.56
1990	−0.53	0.09	0.38	0.50	2.07	0.21	−2.28	−0.58
1991	−0.53	0.09	0.38	0.58	2.39	0.25	−2.17	−0.60
1995	−0.53	0.08	0.39	0.82	3.61	0.40	−1.80	−0.68
1999	−0.53	0.07	0.39	1.01	4.71	0.52	−1.53	−0.74
Long-run	−0.55	0.05	0.41	1.50	13.50	0.88	0.37	−0.84

	U.S. Variables				Japanese Variables			
	S	I	K	W	S	I	K	W
1985	0.03	0.07	0.07	0.03	0.03	0.05	0.05	0.03
1986	0.03	0.07	0.15	0.06	0.03	0.05	0.11	0.06
1987	0.04	0.07	0.22	0.10	0.04	0.05	0.16	0.10
1988	0.04	0.07	0.29	0.13	0.04	0.06	0.21	0.14
1989	0.04	0.07	0.35	0.17	0.04	0.06	0.26	0.17
1990	0.04	0.07	0.42	0.21	0.04	0.06	0.31	0.21
1991	0.04	0.07	0.48	0.24	0.04	0.05	0.35	0.25
1995	0.04	0.07	0.69	0.39	0.05	0.05	0.52	0.40
1999	0.05	0.07	0.87	0.52	0.05	0.05	0.66	0.54
Long-run	0.03	0.04	1.38	1.03	0.04	0.03	1.09	1.20

[a]Percentage deviation from baseline.
[b]Deviation from baseline, in percentage points.

In addition to simulating the effects of hypothetical fiscal deficit reductions that begin in 1985, it is also of interest to see the extent to which shifts in fiscal positions in the three largest industrial economies since 1980 help to explain the interest rate and exchange rate changes that have occurred since then. Our model is intentionally an incomplete description of the forces at work—monetary policy is not included explicitly, nor are Keynesian output effects. Thus this simulation may help to isolate and quantify the importance of medium-term saving and investment behavior, relative to these other factors, in explaining recent history.

The issue of how much of the dollar's strength can be attributed to fiscal policy shifts, and the extent to which such fiscal changes also explain high real interest rates both in the United States and elsewhere, has been addressed in several recent papers. Blanchard and Summers

Table 2.6   **Simulation of a Japanese Fiscal Deficit Reduction Equal to One Percent of Capacity Output, Starting in 1985: Deviations from Baseline,** as percent of baseline capacity output

Year	Japanese Variables							
	S	I	CA	K	F	W	$REEX$[a]	R[b]
1985	−0.54	0.07	0.40	0.07	0.40	0.04	−3.31	−0.55
1986	−0.53	0.07	0.40	0.14	0.78	0.08	−2.02	−0.59
1987	−0.53	0.07	0.40	0.20	1.16	0.13	−1.91	−0.63
1988	−0.53	0.07	0.40	0.27	1.53	0.17	−1.81	−0.67
1989	−0.52	0.07	0.41	0.33	1.89	0.22	−1.72	−0.70
1990	−0.52	0.07	0.41	0.45	2.25	0.26	−1.63	−0.73
1991	−0.52	0.07	0.41	0.50	2.59	0.31	−1.54	−0.76
1995	−0.52	0.07	0.42	0.66	3.89	0.50	−1.22	−0.86
1999	−0.51	0.06	0.42	0.83	5.07	0.68	−0.93	−0.93
Long-run	−0.53	0.04	0.43	1.38	14.31	1.51	1.75	−1.06

	U.S. Variables				German Variables			
	S	I	K	W	S	I	K	W
1985	0.04	0.09	0.09	0.04	0.04	0.12	0.12	0.04
1986	0.04	0.09	0.19	0.08	0.04	0.12	0.23	0.08
1987	0.05	0.09	0.28	0.12	0.05	0.12	0.34	0.13
1988	0.05	0.09	0.36	0.17	0.05	0.11	0.44	0.17
1989	0.05	0.09	0.44	0.21	0.05	0.11	0.54	0.22
1990	0.05	0.09	0.53	0.26	0.05	0.11	1.64	0.27
1991	0.05	0.09	0.60	0.31	0.05	0.11	1.73	0.32
1995	0.06	0.09	0.88	0.49	0.06	0.10	1.03	0.54
1999	0.06	0.08	1.10	0.65	0.05	0.09	1.28	0.65
Long-run	0.04	0.05	1.75	1.29	0.03	0.06	1.90	1.12

[a]Percentage deviation from baseline.
[b]Deviation from baseline, in percentage points.

(1984) consider a number of explanations for high real interest rates, among them fiscal deficits. They argue that even though the U.S. deficit shows an increase of 3.9 percentage points of GNP over the period 1978–85,[16] fiscal contraction in other countries implies an increase of only 0.8 percentage points for the six largest OECD countries (Blanchard and Summers 1984, 298). Adjusting deficits for inflation and for cyclical position and allowing for anticipated future deficits leads them to conclude: "On balance, therefore, we find no evidence that fiscal policy in the OECD as a whole is responsible, through its effect on saving, for high long real rates" (Blanchard and Summers 1984, 302).

Another recent paper examines the consequences of the "Mundell-Reagan mix of fiscal expansion and monetary contraction" (Sachs 1985, 119), in particular its effect on the U.S. dollar. Simulations of a small global macroeconomic model, as well as other evidence presented by

Sachs, tends to support the view that the U.S. monetary/fiscal policy mix—even accompanied by fiscal contraction in the rest of the OECD—goes a long way toward explaining developments in financial and exchange markets in the last few years. The model simulation assumes "a sustained U.S. debt-financed fiscal expansion of 4 percent of GNP; a sustained ROECD [rest of the OECD area] fiscal contraction of 2 percent of ROECD GNP; a substantial tightening of U.S. monetary policy; and no change in ROECD monetary policy. . . . The dollar appreciates by 39.4 percent relative to the ECU, and U.S. short-term real interest rates rise by 8.0 percentage points relative to abroad" (Sachs 1985, 174).

One reason for the difference in the conclusions of these two papers is clearly disagreement concerning the extent of shifts in the stance of fiscal policy—both the stance of current policy and that of expected future policy. We will not attempt to shed any light on that particular issue. Rather we will see the extent to which our model corroborates the results obtained by Sachs. It should be stressed again that our model is classical in its foundations and does not include either the output effects obtained by Sachs or the effects of the monetary contraction in the United States that Sachs assumes.

Table 2.7 presents simulation results for a combined shift in fiscal policy toward expansion in the United States and contraction in Japan and Germany. For simplicity, these changes are assumed to be implemented in their entirety in 1981. No attempt is made here to capture the gradual shifts in fiscal stance that have actually occurred since 1981 (International Monetary Fund 1985, Appendix table 15), nor is the question addressed as to whether the gradual changes that did occur were fully anticipated in 1981 or subsequently. Rather, the goal is merely to gauge whether the direction and magnitude of changes predicted by the model are consistent with average historical experience since the beginning of the decade.

It can be seen that the simulation results in table 2.7 are broadly consistent with those of Sachs and with historical experience, though they differ in a number of details. First, the size of the simulated real appreciation of the dollar is 25%. This compares with an actual appreciation of about 57% from the dollar's trough in 1980 to the peak of early 1985 (International Monetary Fund 1985, 8). Alternatively, if the dollar's real value during 1985 is compared to its average value for the decade 1974–83, the actual net appreciation is 33%. The simulated appreciation is also considerably less than that of Sachs, which is not surprising since it does not account for a tightening of U.S. monetary policy. As in Sachs, the simulated path involves a large initial overshoot and then a gradual decline, whereas the U.S. dollar appreciated nearly continuously from 1980 to early in 1985.

Table 2.7   **Simulation of a U.S. Fiscal Expansion Equal to Four Percent of Capacity Output, and German and Japanese Fiscal Contraction Equal to Two Percent of Capacity Output, All Occurring in 1981: Deviations from Baseline,** as percent of baseline capacity output

Country/ date	DEF	S	I	CA	REER[a]	R[b]
United States						
1981	4.00	2.04	−0.63	−1.33	24.4	3.66
1982	4.00	2.01	−0.63	−1.36	12.9	3.94
1983	4.00	1.99	−0.63	−1.38	11.7	4.21
1984	4.00	1.98	−0.63	−1.39	10.4	4.46
1985	4.00	1.96	−0.62	−1.41	9.2	4.70
Germany						
1981	−2.00	−1.42	−0.79	1.38	−26.0	3.66
1982	−2.00	−1.44	−0.78	1.33	−6.7	3.94
1983	−2.00	−1.47	−0.77	1.30	−5.2	4.21
1984	−2.00	−1.49	−0.76	1.27	−3.9	4.46
1985	−2.00	−1.50	−0.74	1.24	−2.6	4.70
Japan						
1981	−2.00	−1.42	−0.46	1.04	−8.0	3.66
1982	−2.00	−1.44	−0.46	1.02	−3.5	3.94
1983	−2.00	−1.46	−0.47	1.01	−2.8	4.21
1984	−2.00	−1.48	−0.47	0.99	−2.0	4.46
1985	−2.00	−1.49	−0.47	0.98	−1.4	4.70

[a]Percentage deviation from baseline.
[b]Deviation from baseline, in percentage points.

Second, the extent of the simulated rise in real interst rates—initially almost 4 percentage points and growing to almost 5% after five years—compares to an increase of about 8 percentage points that was observed in the United States in 1981 (International Monetary Fund 1985, 18); the rise in other countries has been closer to our figures, however. All in all, if one accepts the size of the fiscal shifts assumed by the simulation, then the view that fiscal policy changes help to explain the direction and rough order of magnitude of the net movements in real interest rates in the 1980s receives strong support.

Finally, the simulation results are consistent with some—but not all—of the broad patterns of saving and investment flows among major industrial countries in recent years. Our assumed fiscal shifts produce a substantial worsening in the model—by almost 1.5% of capacity output—in the U.S. current-account balance, a similar improvement in the German position, and an improvement of the Japanese position by 1%. These changes in fact understate the shifts in current account positions that have occurred since 1981 for the United States and Japan: from a position of near balance in that year, the United States moved to a current-account deficit of almost 4% of GNP by 1985, and Japan to a surplus of a like amount. The model does not capture other changes that are important here; in particular, it does not take account of the impact of tax changes in the United States that helped to stimulate investment, or of the possibility of a general improvement in the productivity of U.S. enterprises. Nor does it allow for possible effects of financial liberalization in Japan on saving and on capital outflows. The estimation residuals give some indication of the importance of these omitted factors, at least until the end of the sample period in 1983. For 1983, the residuals are in fact not unusually large, except for Japanese private saving, which is underpredicted by about one-half of 1% of capacity output. It is not the case that U.S. investment is underpredicted, as might occur if either tax changes or a general improvement in expected productivity since 1981 have provided an unusual stimulus to investment. In fact, our equation slightly overpredicts U.S. investment in 1983, but by a negligible amount, 0.01% of capacity output. In contrast, we underpredict both German and Japanese investment in that year.

We have until now assumed in the simulations that expectations of future exchange rate changes are not affected by the change in fiscal policies, despite the fact that the U.S. dollar depreciates continually from the second year of the simulation onward. In addition, we have not taken account of the fact that changes in real interest rates and exchange rates give rise to valuation effects on wealth. In order to examine the importance of these two assumptions, we perform two additional simulations. In the first, we assume that government debt takes the form of consols and that net foreign claims are in foreign currencies; furthermore, households are assumed to revalue their beginning-of-period stocks of these assets fully to reflect current values of the real interest rate R and real exchange rate $REEX$. In particular, lagged wealth in equation (1) of table 2.3 (the term multiplied by $b3_i$ and divided by YC_i) is now calculated as

$$\phi_i[R_i(-1)/R_i]B_i(-1) + K_i(-1) + [REEX_i(-1)/REEX_i]F_i(-1).$$

Equations (8) and (9) are similarly modified. In the second additional simulation, perfect foresight is imposed on both exchange rate and interest rate expectations. Interest rate expectations appear in the version of the model with valuation effects because the bond rate is now assumed to be the yield on a perpetual bond, while the expected exchange rate in the interest parity condition, equation (11) of table 2.3, is for next period's rate. We therefore add an arbitrage condition implying that holding-period yields on long-term interest rates, R, equal those on one-period bonds, say RS:

$$R_i - R_i(+1)/R_i = RS_i.$$

The exchange rate expectations that appear in the interest parity condition are for bilateral exchange rates against the U.S. dollar. This version of the model therefore must also contain equations relating real *effective* exchange rate movements to the real *bilateral* rates of the yen, the deutsche mark, and the "rest-of-world" currency against the U.S. dollar, using the weights that define the real effective exchange rate indexes. The effective exchange rate for the rest-of-the-world sector has been assumed constant in the calculation of the *ROW* interest rate, but its bilateral rate does move against the dollar.

The results of these additional simulations are compared in figure 2.4 to the static expectations results without valuation effects of table 2.7. It can be seen that though interest rate patterns are considerably different, the U.S. real effective exchange rate has substantially the same path, after a somewhat smaller initial appreciation of 22%. Valuation effects reduce the size of the interest rate response to an increase in the fiscal deficit because they reduce initial wealth, thus creating an incentive for the private sector to increase saving. Making endogenous the expectations of real exchange rate movements drives a wedge between U.S. and foreign rates, allowing initial effects to reflect national saving and investment movements: U.S. rates rise more, while in Germany and Japan, where there is a fiscal contraction, real interest rates rise much less than in the static expectations case with valuation effects. The ultimate effects in our model will be the same under static and rational expectations, and with and without valuation effects, since in all three cases real exchange rates and real interest rates eventually settle down to constant levels, and hence interest rates in the three countries must rise by the same amount in the long run.

In summary, adding valuation effects and rational exchange rate expectations to the model does not change the orders of magnitude of the simulated changes in interest rates. Furthermore, our conclusions concerning the size of the exchange rate movements induced by fiscal policy shifts are invariant to the expectations alternatives considered here. Whether static or rational expectations are assumed, autonomous shifts reflecting the size (but not the timing) of fiscal expansion in the United States since 1980 and restraint in Germany and Japan are simulated to result in strong initial upward pressure on the real value of the U.S. dollar.

The timing of exchange rate movements, in response to a simulated fiscal shock, is similar in all these simulations; it involves an initial overshoot, rather than the gradual rise of the dollar against other major currencies that has occurred since 1980. It is worth noting that if we had assumed a more gradual (and realistic) change in the stance of fiscal policies spread out over 1981–85, instead of making the entire shift occur in the first year, the simulated path of the U.S. dollar would

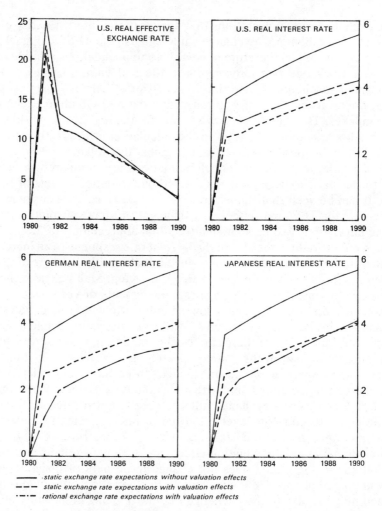

Fig. 2.4   Simulated changes in the U.S. real exchange rate and in real interest rates in response to a U.S. fiscal expansion and a German and Japanese fiscal contraction occurring in 1981: deviation from baseline

have more closely matched the persistent appreciation that actually took place over this period. A number of other factors—particularly shifts in monetary policy and in relative cyclical positions—have also been important determinants of the timing of the interest rate and exchange rate changes. Nevertheless, the basic conclusion of this simulation is that a shift in the pattern of fiscal positions of the magnitude that has actually occurred among the largest industrial countries is a major factor responsible for the net size of the interest and exchange rate changes that took place among them during the first half of this decade.

2.5 Summary and Conclusions

In order to order a comprehensive explanation of the relation between the real exchange rate and the balance of payments, it is necessary to evaluate three interrelated mechanisms: the effect of changes
in competitiveness on the current account; the impact of shifts in interest rates, expectations, and other factors on international asset portfolios; and the effect of autonomous changes in the saving-investment
balance on the level of desired capital transfers among countries. Both
the qualitative and quantitative aspects of the first mechanism have
been thoroughly investigated over the last 20 years and are well understood. The theoretical aspects of the second mechanism have been
analyzed extensively since the mid-1970s, with the development of
portfolio balance models of exchange rate determination. Although the
problems of specifying the determinants of exchange rate expectations
have led to intractable empirical difficulties, these models have provided many important insights into the process of exchange rate determination. The purpose of this paper has been to suggest that the
final mechanism, saving-investment shifts, may also yield important
insights into the behavior of real exchange rates, particularly at times
that are dominated by major autonomous disturbances in the medium-
term flows of national saving and investment, or in preferences regarding net international capital transfers. A number of points are worth
noting in the context of this argument.

First, as section 2.2 has served to show, the theoretical underpinnings
of the latter mechanism are to be found in the neoclassical theory of
international capital transfers. In focusing on the response of real capital movement to disturbances in national saving-investment balances,
this explanation implies quite a different set of causal linkages between
the exchange rate and the current account than does the more popular
explanation based on the responsiveness of import and export demands
to autonomous changes in relative prices. At times when economic
developments are dominated by large autonomous changes in national
saving and investment balances—particularly those induced by shifts
in public sector fiscal positions—the exchange rate and current-account
effects of such disturbances may be expected to exert an overriding
influence on the level of the real exchange rate.

The empirical model described in sections 2.3 and 2.4 tends to confirm the view that the directions and orders of magnitude of movements
in real exchange rates and real interest rates in major industrial countries are related to shifts in fiscal positions in the manner we have
described. Our estimated saving equations imply that changes in fiscal
deficits are not offset one-for-one by changes in private saving; consequently, these fiscal shifts require equilibrating movements in the
pattern of real exchange rates and, to the extent that the global balance
between saving and investment has altered, in the level of real interest

rates. The magnitude of the resulting exchange rate and interest rate movements depends on a number of factors; the model includes estimated investment functions and merchandise trade equations for the three major industrial countries as well as an equation explaining aggregate saving (net of investment) by the rest of the world. Simulated changes in fiscal deficits equal to 1% of a country's capacity GDP—well within historical experience—produce, in our model, sizable movements in these interest rates and exchange rates. The model predicts that the exchange rate movements are largest when the fiscal change is first implemented and are later reversed as trade flows adjust gradually to relative prices and as asset stocks—physical capital, government debt, and claims on foreigners—move over time to their new equilibrium levels. The eventual equilibrium change of the real exchange rate in response to a fiscal contraction may involve either an appreciation or a depreciation, depending on the ultimate effect of the shock on the balance on investment earnings from abroad.

In an attempt to compare these movements with recent experience, we subjected the model to a stylized pattern of fiscal policy shifts that broadly describes the net size of the changes in three major industrial countries since the beginning of this decade, namely a move to fiscal expansion in the United States and fiscal contractions in the Federal Republic of Germany and in Japan (Sachs 1985). The size of the simulated response of exchange rates—an initial appreciation of the U.S. dollar in real terms of about 25%—and of U.S. real interest rates—an initial rise of three or four percentage points, depending on assumptions concerning exchange rate expectations and valuation effects—is a sizable fraction of the changes observed since 1981. It is clear, however, that other factors not captured by the model, such as cyclical effects, uncertainty about the future stance of fiscal policy, "safe havens," and monetary policy effects, are part of a more complete explanation.

The model may nevertheless help in evaluating whether observed exchange rate patterns are related to fundamental policy factors, rather than to portfolio shifts or the volatility of expectations. A crucial issue in macroeconomic policy is that of determining the pattern of current-account balances and real exchange rates among industrial countries that would be sustainable in the medium term (Artus and Knight 1984). Standard portfolio balance models have not yielded many practical insights into this problem. The present model, because it considers saving and investment decisions in the context of longer-term asset stock equilibrium, may help to evaluate sustainable levels of current accounts and real exchange rates and how they depend on one important set of determinants, the stance of fiscal policies in major countries.

Appendix
Data Sources

Except where noted otherwise, all flow data are taken from the national accounts of the country concerned. Sources: Data Resources Inc. (DRI) for the United States; and Organization for Economic Cooperation and Development (OECD) *National Accounts,* 1960–77 and 1971–83, for the Federal Republic of Germany and Japan. Real flows and stocks are valued at 1980 local currency prices.

Variables for the United States, the Federal Republic of Germany, and Japan ($i = US, GE, JA$)

CA_i National accounts net exports of goods and services divided by the GDP deflator.

B_i Real government net debt, calculated by cumulating general government fiscal deficits from benchmark figures, based on debt/GDP ratios in 1982 (Muller and Price 1984): 23.6% for the United States, 23.4% for Japan, and 19.8% for the Federal Republic of Germany. The net debt series was then divided by the GDP deflator.

DEF_i Real general government deficit corrected for inflation, calculated as $B_i - B_i(-1)$.

F_i Real net foreign asset position, calculated by cumulating CA_i, using benchmark figures for nominal net claims on foreigners valued in local currency at the end of 1982, and divided by the 1982 GDP deflator. For the United States, the benchmark is $149.5 billion (Department of Commerce, *Survey of Current Business,* June 1984, p. 75); for Germany DM 66.5 billion (*Monthly Report of the Deutsche Bundesbank,* October 1984, p. 35); and for Japan $24.7 billion (Bank of Japan, *Economic Statistics Annual,* 1983, p. 248).

GAP_i Output gap, as a percentage of capacity output: equals actual GDP divided by capacity output (YC_i) minus one. As YC_i is calculated, GAP_i is the same as the output gap in manufacturing (Artus 1977).

$GAPF_i$ Foreign output gap: actual GDP for 9 industrial countries (excluding the country concerned) divided by the corresponding potential output, minus one. The 10 countries are the United States, Japan, Germany, the United Kingdom, France, Italy, Canada, Belgium, the Netherlands, and Sweden.

I_i Real private net investment, residential plus nonresidential.

K_i Real private net capital stock. For the United States it was calculated as the sum of the nonresidential and residential real stocks, minus the government residential stock (Source: DRI). For the Federal Republic of Germany and Japan, K_i was calculated by cumulating I_i using a benchmark figure. For the Federal Republic of Germany this figure was the 1970 total net capital stock minus the 1970 government capital stock (OECD), *Flows and Stocks of Fixed Capital, 1955–80*). For Japan, where a real net capital stock figure was not available, preliminary estimation of an investment equation chose the value of the 1960 capital/GDP ratio (3.18) that maximized the fit of the equation.

MV_i Volume of non-oil merchandise imports, in real, local-currency terms. Source: International Monetary Fund.

R_i Real long-term interest rate, calculated as the nominal long-term government bond rate (Source: IMF, *International Financial Statistics*) minus the percentage change in the GDP deflator. The result was divided by 100 to get an interest rate expressed as a decimal fraction.

$REEX_i$ Real effective exchange rate index, 1980 = 1 (increase indicates appreciation); calculated as the country's normalized unit labor costs (NULC) relative to a weighted average of its competitors' NULC, in a common currency (Source: IMF, *International Financial Statistics*).

RES_i Residual current account item, equal to the oil trade balance, the balance on services excluding investment income, and unilateral transfers. Calculated as $CA_i - XV_i + MV_i - R_i F_i(-1)$.

S_i Real net private saving, calculated as $CA_i + I_i + DEF_i$.

XV_i Volume of non-oil merchandise exports, in real, local-currency terms. Source: International Monetary Fund, staff estimates.

W_i Real private sector net wealth, calculated as $\phi_i B_i + K_i + F_i$.

YC_i Capacity GDP: calculated by applying the gap between actual and potential manufacturing output (Artus 1977) to actual GDP.

Variables for Germany and Japan

$ERDOT_i$ Expected rate of change of the bilateral real exchange rate against the U.S. dollar (depreciation, if positive): calculated as $R_{US} - R_i$.

Variables for the Rest of the World (ROW)

CAROW   Proxy for the *ROW* real current balance, calculated as $-(CAUS + CAGE/1.815 + CAJA/225.82)$: denominators contain 1980 bilateral rates against the dollar of the deutsche mark and the yen.

RROW   Real interest rate, calculated as a GDP-weighted average of R_{US}, R_{GE}, and R_{JA}.

YCROW   Capacity output, in 1980 U.S. dollars, calculated by aggregating the remaining seven out of our sample of ten industrial countries.

Notes

1. Metzler (1960, 232–33) anticipated a point that is emphasized by the recent literature when he observed: "I would say that the elasticity of demand [for imports] does not determine the degree to which the balance of trade expands to meet a given deficit; this depends, rather, upon internal conditions such as the slopes of the saving and investment schedules, relative to the slope of the capital outflow. . . . The elasticities of demand for imports govern merely the changes in terms of trade needed to get the balance of trade required for equilibrium."

2. Our analysis is intended to refer to the largest industrial economies. Furthermore, it specifically excludes cases where a country's initial fiscal position is viewed as unsustainable, either because it implies a continuously rising ratio of government debt to GNP (Masson 1985) or because the initial outstanding stock of official foreign debt poses significant "sovereign credit risk" problems.

3. This is so even though, as Buiter (1983) has rightly emphasized, both the time path and the steady-state effects of shifts in fiscal policy depend crucially on the specific types of public sector spending and tax changes by which they are implemented.

4. This highly restrictive assumption is relaxed in section 2.3.

5. The relationship between integration of national capital markets and the extent national saving and investment move together has been considered by Feldstein and Horioka (1980) and a number of subsequent authors. Murphy (1984) has shown that if countries do not face a perfectly elastic supply of capital because they have a non-negligible effect on the world rate of interest, then there will be an association between national saving and investment despite perfect capital mobility. Frankel (1985) points out that even for a small country domestic crowding out occurs in response to a fiscal shock unless both capital market integration *and* goods market integration prevail, the latter condition being equivalent to purchasing power parity.

6. It is assumed that governments levy taxes on their own residents only, and that taxes are lump-sum, so that they modify neither the return to labor nor that to capital.

7. In general, φ need not be constant, and will depend on the paths of taxes and interest rates. Let *H* be human wealth and *W* financial wealth, defined as follows (Blanchard 1985, 239):

$$H(t) = \int_t^\infty [Y(s) - T(s)]e^{-\int_t^s (r(v) + p)dv}ds$$

$$\equiv \Pi(Y - T; r + p)$$

$$W(t) = B(t) + C(t)$$

where Y is noninterest income, T lump-sum taxes, B government bonds, C other forms of financial wealth, and Π the present-value operator (Blanchard and Summers 1984, 317). The government's budget constraint in integral form is

$$B(t) = \int_t^\infty [T(s) - G(s)]e^{-\int_t^s r(v)dv} ds$$

$$\equiv \Pi(T - G; r).$$

Using the government's budget constraint, we can express H in terms of current holdings of government debt and future government *spending,* not taxes:

$$H = \Pi(Y; r + p) - \Pi(T; r + p)$$

$$= \Pi(Y; r + p) - (1 - \phi)\Pi(G; r) - (1 - \phi)B$$

where

$$\phi = 1 - \Pi(T; r + p)/\Pi(T; r).$$

We can now define new measures of human and financial wealth as follows:

$$\bar{H} = \Pi(Y; r + p) - (1 - \phi)\Pi(G; r)$$
$$\bar{W} = \phi B + C.$$

If $r(s)$, $T(s)$ and $G(s)$ are constant for $t \leq s < \infty$, then

$$\phi = 1 - r/(r + p)$$
$$\bar{H} = \Pi(Y - G; r + p).$$

8. Since a change in the real exchange rate has a valuation effect as well as a volume effect on N, our prior that $N_\epsilon > 0$ entails the assumption that the Marshall-Lerner condition is fulfilled. Specifically, $N_\epsilon > 0$ requires that $\delta\eta_\epsilon + \mu_\epsilon > 1$ where η_ϵ is the elasticity of the volume of home-country gross exports (X) with respect to ϵ, μ_ϵ is the absolute value of the corresponding elasticity of *ROW* gross exports X^*, and $\delta = X/\epsilon X^*$ is the initial ratio of home to foreign exports, expressed in a common numeraire.

9. The relevant modification is that $S(R)$ is only the interest-sensitive component of private saving, and ϕD represents the net effect of government fiscal policy on *total* (private plus public) national saving, given the value of the Ricardian equivalence parameter ϕ.

10. Wallich (1983) refers to the fact that an increase in the home country's fiscal deficit will induce a capital inflow because it tends to raise domestic interest rates "relative to foreign rates." It is certainly probable that an increase in the home country's fiscal deficit will raise its real interest rate relative to that prevailing abroad, either because domestic and foreign financial assets are not viewed by wealth-holders as perfect substitutes, or because investors expect a real exchange rate depreciation. However, even if interest rates are assumed equal at home and abroad, as in the simple model discussed here, the new equilibrium will involve an appreciation of the home currency as a

result of an increase in its fiscal deficit. It will also be true that interest rates in *both* countries will be higher.

11. Also note that a one unit increase in the *ROW* fiscal deficit would increase the world interest rate by the same amount as a one unit increase in the domestic deficit only if $\phi = \phi^*$.

12. Published data on the real capital stock are calculated by cumulating real gross investment and subtracting physical depreciation; we have not attempted to measure the *market value* of the capital stock, as valued, for instance, in the stock market. To calculate real government debt, we cumulate nominal deficits and divide by the GDP deflator; accounting for valuation changes requires knowledge of the maturity structure of the government debt. Under the assumption made here that all government debt takes the form of one-period bonds, there are no valuation effects of changes in the real interest rate on the real stock of government debt. Finally, real net claims on foreigners are obtained by cumulating current account surpluses and dividing by the GDP deflator. There is an implicit assumption that foreign claims and liabilities are in domestic currency, otherwise there would be a valuation effect associated with changes in the exchange rate. Naturally this cannot be true of all countries, and there is a residual region in the model whose net claims must therefore be in foreign currency. The sensitivity of the results to valuation effects on the stocks of government debt and net claims on foreigners is examined in section 2.4.

13. In the estimation work that follows, the $ERDOT_i$ are effectively treated as exogenous variables. However, the simulation model is later used to study the effects of changes in exchange rate expectations.

14. In particular, they yielded the implausible result that fiscal contraction in Germany and Japan would lead to larger falls in the general level of interest rates than an equal contraction (expressed as a ratio to capacity output) in the United States.

15. This empirical result is generally regarded as counterintuitive. In a recent paper, however, Bernheim and Shoven (1985) present evidence that during the past few years net contributions to pension funds, which make up a large proportion of total private saving in the United States, have tended to fall as real interest rates increased. This implies a negative relation between real interest rates and private saving in the United States. The negative relation occurs because roughly 70% of pension fund assets are in "defined-benefit" plans for which, other things equal, a rise in real interest rates allows firms to finance the benefits stipulated by the plan with a lower level of corporate contributions.

16. Figures for 1984–85 were taken from OECD estimates.

References

Artus, Jacques R. 1977. Measures of potential output in manufacturing for eight industrial countries, 1955–78. International Monetary Fund *Staff Papers* 24 (March): 1–35.

Artus, Jacques R., and Malcolm D. Knight. 1984. Issues in the assessment of exchange rates of industrial countries. International Monetary Fund Occasional Paper no. 29 (July).

Barro, Robert J. 1974. Are government bonds net wealth? *Journal of Political Economy* 82, no. 6 (November-December): 1095–1117.

Bernheim, Douglas, and John Shoven. 1985. Pension funding and saving. National Bureau of Economic Research Working Paper no. 1622.

Blanchard, Olivier. 1985. Debt, deficits, and finite horizons. *Journal of Political Economy* 93, no. 2 (April): 233–47.

Blanchard, Olivier, and Lawrence H. Summers. 1984. Perspectives on high world real interest rates. *Brooking Papers on Economic Activity* 2:273–324.

Branson, William, Hannu Halttunen, and Paul Masson. 1977. Exchange rates in the short run: The dollar-deutsche-mark rate. *European Economic Review* 10 (December): 303–24.

Buiter, Willem H. 1983. The measurement of public sector deficits and its implications for policy evaluation and design. International Monetary Fund *Staff Papers* 30 (June): 306–49.

Buiter, Willem H., and James Tobin. 1979. Debt neutrality: A brief review of doctrine and evidence. In *Social security versus private saving,* ed. George M. von Furstenberg. Cambridge, Mass.: Ballinger.

Carmichael, Jeffrey. 1982. On Barro's theorem of debt neutrality: The irrelevance of net wealth. *American Economic Review* 72 (March): 202–13.

Dornbusch, Rudiger. 1975. A portfolio balance model of the open economy. *Journal of Monetary Economics* 1, no. 1 (January): 3–20.

———. 1976. Expectations and exchange rate dynamics. *Journal of Political Economy* 84, no. 6 (December): 1161–76.

Dornbusch, Rudiger, and Stanley Fischer. 1980. Exchange rates and the current account. *American Economic Review* 70 (December): 960–71.

Feldstein, Martin, and C. Horioka. 1980. Domestic saving and international capital flows. *Economic Journal* 90 (June): 314–29.

Frankel, Jeffrey A. 1985. International capital mobility and crowding out in the U.S. economy: Imperfect integration of financial markets or of goods markets? Paper presented to a conference at the Federal Reserve Bank of St. Louis, October 11–12.

Frenkel, Jacob, and Assaf Razin. 1984. Budget deficits and rates of interest in the world economy. National Bureau of Economic Research Working Paper no. 1354 (May).

———. 1985a. Government spending, debt, and international economic interdependence. *Economic Journal* 95 (September): 619–36.

———. 1985b. Fiscal expenditures and international economic interdependence. In *International economic policy coordination,* ed. Willem Buiter and Richard C. Marston. Cambridge: Cambridge University Press.

Frenkel, Jacob, and Carlos Rodriguez. 1982. Exchange rate dynamics and the overshooting hypothesis. International Monetary Fund *Staff Papers* 29 (March): 1–30.

Girton, Lance, and Dale Henderson. 1977. Central bank operations in foreign and domestic assets under fixed and flexible exchange rates. In *The effects of exchange rate adjustment,* ed. P. B. Clark, D. E. Logue, and R. J. Sweeney. Washington: Government Printing Office.

Goldstein, Morris, and Mohsin S. Khan. 1985. Income and price effects in foreign trade. In *Handbook of international economics,* vol. 2, ed. Ronald W. Jones and Peter B. Kenen. Amsterdam: North-Holland.

Gould, J. P. 1968. Adjustment costs and the theory of investment of the firm. *Review of Economic Studies* 35 (January): 47–55.

Helliwell, John F., and Tim Padmore. Empirical studies of macroeconomic interdependence. In *Handbook of international economics,* vol. 2, ed. Ronald W. Jones and Peter B. Kenen. Amsterdam: North-Holland.

International Monetary Fund. 1985. *World Economic Outlook* (October).

Jump, Greg. 1980. Interest rates, inflation expectations, and spurious elements in measured saving. *American Economic Review* 70 (December): 990–1004.

Kochin, Lewis. 1974. Are future taxes anticipated by consumers? *Journal of Money, Credit, and Banking* 6 (August): 385–94.

Kouri, Pentti, and Michael Porter. 1974. International capital flows and portfolio equilibrium. *Journal of Political Economy* 82 (May-June): 443–67.

Laursen, Svendt, and Lloyd A. Metzler. 1950. Flexible exchange rates and the theory of employment. *Review of Economics and Statistics* 32 (November): 281–99.

Masson, Paul R. 1985. The sustainability of fiscal deficits. International Monetary Fund *Staff Papers* 32 (December): 577–605.

Metzler, Lloyd A. 1951. Wealth, saving, and the rate of interest. *Journal of Political Economy* 59 (April): 93–116.

———. 1960. The process of international adjustment under conditions of full employment: A Keynesian view. Paper delivered before the Econometric Society, December.

Muller, Patrice, and Robert W. R. Price. 1984. Structural budget indicators and the interpretation of fiscal policy stance in OECD countries. *OECD Economic Studies,* no. 3 (Autumn): 27–72.

Mundell, Robert A. 1963. Capital mobility and stabilization policy under fixed and flexible exchange rates. *Canadian Journal of Economics and Political Science* 29 (November): 303–24.

Murphy, Robert G. 1984. Capital mobility and the relationship between saving and investment rates in OECD countries. *Journal of International Money and Finance* 3, no. 3 (December): 327–42.

Mussa, Michael. 1976. *A Study in macroeconomics.* Amsterdam: North-Holland.

Sachs, Jeffrey D. 1981. The current account and macroeconomic adjustment in the 1970s. *Brookings Papers on Economic Activity* 1:201–68.

———. 1985. The dollar and policy mix: 1985. *Brookings Papers on Economic Activity* 1:117–97.

Sachs, Jeffrey D., and Charles Wyplosz. 1984. Real exchange rate effects of fiscal policy. National Bureau of Economic Research Working Paper no. 1255 (January).

Seater, John. 1982. Are future taxes discounted? *Journal of Money, Credit, and Banking* 14 (August): 376–89.

Spencer, Grant H. 1984. The World Trade Model: Revised estimates. International Monetary Fund *Staff Papers* 31 (September): 469–98.

Svensson, Lars E. O., and Assaf Razin. 1983. The terms of trade effect and the current amount: The Harberger-Laursen-Metzler effect. *Journal of Political Economy* 91 (February): 97–125.

Tanner, Ernest. 1979. An empirical investigation of tax discounting. *Journal of Money, Credit, and Banking* 11 (May): 214–18.

Wallich, Henry C. 1983. *Journal of Commerce* (August 19).

Comment   Olivier Jean Blanchard

This paper addresses the most interesting question in international fiscal economics today. Namely, how much of the movement in real interest

Olivier Jean Blanchard is professor of economics at MIT and a research associate of the National Bureau of Economic Research.

rates and exchange rates of the last five years is due to disequilibrium, Mundell-Fleming, effects of the international fiscal mix, and how much is due instead to equilibrium, full employment investment-savings, effects of that mix? The question is crucial because how we answer it determines how we forecast the future. Put crudely, disequilibrium effects cannot last very long while equilibrium effects may be with us for the foreseeable future.

The strategy of the paper is to ask: Supposing that there had been no disequilibrium effects in the last five years, that prices and wages had been flexible enough to insure full employment in the world and to imply that monetary policy did not affect real rates—would interest rates and exchange rates have moved as much as they did? Masson and Knight conclude that much of the movement is consistent with an equilibrium story. Even if their conclusion is correct, it does not logically follow that disequilibrium effects have been unimportant; but it gives us some insights as to the potential importance of the equilibrium factors. I like the strategy, but I have enough reservations about the execution that I am somewhat skeptical of the conclusions.

Their paper has two parts. The first is a useful review of the channels through which the fiscal mix affects interest rates and exchange rates in the world. The second is the estimation and simulation of a world model. I shall discuss both of them in turn.

The Fiscal Mix, Interest Rates, and Exchange Rates

We now have a fairly good understanding of the way the world fiscal mix affects interest rates and exchange rates through equilibrium channels. But the theory ends up with question marks on the signs of many of the effects, and this is precisely where an empirical effort, such as the one presented in the paper, can be useful. Careful empirical estimates may allow us to sign some of these theoretically ambiguous effects. Let me therefore briefly review the main channels that have been identified, with a particular emphasis on the question marks.

Let us think of two "countries," the United States and the rest of the world, *ROW,* and consider the effects of a U.S. fiscal expansion under flexible prices. Let us start with the short-run effects. A U.S. fiscal expansion increases the U.S. demand and thus the world demand for goods, putting pressure on interest rates; the world interest rate therefore increases. In addition, the relative demand for U.S. goods most likely increases, leading to an increase in their relative price, a real U.S. dollar appreciation. Using figure 2.5 from the paper (which itself reproduces that in Dornbusch [1983]), and denoting *ROW* variables with asterisks, the U.S. goods market equilibrium locus is given by GG, and the *ROW* equilibrium locus by G^*G^*. A U.S. fiscal expansion increases demand, increasing the interest rate r at any exchange

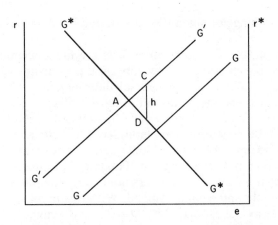

Fig. 2.5   Fiscal policy, interest, and exchange rates

rate, and shifting *GG* to *G'G'*. Under interest arbitrage $r = r^*$, this shift leads to lower *e* and higher *r* and r^*. So far so good and the effects are unambiguous.

In the medium and the long term, four stock-flow effects come into action.[1] The first is the increase in U.S. public debt, due to the accumulation of deficits. Like the initial deficits, this increases world demand and the relative demand for U.S. goods, leading to further pressure on interest rates and the dollar.

The second is the transfer of wealth implied by the current account deficit of the U.S. from the U.S. to the *ROW*. This transfer decreases U.S. wealth relative to *ROW* wealth, decreasing the relative demand for U.S. goods and thus leading to dollar depreciation. In figure 2.5, *GG* moves from *G'G'* back to the right, while G^*G^* moves to the left. The impact on interest rates is ambiguous.

The third effect comes from capital accumulation. The initial increase in interest rates leads to a slowdown in capital accumulation over time, further reducing supply in both countries. This is likely to further increase interest rates but has ambiguous effects on the exchange rate.

The fourth effect arises from the increase in the proportion of U.S. debt in portfolios. If U.S. and foreign debt are not perfect substitutes, such an increase will require an increase in the premium on U.S. debt. The effect on interest rates and exchange rates can also be analyzed using figure 2.5. Starting from point A, consider an increase in the U.S. debt to *ROW* debt ratio, which requires an increase in the premium of *h*. The new equilibrium, in which $r = r^* + h$ is given by points C and D. The U.S. interest rate is higher, the *ROW* rate lower, and the dollar depreciates. The Masson-Knight paper ignores this effect and is prob-

1. Sachs and Wyplosz (1984) focus on these aspects.

ably right in doing so, given the lack of empirical success in isolating it.

To summarize, while short-run effects are fairly unambiguous, medium- and long-run effects, especially on the exchange rate front, are much less so.[2] What are the crucial determinants of the signs and magnitudes of these medium- and long-run effects? The main one is the degree to which fiscal policy affects demand in the first place, or equivalently the degree of non-neutrality of deficits and debt. For the rest, it depends on whether one focuses on interest rates or exchange rates, the medium or the long run. For long-run interest rate effects, for example, the central parameters are clearly the interest elasticities of wealth supply and capital demand. With this in mind, let us look at the empirical model estimated by Masson and Knight.

Empirical estimates

Obviously, Masson and Knight cannot build a large empirical model. They build a simple model with three equations for each country: an investment equation, a savings equation, and a trade balance equation. I have no quarrel with this choice.

They then use and estimate simple linear specifications which, ignoring disequilibrium terms, relate the savings income ratio to the wealth income ratio and the interest rate, and the investment output ratio to the capital output ratio and the interest rate. Anybody who has estimated either consumption or investment functions will be skeptical of the ability of such specifications to capture interest elasticities of wealth and capital accurately; the difficulties of finding either an effect of user cost—let alone of the interest rate—on investment or of the interest rate on savings are well documented. And the results of the paper will do little to reassure the skeptics. I shall limit myself to two examples:

The estimated interest elasticity of savings is negative[3]; this in turn implies a negative interest elasticity of wealth. It is a result with strong implications for their simulations as it implies very large movements of interest rates in response to deficits. This negative elasticity is, despite what the authors state, a result which is at sharp variance with theory. Summers (1981) has shown that the often heard statement that income and substitution effects of interest rate changes on savings can easily cancel is only appropriate in models in which people receive labor income on the first day of their working life. In models with more

2. With forward-looking expectations, the ambiguity about the medium and long runs may well carry over to the short run. But the paper stays clear of that issue.
3. The logic behind constraining the coefficient on interest rates to be the same across countries is not compelling. Either the countries are the same, in which case all coefficients should be constrained to be identical, or they are not, in which case it is difficult to see why this would affect all coefficients except this one.

realistic life cycle assumptions, the wealth elasticity is likely to be positive, even if the elasticity of substitution between consumption at different points in time is very low.

The estimated investment equation, say for the U.S., implies that an increase in the real rate from 5 to 10% decreases the ratio of investment to GNP by 1% and decreases the capital output ratio ultimately by 8%. Is this reasonable? If we assumed Cobb Douglas production, which is often thought to be a decent approximation to the long-run production function, and a depreciation rate of 10%, the decrease in the capital output ratio in response to this doubling of the real rate would be of 33%. Here again, their estimates of the interest elasticity of capital imply substantially more movement in interest rates than what theory would predict. Indeed, for all three countries, the interest elasticity of net savings (savings minus investment) appears not to be significantly different from zero.[4]

The arguments above suggest that the model overestimates the effect of a given increase in aggregate demand on interest rates. At the same time, it may well be that the model underestimates the effect of fiscal policy on demand. This is because it treats ϕ, the degree to which debt is net wealth as given and constant throughout; but theory suggests that this is unlikely to be true. Debt is surely much more net wealth if agents anticipate not to repay taxes during their lifetime than if they anticipate a sharp increase in taxes in the near future. Gramm-Rudman has surely decreased ϕ drastically, and this was indeed reflected right away in interest rates and exchange rates. But ϕ may still be much higher than in the 1970s, and higher than the sample estimate of .42 given in the table.

Within their strategy, what could Masson and Knight have done? I think they should have asked less of their data and relied more on theory and estimates obtained by others using better data sets and better specifications. The exact mix of specification, estimation, and theft is largely a matter of taste. I would, for example, have specified the investment function by forcing it to imply a reasonable long-run production function—say Cobb Douglas—and letting the data determine only the process of adjustment, which they can do quite accurately. I would have relied on a tighter specification of consumption such as that used and estimated by Hayashi (1982), which has well understood steady-state implications. This would surely not resolve all difficulties; the unfortunate fact is that we do not know much about the interest elasticity of wealth—probably not enough to give a precise answer to the question asked in this paper.

---

4. To be sure that this was the case, one would need to know the covariance of the estimates of the two elasticities, which is not reported in the paper.

References

Dornbusch, Rudiger. 1983. Comment of J. Shafer and B. Loopesko, "Floating exchange rates after ten years." Brookings Papers on Economic Activity, 1983-1, pp. 79–85.
Hayashi, Fumio. 1982. The permanent income hypothesis: Estimation and testing by instrumental variables. *Journal of Political Economy* 90 (October): 895–916.
Sachs, Jeffrey, and Charles Wyplosz. 1984. Real exchange rate effects of fiscal policy. National Bureau of Economic Research Working Paper no. 1255 Cambridge.

Comment   Rudiger Dornbusch

This paper proposes an ambitious task: the empirical implementation of a modern, micro-based saving and investment approach to trade imbalances and the real exchange rate. This interpretation of the Mundell-Flemming paradigm in new clothes, while well-established from countless discussions in the past three years and known in Washington as the Feldstein doctrine, is in fact quite difficult. Any model based on an uncompromising approach to microeconomic foundations must cast the forward-looking, tax-paying household in a multi-country setting. The paper does not quite come to grips with this hard task— all the language is right, but the equations are neither of the new classical kind, nor quite the old Keynesian ones. Both camps thus are left with their appetites whetted and their bellies half-empty and rumbling. But even if the particular channels of transmission and their stability remain open to question, the paper offers important empirical evidence which, along with recent work by Hutchinson and Throop (1985) and Feldstein (1986), highlights the impact of budget deficits on real exchange rates.

The Issue

The basic proposition of the paper is that large shifts in national structural budgets in the past ten years, not monetary policy changes, explain the real appreciation of the dollar. Table 2.8 shows the cumulative changes from 1981 to 1985 in the structural budget surpluses and in the real exchange rates for the United States, Japan, and Germany.

The explanation can easily be seen with the help of figure 2.6 (see Dornbusch [1983a, 83–85]). Along *II* the home country's goods market clears: increased real interest rates depress world demand for domestic

Rudiger Dornbusch is the Ford International Professor of Economics in the Department of Economics, Massachusetts Institute of Technology.

Table 2.8   **Structural Budgets and Real Exchange Rates: 1981–85 (Cumulative Percentage Change)**

	Structural Budget	Real Exchange Rate
United States	−3.0	21.1
Japan	2.2	−7.8
Germany	3.4	−2.0

Source: OECD and Morgan Guaranty.
Note: Structural and inflation adjusted, cumulative shift in discretionary fiscal policy.

output and therefore require, for market equilibrium, a real depreciation. Along $I*I*$ the foreign goods market clears. Here higher real
interest rates, by symmetry, require an increase in the relative price
of domestic goods or real appreciation. A fiscal expansion at home,
assuming that it falls entirely on domestic goods, shifts II up and to
the left, leading to a new equilibrium at E' with higher world interest
rates and a real appreciation of the home country's currency. It is worth
recording that this 1983 analysis interpreted both the dollar appreciation
and anticipated the dollar decline that would come with prospective
fiscal consolidation. I noted at the time:

> These prospective changes in interest rates and exchange rates (due
> to an anticipated fiscal expansion) are anticipated under rational ex-
> pectations and show up in higher long-term real interest rates and in
> dollar appreciation. The forward-looking nature of assets markets,
> however, makes recovery much more difficult. If this analysis is

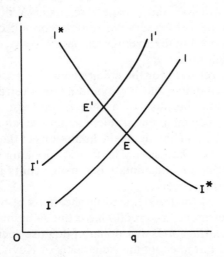

Fig. 2.6   The effect of a fiscal expansion

correct, a move toward smaller long-run, not cyclical, deficits would lead to a collapse of the dollar. The analysis emphasizes the peculiar and central effects of fiscal policy under flexible exchange rates.

Theory

At the theoretical level there are several objections to the Knight-Masson analysis. These objectives invalidate the claim that this analysis offers an implementation of the modern approach.

- There is a lack of integration of the trade sector and the savings-investment sector. While the savings-investment equations are based on intertemporal optimization considerations, the trade equations are of the most orthodox variety, with real exchange rates, a time trend, and cyclical variables determining trade flows. There is no appearance here at all of wealth, budget deficit spillovers, or real interest rates. Of course, that does not make sense since the same household that reduces demand for domestic goods in response to increased interest rates will also ordinarily reduce demand for imports. The same argument applies to the impact of changes in investment spending on trade flows. The failure to carry the optimizing considerations over to the critical trade block has bearing on the interpretation of the empirical findings.
- The treatment of the wealth implications of fiscal policy is entirely inappropriate. The Barro-Blanchard mortal taxpayer is concerned with the exact timing of *future* taxes. The current stock of debt and the current budget deficit are not sufficient statistics to judge the impact of fiscal policy. It is the essence of the modern approach that the public should look forward to ask whether they themselves or someone else will pay the prospective taxes. Will Kemp-Roth be followed on the heels by a Gramm-Rudman or is fiscal consolidation sufficiently remote for the average taxpayer to discount future consolidation at high rates?

  This is highly relevant for the empirical analysis: even as the structural deficit is widening, the household already retrenches, contrary to Knight-Masson, because of a shift toward fiscal consolidation. Knight-Masson recognize the problem in note seven of their text, but their own presentation highlights the limitations of the analysis carried in the main body of the paper. The forward-looking variables simply cannot be modeled as constants when major shifts in the future tax and spending profile occur.
- There is no regard for the demand implications of the budget. Does a dollar of investment tax credits have the same impact on *current* demand for *domestic* goods as a dollar of defense spending or a dollar of estate taxes? Large econometric models of Keynesian persuasion or the Tel Aviv School would make much out of the difference.

• The forward-looking taxpayer asset-holder has little scope for action in the Masson-Knight model. At the end of 1984, U.S. national net worth amounted to $11,700 billion and the public debt outstanding was about $1,000 billion. This suggests that the role of other assets, specifically the value of the capital stock, should be central to the analysis. A good week on the stock market, after all, has more of an impact on wealth than a full year of deficits. This point simply cannot be neglected. Empirically it implies that the capital stock cannot be carried at replacement cost but must be carried at market value to capture the impact of valuation on saving and investment.[1]

• The treatment of interest rates is inappropriate. In an intertemporal context where relative prices appear, distinction between permanent and transitory changes in real interest rates is necessary. In a country where deficits have led to real appreciation, there is an expectation of real depreciation and hence real interest rates are perceived by households as being high. The converse is true for the country that is lending. On the investment side this point is important since the real user cost of capital may be affected by terms of trade changes.[2]

The Central Empirical Issue

The overriding objection to the empirical implementation arises from the introduction of cyclical variables in the saving and investment equation. In the theoretical section, without any justification in terms of the underlying microeconomic theory, saving is made a function of *current* real GNP, as is the desired stock of capital and hence investment. This formulation implies that in the actual equations for saving and investment the variable *GAP* appears as an explanatory variable. In the same manner, inclusion of the actual deficit as a regressor introduces an endogenous cyclical variable in place of the theoretically more appropriate cyclically adjusted deficit.

The uncompromising microeconomic approach has no room for such a formulation. The forward-looking household bases saving decisions on the relation between actual assets relative to the present value of human wealth. Of course, the present value of human wealth and current real GNP are not the same. Likewise, investment decisions of the optimizing capital-user and the investment producing industries, in a context of adjustment costs, are based on the structural parameters characterizing technology and on the perspective cost of capital, not on output. By assumption these firms are price takers. If demand were to matter, a model of imperfect competition would need to be offered

1. See, for example, Blanchard (1981) and Dornbusch and Dantas (1984).
2. See Obstfeld (1983), Svensson and Razin (1985), and Dornbusch (1985a, 1985b, 1986).

and there is simply no question that the path of future demand, not current output, would be the relevant explanatory variable.

It is well-known that empirically cyclical variables do more of the work than they should be doing by the standards of uncompromising microeconomic approaches.[3] Liquidity constraints and accelerator effects provide an explanation. These effects, one must assume, provide significance in the Knight-Masson estimations. Therefore it is entirely inappropriate to read the evidence as a test of an uncompromising microeconomic approach. The results are a faithful rendition of the standard Keynesian model. There appears to be no recognition of this issue in the Knight-Masson analysis.

Concluding Remarks

The Knight-Masson paper is an ambitious, welcome addition to the empirical literature on open economy macroeconomics. That literature remains scarce, imperfect, and easy to take issue with. Criticism at this stage is unavoidable but also altogether appropriate for two reasons. First it identifies what exactly we know and sharpens the debate. Second, by contrasting alternative paradigms, it is quite obvious that, for the time being, the uncompromising microeconomic approach (even with the Blanchard Amendment) remains at best a promising research agenda, but most assuredly does not command a shred of empirical evidence in its support.

References

Blanchard, O. 1981. Output, the stock market and interest rates. *American Economic Review* 71, no. 1 (March): 132–43

Dornbusch, R. 1983a. Floating exchange rates ten years after: Comment. *Brookings Papers on Economic Activity* 1: 79–85

———. 1983b. Real interest rates, home goods and optimal external borrowing. *Journal of Political Economy* 91, no. 1 (February): 141–53

———. 1985a. Intergenerational and international trade. *Journal of International Economics* 18, no. 1/2 (February): 123–39

———. 1985b. External debt, budget deficits and disequilibrium exchange rates. In *International debt and the developing countries,* ed. G. Smith and J. Cuddington. World Bank. Washington, D.C.

Dornbusch, R., and Dantas, D. 1984. Anticipated fiscal policy and the term structure of interest. NBER Working Paper no. 1518.

Dornbusch, R. 1986. *Debtors, Debts, and Deficits.* Cambridge, Mass.: MIT Press.

Feldstein, M. 1986. The dollar and U.S. budget deficits. NBER Conference on Macroeconomic Policy. Cambridge, Mass.

---

3. See, for example, Flavin (1985).

Flavin, M. 1985. Excess sensitivity of consumption to current income: Liquidity constraints or myopia? *Canadian Journal of Economics* 1 (February): 117–36

Giovannini, A. 1984. "Fiscal Policy and the External Balance." Chapter in an unpublished Ph.D. dissertation, Massachusetts Institute of Technology.

Hutchinson, M., and Throop, A. 1985. U.S. budget deficits and the real value of the dollar. Federal Reserve Bank of San Francisco, *Economic Review,* no. 4 (Fall): 26–43

Obstfeld, M. 1983. Intertemporal price speculation and the optimal current account deficit. *Journal of International Money and Finance* 2, no. 2: 135–45.

Svensson, L., and Razin, A. 1983. The terms of trade effect, and the current account. *Journal of Political Economy* 91, no. 1 (February): 97–125.

Sachs, J., and Wyplosz, C. 1984. Real exchange rate effects of fiscal policy. NBER Working Paper no. 1255.

3 Coordination of Monetary and Fiscal Policies in the Industrial Economies

Warwick J. McKibbin and Jeffrey D. Sachs

3.1 Introduction

The volatility of the world economy since the breakdown of the Bretton Woods par value system of exchange rates has led many policymakers and economists to call for reform of the international monetary system. Many economists have argued that domestic macroeconomic policies in the major OECD economies should be geared, at least in part, to maintaining exchange rates within ranges set cooperatively among the major countries. Proposals vary from the "target zone" system, as advocated by Williamson (1983) and Roosa (1984), to a much more stringent system of fixed exchange rates, as advocated by McKinnon (1984). There are several possible arguments in the case for a return to a more managed system, as described in recent surveys by Obstfeld (1985) and Sachs (1985b). One crucial argument has been that the equilibrium of noncooperative macroeconomic policymaking under flexible exchange rates is likely to be inefficient, as countries fail to take into account the external effects of their policies on their trading partners. More rigid rules of the game, as embodied in a managed exchange rate system, are seen as a way to reduce the inducements to beggar-thy-neighbor policies. It has been frequently noted that there are many institutional forms that greater cooperation might take, ranging from the give-and-take of bargaining at economic summit meetings

Warwick J. McKibbin is an economist at the Reserve Bank of Australia. Jeffrey D. Sachs is professor of economics at Harvard University and a research associate at the National Bureau of Economic Research.

The authors thank William Branson and Robert Flood for helpful comments and DRI for computing facilities. Warwick McKibbin thanks the Reserve Bank of Australia for financial support. Any views expressed in this paper do not necessarily reflect those of the institutions with which the authors are affiliated.

to the implicit form of cooperation that takes place when each country adheres to externally imposed exchange rate targets. The exchange rate alternative is seen as particularly attractive in that it reduces the needs for constant, face-to-face bargaining. The hope is that, by changing rules of the game, policymakers can then be free to act independently (i.e., noncooperatively) within the confines of the international agreement. Tighter margins for exchange rate fluctuations might eliminate the most noxious forms of international competition, in the same way that the General Agreement on Tariffs and Trade has significantly reduced the international competition via tariff setting.

There are of course limits to the gains that will be achieved by a change in the international rules of the game. Every set of exchange arrangements will generate its own forms of strategic behavior, which will tend to cause some forms of inefficient strategic behavior. For example, while much of recent writing in this area has considered the gaming aspects of flexible exchange rates (see Canzoneri and Gray 1985, and Buiter and Marston 1985), many other studies have shown that similar strategic issues arise in fixed exchange rate systems. Indeed, the original analytical work in this area, by Hamada (1974), considered the case of monetary management under a fixed exchange rate regime. Even the classical gold standard, the self-regulating system par excellence, offered up incentives for inefficient strategic behavior, as argued by Eichengreen (1985) and Matsuyama (1985). An important task of research in this area is to make quantitative judgments about the gains and losses from alternative forms of exchange rate management.

This paper studies the properties of four alternative international monetary regimes, with respect both to their operating characteristics and to the incentives for strategic behavior under each regime. We consider alternatively a floating exchange rate system and three forms of fixed exchange rate systems. In the floating rate system, we assume that policymakers in each country can choose monetary and fiscal instruments in order to maximize a national social welfare function, without having to gear the policy choices to a particular exchange rate target. In the fixed exchange rate systems, some or all of the countries are required to peg the exchange rate as a side condition on their policy actions. We then study the implications of the exchange rate constraints. However, we do not ask the more fundamental question whether the exchange rate system itself would be viable or whether the countries would instead choose to bow out of the arrangement.

As is well known, a fixed exchange rate system must be specified by much more than the constraint that bilateral or multilateral rates be fixed. It is crucial to specify which countries have the obligation to intervene in order to preserve a given peg. The so-called $N-1$ problem underlines the fact that in a fixed regime of N countries, only $N-1$ countries need to undertake the obligation to stabilize. The Nth country, presumably, can act without direct regard for the consequences of its policies on the exchange rate. The "problem," generally speaking, is to decide how the responsibilities for pegging are allocated among the countries.

We consider three alternatives that are widely discussed. The first is an asymmetric "dollar standard," in which the United States assumes no responsibility in pegging the exchange rate, while the other countries (specifically Japan, and the rest of the OECD, which we call the ROECD) both peg to the dollar. This system, making the United States the Nth country, is considered by many to be a reasonable description of how the Bretton Woods system actually operated (see Swoboda 1978). In fact, it should be remembered that under the Bretton Woods arrangement, the United States had the side condition to peg the dollar price of gold at $35 per ounce, though it is difficult to find an important effect of this constraint on U.S. policy actions through most of the Bretton Woods period.

The other two systems that we study are symmetric solutions to the $N-1$ problem, à la gold standard. Recently, McKinnon (1984) has proposed a fixed exchange rate arrangement for the United States, Germany, and Japan, in which the cross rates among these countries are fixed, and in which the weighted sum of the money stocks of the three countries is to be held constant. This means that any expansion of money in one country must be matched by a compensating contraction in the other countries. Note that a strict gold standard, with a constant world stock of gold reserves, would work this way: any increase in money in one country (backed 100% by gold reserves) would necessarily require a contraction in money in the rest of the world. Subject to this monetary constraint, the countries would be free to pursue independent fiscal policies.

This monetary standard is extremely strict in making the aggregate stock of world money invariant to underlying conditions. As a third fixed exchange rate arrangement, we experiment with a modified McKinnon plan (dubbed McKinnon II), in which the exchange rates across regions are fixed, but in which the weighted world money stock is controlled cooperatively by the participating countries to forestall large swings in world economic activity. Using a numerical model later, we attempt to find an equilibrium set of rules for fiscal policy in each country and for the global money stock, which has the following properties: the fiscal rules are optimal for each country, taking as given the fiscal rules in the other countries and the rule for the management of the global money stock, while at the same time the cooperative money rule is optimal, taking as given the fiscal rules in each of the countries.

Within each of these exchange rate systems, we analyze the behavior and characteristics of fiscal policy and examine the way changes in the rules of the game affect the incentives to use fiscal and monetary policies. In particular, we seek to determine whether the various inefficiencies of floating rates caused by the strategic behavior of individual countries can be muted by a move to a more managed system. Under various circumstances, a move to managed rates can indeed blunt the inefficient deployment of fiscal policies, but we also find that there are many circumstances in which the introduction of fixed rates would itself lead to serious inefficiencies of other sorts. As is common in this kind of research, the desirability of one type of monetary arrangement over another will depend to an important extent on the nature of the underlying shocks hitting the world economy.

In section 3.2 we examine the transmission of fiscal policies under alternative exchange rate arrangements, using an extremely simple version of the Mundell-Fleming model for heuristic purposes. We then move on to a large-scale empirical model of the world economy in section 3.3, in which the same fiscal experiments are performed. We find that the cross-country transmission of fiscal policy is affected in crucial quantitative ways according to the global monetary arrangements in which the fiscal expansion takes place. In section 3.4 we take up the strategic aspects of monetary and fiscal policies under the alternative monetary arrangements that we are examining, and present illustrations in which a return to fixed rates would indeed raise the efficiency of macroeconomic management. In section 3.5 the large-scale empirical model is then used to study strategic aspects of policymaking in a differential game format. We examine a game of disinflation, in which all of the major economies begin the game with an excessively high inflation rate and in which all then use monetary and fiscal policies (subject to the rules of the exchange regime) in order to disinflate optimally. Once again we confirm the crucial quantitative importance of alternative exchange regimes for policy choices and macroeconomic outcomes. Finally, in section 3.6 we introduce a useful methodology for judging the long-run efficiency of alternative forms of monetary arrangements. Some concluding remarks are offered in section 3.7.

3.2   Fiscal Policy Transmission in a Simple Mundell-Fleming Model

We now introduce a simple, static, two-country model in order to illustrate the implications for fiscal policy of alternative monetary regimes. We introduce the barest-bones model here for illustrative purposes only, since in section 3.3 we study a richly specified and empirically calibrated model of the world economy. It turns out, however,

that even the simplest fixed-price model can give us a good understanding of the properties of the short-run policy multipliers in the
large-scale model.

Consider the following standard setup, as in Mundell (1968). We
assume that domestic and foreign goods prices (p and p^*) are fixed,
and that there is perfect capital mobility ($i = i^*$). The exchange rate
(e) between the two countries is in units of the home currency per unit
of foreign currency. An asterisk (*) denotes foreign country. The model
is specified with two money demand equations, and two IS curves. The
notation is standard: m is (log) money balances; p is (log) prices; q is
(log) output; i is the nominal interest rate; and g is the measure of fiscal
policy. The equations are as follows:

(1)
$$m - p = \phi q - \beta i$$

(2)
$$m^* - p^* = \phi q^* - \beta i$$

(3)
$$q = -\delta(p - e - p^*) - \sigma i + \lambda g + \gamma q^*$$

(4)
$$q^* = \delta(p - e - p^*) - \sigma i + \lambda g^* + \gamma q$$

We assume, as is standard, that the interaction term in the IS equations,
γ, is positive and less than one in value. We consider four monetary
regimes and study the fiscal policy multipliers in each case. The regimes
are:

(a) floating exchange rate (the change in the exchange rate, de, is
    unrestricted, and pure fiscal policy is studied with $dm = dm^* = 0$);
(b) dollar standard (U.S. monetary policy is held fixed, so that $dm = 0$
    and the foreign money supply adjusts endogenously so that $de = 0$);
(c) McKinnon rule (the exchange rate is fixed, $de = 0$, and a weighted
    average of the money stocks $m^w = \alpha m + (1 - \alpha) m^*$ is held fixed);
(d) modified McKinnon rule ($de = 0$, m^w is allowed to change).

We now turn to the fiscal policy multipliers.

(a)   Floating exchange rate

The system (1)–(4) is differentiated and solved. The multipliers for
fiscal and monetary policy are:

$$dq = \frac{\lambda}{2[1 - \gamma + \sigma\phi/\beta]} (dg + dg^*)$$

$$+ \frac{1 - \gamma + 2\sigma\phi/\beta}{2\phi[1 - \gamma + \sigma\phi/\beta]} dm - \frac{1 - \gamma}{2\phi[1 - \gamma + \sigma\phi/\beta]} dm^*$$

$$dq^* = \frac{\lambda}{2[1 - \gamma + \sigma\phi/\beta]} (dg + dg^*)$$

$$-\frac{1 - \gamma}{2\phi[1 - \gamma + \sigma\phi/\beta]}\, dm + \frac{1 - \gamma + 2\sigma\phi/\beta}{2\phi[1 - \gamma + \sigma\phi/\beta]}\, dm^*$$

$$de = \frac{\lambda}{2\delta}(dg^* - dg) - \frac{1 - \gamma}{2\delta\phi}(dm^* - dm)$$

In this symmetric case fiscal policy is positively transmitted across countries (given that $\gamma < 1$) with the country having the largest fiscal expansion experiencing an appreciation of its currency. Monetary policy is negatively transmitted, since a money supply expansion at home causes the exchange rate to depreciate, and thereby shifts demand from the foreign country to the home market.

(b) Dollar standard

The system is again solved, this time using the assumptions that $de = 0$, dm exogenous and dm^* endogenous. In this case we find:

$$dq = \frac{\lambda}{\Delta}(dg + \gamma\, dg^*) + \frac{\sigma(1 + \gamma)/\beta}{\Delta}\, dm$$

$$dq^* = \frac{\lambda[\gamma - \sigma\phi/\beta]}{\Delta}\, dg + \frac{\lambda\,[1 + \phi\sigma/\beta]}{\Delta}\, dg^* + \frac{\sigma(1 + \gamma)/\beta}{\Delta}\, dm$$

$$dm^* = \frac{\phi\lambda[\gamma - \sigma\phi/\beta - 1]}{\Delta}\, dg + \frac{\phi\lambda[1 - \gamma + \phi\sigma/\beta]}{\Delta}\, dg^* + dm$$

where

$$\Delta = [1 - \gamma^2 + (\phi/\beta)(1 + \gamma)\,] > 0$$

A foreign fiscal expansion is again transmitted positively to the home country, while a domestic fiscal expansion will actually be negatively transmitted if $\sigma\phi > \beta\gamma$. This surprising result occurs because the fiscal expansion by the home country tends to appreciate the currency. The foreign country is thereby required to undertake a monetary contraction in order to prevent its currency from depreciating. The contractionary effects of this endogenous monetary response can be sufficient to offset the normal expansionary effect coming through a rise in exports to the home country. Note that a rise in home-country money, $dm > 0$, raises output in both countries and induces a corresponding increase in the foreign money supply.

There is admittedly something artificial in the way we study this case, in that g and g^* are assumed to be exogenous, so that m^* is the "automatic" instrument that the foreign country uses to peg the exchange rate. If, for example, we were instead to assume that g^* is altered to keep $de = 0$, then a home fiscal expansion ($dg > 0$) would necessarily raise foreign output. In the later empirical sections, the foreign country chooses the combination of dg^* and dm^* optimally in order to maximize a social welfare function, subject to the constraint that $de = 0$.

(c)   McKinnon rule

In the fixed exchange rate regime proposed by McKinnon (1984), the exchange rate between the major countries would be fixed, together with an exogenously set growth rate of a weighted average world money stock. The implications of this regime for fiscal policy in this simple model can be found by setting $dm^w = \alpha dm + (1-\alpha)dm^*$ as an exogenous variable, and requiring that $de = dm^w = 0$. Monetary policy in both countries is endogenous. Doing this we find:

$$dq = \frac{\lambda}{\theta} dg + \frac{\lambda \left[\gamma\beta/\phi(1-\alpha) - \sigma\right]}{\theta \left[\sigma + \beta/\phi(1-\alpha)\right]} dg^*$$

$$dq^* = \frac{\lambda}{\theta^*} dg^* + \frac{\lambda \left[\gamma\beta/\phi\alpha - \sigma\right]}{\theta \left[\sigma + \beta/\phi\alpha\right]} dg$$

where
$$\theta = 1 - \gamma^2 + \frac{(1 + \gamma)\sigma[\gamma + \alpha/(1-\alpha)]}{[\sigma + \beta/\phi(1-\alpha)]}$$

$$\theta^* = 1 - \gamma^2 + \frac{(1 + \gamma)\sigma[\gamma + (1-\alpha)/\alpha]}{[\sigma + \beta/\phi\alpha]}$$

In this case both home and foreign fiscal policies will be negatively transmitted if $\sigma\phi(1 - \alpha) > \gamma\beta$ for a foreign expansion and $\sigma\phi\alpha > \gamma\beta$ for a domestic expansion.

The form of the monetary regime has been shown to have important implications for the transmission of fiscal policy in the world economy. Later, we will see that the nature of the transmission will have important consequences for policy coordination among the major economies. In the next section we use a large-scale simulation model in an attempt to better quantify the fiscal policy multipliers.

3.3   Fiscal policy in an Empirical Model

In this section we use the MSG (McKibbin-Sachs Global) simulation model to examine the international transmission of fiscal policy. The MSG model was developed in Sachs and McKibbin (1985). The reader is also referred to recent papers by Ishii, McKibbin, and Sachs (1985), McKibbin and Sachs (1985) and Sachs (1985a) for several applications and refinements. The model is a rational-expectations, dynamic general equilibrium macroeconomic model of the world economy. A full list of equations is provided in the Appendix. The world economy is divided into five regions consisting of the United States, Japan, the ROECD, the Organization of Petroleum Exporting Countries (OPEC), and the non-oil developing countries. Each region is linked via flows of goods and assets. Stock-flow relationships and intertemporal budget constraints are carefully observed. Budget deficits cumulate into a stock of government debt which must eventually be financed, while current account deficits cumulate into a stock of foreign debt. Asset markets are forward-looking, so that the exchange rate and long-term interest rate are conditioned by the entire future path of policy.

There are equations for the internal macroeconomic structure of the three industrialized regions of the United States, the ROECD, and Japan, while the OPEC and developing-country regions have only their foreign trade and financial structures incorporated. Each region produces a good that is an imperfect substitute in the consumption baskets of each of the other regions. Consumption of each good therefore depends on income and relative prices. Private absorption depends on financial wealth, disposable income, and long-term and short-term real interest rates along conventional lines. Nominal wages are predetermined in each period, with the nominal wage change between periods a function of lagged consumer price inflation, the output gap, and the change in the output gap. With the assumption that the gross domestic product (GDP) deflator is a fixed markup over wages, we derive a standard Phillips curve equation. In essence, the model is a generalized version of the Dornbusch (1976) model, in which the goods markets clear less rapidly than the asset markets.

Residents in different countries hold their own country's assets as well as foreign assets (except foreign money), based on the relative expected rates of return, with expectations being formed rationally. While we specify the asset demand functions in a general portfolio balance fashion, the parameter values that we impose make the model behave almost as if assets were perfect substitutes. Money demand is specified according to a standard transactions-demand formulation.

The model is parameterized using actual 1983 trade shares and asset stocks. Behavioral parameters are chosen to be consistent with values found in the empirical literature. We have shown elsewhere (see Sachs 1985a) that the model is able to explain much of the macroeconomic experience of the 1980s, including the strong dollar and trade imbalances by shifts in macroeconomic policies in the United States, Japan, and the ROECD.

We simulate nonlinear and linear versions of the model using numerical techniques which take into account the forward-looking variables in the model. Specifically we use a procedure described by Fair and Taylor (1983). The linearized version of the model is amenable to policy-optimization exercises and has previously been used to consider the gains to policy coordination using dynamic game theory techniques (see Sachs and McKibbin 1985). Throughout the paper we use the linearized version of the model because of the reliance on dynamic programming in later sections. We have verified in earlier work that there is little difference between the policy multipliers in the linearized and nonlinear versions of the model in the exercises studied here.

We simulate a fiscal expansion by assuming a permanent 1% of GNP increase in real government expenditure on domestic goods, commencing in 1984, which is financed by government debt. We assume that the expenditure increase is permanent, and expected on impact to be permanent, with the budget deficit remaining 1% of GNP above the baseline path. Because of rising interest payments on the accumulating public debt, the deficit would tend to grow over time in the absence of compensating cuts in expenditure or increases in taxes. We assume that over time the increase in interest repayments is paid for through higher tax revenues. Note that the economies all possess a steady state growth rate of 3% per annum. In steady-state equilibrium, a constant deficit is compatible with a fixed debt–GDP ratio as long as the increase in debt due to the deficit causes the total debt stock to grow at the 3% annual rate. This requirement means that the steady-state debt–GDP ratio equals the steady-state deficit–GDP ratio divided by 0.03. For example, a permanent increase in the budget deficit, which raises the deficit from zero to 1% of GDP, causes the steady-state debt–GDP ratio to rise from zero to 33% of GDP.

Table 3.1 contains the results for a fiscal expansion in the United States under a pure floating exchange rate. Real GNP, the exchange rate, and money supply are recorded as a percentage deviation from the initial baseline, while the trade deficit and budget deficit are both reported as deviations from the baseline in percent of potential GNP. Inflation and the nominal interest rate are shown as percentage point deviations from the baseline (indicate with D). The absence of Ricardian consumers and the presence of price stickiness is obvious in the results. The real output multiplier follows a familiar hump shape: output rises initially, but over time rising interest rates, rising prices, a strong dollar, and rising taxes to finance the growing debt burden crowd out the fiscal stimulus. Crowding out is complete by 1989. Note that the dollar appreciates on impact by 3.3% against the Ecu (the currency of the ROECD) and the yen. Interest rates rise throughout the world, although by more in the United States than abroad. The differential in large part captures the expectation of a future depreciation of the U.S. dollar (remember, though, that because of the portfolio balance assumptions, there is also a slight and growing risk premium on dollar-denominated assets). The fiscal impulse is positively transmitted to the rest of the world as Japanese and ROECD trade balances improve, thanks both to the demand stimulus from higher U.S. output and to the strong dollar. The positive transmission quickly fades as rising world interest rates have their effect. Note that inflation initially falls in the United States. This result follows from our somewhat artificial assumption that home

Table 3.1   **U.S. Fiscal Expansion under a Flexible Exchange Rate**

		1984	1985	1986	1987	1988	1989
U.S. economy							
Real GNP	%	0.9	0.9	0.6	0.4	0.1	−0.1
Inflation	D	−0.2	0.2	0.3	0.4	0.4	0.4
Nominal interest rate	D	0.8	1.1	1.4	1.7	2.0	2.2
Exchange rate (Ecu/$)	%	3.3	3.2	3.4	3.4	3.3	3.2
Trade balance	%GNP	−0.4	−0.4	−0.4	−0.4	−0.4	−0.4
Budget deficit	%GNP	1.0	1.0	1.0	1.0	1.0	1.0
Money supply	%	0.0	0.0	0.0	0.0	0.0	0.0
Japanese economy							
Real GNP	%	0.6	0.2	0.1	−0.1	−0.2	−0.2
Inflation	D	0.2	0.4	0.3	0.3	0.3	0.2
Nominal interest rate	D	0.6	1.1	1.2	1.5	1.6	1.7
Exchange rate (yen/$)	%	3.3	3.1	3.2	3.2	3.1	2.9
Trade balance	%GNP	0.3	0.2	0.2	0.2	0.2	0.2
Budget deficit	%GNP	0.0	0.0	0.0	0.0	0.0	0.0
Money supply	%	0.0	0.0	0.0	0.0	0.0	0.0
ROECD economies							
Real GNP	%	0.8	0.1	0.0	−0.2	−0.3	−0.4
Inflation	D	0.2	0.5	0.3	0.3	0.2	0.2
Nominal interest rate	D	0.7	1.2	1.3	1.5	1.6	1.6
Trade balance	%GNP	0.3	0.3	0.3	0.3	0.3	0.3
Budget deficit	%GNP	0.0	0.0	0.0	0.0	0.0	0.0
Money supply	%	0.0	0.0	0.0	0.0	0.0	0.0

goods prices do not respond at all within the first year to higher domestic output, while import prices fall in response to the appreciation of the dollar.

Table 3.2 contains corresponding results for an ROECD fiscal expansion under a flexible exchange rate. The results are similar to those for the U.S. fiscal stimulus, with a positive transmission of output to the United States and Japan. The ROECD exchange rate appreciates against the dollar by 3.4% on impact, and against the yen by 3.1% on impact.

The results for a U.S. fiscal expansion under a dollar standard regime are shown next in table 3.3. In specifying this regime, we make several crucial assumptions. First, the comparative dynamic exercises assume that the non-U.S. economies peg their exchange rates to the dollar via monetary rather than fiscal policy. In other words, the U.S. fiscal multipliers assume that foreign fiscal policies are held fixed, while foreign monetary policies are wholly endogenous. Second, the form of monetary intervention must be made clear. The authorities could choose to stabilize the exchange rate with intervention on the foreign exchange markets or via intervention in the domestic credit markets (e.g., open-market operations, rediscounting, etc.). In a world of perfect capital

Table 3.2   **ROECD Fiscal Expansion under a Flexible Exchange Rate**

		1984	1985	1986	1987	1988	1989
U.S. economy							
Real GNP	%	0.7	0.2	0.1	−0.2	−0.3	−0.5
Inflation	D	0.2	0.4	0.4	0.4	0.3	0.2
Nominal interest rate	D	0.6	1.2	1.4	1.6	1.7	1.7
Exchange rate (Ecu/$)	%	−3.4	−3.1	−3.1	−2.9	−2.6	−2.3
Trade balance	%GNP	0.3	0.3	0.3	0.3	0.3	0.3
Budget deficit	%GNP	0.0	0.0	0.0	0.0	0.0	0.0
Money supply	%	0.0	0.0	0.0	0.0	0.0	0.0
Japanese economy							
Real GNP	%	0.5	0.1	0.1	−0.1	−0.2	−0.4
Inflation	D	0.2	0.4	0.3	0.3	0.2	0.1
Nominal interest rate	D	0.4	1.0	1.2	1.4	1.4	1.4
Exchange rate (yen/$)	%	−0.3	−0.4	−0.5	−0.6	−0.7	−0.8
Trade balance	%GNP	0.3	0.3	0.3	0.2	0.2	0.1
Budget deficit	%GNP	0.0	0.0	0.0	0.0	0.0	0.0
Money supply	%	0.0	0.0	0.0	0.0	0.0	0.0
ROECD economies							
Real GNP	%	1.1	1.1	0.7	0.4	0.0	−0.4
Inflation	D	−0.2	0.3	0.5	0.6	0.5	0.5
Nominal interest rate	D	0.9	1.4	2.0	2.4	2.6	2.8
Trade balance	%GNP	−0.4	−0.3	−0.3	−0.3	−0.3	−0.3
Budget deficit	%GNP	1.0	1.0	1.0	1.0	1.0	1.0
Money supply	%	0.0	0.0	0.0	0.0	0.0	0.0

mobility, all of these alternatives would be identical from the point of view of macroeconomic outcomes, while in a world of imperfect capital mobility, differences will arise depending on the nature of exchange rate pegging. Since our model assumes very high, though not fully perfect, substitutability, the choice of intervention mechanism is quantitatively of some, but only minor, importance. In fact, in all of our specifications used in the paper, we assume that the exchange rate is stabilized through interventions in the domestic money market.

Several results are striking. The first is the negative transmission of the U.S. fiscal expansion to the rest of the world. In this case both Japan and the ROECD adopt severely contractionary monetary policies in order to maintain the fixed exchange rate. The result is severe recession in both regions. The recessionary effect of the contractionary monetary policies quickly feeds back to the United States, and does much to dampen the U.S. fiscal multiplier (it turns negative by 1987). The asymmetry in the dollar standard regime is illustrated in table 3.4, which shows the results for an ROECD fiscal expansion. In contrast to the U.S. fiscal expansion, the ROECD fiscal expansion is positively transmitted to the rest of the world. The Ecu tends to appreciate, so that the ROECD monetary authorities are compelled to expand the

Table 3.3   **U.S. Fiscal Expansion under a Dollar Standard**

		1984	1985	1986	1987	1988	1989
U.S. economy							
Real GNP	%	1.7	0.6	0.1	−0.4	−0.5	−0.3
Inflation	D	0.0	0.6	0.3	0.1	−0.2	−0.4
Nominal interest rate	D	1.4	2.0	1.8	1.4	0.9	0.4
Exchange rate (Ecu/$)	%	0.0	0.0	0.0	0.0	0.0	0.0
Trade balance	%GNP	−0.3	−0.4	−0.6	−0.7	−0.8	−0.8
Budget deficit	%GNP	1.0	1.0	1.0	1.0	1.0	1.0
Money supply	%	0.0	0.0	0.0	0.0	0.0	0.0
Japanese economy							
Real GNP	%	−1.0	−1.6	−1.6	−1.4	−0.8	0.0
Inflation	D	0.0	−0.5	−0.9	−1.2	−1.4	−1.3
Nominal interest rate	D	1.4	1.9	1.7	1.3	0.8	0.2
Exchange rate (yen/$)	%	0.0	0.0	0.0	0.0	0.0	0.0
Trade balance	%GNP	0.1	0.1	0.1	0.1	0.2	0.3
Budget deficit	%GNP	0.0	0.0	0.0	0.0	0.0	0.0
Money supply	%	−1.0	−2.5	−3.8	−4.9	−5.8	−6.4
ROECD economies							
Real GNP	%	−2.1	−3.2	−2.7	−1.6	0.2	2.4
Inflation	D	0.0	−0.8	−1.5	−1.9	−1.9	−1.4
Nominal interest rate	D	1.4	1.9	1.7	1.2	0.5	0.0
Trade balance	%GNP	0.2	0.4	0.5	0.6	0.6	0.5
Budget deficit	%GNP	0.0	0.0	0.0	0.0	0.0	0.0
Money supply	%	−1.4	−3.6	−5.7	−7.2	−8.0	−7.8

domestic money supply. This leads to an enormous expansion in the ROECD and positive transmission to the other economies.

Table 3.5 illustrates the consequence of a fiscal expansion under the McKinnon rule. In this case we study the effects of a fiscal expansion under the assumption that a geometric weighted average of the money supplies in the United States, the ROECD, and Japan is fixed, and that the exchange rates are similarly fixed. The weights used (somewhat arbitrarily) are the GNP weights for 1983. In this case, as with the U.S. expansion under the dollar standard, the transmission of fiscal policy is negative. Once again, the non-U.S. economies are compelled to contract their money stocks while the United States expands its money stock. The result is a rise in interest rates abroad that is sufficient to overwhelm the direct effects of the U.S. stimulus. The extent of the recession abroad is less than in the dollar standard, since, in the McKinnon case, the United States is compelled to expand its money supply in line with the fiscal expansion.

The effects of an ROECD fiscal expansion under the McKinnon rule are shown in table 3.6. Now the ROECD fiscal expansion is negatively transmitted to the rest of the world. Clearly, the McKinnon rule on world money supplies imposes more symmetry than does the dollar

Table 3.4   **ROECD Fiscal Expansion under a Dollar Standard**

		1984	1985	1986	1987	1988	1989
U.S. economy							
Real GNP	%	0.1	0.5	0.6	0.5	0.1	−0.5
Inflation	D	0.0	0.2	0.5	0.7	0.9	0.8
Nominal interest rate	D	0.1	0.6	1.3	2.2	3.0	3.4
Exchange rate (Ecu/$)	%	0.0	0.0	0.0	0.0	0.0	0.0
Trade balance	%GNP	0.3	0.4	0.6	0.7	0.7	0.6
Budget deficit	%GNP	0.0	0.0	0.0	0.0	0.0	0.0
Money supply	%	0.0	0.0	0.0	0.0	0.0	0.0
Japanese economy							
Real GNP	%	0.6	0.9	0.8	0.6	0.1	−0.5
Inflation	D	0.1	0.4	0.7	1.0	1.1	0.9
Nominal interest rate	D	0.1	0.5	1.2	2.0	2.7	3.0
Exchange rate (yen/$)	%	0.0	0.0	0.0	0.0	0.0	0.0
Trade balance	%GNP	0.2	0.4	0.5	0.5	0.5	0.3
Budget deficit	%GNP	0.0	0.0	0.0	0.0	0.0	0.0
Money supply	%	0.2	0.6	0.9	1.2	1.4	1.6
ROECD economies							
Real GNP	%	4.7	4.5	3.2	1.1	−1.6	−4.3
Inflation	D	0.1	1.8	2.6	2.8	2.4	1.5
Nominal interest rate	D	0.1	0.8	1.7	2.8	3.8	4.4
Trade balance	%GNP	−0.3	−0.4	−0.5	−0.6	−0.6	−0.6
Budget deficit	%GNP	1.0	1.0	1.0	1.0	1.0	1.0
Money supply	%	1.7	4.2	6.2	7.5	7.8	7.0

rule. In the case of an ROECD fiscal expansion under the McKinnon rule, the United States and Japan contract monetary policy and the ROECD expands monetary policy in order to maintain the fixed exchange rate. The consequence of the contractionary monetary policies is to cause a recession in Japan and the United States.

3.4   Implications of the Exchange Regime for Strategic Interactions of Monetary and Fiscal Policy

As we noted in the beginning, one of the most attractive aspects of monetary reform is the possibility of reducing the inefficient strategic behavior of national macroeconomic authorities. It is well known that if policymakers in the United States, the ROECD, and Japan independently select their monetary and fiscal policies, taking as given the actions of the other countries, the resulting (Nash) equilibrium of macroeconomic policies is likely to be inefficient, in the sense that another vector of policy parameters could simultaneously raise the level of social welfare in all of the countries. In this brief theoretical section, we illustrate how a change of regime might make the independent actions of national policymakers more efficient.

Table 3.5   **U.S. Fiscal Expansion under the McKinnon Rule**

		1984	1985	1986	1987	1988	1989
U.S. economy							
Real GNP	%	2.3	1.9	1.4	0.7	0.0	−0.8
Inflation	D	0.0	0.9	1.1	1.1	1.0	0.8
Nominal interest rate	D	0.6	1.0	1.3	1.5	1.7	1.9
Exchange rate (Ecu/$)	%	0.0	0.0	0.0	0.0	0.0	0.0
Trade balance	%GNP	−0.2	−0.3	−0.4	−0.6	−0.7	−0.7
Budget deficit	%GNP	1.0	1.0	1.0	1.0	1.0	1.0
Money supply	%	0.6	1.5	2.4	3.1	3.6	3.8
Japanese economy							
Real GNP	%	−0.2	−0.4	−0.4	−0.3	−0.2	−0.1
Inflation	D	0.0	0.0	−0.1	−0.2	−0.2	−0.2
Nominal interest rate	D	0.6	1.0	1.2	1.4	1.5	1.6
Exchange rate (yen/$)	%	0.0	0.0	0.0	0.0	0.0	0.0
Trade balance	%GNP	0.1	0.2	0.2	0.2	0.3	0.3
Budget deficit	%GNP	0.0	0.0	0.0	0.0	0.0	0.0
Money supply	%	−0.4	−0.8	−1.3	−1.7	−2.1	−2.3
ROECD economies							
Real GNP	%	−0.5	−0.9	−0.7	−0.5	−0.1	0.4
Inflation	D	0.0	−0.2	−0.3	−0.4	−0.3	−0.2
Nominal interest rate	D	0.6	1.0	1.2	1.4	1.5	1.5
Trade balance	%GNP	0.2	0.3	0.4	0.4	0.5	0.5
Budget deficit	%GNP	0.0	0.0	0.0	0.0	0.0	0.0
Money supply	%	−0.5	−1.2	−1.9	−2.5	−2.9	−3.0

Consider a hypothetical situation in which two symmetric countries choose monetary and fiscal policies to maximize a social welfare function in output, in the fiscal deficit, and in the level of prices (in the dynamic model, the target will be the inflation rate). For simplicity, we assume that the welfare functions are identical and of the following quadratic form:

$$(5) \qquad W = -(q^2 + \mu\, p_c^2 + \nu\, g^2),$$

where p_c is the (log) level of consumer prices (the foreign welfare function is of course a function of the corresponding foreign variables). The bliss points for each country are zero levels of (log) output, consumer prices, and fiscal expenditure. We use the earlier static model of section 3.2, with the addition that consumer prices in each country are a weighted average of home prices and import prices (valued in domestic currency):

$$p_c = \eta\, p + (1 - \eta)\, (p^* + e)$$
$$p_c^* = \eta\, p^* + (1 - \eta)\, (p - e)$$

Table 3.6   **ROECD Fiscal Expansion under the McKinnon Rule**

		1984	1985	1986	1987	1988	1989
U.S. economy							
Real GNP	%	−0.6	−0.8	−0.6	−0.3	0.0	0.4
Inflation	D	0.0	−0.1	−0.2	−0.2	−0.2	−0.1
Nominal interest rate	D	0.9	1.5	1.8	2.0	2.0	1.9
Exchange rate (Ecu/$)	%	0.0	0.0	0.0	0.0	0.0	0.0
Trade balance	%GNP	0.2	0.3	0.4	0.5	0.6	0.5
Budget deficit	%GNP	0.0	0.0	0.0	0.0	0.0	0.0
Money supply	%	−0.6	−1.5	−2.2	−2.7	−2.9	−2.8
Japanese economy							
Real GNP	%	−0.2	−0.4	−0.3	−0.2	−0.1	0.0
Inflation	D	0.1	0.0	0.0	0.0	0.0	0.0
Nominal interest rate	D	0.9	1.4	1.7	1.8	1.8	1.6
Exchange rate (yen/$)	%	0.0	0.0	0.0	0.0	0.0	0.0
Trade balance	%GNP	0.2	0.3	0.4	0.4	0.4	0.3
Budget deficit	%GNP	0.0	0.0	0.0	0.0	0.0	0.0
Money supply	%	−0.5	−1.0	−1.5	−1.7	−1.8	−1.7
ROECD economies							
Real GNP	%	3.1	2.3	1.5	0.4	−0.8	−1.8
Inflation	D	0.0	1.2	1.4	1.4	1.1	0.7
Nominal interest rate	D	0.9	1.6	2.1	2.5	2.7	2.8
Trade balance	%GNP	−0.2	−0.3	−0.4	−0.5	−0.6	−0.6
Budget deficit	%GNP	1.0	1.0	1.0	1.0	1.0	1.0
Money supply	%	0.8	1.8	2.7	3.3	3.5	3.4

Maintaining the assumption that domestic and foreign output prices are fixed, with $p = p^* = p_0 > 0$, we see that fluctuation in the exchange rate is the only factor that can cause p_c and p_c^* to change in the short run.

In the case of symmetric countries, it will necessarily be the case that the exchange rate equals zero ($e = 0$). Given this fact, consumer prices in each country are fixed at the level p_0. Since p_c cannot be reduced in both countries simultaneously, the best symmetric solution is merely to live with the fact that p_c is above the bliss level, and then to set $g = g^* = 0$, and $m = m^* = p_0$, so that output is kept at $q = q^* = 0$. In other words, the economies should sit at "full employment" and zero budget deficit, suffering the inevitable fact that consumer prices are above their bliss level.

Unfortunately, in noncooperative policymaking under floating exchange rates, this efficient equilibrium will not be reached. Each country's policy authorities will believe that a strong currency option is available that will allow them to reduce p_c, and therefore to import price stability (and to export inflation!). Each country will therefore aim its monetary policy in a contractionary direction and its fiscal policy in an expansionary direction in order to exploit the possible anti-inflationary gains of a strong currency. Of course, this noncooperative outcome has all the trappings of a prisoners' dilemma game, in that the two symmetric countries will be unable, simultaneously, to enjoy a strong currency vis-à-vis each other! The results of the noncooperative game will therefore be (1) a policy mix geared toward fiscal expansion cum monetary contraction, with a socially undesirable level of fiscal deficits; (2) overly contractionary policies in total, with output reduced below the efficient symmetric level of $q = q^* = 0$; and (3) an exchange rate $e = 0$, with $p_c = p_c^* = p_0$, i.e., no success in either country of manipulating the exchange rate to its own advantage.

These results are easy to confirm algebraically. The home country maximizes the social welfare function (eq. 5) with respect to m and g, taking as given the level of m^* and g^*. The foreign country makes the comparable policy analysis, arriving at values of m^* and g^*, taking as given m and g. At the Nash equilibrium in this symmetric case, $m = m^*$ and $g = g^*$, with the specific values of the target variables given as follows (note that the multipliers dy/dx in the equations are as given in the derivations in section 3.2):

$$q = q^* = -[\mu \, p_0 \, (1 - \eta)(de/dm)]/(dq/dm) < 0$$

$$p_c = p_c^* = p_0 > 0$$

$$g = g^* = -[q \, (dq/dg) + \mu \, p \, (1 - \eta)(de/dg)]/v > 0$$

Remember that $de/dm > 0$, $de/dg < 0$, $dq/dm > 0$, $dq/dg > 0$, in order to derive the signs of the preceding expressions. Thus, output is below zero, while government spending is above zero. By simple substitution, it is easy to see that $m = m^* < p_0$. In sum we have established the early conclusions: m is too tight and g is too loose relative to the efficient equilibrium, and aggregate demand overall is too tight (since $q = q^* < 0$).

It is important to note that the inefficiency in this game would hold if the players had only one instrument, either m or g, instead of two. If m and m^* were fixed, with the authorities setting g and g^*, there would still be a bias toward inefficiently large fiscal deficits, whereas if g and g^* are fixed while the game is played with m and m^*, then the bias is toward overcontractionary policies. In both cases, the countries attempt to manipulate the exchange rate in their favor (i.e., toward an appreciation).

Now, consider how this game would be played under the McKinnon standard. In that case, policymakers choose only g and g^*, since monetary policy is set according to the two rules that m^w is fixed and that the exchange rate is fixed (in this case at $e = 0$). The cooperative optimum equilibrium is again the same, with $q = q^* = 0$, $g = g^* = 0$, and $p_c = p_c^* = p_0$. To achieve this equilibrium, m^w should be set at p_0, and fiscal policy in both countries should be set at zero.

Assume now that the McKinnon rule is in place, but with each fiscal policy authority free to choose the level of fiscal spending in a noncooperative way. Suppose also that m^w is fixed exogenously at p_0 (more on this assumption in a moment). It now turns out that the independent actions of the fiscal authorities will lead to the social optimum. The policymaker has no incentive to try to deviate from the point of zero fiscal expenditure. Higher fiscal spending no longer improves the price performance, as it did under the floating system, since now the exchange rate is fixed at zero. Therefore fiscal expenditure merely worsens the budget deficit without any compensating benefits. These results are verified formally by maximizing the social welfare function at home with respect to g, and abroad with respect to g^*. It is easy to verify that $g = g^* = 0$ constitutes a Nash equilibrium.

To see this formally, we simply differentiate the utility function with respect to g, and set the results equal to zero. Under the McKinnon rule, $de/dg = 0$, so that the result of differentiation is: $dW/dg = 0 = -[q(dq/dg) + vg]$. With m^w at p_0, and $g^* = 0$, this first-order condition is satisfied at $q = 0$ and $g = 0$. The same result holds for the foreign country when $g = 0$, so that the pair $g = g^* = 0$ constitutes a Nash equilibrium.

Thus, we have a case in which a change in monetary regime eliminates the inefficient strategic interactions of the two governments. The essential inefficiency of the game under floating exchange rates resulted from the fact that the two sides had inconsistent exchange rate targets, which obviously could not be simultaneously satisfied. Under the McKinnon rule, neither player attempts or is able to influence the exchange rate in his favor. It must be stressed that the efficiency of the McKinnon solution relied heavily on two facts. First, it was assumed that the world money stock m^w was at the global optimum. In fact, McKinnon has opted for a fixed level of m^w in most discussions of his proposal, and there is no reason to believe that the selected value of m^w would necessarily be at an efficient level. Second, the symmetry of the model and the symmetry of the "shock" (both countries had prices equally above the optimum) meant that the exchange rate did not have to adjust in order to adapt efficiently to the shock. In later sections we will study asymmetric cases, in which efficiency requires a change in the nominal exchange rate.

3.5 Strategic Interactions under Alternative Regimes in the MSG Model

We now employ the large-scale simulation model to study strategic interactions in the dynamic case. For this purpose we use two methodologies. In the first, we place the countries in a particular historical situation and study the optimal strategies of each country over time. A benchmark "cooperative" equilibrium is used as a benchmark with which to compare the performance in the alternative monetary regimes. In the second and more novel approach, introduced in section 3.6, we study the asymptotic properties of the system under alternative exchange arrangements. In that case we assume that the system is buffeted through time by various stochastic disturbances, in output markets, money markets, and elsewhere. Using a technique described in that section, we can calculate the steady-state variance/covariance structure of the target variables in each exchange regime, and thereby measure the average operating properties of each system. In general, the MSG model is particularly well suited to this kind of analysis, since the model is easily reducible to a first-order difference equation system, which is easy to analyze using standard techniques of dynamic analysis.

To study the dynamic games involved in setting national policy, we specify a social welfare function for each of the three OECD regions. Social welfare in each region is specified as a function of various macroeconomic targets, such as the inflation rates, the GDP gap, the current account deficit, and the budget deficit. The intertemporal social welfare functions are written as additively separable quadratic functions of the targets in each period. The specific form that we employ makes social welfare a function of the output gap Q, consumer price index inflation π, the current account deficit as a percent of GDP, denoted CA, and the level of the budget deficit relative to GDP, denoted D. The specific function that we employ is as follows:

$$(6) \qquad W = - \sum_{t=0}^{\infty} \delta^t [0.5 \ Q_t^2 + \pi_t^2 + 0.5 \ CA_t^2 + 0.6 \ D_t^2]$$

δ is the social rate-of-time discount. Clearly, macroeconomic bliss is achieved when the GDP gap is zero, CPI inflation is zero, the current account is in balance, and the budget is in balance.

Corresponding welfare functions are assumed for the ROECD and Japan. A couple of preliminary comments should be made about this welfare function. First, the results are obviously specific to a given numerical specification. The inefficiency of a strategic noncooperative interaction will depend quantitatively on the weights attached to the countries' target variables. In the simple example of the section 3.4, for example, the inefficiency resulted from the fact that both countries were attempting simultaneously to reduce their price levels via exchange rate appreciation. The inefficiency of the noncooperative solution in that case depends crucially on the relative weight placed by the countries on the inflation target. For purposes of study of our large-scale model, we have not yet determined any way to study the dynamic games except through the specification of particular loss functions. The second point is that the loss function relates to macroeconomic targets (inflation, unemployment, etc.) rather than to more basic categories of real consumption over time. Our model does not have strong enough microeconomic foundations at this point to write policy targets in terms of the "primitives" of consumption expenditure, as might be desirable in a more sophisticated treatment.

Using results of dynamic game theory, we calculate (with numerical dynamic programming methods) a set of fiscal policy rules in the three OECD regions that have the following equilibrium property: the rules for each country are optimal for the given country (in that they maximize the dynamic social welfare function), taking as given the rules that are being employed in the other regions. A more rigorous statement of the equilibrium conditions and a discussion of the solution technique is given in Oudiz and Sachs (1985). The optimum we calculate is time consistent. That is, there is no incentive to choose a different set of policies if the optimization problem is solved again at some point in the future. The policies are therefore also credible to the forward-looking private agents and other countries in the model. We have shown elsewhere (see Sachs and McKibbin 1985), that, as in the static model of the section 3.4, such an equilibrium does not necessarily yield very attractive outcomes. These rules will likely contain some types of beggar-thy-neighbor policies and will therefore show some of the disadvantages of the classic prisoners' dilemma. For example, in the case where both monetary and fiscal policies are chosen according to such rules under a flexible exchange rate regime, we will see that the equilibrium rules are likely to produce excessive budget deficits and high real interest rates in an inflationary environment, just as we found for the static model.

It is therefore very likely that the social welfare of all of the countries can be enhanced by a different set of policies, chosen cooperatively. We can find such a set new rules by assuming that a single "world" planner maximizes a single social welfare function, which is a weighted average of the social welfare functions of the United States, Japan, and the ROECD, where the weights are GNP shares. The result of this global optimization is a new set of rules that avoids prisoners' dilemmas. These optimal "cooperative" rules can then be compared with the "noncooperative" rules found in the first stage. In general, it will be the case that "cooperative" policies result in some form of managed float, in that global efficiency of policy setting will almost surely require changes in the nominal exchange rates of the three countries in the course of macroeconomic adjustment.

We use this technique to generate noncooperative rules for fiscal policy, given the monetary regime in place, as well as a set of cooperative rules. In the case of the flexible exchange rate regime, we assume that policymakers choose *both* monetary and fiscal policies to reach targets for output, inflation, the current account, and budget deficits. In the dollar standard case the United States is allowed to optimize on both monetary and fiscal policies, whereas Japan and the ROECD are only given the option of choosing fiscal policy. Their money supplies are made endogenous and are set at the levels necessary to keep the exchange rate unchanged, given the levels of the state variables of the world economy, and given the levels of their own fiscal policies and of the monetary and fiscal policies in the other economies. In the McKinnon regime, each region chooses fiscal policy to reach its given targets. In the "simple" McKinnon regime, the global money stock is held fixed, while in the "modified" McKinnon regime, the three regions cooperatively set the global money stock, m^w, while they choose their fiscal policies independently. In each case the dynamic welfare function is the one we have just introduced.

A word must be said about how we implement the modified McKinnon regime. Remember that, in that case, the global money stock is set cooperatively, while the individual countries set the fiscal policies noncooperatively. To find a "good" rule for the global money stock, we employed the following iterative procedure. We found the rule for global money that maximizes a global social welfare function (a GNP-weighted average of the individual region social welfare functions) assuming that fiscal policies were also chosen cooperatively. Then, given the resulting rule for global money, we let the individual policymakers choose optimal fiscal policies in a noncooperative manner. Taking as given these resulting rules for fiscal policy, we then recalculated an optimal cooperative rule for global money, and used that one as the rule to control the evolution of m^w. Ideally, the linear rule should be found for m^w that maximizes the global welfare, subject to the constraint that the fiscal rules are chosen uncooperatively by the separate regions. This formulation would make the cooperative monetary authorities Stackelberg leaders with respect to the fiscal authorities of the individual countries. Unfortunately we have not yet been able to implement this more ambitious approach.

As a formal matter, the MSG model can be written in a standard state space representation in the following way:

(7) $$X_{t+1} = AX_t + Be_t + CU_t + Z\epsilon_t$$

(8) $$_t(e_{t+1}) = DX_t + Fe_t + GU_t + W\epsilon_t$$

(9) $$\tau_t = MX_t + Le_t + NU_t + O\epsilon_t$$

where:

X_{t+1} is a vector of state variables (in this case 37×1)
U_t is a vector of control variables
e_t is a vector of nonpredetermined (or "jumping") variables
τ_t is a vector of target variables
ϵ_t is a vector of stochastic shocks (6×1)
$_t(e_{t+1})$ is the expectation taken at time t of the jumping variables at time $t+1$ based on information available at time t

The model variables are divided into state variables X_t, historically given at any moment; "jumping" or forward-looking variables e_t, which are fixed in order to place the system on the stable dynamic manifold; control variables U_t including fiscal and monetary policies; and stochastic shocks ϵ_t. Assuming that in each period the policy variables must be set before the stochastic shocks are observed, the policy rules are all written in the form:

$$(10) \qquad U_t = \Gamma X_t$$

In other words, the general specification of rules links the control variables to the state variables in any period via a fixed set of linear rules. Of course, the linearity results from the assumption of linearity of the underlying model and the assumption of a quadratic social welfare function in each region.

The dynamic game that we study in this section has the policy authorities all confronting an unanticipated jump in nominal wage inflation of 10% per year, after being on a baseline path of zero inflation, zero GDP gap, budget balance, and current account balance. The shock hits in 1984, raising domestic prices in the year by 10% and setting in motion several years of high inflation, given the inflationary momentum built into the Phillips curve equation (which makes current nominal wage change a function of lagged nominal price change). In each region, monetary and fiscal policies are deployed in order to engineer an optimal rate of disinflation, subject to the social welfare function (which trades off output, inflation, budget, and current account deficits) and subject to the policy rules taken abroad. In this analysis we assume that the system is nonstochastic (that is, all ϵ are zero), returning to the stochastic case in the section 3.6, when we look at the steady-state operating properties of the alternative regimes.

Table 3.7 illustrates the case of optimal cooperative disinflation. Since all countries begin with a shock of 10% wage inflation, it is optimal to pursue tight macroeconomic policies in order to bring inflation down to zero in the period of a few years. In this case, the nominal money stock growth is kept low and falling, so that real money balances (not shown) fall sharply in the early period of disinflation. Since domestic prices in each of the three regions has risen by 10% in 1984, the fact

Table 3.7   **Cooperative Response to an Inflationary Shock under a Flexible Exchange Rate**

		1984	1985	1986	1987	1988	1989
U.S. economy							
Real GNP	%	−10.1	−8.0	−6.4	−5.2	−4.1	−3.3
Inflation	D	10.0	5.9	4.8	3.8	3.0	2.4
Nominal interest rate	D	15.4	12.3	9.7	7.6	6.1	5.0
Exchange rate (Ecu/$)	%	0.6	0.0	−0.5	−1.0	−1.4	−1.9
Trade balance	%GNP	0.2	0.2	0.1	0.1	0.1	0.1
Budget deficit	%GNP	−0.5	−0.3	−0.2	−0.1	−0.1	0.0
Money supply	%	−0.8	2.0	6.9	12.2	17.0	21.2
Japanese economy							
Real GNP	%	−9.8	−7.9	−6.4	−5.1	−4.2	−3.4
Inflation	D	9.2	5.4	4.4	3.5	2.9	2.3
Nominal interest rate	D	16.1	12.9	10.0	7.8	6.2	4.9
Exchange rate (yen/$)	%	−5.1	−4.5	−3.9	−3.5	−3.3	−3.1
Trade balance	%GNP	−0.8	−0.6	−0.6	−0.5	−0.4	−0.2
Budget deficit	%GNP	−0.8	−0.5	−0.4	−0.3	−0.3	−0.2
Money supply	%	−1.1	0.8	5.3	10.3	15.0	19.0
ROECD economies							
Real GNP	%	−10.3	−8.0	−6.4	−5.1	−4.0	−3.2
Inflation	D	9.9	5.8	4.6	3.6	2.9	2.3
Nominal interest rate	D	14.8	11.6	8.9	6.8	5.3	4.2
Trade balance	%GNP	0.4	0.2	−0.1	−0.2	−0.3	−0.2
Budget deficit	%GNP	0.0	0.0	0.0	0.0	0.0	−0.1
Money supply	%	−0.5	2.3	7.3	12.6	17.4	21.4

that nominal money stocks are falling in 1984 relative to the baseline means that real money balances are declining by more than 10% in 1984, i.e., that monetary policy is highly nonaccommodative in the year of the price shock. Also, fiscal policy is restrictive in the United States (where there is a surplus of 0.5% of GNP in 1984), and Japan (where there is a surplus of 0.8% of GNP), while fiscal policy is neutral in the ROECD. In all countries there is a sharp recession in 1984 of about 10% of GDP relative to potential, and actual GDP reapproaches its potential level only slowly over time. Note that, because of the monetary stringency, there is a sharp rise in nominal short-term interest rates, with interest rates in 1984 rising by 15.4 percentage points in the United States, by 16.1 percentage points in Japan, and by 14.8 percentage points in the ROECD. Interest rates fall gradually over time, in line with the gradual disinflation.

Table 3.7 shows the optimal cooperative response. Table 3.8 shows what happens when policy makers act independently and noncooperatively, under a regime of floating exchange rates. Suddenly, everybody tries to maintain a strong currency in order to help fight off the infla-

Table 3.8   Noncooperative Response to an Inflationary Shock under a Flexible Exchange Rate

		1984	1985	1986	1987	1988	1989
U.S. economy							
Real GNP	%	−10.2	−8.0	−6.4	−5.2	−4.1	−3.3
Inflation	D	9.9	5.9	4.7	3.8	3.0	2.4
Nominal interest rate	D	19.3	14.7	11.8	9.4	7.7	6.3
Exchange rate (Ecu/$)	%	1.5	0.5	−0.1	−0.7	−1.2	−1.7
Trade balance	%GNP	0.2	0.1	0.1	0.1	0.1	0.1
Budget deficit	%GNP	1.3	0.8	0.6	0.6	0.5	0.4
Money supply	%	−2.5	−0.1	4.9	10.3	15.3	19.6
Japanese economy							
Real GNP	%	−10.1	−7.8	−6.3	−5.1	−4.1	−3.3
Inflation	D	9.1	5.3	4.3	3.5	2.8	2.3
Nominal interest rate	D	19.9	15.6	12.7	10.3	8.6	7.3
Exchange rate (yen/$)	%	−5.2	−4.6	−4.1	−3.7	−3.5	−3.3
Trade balance	%GNP	−0.7	−0.6	−0.5	−0.5	−0.4	−0.3
Budget deficit	%GNP	1.4	0.9	0.7	0.6	0.5	0.5
Money supply	%	−2.9	−1.4	2.8	7.8	12.5	16.6
ROECD economies							
Real GNP	%	−10.3	−8.0	−6.3	−5.0	−4.0	−3.2
Inflation	D	10.0	5.8	4.6	3.7	2.9	2.3
Nominal interest rate	D	18.3	14.0	11.1	8.9	7.2	5.9
Trade balance	%GNP	0.6	0.3	0.0	−0.2	−0.3	−0.3
Budget deficit	%GNP	1.6	1.0	0.8	0.6	0.5	0.5
Money supply	%	−2.1	0.5	5.5	10.9	15.8	19.9

tionary shock. Each country therefore has more expansionary fiscal policy than in the cooperative solution (the United States, for example, runs a budget deficit of 1.3% of GNP in 1984) and has more contractionary monetary policy than in the cooperative case. The result is that noncooperation under floating leads to very high world interest rates, since the whole world is tilted toward fiscal expansion and monetary contraction. U.S. nominal interest rates jump by 19.3 percentage points in the noncooperative floating rate case, whereas they increased by only 14.8 percentage points in the cooperative policy response.

In tables 3.9 and 3.10 we ask what happens when the same shock occurs in a regime of fixed exchange rates, first under a dollar standard and then under a modified McKinnon rule. The notable point about the dollar standard is that the United States still has an incentive to pursue fiscal expansion and monetary contraction, just as under the floating rate case. A fiscal expansion in the United States reduces output abroad (we noted the negative transmission in sections 3.2 and 3.3), and thereby lowers foreign inflation. Lower foreign inflation in turn lowers U.S. import prices. Similarly, a U.S. monetary contraction has the same side-effect.

Table 3.9   **Noncooperative Response to an Inflationary Shock under a Dollar Standard**

		1984	1985	1986	1987	1988	1989
U.S. economy							
Real GNP	%	−10.5	−8.3	−6.6	−5.2	−4.1	−3.3
Inflation	D	9.9	5.7	4.5	3.5	2.8	2.2
Nominal interest rate	D	22.8	18.1	14.4	11.5	9.3	7.6
Exchange rate (Ecu/$)	%	0.0	0.0	0.0	0.0	0.0	0.0
Trade balance	%GNP	0.2	0.1	0.0	0.0	−0.1	0.0
Budget deficit	%GNP	2.8	2.2	1.9	1.5	1.3	1.1
Money supply	%	−4.2	−2.7	2.0	7.5	12.7	17.1
Japanese economy							
Real GNP	%	−9.8	−7.7	−6.2	−5.0	−4.1	−3.4
Inflation	D	9.7	5.8	4.7	3.7	3.0	2.4
Nominal interest rate	D	22.8	18.2	14.6	11.7	9.6	8.0
Exchange rate (yen/$)	%	0.0	0.0	0.0	0.0	0.0	0.0
Trade balance	%GNP	0.1	0.0	−0.2	−0.3	−0.4	−0.4
Budget deficit	%GNP	1.3	0.9	0.7	0.6	0.6	0.5
Money supply	%	−4.1	−2.5	2.4	7.9	13.1	17.6
ROECD economies							
Real GNP	%	−10.7	−8.1	−6.3	−4.8	−3.8	−2.9
Inflation	D	9.8	5.6	4.5	3.6	2.9	2.4
Nominal interest rate	D	22.8	18.4	15.0	12.3	10.2	8.6
Trade balance	%GNP	0.4	0.2	0.0	−0.2	−0.3	−0.3
Budget deficit	%GNP	4.4	3.2	2.5	1.9	1.4	1.0
Money supply	%	−4.3	−2.9	1.7	7.2	12.4	17.0

Thus, the United States, as center of the monetary system, shifts its policy mix in a direction intended to promote very sharp disinflation abroad. In the other countries, expansionary budget policies are undertaken defensively, in order to limit the extent of disinflation and economic contraction implicit in the U.S. policies. The result is that, like the floating rate case, each country is led to pursue a policy mix of large budget deficits and very contractionary monetary policies. World interest rates shoot up, and the world falls into recession.

Table 3.10, under the modified McKinnon regime, shows the advantage of this regime in fighting a global inflationary shock. As we saw in the theoretical analysis of section 3.4, countries no longer have the incentive to run large budget deficits under the McKinnon regime, since they know that they cannot get disinflationary benefits from such a policy mix. Therefore they all choose to have lower budget deficits than in the noncooperative equilibrium under floating, and than in the noncooperative equilibrium under the dollar standard. In this sense, the shift in regime almost substitutes for the cooperation assumed in table 3.7. World interest rates rise much less under the modified McKinnon plan than under the other noncooperative regimes.

Table 3.10   **Noncooperative Response to an Inflationary Shock under the McKinnon Rule**

		1984	1985	1986	1987	1988	1989
U.S. economy							
Real GNP	%	−10.0	−8.0	−6.5	−5.2	−4.2	−3.4
Inflation	D	9.9	5.9	4.7	3.7	3.0	2.3
Nominal interest rate	D	16.6	13.3	10.6	8.4	6.8	5.6
Exchange rate (Ecu/$)	%	0.0	0.0	0.0	0.0	0.0	0.0
Trade balance	%GNP	0.1	0.1	0.0	0.0	0.0	0.0
Budget deficit	%GNP	0.2	0.3	0.4	0.4	0.4	0.4
Money supply	%	−1.2	1.2	6.0	11.2	16.0	20.1
Japanese economy							
Real GNP	%	−8.3	−7.0	−6.0	−5.1	−4.4	−3.8
Inflation	D	9.7	6.3	5.2	4.2	3.3	2.6
Nominal interest rate	D	16.6	13.1	10.2	7.9	6.2	5.0
Exchange rate (yen/$)	%	0.0	0.0	0.0	0.0	0.0	0.0
Trade balance	%GNP	−0.1	−0.3	−0.4	−0.5	−0.5	−0.5
Budget deficit	%GNP	−1.3	−1.1	−0.9	−0.7	−0.4	−0.2
Money supply	%	−0.7	2.4	7.7	13.2	18.3	22.5
OECD economies							
Real GNP	%	−10.5	−8.1	−6.3	−5.0	−3.9	−3.0
Inflation	D	9.8	5.7	4.5	3.7	3.0	2.4
Nominal interest rate	D	16.6	13.3	10.6	8.4	6.8	5.6
Trade balance	%GNP	0.3	0.1	0.0	−0.1	−0.1	−0.1
Budget deficit	%GNP	1.2	0.9	0.7	0.5	0.2	0.1
Money supply	%	−1.4	0.8	5.6	10.8	15.7	19.9

We can make a formal comparison of the outcomes of the four regimes by measuring the intertemporal welfare function, starting in 1984, for all of the countries, given the different adjustment paths. The results of this comparison are as follows:

	U.S.	Japan	ROECD
Cooperative case	−14.884	−13.416	−14.626
Noncooperative case	−14.983	−13.441	−14.886
Dollar standard	−15.381	−14.286	−15.644
Modified McKinnon	−14.739	−14.239	−14.695

Comparing the noncooperative with the cooperative case we see that each country has a lower loss under cooperation. The dollar standard leads uniformly to the largest loss. For the United States and the ROECD, the McKinnon rule performs well relative to the noncooperative case, but it is worse for Japan. The ranking of noncooperation and the McKinnon rule is therefore ambiguous.

The results have shown that national welfare in responding to an exogenous shock will be altered by the nature of the monetary regime, and that at least for one shock (a global inflationary disturbance), the symmetric fixed exchange rate regime envisioned by McKinnon might have some merit. However, it is extremely inappropriate to draw conclusions about the relative merits of exchange rate regimes from one type of shock. In the next section we enrich the comparison among regimes by using a technique that allows us to examine regime performance under a variety of disturbances.

3.6   Asymptotic Properties of Alternative Regimes

Our second approach to comparing interactions under alternative exchange regimes uses a technique developed in McKibbin and Sachs (1985), in which we calculate the steady-state variances of a set of targets when the model is subject to a range of stochastic shocks, and when national policymakers optimize their policy choices with respect to a social welfare function. Related methods have been employed by Currie and Levine (1985). In the illustration in this section, the stochastic shocks are included in equations for aggregate demand, prices, and money demand in both the United States and the ROECD. It is assumed that in each period the shocks hit after the policies are in place, so that the policy choices are not conditioned on the realizations of the disturbances hitting the system within the period.

Under our assumption of an additively separable, quadratic social welfare function, average operating welfare of an economy in a particular monetary regime can be written in terms of the variances and covariances of the target variables under the particular regime. The numerical techniques in this section allow us to determine the asymptotic variance/covariance matrices for the target variables for each of the countries, and thereby to determine the average welfare levels of the economies under each of the regimes. For each regime, we proceed as follows. Optimal rules of adjustment, in the form

$$U_t^i = \Gamma^i X_t \qquad\qquad i = \text{United States, ROECD, and Japan}$$

are calculated for each country, using the dynamic programming solutions shown in section 3.5. We may then substitute these rules back into the structural equations of the model. Given the asymptotic variance/covariance structure of the shocks, we can then solve for the asymptotic variance/covariance structure of the target variables. Given these results, it is possible to calculate the asymptotic level of expected welfare for each country under each regime by a method described later in this section. In this way we can find out which regimes are most attractive independent of the initial conditions of the economy, in other words, in the long-run operating characteristics.

Since the technique is somewhat technical, it is worth spelling out in some detail. Once again, we begin with the state-space representation of the model, as reproduced here from equations 7 to 9:

(7')
$$X_{t+1} = AX_t + Be_t + CU_t + Z\epsilon$$

(8')
$$_t(e_{t+1}) = DX_t + Fe_t + GU_t + W\epsilon_t$$

(9')
$$\tau_t = MX_t + Le_t + NU_t + O\epsilon_t$$

We now make several assumptions about the stochastic disturbances. They all enter additively so certainty equivalence holds. All shocks have persistent effects in the model. This is because the shocks enter into dynamic equations which cause the effects of the shocks to propagate over time. The shocks to the aggregate demand equation (ϵ^a) are entered explicitly in the following way:

$$\mu_{t+1} = .75 (\mu_t) + \epsilon^a{}_t$$

where μ_t becomes part of the state vector X_t.

The other shocks, although serially uncorrelated, are persistent because of the dynamic specification of the model: the price shocks are built into a wage-price spiral in the model, and disturbances to money demand affect future money demand because of a lagged adjustment specification of the money demand equation (which makes the future demand for real money balances a function of the lagged level of real money balances).

The shocks also satisfy the following conditions:

$$E_{t-1}(\epsilon_t) = 0$$
$$E_{t-1}(\epsilon_t \epsilon_t{}^T) = \Sigma$$

Policy rules are written in the form:

(10')
$$U_t = \Gamma_1 X_t$$

where U_t is the stacked vector consisting of the policy instruments of the individual regions, U_t^i, $i =$ United States, ROECD, and Japan.

The policy rule may be the result of an optimization procedure (the case that we study in this section), or may be chosen by some other arbitrary technique. In other words, the technique in the section can be used to analyze each individual's favorite "optimal" policy rule, whether or not that rule is derived from a formal optimization procedure.

Given a specification of a policy rule, and given the structural equations of the system in equations (7') to (9'), we find the stable manifold for the "jumping" variables e_t:

(11)
$$e_t = H_1 X_t + H_2 \epsilon_t$$

(This equation can be derived through various procedures, including the closed-form solutions of Blanchard and Kahn [1980], or by various iterative techniques, one of which we have developed and used here). Then, by substituting (11) into (7'):

$$(12) \qquad X_{t+1} = \bar{A} X_t + \bar{Z} \epsilon_t$$

where

$$\bar{A} = A + BH_1 + C\Gamma_1$$

and

$$\bar{Z} = Z + BH_2$$

With the system written in the canonical form of a first-order stochastic difference equation, as in (12), it is straightforward, though tedious, to calculate the asymptotic variance/covariance structure of the state variables X. Once these are calculated, it is possible to use the equation for the target variables τ, in order to calculate the variance/covariance matrix of the target variables. A full description of the numerical techniques used to get to this point is provided in McKibbin and Sachs (1985).

Once the variance/covariance matrix of the target variables is known, we can also calculate the expected utility loss given some arbitrary welfare function.

$$\text{Let } \Pi = E(\tau\tau^T), \text{ and utility } U = \sum_{t=0}^{\infty} \beta^t \tau^T W\tau$$

where W is a diagonal matrix with weights for each target along the diagonal. Then,

$$(13) \qquad E(\tau^T W\tau) = TrE(W\tau\tau^T) = Tr(W\Pi).$$

Thus we find

$$(14) \qquad E(U) = Tr(W\Pi)/(1 - \beta)$$

Using the procedures just outlined we can now calculate the variance of targets under the alternative monetary regimes. For each regime, we calculate optimal policy rules of the form given in equation (10), and then we derive the asymptotic variance/covariance structures of the target variables. Rather than summarizing the results by presenting a single expected welfare level for each regime, as in equation (14), we instead report the asymptotic variances of the key variables, so that the reader can see how well the alternative regimes do in stabilizing the target variables in the world economy. (For convenience, the results are actually reported as standard deviations, rather than variances.)

These results are reported in tables 3.11 to 3.13, which present the standard deviations of output, inflation, the current account and the fiscal deficit in the United States and the ROECD, given shocks to

Table 3.11   **Standard Deviation of Targets under Aggregate Demand Shocks**

	Pure float	Cooperative float	Noncooperative float	McKinnon I	McKinnon II
			U.S. Demand Shock		
U.S.					
Output	2.164	1.534	1.490	3.253	3.197
Inflation	0.932	0.539	0.508	1.276	1.221
Current account	0.678	0.584	0.636	0.590	0.629
Fiscal deficit	0.010	0.255	0.108	1.518	1.382
ROECD					
Output	1.039	0.729	0.764	0.950	0.995
Inflation	0.621	0.433	0.458	0.372	0.525
Current account	0.557	0.474	0.525	0.497	0.530
Fiscal deficit	0.002	0.048	0.093	0.506	0.905
			ROECD Demand Shock		
U.S.					
Output	1.031	0.629	0.627	0.651	0.673
Inflation	0.648	0.408	0.406	0.217	0.376
Current account	0.251	0.236	0.234	0.222	0.352
Fiscal deficit	0.015	0.053	0.089	0.355	0.803
ROECD					
Output	2.114	1.383	1.382	3.636	3.554
Inflation	0.929	0.456	0.456	1.407	1.342
Current account	0.300	0.319	0.329	0.352	0.498
Fiscal deficit	0.003	0.037	0.054	1.635	1.168

aggregate demand, prices, and monetary velocity in each of these regions. Each row of numbers in the tables correspond to the asymptotic standard error of each target when the economy is subject to a given stochastic shock, within a given monetary regime. Results are reported for five types of monetary regimes: (1) a pure float, in which no policy actions are taken in any country (i.e., pure laissez-faire); (2) a cooperative float, in which all of the instruments in all of the countries are cooperatively controlled by a central authority, who maximizes a weighted sum of regional utilities; (3) a noncooperative float, in which monetary and fiscal policies are selected in a noncooperative way by the macroeconomic authorities in each of the countries; (4) the simple

Table 3.12   Standard Deviation of Targets under Price Shocks

	Pure float	Cooperative float	Noncooperative float	McKinnon I	McKinnon II
			U.S. Price Shock		
U.S.					
Output	2.723	1.771	1.783	2.465	2.187
Inflation	1.229	1.418	1.418	1.415	1.439
Current account	0.377	0.266	0.278	0.692	0.670
Fiscal deficit	0.012	0.083	0.150	1.346	1.111
ROECD					
Output	0.517	0.198	0.185	0.318	0.399
Inflation	0.374	0.163	0.157	0.236	0.562
Current account	0.295	0.212	0.229	0.585	0.578
Fiscal deficit	0.002	0.119	0.040	0.419	0.812
			ROECD Price Shock		
U.S.					
Output	0.664	0.274	0.230	0.302	0.280
Inflation	0.417	0.207	0.176	0.153	0.530
Current account	0.149	0.134	0.092	0.235	0.469
Fiscal deficit	0.005	0.118	0.044	0.310	0.758
ROECD					
Output	2.972	1.899	1.922	2.952	2.624
Inflation	1.281	1.482	1.504	1.637	1.597
Current account	0.164	0.171	0.139	0.350	0.566
Fiscal deficit	0.001	0.159	0.202	1.745	1.189

McKinnon rule (I), with fixed exchange rates and a constant level of global money; and (5) a modified McKinnon rule (II), in which the global money is cooperatively controlled in the way outlined in section 3.5.

Consider, for example, the effects of a unit shock to U.S. aggregate demand, under the alternative regimes given in table 3.11. The standard deviation of the shock itself is 1% of U.S. GDP (the corresponding shock in the ROECD has a standard deviation of one percent of ROECD GDP). Under a pure laissez-faire float, (denoted ''pure float'' in the

Table 3.13   **Standard Deviation of Targets under Money Velocity Shocks**

	Pure float	Cooperative float	Noncooperative float	McKinnon I	McKinnon II
			U.S. Money Shock		
U.S.					
Output	1.628	1.546	1.550	0.631	0.633
Inflation	0.505	0.604	0.607	0.233	0.276
Current account	0.162	0.168	0.174	0.077	0.063
Fiscal deficit	0.001	0.041	0.070	0.164	0.019
ROECD					
Output	0.272	0.122	0.126	0.936	0.888
Inflation	0.112	0.046	0.048	0.337	0.347
Current account	0.153	0.162	0.168	0.094	0.081
Fiscal deficit	0.000	0.055	0.006	0.267	0.060
			ROECD Money Shock		
U.S.					
Output	0.291	0.060	0.039	0.629	0.630
Inflation	0.113	0.068	0.055	0.234	0.275
Current account	0.068	0.058	0.033	0.079	0.063
Fiscal deficit	0.002	0.071	0.015	0.172	0.019
ROECD					
Output	2.184	1.955	1.976	0.935	0.885
Inflation	0.666	0.772	0.787	0.339	0.346
Current account	0.086	0.068	0.054	0.094	0.081
Fiscal deficit	0.001	0.086	0.108	0.284	0.060

table), the unit shock to aggregate demand induces an asymptotic standard deviation in real output in the United States of 2.164% of GDP. Under a global cooperative arrangement, the standard deviation is reduced to 1.534% of U.S. GDP. If the United States is stabilizing by itself, in a noncooperative flexible exchange rate regime, and if the stabilization is such as to minimize the social welfare function introduced earlier, then the variability of U.S. GDP due to pure demand shocks is reduced still further, to 1.490% of U.S. GDP. The shock, of course, also induces fluctuations in inflation and in the current account-

GDP ratio (the table records the standard deviation of both of these variables when measured in percentage points; i.e., the standard deviation of 0.932 in U.S. inflation signifies a standard deviation of just under one percentage point of annual inflation).

The key point in table 3.11 is that the fixed exchange rate systems (McKinnon I and McKinnon II) are destabilizing for the real GDPs of both the United States and the ROECD when U.S. aggregate demand is hit by stochastic shocks. In a floating rate system, some of the demand shock is automatically muted as the floating rate appreciates and thereby shifts some of aggregate demand abroad. Under the McKinnon rule, however, if the United States is hit by a positive aggregate demand shock, the U.S. money supply automatically expands, enough to forestall any appreciation of the exchange rate. The demand shock is then magnified in the United States, as it is amplified by a monetary expansion. Abroad, we have already seen, the foreign money supply contracts under the rules of the game, and the foreign economy actually slumps. For this kind of shock, it doesn't really matter whether the global money stock is fixed (as in the McKinnon I) or varied cooperatively (as in McKinnon II), though it is not clear to us why there is not more gain to a coordinated monetary response. Note, finally, that some policy is better than none, since the cooperative and noncooperative floating rate policies dominate the laissez-faire response in all cases.

When we turn our attention to price shocks, in table 3.12, little of this conclusion is changed. In almost all cases, cooperative or noncooperative floating is better than either laissez-faire or a fixed exchange rate. This result is really not surprising, in that a nominal price or wage shock in one country (due, for example, to a temporary productivity decline, to wage militancy, etc.) is best absorbed in the world markets through a depreciation of the currency of the inflating country. In this way, there is a substantial gain in the stability of real output, with only a slight decline in the stability of the inflation rate (note that the laissez-faire policies and the pure McKinnon rule have a very slightly lower variance of inflation than do the floating rate rules).

Why is it that the McKinnon rule seemed stabilizing in the inflation game of section 3.5, but seems rather unattractive in the present context? The reason is that the previous game studied a case in which all countries simultaneously are faced with a price shock, whereas in table 3.12 the price shocks in the United States or the ROECD are considered to be independently distributed. This distinction is potentially very important in that when the price shocks are independent, it is useful to allow for nominal exchange rate variability across the countries, while when the shocks are highly correlated, the need for exchange rate movements is very much reduced, and the benefit to reducing cross-country strategic actions that cancel each other out, is likewise increased. For that reason, the methodology in this section is somewhat biased against a fixed exchange rate system.

Table 3.13 refers to velocity shocks in the money demand equations in the United States and the ROECD. Once again, we study the case in which the shocks are independently distributed. Now we have an interesting and intuitively plausible finding: a fixed rate regime stabilizes the economy of the country that experiences the monetary shock, but destabilizes the economy of the other country. Consider concretely what happens when U.S. money demand rises, under the alternative systems (remember that the shock is unobserved within the period that it occurs). Under floating rates, the economy with rising money demand experiences a currency appreciation and a corresponding decline in aggregate demand, resulting from the fall in national competitiveness. The other economies experience either a modest gain or fall in output: competitiveness improves, but export markets shrink since the economy with rising money demand goes into recession. Now, under a McKinnon rule, the economy with rising money demand would automatically have an accommodating increase in money, as the monetary authority expands money enough to keep the exchange rate pegged. The other economy, however, would be forced to contract the money supply under the rules of the game, so that its economy could be greatly destabilized.

Once again, the conclusions would look much more appealing to the McKinnon rule once we allow for a negative correlation across countries in the money shocks. Suppose, for example, that the money shocks in the United States and the ROECD are perfectly negatively correlated. The results for this case are given in table 3.14. In this case the McKinnon rule is close to being perfectly stabilizing, since the country with expanding money demand automatically has a rising money supply, while the country with the contracting money demand automatically has a falling money supply. The other regimes perform far worse than the McKinnon rule for this particular type of shock, which indeed is the type of shock stressed by McKinnon.

A full analysis of the costs and benefits of the alternative systems would require a more complete investigation of the covariance structure of the underlying shocks, something that we hope to do in future work.

3.7 Conclusions

This chapter has analyzed the implications of alternative monetary regimes in the OECD for the transmission of fiscal policy and for the efficiency of strategic interactions across the major OECD economies. While the work is tentative, we have already arrived at several useful

Table 3.14   Standard Deviation of Targets under Negatively Correlated U.S. and ROECD Money Shocks

	Pure float	Cooperative float	Noncooperative float	McKinnon I	McKinnon II
U.S.					
Output	1.608	1.490	1.518	0.002	0.002
Inflation	0.430	0.549	0.569	0.001	0.001
Current account	0.174	0.188	0.176	0.000	0.000
Fiscal deficit	0.004	0.111	0.058	0.000	0.000
ROECD					
Output	2.386	2.076	2.101	0.003	0.003
Inflation	0.680	0.794	0.812	0.001	0.001
Current account	0.135	0.173	0.164	0.000	0.000
Fiscal deficit	0.001	0.141	0.103	0.001	0.000

conclusions. First, the nature of fiscal interactions will vary greatly depending on the nature of the monetary regime. Under floating exchange rates, transmission of fiscal policy tends to be positive, while under a fixed rate system, of the sort propounded by McKinnon, fiscal policy can actually be negatively transmitted. In asymmetric monetary systems, such as a dollar standard, U.S. fiscal policy may well be negatively transmitted, while foreign fiscal policy is almost surely positively transmitted to the United States. These theoretical findings are supported by simulation experiments in a large-scale multiregion model of the world economy (the MSG model). The quantitative estimates show that negative transmission of fiscal policy under a fixed exchange rate regime is more than a theoretical curiosity and is at the least a real empirical possibility, if not likelihood.

One of the alleged advantages of a move to fixed exchange rates is that it would mute the incentives for beggar-thy-neighbor policies under flexible exchange rates. We illustrated that proposition in two ways, first using a simple theoretical model, and, second, by examining a differential game in which the large three OECD regions all inherit a high inflation rate and then use macroeconomic policies in the attempt to pursue an optimal disinflation. As we show, the noncooperative floating regime tends to create an incentive toward fiscal expansion and monetary contraction that is inefficient from the point of view of the social welfare functions in the individual countries.

A new methodology is used at the end to examine the "average" operating properties of the alternative systems. The question of which system is best is shown to depend on which stochastic disturbances are dominant, a standard result in the analysis of fixed versus flexible rates. The results, on the whole, are relatively hostile to fixed exchange rates, but that might depend on our specification of the shocks. As is described in the text, price shocks that are positively correlated across countries, or money demand shocks that are negatively correlated across countries, will both tend to be relatively well handled by fixed exchange rate regimes.

Appendix
MSG Model of the World Economy

U.S. Equations

$$Q^U = D^U + G^U + (C_O^U + C_U^U + C_L^U + C_U^P) - (\Lambda^O C_O^U + \Lambda^J C_J^U + \Lambda^L C_L^U + \Lambda^P C_P^U)$$

$$\Lambda^O = P^O E^O / P^U$$

$$\Lambda^J = P^J E^J / P^U$$

$$\Lambda^L = P^L / P^U$$

$$\Lambda^P = P^P / P^U$$

$$D^U = (1 - s)(Q^U - T^U) + \delta H^U - .5 v r^U - .5 v R^U$$

$$H^U = B^U + A_L^U - A_O^U - A_U^P - A_U^L$$

$$B_{t+1}^U = (B_t^U + DEF_t^U)/(1 + n)$$

$$DEF^U = G^U + r^U B^U - v^U B_L^U - T^U$$

$$M_t^U / P_t^U = \{Q_t^{U\Phi}(1 + i_t^U)^{-\beta}\}^{.5} \{M_{t-1}^U / P_{t-1}^U\}^{.5}$$

$$i_t^U = r_t^U + \pi_{t+1}^U$$

$$r_t^U = R_t^U - ({}_t R_{t+1}^U - R_t^U)/R_t^U$$

$$v_t^U = .13 r_t^U + .82 v_{t-1}^U$$

$$\pi_{t+1}^U = (P_{t+1}^U - P_t^U)/P_t^U$$

$$\pi_{t+1}^{CU} = (P_{t+1}^{CU} - P_t^{CU})/P_t^{CU}$$

$$\pi_{t+1}^U = \pi_t^{CU} + \Omega Q_t^U + \tau(Q_t^U - Q_{t-1}^U)$$

$$P^{CU} = (P^U)^{\gamma_1}(P^O E^O)^{\gamma_2}(P^L)^{\gamma_3}(P^J E^J)^{\gamma_4}(P^P)^{(1-\gamma_1-\gamma_2-\gamma_3-\gamma_4)}$$

$$C^U_O = \alpha_O(D^U + G^U)(\Lambda^O)^{-1.5}$$

$$C^U_L = \alpha_1(D^U + G^U)(\Lambda^L)^{-1.0}$$

$$C^U_P = \alpha_2(D^U + G^U)(\Lambda^P)^{-0.2}$$

$$C^U_J = \alpha_3(D^U + G^U)(\Lambda^J)^{-1.5}$$

$$TB^U = (C^U_O + C^U_L + C^U_P + C^U_J) - (C^U_O \Lambda^O + C^U_L \Lambda^L + C^U_P \Lambda^P + C^U_J \Lambda^J)$$

Japan Equations

$$Q^J = D^J + G^J + (C^U_J + C^O_J + C^L_J + C^P_J) - (C^J_U + C^J_O \Lambda^O + C^J_L \Lambda^L + C^J_P \Lambda^P)/\Lambda^J$$

$$D^J = (1 - s^J)(Q^J - T^J) - vr^J + \delta H^J$$

$$H^J = B^J + A^J_U/\Lambda^J + A^J_{LJ} + A^J_{LU}/\Lambda^J - A^P_J$$

$$B^J_{t+1} = (B^J_t + \mathrm{DEF}^J_t)/(1 + n)$$

$$\mathrm{DEF}^J = G^J + r^J B^J - v^J B^J_L - T^J$$

$$M^J_t/P^J_t = \{Q^{J\Phi}_t(1 + i^J_t)^{-\beta}\}^{.5} \{M^J_{t-1}/P^J_{t-1}\}^{.5}$$

$$i^J_t = r^J_t + \pi^J_{t+1}$$

$$v^J_t = .82v^J_{t-1} + .13r^J_t$$

$$\pi^J_{t+1} = (P^J_{t+1} - P^J_t)/P^J_t$$

$$\pi^{CJ}_{t+1} = (P^{CJ}_{t+1} - P^{CJ}_t)/P^{CJ}_t$$

$$\pi^J_{t+1} = \pi^{CJ}_t + \Omega Q^J_t + \tau(Q^J_t - Q^J_{t-1})$$

$$P^{CJ} = (P^J)^{\gamma_5}(P^U/E^J)^{\gamma_6}(P^O E^O/E^J)^{\gamma_7}(P^L/E^J)^{\gamma_8}(P^P/E^J)^{(1-\gamma_5-\gamma_6-\gamma_7-\gamma_8)}$$

$$C^J_U = \alpha_4(D^J + G^J)(\Lambda^J)^{1.5}$$

$$C^J_O = \alpha_5(D^J + G^J)(\Lambda^O/\Lambda^J)^{-1.5}$$

$$C^J_L = \alpha_6(D^J + G^J)(\Lambda^L/\Lambda^J)^{-1.0}$$

$$C^J_P = \alpha_7(D^J + G^J)(\Lambda^P/\Lambda^J)^{-0.2}$$

$$TB^J = \Lambda^J(C^U_J + C^O_J + C^L_J + C^P_J) - (C^J_U + \Lambda^O C^J_O + \Lambda^L C^J_L + \Lambda^P C^J_P)$$

$$A^J_{Ut+1} = (A^J_{Ut} + CA^J_t)/(1 + n) - [(A^J_{LJt+1}\Lambda^J_t + A^J_{LUt+1} + B^J_{Lt+1}\Lambda^J_t - A^P_{Jt+1}\Lambda^J_t) - (A^J_{LJt}\Lambda^J_t + A^J_{LUt} + B^J_{Lt}\Lambda^J_t - A^P_{Jt}\Lambda^J_t)/(1 + n)]$$

$$CA^J = TB^J + r^U(A^J_U + A^J_{LU}) + r^J\Lambda^J A^J_{LJ} + v^J\Lambda^J B^J_L - r^J\Lambda^J A^P_J$$

$$(A^J_{Ut} + A^J_{LUt})/\Lambda^J_t = \sigma^J[r^U_t - r^J_t - ({}_t\Lambda^J_{t+1} - \Lambda^J_t)/\Lambda^J_t] + \theta H^J_t$$

ROECD Equations

$$Q^O = D^O + G^O + (C^Y_O + C^L_O + C^P_O + C^J_O) - (C^Y_O + C^J_O\Lambda^J$$
$$+ C^L_O\Lambda^L + C^P_O\Lambda^P)/\Lambda^O$$

$$D^O = (1 - s)(Q^O - T^O) - vr^O + \delta H^O$$

$$H^O = B^O + A^O_U/\Lambda^O + A^O_L - A^P_O/\Lambda^O$$

$$B^O_{t+1} = (B^O_t + \text{DEF}^O_t)/(1 + n)$$

$$\text{DEF}^O = G^O + r^O B^O - v^O B^O_U - T^O$$

$$M^O_t/P^O_t = \{Q^{O\phi}_t(1 + i^O_t)^{-\beta}\}^{.5}\{M^O_{t-1}/P^O_{t-1}\}^{.5}$$

$$i^O_t = r^O_t + \pi^O_{t+1}$$

$$v^O_t = .13r^O_t + .82v^O_{t-1}$$

$$\pi^O_{t+1} = (P^O_{t+1} - P^O_t)/P^O_t$$

$$\pi^{CO}_{t+1} = (P^{CO}_{t+1} - P^{CO}_t)/P^{CO}_t$$

$$\pi^O_{t+1} = \pi^{CO}_t + \Omega Q^O_t + \tau(Q^O_t - Q^O_{t-1})$$

$$P^{CO} = (P^O)^{\gamma 9}(P^U/E^O)^{\gamma 10}(P^L/E^O)^{\gamma 11}(P^J E^J/E^O)^{\gamma 12}(P^P/E^O)^{(1 - \gamma 9 - \gamma 10 - \gamma 11 - \gamma 12)}$$

$$C^Y_O = \alpha_8(D^O + G^O)(\Lambda^O)^{1.5}$$

$$C^J_O = \alpha_9(D^O + G^O)(\Lambda^J/\Lambda^O)^{-1.5}$$

$$C^L_O = \alpha_{10}(D^O + G^O)(\Lambda^L/\Lambda^O)^{-1.0}$$

$$C^P_O = \alpha_{11}(D^O + G^O)(\Lambda^P/\Lambda^O)^{-0.2}$$

$$TB^O = (C^Y_O + C^L_O + C^P_O + C^J_O) - (C^Y_O + C^J_O\Lambda^J + C^L_O\Lambda^L$$
$$+ C^P_O\Lambda^P)/\Lambda^O$$

$$A^O_{Ut+1} = (A^O_{Ut} + CA^O_t)/(1 + n) - [(A^P_O + B^O_U)_{t+1}\Lambda^O_t$$
$$- (A^P_O + B^O_U)_t\Lambda^O/(1 + n) - A^P_{Ot+1} + A^P_{Ot}/(1 + n)]$$

$$CA^O = (A^Y_O - A^P_O)r^U + (A^L_O\Lambda^O)r^O + (B^O_U\Lambda^O)v^O + TB^O\Lambda^O$$

$$(A^Y_O - A^P_O)_t/\Lambda^O_t = \sigma[r^U_t - r^O_t - ({}_t\Lambda^O_{t+1} - \Lambda^O_t)/\Lambda^O_t] + \theta H^O_t$$

LDC Equations

$$P^L = (P^U)^{\eta 1}(P^O E^O)^{\eta 2}(P^J E^J)^{-\eta 3}(P^P)^{(1 - \eta 1 - \eta 2 - \eta 3)} (C^Y_L + C^O_L + C^P_L + C^J_L)^{\gamma L}$$

$$C^Y_L = \eta_1(C^Y_L + \Lambda^O C^O_L + \Lambda^P C^P_L + \Lambda^J C^J_L)$$

$$C^O_L = \eta_2(C^Y_L + \Lambda^O C^O_L + \Lambda^P C^P_L + \Lambda^J C^J_L)/\Lambda^O$$

$$C^J_L = \eta_3(C^Y_L + \Lambda^O C^O_L + \Lambda^P C^P_L + \Lambda^J C^J_L)/\Lambda^J$$

$$C^P_L = (1 - \eta_1 - \eta_2 - \eta_3)(C^Y_L + \Lambda^O C^O_L + \Lambda^P C^P_L + \Lambda^J C^J_L)/\Lambda^P$$

$$TB^L = \Lambda^L(C^U_L + C^O_L + C^P_L + C^J_L) - C^U_L - \Lambda^O C^O_L - \Lambda^P C^P_L - \Lambda^J C^J_L$$

$$CA^L_t = \omega CA^L_{t-1} + \epsilon\{\text{DEBT}_t - \xi\Lambda^L_t(C^O_{Lt} + C^U_{Lt} + C^P_{Lt} + C^J_{Lt}) \cdot [1 + n(1 - \omega)/\epsilon]\}$$

$$\text{DEBT}_t = A^U_L + (A^O_L\Lambda^O) + A^P_L + B^U_L + (B^O_L\Lambda^O) + A^J_{LU} + A^J_{LJ}\Lambda^J + B^J_L\Lambda^J$$

$$B^U_{Lt+1} = B^U_{Lt} + .1[A^U_{Lt+1}(1 + n) - A^U_{Lt}]$$

$$B^O_{Lt+1} = B^O_{Lt} + .1[A^O_{Lt+1}(1 + n) - A^O_{Lt}]$$

$$\Lambda^J_t B^J_{Lt+1} = \Lambda^J_t B^J_{Lt} + .1[(A^J_{LJt+1}\Lambda^J_t + A^J_{LUt+1})(1 + n) - (A^J_{LJt}\Lambda^J_t + A^J_{LUt})]$$

$$A^O_{Lt+1}\Lambda^O_t = \{a_1[(A^U_{Lt+1} + A^O_{Lt+1}\Lambda^O_t + A^P_{Lt+1} + A^J_{LJt+1}\Lambda^J_t + A^J_{LUt+1})(1 + n) - (A^U_{Lt} + A^O_{Lt}\Lambda^O_t + A^P_{Lt} + A^J_{LJt}\Lambda^J_t + A^J_{LUt})] + A^O_{Lt}\Lambda^O_t\}/(1 + n)$$

$$A^P_{Lt+1} = \{a_2[(A^U_{Lt+1} + A^O_{Lt+1}\Lambda^O_t + A^P_{Lt+1} + A^J_{LJt+1}\Lambda^J_t + A^J_{LUt+1}) \cdot (1 + n) - (A^U_{Lt} + A^O_{Lt}\Lambda^O_t + A^P_{Lt} + A^J_{LJt}\Lambda^J_t + A^J_{LUt})] + A^P_{Lt}\}/(1 + n)$$

$$A^J_{LJt+1}\Lambda^J_t = \{a_3[(A^J_{Lt+1} + A^J_{LJt+1}\Lambda^J_t + A^J_{LUt+1} + A^O_{Lt+1}\Lambda^O_t + A^P_{Lt+1})(1 + n) - (A^U_{Lt} + A^J_{LJt}\Lambda^J_t + A^J_{LUt} + A^O_{Lt}\Lambda^O_t + A^P_{Lt})] + A^J_{LJt}\Lambda^J_t\}/(1 + n)$$

$$A^J_{LUt+1} = \{a_4[(A^U_{Lt+1} + A^J_{LJt+1}\Lambda^J_t + A^J_{LUt+1} + A^O_{Lt+1}\Lambda^O_t + A^P_{Lt+1}) (1 + n) - (A^U_{Lt} + A^J_{LJt}\Lambda^J_t + A^J_{LUt} + A^O_{Lt}\Lambda^O_t + A^P_{Lt})] + A^J_{LUt}\}/(1 + n)$$

$$A^U_{Lt+1} = (A^U_{Lt} + CA^L_t)/(1 + n) - [(A^J_{LJt+1}\Lambda^J_t + A^J_{LUt+1} + A^O_{Lt+1}\Lambda^O_t + A^P_{Lt+1} + B^U_{Lt+1} + B^J_{Lt+1}\Lambda^J_t + B^O_{Lt+1}\Lambda^O_t) - (A^J_{LJt}\Lambda^J_t + A^J_{LUt} + A^O_{Lt}\Lambda^O_t + A^P_{Lt} + B^U_{Lt} + B^J_{Lt}\Lambda^J_t + B^O_{Lt}\Lambda^O_t)/(1 + n)]$$

OPEC Equations

$$PP = (P^U)^{\eta_4}(P^O E^O)^{\eta_5}(P^J E^J)^{\eta_6}(P^L)^{(1 - \eta_4 - \eta_5 - \eta_6)} (C^U_P + C^O_P + C^L_P + C^J_P)^{\gamma P}$$

$$C^P_U = \eta_4(C^P_U + \Lambda^O C^P_O + \Lambda^L C^P_L + \Lambda^J C^P_J)$$

$$C^P_O = \eta_5(C^P_U + \Lambda^O C^P_O + \Lambda^L C^P_L + \Lambda^J C^P_J)/\Lambda^O$$

$$C^P_J = \eta_6(C^P_U + \Lambda^O C^P_O + \Lambda^L C^P_L + \Lambda^J C^P_J)/\Lambda^J$$

$$C^P_L = (1 - \eta_4 - \eta_5 - \eta_6)(C^P_U + \Lambda^O C^P_O + \Lambda^L C^P_L + \Lambda^J C^P_J)/\Lambda^L$$

$$H^P = A^P_U + A^P_O + A^P_L + A^P_J\Lambda^J$$

$$TB^P = \Lambda^P(C^U_P + C^O_P + C^L_P + C^J_P) - C^P_U - \Lambda^O C^P_O - \Lambda^L C^P_L - \Lambda^J C^P_J$$

$$CA^P_t = \zeta[\psi(C^U_P + C^O_P + C^L_P + C^J_P)_t(PP/P^U)_t - H^P_{t-1}] + nH^P_{t-1}$$

$$A^P_{Ut+1} = (A^P_{Ut} + CA^P_t)/(1 + n) - [(A^P_O + A^P_L)_{t+1} + A^P_{Jt+1}\Lambda^J_t$$
$$- (A^P_O + A^P_L + A^P_J\Lambda^J)_t/(1 + n)]$$

$$A^P_{Ot+1} = \{b_1[(A^P_U + A^P_O + A^P_L + A^P_J\Lambda^J_t)_{t+1}(1 + n)$$
$$- (A^P_U + A^P_O + A^P_L + A^P_J\Lambda^P)_t] + A^P_{Ot}\}/(1 + n)$$

$$A^P_{Jt+1}\Lambda^J_t = \{b_2[(A^P_U + A^P_O + A^P_L + A^P_J\Lambda^J t)_{t+1}(1 + n)$$
$$- (A^P_U + A^P_O + A^P_L + A^P_J\Lambda^J)_t] + A^P_{Jt}\Lambda^J_t\}/(1 + n)$$

Definitions

A^i_j	Claims on country j held by private creditors in country i
B^i_j	Claims on country j held by official creditors in country i
B^i	Government debt of country i
C^i_j	Consumption by country i of the output of country j
CA	Current account
D	Domestic absorption
DEBT	Developing country debt
DEF	Government deficit
E^O	Exchange rate (\$/Ecu)
E^J	Exchange rate (\$/yen)
G	Government expenditure
H	Real financial wealth
i	Nominal interest rate
M	Nominal money supply
n	Growth rate
P^i	Price level of country i goods
P^C	Consumer price index
π_t	Domestic price inflation
π^C_t	Consumer price inflation
Q	Gross domestic product
r	Real short interest rate
R	Real long interest rate
T	Taxes
TB	Trade balance
v	Concessional real interest rate
Λ	Real exchange rate
$_tX_{t+1}$	Expectation of X_{t+1} based on period t information

Superscripts and Subscripts

U	United States
O	Rest of OECD
J	Japan
L	Developing Countries
P	OPEC

Parameter Values

S	$= 0.3$	γ_6	$= 0.022$	α_7	$= 0.039$	γ_L	$= 0.5$
S^J	$= 0.5$	γ_7	$= 0.020$	α_8	$= 0.032$	γ_P	$= 0.5$
ν	$= 0.2$	γ_8	$= 0.026$	α_9	$= 0.010$	a_1	$= 0.110$
δ	$= 0.1$	γ_9	$= 0.911$	α_{10}	$= 0.028$	a_2	$= 0.230$
n	$= 0.03$	γ_{10}	$= 0.032$	α_{11}	$= 0.019$	a_3	$= 0.010$
ϕ	$= 0.8$	γ_{11}	$= 0.028$	σ	$= 4$	a_4	$= 0.130$
β	$= 0.9$	γ_{12}	$= 0.010$	σ^J	$= 1$	b_1	$= 0.226$
Ω	$= 0.2$	α_0	$= 0.034$	θ	$= 0.5$	b_2	$= 0.070$
τ	$= 0.2$	α_1	$= 0.024$	η_1	$= 0.195$	ω	$= 0.9$
γ_1	$= 0.922$	α_2	$= 0.008$	η_2	$= 0.353$	ϵ	$= 0.3$
γ_2	$= 0.034$	α_3	$= 0.013$	η_3	$= 0.145$	ξ	$= 1.985$
γ_3	$= 0.024$	α_4	$= 0.022$	η_4	$= 0.092$	ψ	$= 1.65$
γ_4	$= 0.013$	α_5	$= 0.020$	η_5	$= 0.323$	ζ	$= 0.29$
γ_5	$= 0.893$	α_6	$= 0.026$	η_6	$= 0.109$		

References

Blanchard, O., and C. Kahn. 1980. The solution of linear difference models under rational expectations. *Econometrica* 48 (5):1305–12.

Buiter, W., and R. Marston. 1985. *International economic policy coordination.* Cambridge: Cambridge Univ. Press.

Canzoneri, M., and J. A. Gray. 1985. Two essays on monetary policy in an interdependent world. *International Economic Review.*

Currie, D., and P. Levine. 1985. Macroeconomic policy design in an interdependent world. In Buiter and Marston (1985), 228–67.

Dornbusch, R. 1976. Expectations and exchange rate dynamics. *Journal of Political Economy* 84, no. 6, (December):1161–76.

Eichengreen, B. 1985. International policy coordination in historical perspective: A view from the interwar years. In Buiter and Marston (1985), 139–78.

Fair, R., and J. Taylor. 1983. Solution and maximum likelihood estimation of dynamic non-linear rational expectations models. *Econometrica* 51 (4):139–78.

Hamada, K. 1974. Alternative exchange rate systems and the interdependence of monetary policies. In Robert Z. Aliber, ed., *National monetary policies and the international financial system,* 13–33. Chicago: Univ. of Chicago Press.

Ishii N., W. McKibbin, and J. Sachs. 1985. The economic policy mix, policy cooperation, and protectionism: Some aspects of macroeconomic interdependence among the United States, Japan, and other OECD countries. *Journal of Policy Modeling* 7 (4):533–572.

Matsuyama, K. 1985. Strategic aspects of the international gold standard. Mimeo, Harvard University.

McKibbin, W., and J. Sachs. 1985. Comparing the global performance of alternative exchange arrangements, *NBER Working Paper* no. 2024, September.

McKinnon, R. 1984. *An international standard for monetary stabilization.*
Policy analyses in international economics, no. 8. Institute for International
Economics. March.

Mundell, R. 1968. *International economics.* New York: Macmillan. Chapter
18.

Obstfeld, M. 1985. Floating exchange rates: Experience and prospects. *Brookings Papers on Economic Activity* 2:369–450.

Oudiz, G., and J. Sachs. 1985. International policy coordination in dynamic
macroeconomic models. In Buiter and Marston (1985), 274–319.

Roosa, R. 1984. Exchange rate arrangements in the eighties. In *The International Monetary System.* Federal Reserve Bank of Boston Conference Series,
no. 28.

Sachs, J. 1985a. The dollar and the policy mix: 1985. *Brookings Papers on
Economic Activity* 85 (1):117–85.

————. 1985b. The case for more managed exchange rates. Paper presented
to the Federal Reserve Bank of Kansas City conference on the U.S. dollar,
Jackson Hole, Wyoming, August 1985.

Sachs, J., and W. McKibbin. 1985. Macroeconomic policies in the OECD and
LDC external adjustment. NBER Working Paper no. 1534, January.

Swoboda, A. 1978. Gold, dollars, Euro-dollars and the world money stock
under fixed exchange rates. *American Economic Review,* September.

Williamson, J. 1983. *The exchange rate system.* Policy analyses in international
economics, no. 5. Washington, D.C.: Institute for International Economics,
September.

Comment   William H. Branson

This paper begins by reviewing some basic analytical results on the
transmission of disturbances between economies under alternative exchange rate regimes. These are the basis for the case for coordination;
it is expected to reduce the negative effects of transmission. The paper
then goes on to report numerical results for simulation using the global
model developed by McKibbin and Sachs, which the authors dub the
MSG model. The model-based results progress from simple illustrations
of transmission in section 3.3 to optimal coordination results in sections
3.5 and 3.6. Readers of the paper should keep in mind that the authors,
while referring to the model as "empirical," are also careful to point
out that the parameters of the model are not estimated but "chosen to
be consistent with values found in the empirical literature" (sec. 3.3).
In a sense, then, the paper is rather more about the model, and less
about the effect of coordination in the world, than would be the case
if the model were actually estimated. By the end of the paper the reader

William H. Branson is professor of economics and international affairs at Princeton
University and research associate at the National Bureau of Economic Research.

knows quite a lot about the model, and may even feel a little overdosed on MSG!

In this comment I offer a brief reader's guide to the paper, with my own views interspersed. This may help to lighten the MSG dosage. The comment ends with some observations on research on coordination, and the place of the McKibbin-Sachs work in this context.

The results of the basic Mundell model for the transmission of fiscal policy are reviewed in section 3.2 under three alternative exchange rate regimes—clean float, all others peg to the dollar, and modified McKinnon, with exchange rates and a weighted average of money stocks fixed. The analytical results are influenced by use of a fixed-price assumption. In the case of the clean float, fiscal policy is positively transmitted; an increase in spending in the United States raises interest rates and appreciates the dollar, giving a stimulus to net exports abroad. The European argument that this effect may be offset by the depressive effect of higher interest rates on investment is ruled out by the fixed-price assumption. In the money market equation (2), if $m^* - p^*$ is fixed, an increase in i requires an increase in q^* to maintain equilibrium. If p^* were permitted to rise, the positive transmission result would become ambiguous.

Under the dollar standard with the U.S. money stock fixed, foreign monetary policy must tighten to keep the dollar from appreciating. This produces an investment effect abroad that may offset the trade effect from the U.S. expansion. The result depends on the sign of $\gamma - \sigma\phi/\beta$, the q^* multiplier under the dollar standard. The econometric results in Branson (1984a, 1984b) suggest that the dollar standard results are most relevant. U.S. monetary policy seems focused on domestic targets, while European policy reacts to the exchange rate.

Under the modified McKinnon rule, exchange rates are fixed along with a weighted average world money supply. So with U.S. fiscal expansion, U.S. monetary policy is also eased, reducing the required tightening abroad to keep the dollar from appreciating. This procedure will work only in a world of perfect asset substitutability where only the ratio of money supplies matters for the exchange rate. This pure monetary model of exchange rate determination is under a heavy empirical cloud, however. In any event, the modified McKinnon rule provides a muted version of the dollar standard results, with negative transmission less likely.

The same experiments are performed in section 3.3 using the MSG simulation model, a computerized version of the dynamized Mundell model of Dornbusch (1976). It has sticky wages and prices, income-constrained consumers, and very high asset substitutability. The specification of the three OECD areas, United States, Japan, rest of OECD (ROECD), is fairly symmetric. This is surprising in view of Sachs's

(1979) own work on the asymmetries in wage behavior across these areas.

Tables 3.1, 3.3, and 3.5 confirm that the MSG computer can indeed reproduce the Dornbusch-Mundell results. With floating rates (table 3.1) and a fixed path of the U.S. money stock, a fiscal expansion in the United States raises interest rates and the Ecu and yen prices of the dollar, but also gives a short-run stimulus to real GNP in Japan and the ROECD. The wage and price reaction reverses this positive transmission after three years. With the dollar standard (table 3.3), the money stock and output fall in Japan and ROECD. Under the modified McKinnon rule (table 3.5), U.S. money increases, so that money tightens less in Japan and the ROECD, and the reduction in output is reduced.

The coordination part of the paper begins in section 3.4 with a two-country example of strategic interaction of policy in a modification of the static Mundell model of section 3.2. The crucial assumptions in this section are the shift to using the CPI with an import component as the price index, and inclusion of the fiscal deficit g explicitly in the welfare function of equation (5), as well as output q and the price index. The standard noncooperative game result is that each country reacts to a common inflation shock by tightening monetary policy and easing fiscal policy to get an offsetting price effect from the exchange rate. Of course they both fail; and, with no predictable effect on the exchange rate, they both end up with tighter money and easier fiscal policy than intended or expected, and a failed attempt at competitive appreciation.

McKibbin and Sachs introduce a suboptimal result for real outputs into the scenario by including the fiscal deficit in the welfare function. Now as each country eases fiscal policy, welfare falls. Note that g and $g*$ enter the welfare function symmetrically around their target levels. The fall in welfare induces each country to ease fiscal policy a little less, and to permit output q to absorb some of the welfare loss.

The inefficiency of this noncooperative game is eliminated by the modified McKinnon rule in this example. The essential argument is that fixing the exchange rate removes the temptation to manipulate it via monetary policy in order to offset an exogenous inflation shock. So there is no attempt to twist monetary and fiscal policy, and no need to trade off q against g in the welfare function. The optimal result is efficiently to swallow the exogenous inflation shock, rather than to attempt to dampen it via a competitive appreciation. The difficulty that arises here is the hidden problem of incentives. What eliminates the incentive for a monetary authority to try to cheat on the system a little? This problem is in the background for the rest of the paper.

In section 3.5, McKibbin and Sachs turn to strategic interactions and coordination using MSG. The welfare function of each area, specified in equation (6), includes both the fiscal deficit and the current account balance explicitly. This implies that the specification of "bliss" includes national saving equal to domestic investment for each area. Inclusion of policy variables explicitly in the welfare function opens the possibility that differentiation among policy choices is built into the results by assumption.

The noncooperative solutions for policy using MSG assume each area chooses its fiscal rule taking the others as given, in the face of a common inflation shock. These are Nash equilibria for each of the monetary regimes. These can be compared with the cooperative regime where a world planner, or the Economic Policy Committee (EPC) of OECD, maximizes a GNP-weighted world welfare index. The non-cooperative dollar standard solution has the United States maximizing on monetary and fiscal policy. This then constrains Japanese and ROECD monetary policy; so they maximize on fiscal policy only. In the modified McKinnon case, the EPC chooses a path for weighted world money, assuming optimal fiscal policies. This fixes world money, and then, in the noncooperative solution, each area chooses fiscal policy independently, taking the others as given. Again, the incentives that bind monetary authorities are not specified.

The MSG results for the common inflation shock are puzzling. Comparison of tables 3.7 and 3.8 for the floating rate cooperative and non-cooperative solution reveals virtually no difference in the output or inflation paths. The main result of noncooperation is the twist toward tighter money and easier fiscal policy with higher interest rates. Presumably the slight superiority of the cooperative case on the welfare measure (section 3.5) comes from inclusion of the fiscal balance in the welfare measure. Comparison of tables 3.8 and 3.9 shows the inferiority of the dollar standard in the face of the inflation shock, but the explanation is not convincing. McKibbin and Sachs argue that the United States attempts to import disinflation in this case by engineering a disinflation abroad using tight money and fiscal ease in the United States. But under the dollar standard in table 3.9, Japanese real GNP and inflation are higher than with the floating rate, and GNP and inflation in the ROECD are about the same. The modified McKinnon rule removes the incentive for competitive appreciation, so the results resemble the cooperative flexible regime. As the welfare scores in section 3.5 show, there is not much difference among the two floating rate cases and the McKinnon rule in the disinflation game.

One of the main lessons from recent work on coordination is that the ranking of regimes depends on the source of disturbances. So in section 3.6 McKibbin and Sachs report the asymptotic variance of MSG under the alternative regimes with stochastic shocks to aggregate demand, the price level, and the velocity of money, in alternatively the United States and the ROECD. In table 3.11 we see that the non-cooperative float seems best for demand shocks, and in table 3.12 the cooperative and noncooperative floats share first place under price shocks. With money velocity shocks in one country, the McKinnon rule stabilizes the economy where the shock originates, by inducing an offsetting money supply response, but destabilizes the other economy. This is shown in table 3.13. But with negative correlation across countries in velocity shocks in table 3.14, the McKinnon rule dominates. This is as it should be, since the rule was designed for a world in which shifts of asset preference across currencies are the dominant source of disturbances.

What does the reader learn in this encounter with the McKibbin-Sachs global model? First, we see that with a heavy dose of MSG we can obtain sensible-looking numerical results that conform to intuition based on simple analytical models. This should increase confidence in the model's usefulness in analyzing policy alternatives. Second, we see that no regime dominates. The results depend on sources of shocks and probably also on the nature of the game that policymakers are playing. This makes it difficult to see how a coordination agreement could be negotiated internationally at the present time. Third, the non-cooperative float looks like a fairly good regime. It would work especially well if central banks could agree to rule out competitive appreciation in the face of inflation shocks.

Research on monetary or macro policy coordination seems to be following three different paths. One is simulation study, taking empirical parameters *and* the institutional framework that would induce policymakers to join the specified cooperative game or set of rules as given. The present paper is on this path. A second is actual empirical work, attempting to estimate better models for the simulation studies to manipulate. The third path is the design of institutions that provide the incentives for policymakers to coordinate in productive ways. Perhaps further work with MSG or its descendants can contribute to this third line of research by developing regimes that offer policymakers such incentives.

References

Branson, W. H. 1984a. Exchange rate policy after a decade of floating. In *Exchange rate theory and practice,* ed. John F. O. Bilson and Richard C. Marston. Chicago: University of Chicago Press.
————. 1984b. A model of exchange-rate determination with policy reaction evidence from monthly data. In *Contemporary macroeconomic modelling,* ed. Pierre Malgrange and Pierre-Alain Muet. London: Basil Blackwell.

Dornbusch, R. 1976. Expectations and exchange rate dynamics. *Journal of Political Economy* 84:1161–76.

Sachs, J. D. (1979), Wages, profits, and macroeconomic adjustment: A comparative study. *Brookings Papers on Economic Activity* 2:269–320.

Comment   Robert P. Flood

In this paper McKibbin and Sachs present some policy simulations using their global model. The model is listed in the paper's appendix, and its construction has been discussed elsewhere. Since the model is not treated specifically here, I will make no specific comments on it. I will, however, make three kinds of general comments about the paper. First, I will list and explain briefly some standard caveats concerning this type of simulation exercise. Second, I will discuss what I think are some problems associated with the arbitrary loss function adopted by the authors. Third, I will discuss a methodological problem with using this type of model for policy evaluation. My comments are all critical, but that should not be taken as a negative evaluation of the work. This paper is state-of-the-art, open-economy policy evaluation and is a quantum leap beyond many of its competitors. I know of no work on this topic that is not subject to similar negative comments. In my view though, the paper illustrates that economists are a long way from being able to give policy advice based on recent ideas. (Such a gap may well be a health steady state.)

Everything I have to say is at some level a variant of the famous Lucas Econometric Policy Evaluation Critique. I think this is to be expected. McKibbin and Sachs have undertaken policy evaluation using a data-based model, and this was precisely the setting for Lucas's critique. Most of the points Lucas made concerning modeling the first moments of agents' beliefs about a model's variables have been answered in the present simulation strategy, so I will take up a few other aspects of the critique.

Some Standard Caveats

Recall that the Lucas Critique is a criticism of the methodology of estimating parameters using data generated under one regime and taking these parameters as being necessarily invariant to policy-regime changes. Lucas's suggested research program to carry out econometric policy evaluation requires that deep structural parameters of tastes and technology be estimated. The hope is that such parameters will be invariant to policy-regime changes.

Robert P. Flood is a professor of economics at Northwestern University and a research associate of the National Bureau of Economic Research.

McKibbin and Sachs have treated parameters such as adjustment speeds in money markets as policy-invariant. I would expect adjustment speeds to be chosen by agents as an optimal response to the economic environment. Parameters such as these may well change radically in response to the various monetary policies simulated in the paper. Therefore, I would have found helpful a report on the sensitivity of the simulations to policy-induced alterations in some of the parameters. An alternative might have been to design the simulated policies so that it can be argued that a policy shift would have little effect on the parameters.

In the appendix the parameterization of the model is given with the parameters treated as fixed numbers. Almost all of these numbers are actually random variables, some probably quite imprecisely estimated, some jointly distributed with other parameters, and some (almost surely) inconsistently estimated according to the model being simulated. I do not think anything can be done easily about these points. Some notion of the confidence intervals of the simulations would have been useful to me with those confidence intervals based on the joint distribution of the parameters. I also would have liked a section persuading me that a reasonable attempt had been made to secure parameter estimates consistent under the simulated model.

Social Welfare

The social welfare function adopted for the dynamic game simulation in section 3.5 is not necessarily consistent with the behavior in the rest on the model. Ideally, the social welfare function would be a policy invariant function of the utilities of the agents responsible for behavior in the rest of the model.

The specific social welfare function adopted in the paper makes the flow of social welfare a quadratic function of the output gap, CPI inflation, the current account as a percentage of GDP, and the budget deficit relative to GDP. The quadratic form implies that optimizing government policy minimizes a linear function of the second moments of these variables. Some assumption about the social welfare function must be made, but why is this a particularly interesting assumption? Some of the variables listed in the chosen function—for example, the current account and the government deficit relative to GDP—are measures of variables that adjust to buffer shocks and would not in general be zero at stochastic "bliss."

My guess is that McKibbin and Sachs adopted their social welfare function on the basis of their observations of statements made by representatives of OECD governments. My fear is that such statements are regime-specific and would be altered under precisely the conditions that would bring about the policy shifts being analyzed. If my view is correct, then even the social welfare function (since it is not derived from deeper considerations) should not be viewed as policy-invariant.

What Do We Mean by Changes in Policy?

The methodology of rational expectations requires that agents have rational beliefs about the moments of variables relevant to their decisions. This presents a new problem for those trying to give policy advice. Under some other assumptions it is sensible to think about introducing a new policy or reviving some long-dormant policy with agents reacting to the policy shift as if it were a complete surprise and as if they thought the policy would never be abandoned. Rational expectations are somewhat more demanding of the would-be policy adviser.

Fully rational agents are rational about policy. They understand that government policy is altered from time to time as dictated by events. The realization of a particular policy is like the realization of any other random variable. When it happens it is a surprise, but it is not an entirely unforeseen surprise. Furthermore, when the policy is realized there is typically no reason for agents to believe that the current policy realization is the final policy realization.

Rational expectations, consequently, lead us to think about policy modeling in a very different way than we thought about it ten or fifteen years ago. Policy is the outcome of a (possibly optimizing) decision process, and policy is set and changed as the state variables relevant to the policy decision process evolve. Consequently, to give policy advice in a rational expectations environment, one must first discover what historical state of the system led to the choice of the current policy and then find out how the state has evolved since the most recent policy choice was made.

McKibbin and Sachs approach policy modeling in the traditional way—an econometric model is used to simulate the effects of new policies taking as fixed the nonpolicy economic environment in which the model was estimated. It seems to me that this approach is internally inconsistent. Why is new policy advice needed unless the economic environment has somehow changed? But if the economic environment has changed, the change should have been incorporated into the economic model.

Final Comments

As I mentioned at the beginning of my comments, the McKibbin and Sachs paper is state-of-the-art policy modeling. Although my comments were all negative, I do not want to give the impression that I know of any work on this topic that is not subject to similar negative comments.

4 Macroeconomic Policy Design in an Interdependent World Economy: An Analysis of Three Contingencies

Willem H. Buiter

4.1 Introduction

In this chapter I take up three policy issues that have been of central concern in recent academic and official discussions of international economic interdependence and macroeconomic policy coordination. They are:

1. What should be the monetary and/or fiscal response in the rest of the industrialized world to a unilateral tightening of U.S. fiscal policy, and what should be the U.S. monetary response to that?

2. What should be the monetary and fiscal response in the industrialized countries to a sudden, large change in an important exchange rate? For concreteness I shall refer to this event as a "collapse of the U.S. dollar."

3. What should be the policy response in the industrialized world to a disappointing real-growth performance?

All three issues are clearly of more than academic interest. In this chapter I attempt to give qualitative answers using a simple analytical model. However simple the individual-country models may be, the

Willem H. Buiter is professor of economics at Yale University and a research associate of the National Bureau of Economic Research.

"Macroeconomic Policy Design in an Interdependent World Economy: An Analysis of Three Contingencies," by Willem H. Buiter was published in IMF *Staff Papers* (September 1986) and appears here by permission of the International Monetary Fund.

This paper was written while I was a consultant in the Research Department of the IMF during the summer of 1985. The topic was suggested to me by Andrew D. Crockett. Malcolm Knight made a number of incisive comments on an earlier draft. The opinions expressed in the paper are my own.

The research reported here is part of the NBER's research program in international studies. Any opinions expressed are those of the author and not those of the National Bureau of Economic Research.

interdependent global economic system very soon grows too large for analytical treatment; numerical simulation methods are called for. Recent work by Sachs (1985) and by Sachs and McKibbin (1985) has demonstrated the usefulness of such an approach. The advantages in terms of intuition and insight from keeping things sufficiently small and transparent to permit a simple algebraic and diagrammatic analysis are such, however, that a first pass at this problem "in two dimensions" is justified.

Section 4.2.1 outlines the simple two-country Dornbusch-style model that has a floating exchange rate, perfect capital mobility, rational exchange-rate expectations, and gradual price adjustment. The long-run or steady-state comparative statics are reviewed in section 4.2.2 while section 4.2.3 characterizes the nature of the dynamic adjustment process. Possible responses to a tightening of U.S. fiscal policy are reviewed in section 4.3. In section 4.4 possible responses to a collapse of the U.S. dollar are considered and section 4.5 deals with the policy implications of a slowdown in world economic activity. Qualifications and conclusions are found in section 4.6.

4.2 An Analytical Approach

4.2.1 The Model

Consider the simple two-country or two-region version of the Dornbusch (1976) open macroeconomic model with a free-floating exchange rate and perfect capital mobility given in equations (1)–(12) below. This model can be viewed as a sluggish-price-adjustment, rational-exchange-rate-expectations version of Mundell's two-country model (Mundell [1968]). Except for some inconsequential differences, this model is the one used by Miller (1982). Turnovsky (1985) has used this model to analyze the effects of a number of anticipated and unanticipated monetary and fiscal shocks. (See also Buiter [1985a] for another application.) All variables other than interest rates are in natural logarithms.

All coefficients are non-negative. Country 1 will be referred to as the United States and country 2 as the rest of the world (ROW).

(1) $m_1 - p_1 = k_1 y_1 - \lambda_1 i_1 + \eta_1$

(2) $y_1 = -\gamma_1 r_1 + \delta_{12}(e + p_2 - p_1) + \epsilon_{12} y_2 + f_1$

(3) $\dot{p}_1 = \psi_1(y_1 - \bar{y}_1) + \dot{m}_1$

(4) $r_1 = i_1 - \dot{p}_1$

(5) $i_1 = i_2 + \dot{e} + \tau_2 - \tau_1$

(6) $m_2 - p_2 = k_2 y_2 - \lambda_2 i_2 + \eta_2$

(7) $y_2 = -\gamma_2 r_2 - \delta_{21}(e + p_2 - p_1) + \epsilon_{21} y_1 + f_2$

(8) $\dot{p}_2 = \psi_2(y_2 - \bar{y}_2) + \dot{m}_2$

(9) $r_2 = i_2 - \dot{p}_2$

(10) $c \equiv e + p_2 - p_1$

(11) $l_1 \equiv m_1 - p_1$

(12) $l_2 \equiv m_2 - p_2$

In these equations m_j is the nominal money stock of country j, p_j its gross domestic product (GDP) deflator, y_j its real output, i_j its nominal interest rate, and r_j its real interest rate; e is the nominal exchange rate, expressed as the number of units of country 1's currency per unit of country 2's currency; f_j is a measure of fiscal stance in country j, τ_j is country j's tax rate on interest income accruing from abroad and its subsidy rate on the interest cost of borrowing from abroad. These taxes drive a wedge between the domestic nominal-interest rate and the interest rate on loans denominated in the same currency overseas. The real exchange rate or competitiveness is c, and l_j is country j's stock of real-money balances.

The model has rational exchange-rate expectations and rational inflation expectations by investors. The exchange rate is set in an efficient, forward-looking asset market. It can make discrete "jumps" at a point in time in response to "news." Domestic costs p_j are predetermined (i.e., given at a point in time), but their rates of change respond to excess demand or supply and "core inflation."

The model will have short-run Keynesian but long-run classical or monetarist features. Each country's demand for real-money balances varies positively with its own national income y_j and negatively with its own nominal interest rate i_j.[1] There is no endogenous direct currency substitution.[2] A shift parameter η_j is added to allow for portfolio shifts. The demand for each country's output depends on its real interest rate r_j, on competitiveness c, on the other country's level of real income, and on the domestic fiscal impulse f_j. Domestic costs are governed by an augmented Phillips curve. The (logarithm of the) level of capacity output $\bar{y}_j$ (or the natural rate of unemployment) in each country is exogenous. The augmentation term in the Phillips curve is taken to be the current rate of growth of the money stock $\dot{m}_j$. This is done merely to permit a simple diagrammatic analysis of the model's properties. More satisfactory ways of modeling the augmentation term are discussed in Buiter and Miller (1982, 1983, 1985).

The two countries are not only linked through competitiveness and activity effects but also directly through an integrated international financial market. Equation (5) represents the condition for (after-tax) uncovered interest parity. U.S. and ROW currency-denominated interest-bearing assets are perfect substitutes in private portfolios. This will be the case if the international financial markets are efficient and if there are risk-neutral speculators.

It will be convenient to represent the essential dynamics of this economic miniworld through three state variables, $l_j, j = 1,2$; real-money balances in each of the two countries; and c, U.S. competitiveness.

4.2.2.   The Long-Run Equilibrium

The long-run comparative statics in this model are completely classical or monetarist. Output in each country is at its exogenously given full employment level, and changes in the levels and growth rates of nominal money stocks are translated into corresponding changes in the levels and proportional rates of change of costs and of the exchange rate. Equation (13a–i) summarizes the long-run equilibrium of this economy.

$$(13a) \qquad\qquad y_i = \bar{y}_i \qquad\qquad i = 1, 2$$

$$(13b) \qquad\qquad \dot{p}_i = \dot{m}_i \qquad\qquad i = 1, 2$$

$$(13c) \qquad\qquad \dot{e} = \dot{m}_1 - \dot{m}_2$$

$$(13d) \qquad\qquad r_1 = r_2 + \tau_2 - \tau_1$$

$$(13e) \qquad c = \frac{1}{\Lambda} [\gamma_1 f_2 - \gamma_2 f_1] - \frac{\gamma_1 \gamma_2}{\Lambda}(\tau_1 - \tau_2)$$
$$+ \frac{(\gamma_2 + \gamma_1 \epsilon_{12})}{\Lambda} \bar{y}_1 - \frac{(\gamma_1 + \gamma_2 \epsilon_{12})}{\Lambda} \bar{y}_2$$

$$(13f) \qquad r_1 = \frac{1}{\Lambda} [\delta_{12} f_2 + \delta_{21} f_1] - \frac{\delta_{12} \gamma_2}{\Lambda} (\tau_1 - \tau_2)$$
$$+ \frac{(\delta_{12}\epsilon_{21} - \delta_{21})}{\Lambda} \bar{y}_1 + \frac{(\delta_{21}\epsilon_{12} - \delta_{12})}{\Lambda} \bar{y}_2$$

$$(13g) \qquad r_2 = \frac{1}{\Lambda} [\delta_{12} f_2 + \delta_{21} f_1] + \frac{\delta_{21} \gamma_1}{\Lambda} (\tau_1 - \tau_2)$$
$$+ \frac{(\delta_{12}\epsilon_{21} - \delta_{21})}{\Lambda} \bar{y}_1 + \frac{(\delta_{21}\epsilon_{12} - \delta_{12})}{\Lambda} \bar{y}_2$$

$$(13h) \quad l_1 = \frac{-\lambda_1}{\Lambda} (\delta_{12} f_2 + \delta_{21} f_1) + \frac{\lambda_1 \delta_{12} \gamma_2}{\Lambda} (\tau_1 - \tau_2) - \lambda_1 \dot{m}_1 + \eta_1$$
$$+ (k_1 - \frac{\lambda_1(\delta_{12}\epsilon_{21} - \delta_{21})}{\Lambda}) \bar{y}_1 - \frac{\lambda_1(\delta_{21}\delta_{21} - \delta_{12})}{\Lambda} \bar{y}_2$$

$$(13i) \quad l_2 = \frac{-\lambda_2}{\Lambda} (\delta_{12} f_2 + \delta_{23} f_1) - \frac{\lambda_2 \delta_{21} \gamma_1}{\Lambda} (\tau_1 - \tau_2) - \lambda_2 \dot{m} + \eta_2$$
$$+ (k_2 - \frac{\lambda_2(\delta_{21}\epsilon_{12} - \delta_{12})}{\Lambda}) \bar{y}_2 - \frac{\lambda_2(\delta_{12}\epsilon_{21} - \delta_{21})}{\Lambda} \bar{y}_1,$$

where

(13j) $$\Lambda = \delta_{21}\gamma_1 + \delta_{12}\gamma_2.$$

In the long run (at full employment), fiscal expansion in the United States worsens U.S. competitiveness while fiscal expansion in the ROW causes U.S. competitiveness to improve.[3] Neither changes in the levels nor in the rates of growth of the nominal money stocks affect real competitiveness or real interest rates. Fiscal expansion in the United States or in the ROW raises the world real interest rate. (Note that the United States and the ROW real interest rates differ only to the extent that U.S. and ROW taxes [subsidies] on foreign interest income [payments] differ.) An increase in $\tau_1 - \tau_2$ lowers the U.S. real interest rate and raises that in the ROW. Competitiveness therefore must move against the United States to restore equilibrium in the market for U.S. output. An increase in $\dot{m}_i$ raises $\dot{p}_i$ and the rate of depreciation of country i's currency by the same amount. A higher nominal interest rate reduces the stock of real-money balances demanded in the long run, if the interest-sensitivity of the demand for real-money balances is nonzero. Given the rate of money growth (and thus the rate of inflation), expansionary fiscal policy in either country, by raising the real interest rate, also raises the nominal interest rate and reduces the demand for real-money balances at home and abroad.

An increase in the level of capacity output ($\bar{y}_i$) of a country is associated with an improvement in its long-run competitiveness. This is required in order for the market to absorb the relatively greater supply of that country's output. If we assume that $\delta_{12}\epsilon_{21} - \delta_{12}$ and $\delta_{21}\epsilon_{12} - \delta_{12}$ are both negative, an increase in the level of capacity output in either country lowers the long-run real interest rate in both countries; the lower real interest rates stimulate demand and bring it back to equality with the larger level of full employment output. Both directly, via the income effect on money demand and indirectly, by lowering the nominal interest rate (since real interest rates decline and money growth is held constant), increased capacity output in either country raises the long-run stock of real-money balances in both countries.

4.2.3. The Dynamic Response to Policy Changes and Exogenous Shocks

The three simultaneous state equations of the unrestricted model are available from the author on request. When the restriction is imposed that the two countries or regions have identical structures, it becomes possible to provide an analytical and diagrammatic exposition of the main policy issues (see Aoki [1981] and Miller [1982]). The assumption of identical structures is of course quite restrictive. All differences in country performance must be attributed solely to different policies, different exogenous shocks, or different initial conditions. A full analysis of two- or three-country models that allows for intercountry differences in the specification of major behavioral relationships will require numerical simulation methods. The simplified two-country model does, however, permit a very transparent first pass at the major policy issues. Symmetry in this model means that $k_1 = k_2 = k; \lambda_1 = \lambda_2 = \lambda;$ $\gamma_1 = \gamma_2 = \gamma; \delta_{12} = \delta_{21} = \delta; \epsilon_{12} = \epsilon_{21} = \epsilon; \psi_1 = \psi_2 = \psi.$

The three simultaneous state equations of the unrestricted model can be decomposed into two independent subsystems when the restriction of identical structures is imposed. A two-dimensional system involves the real exchange rate and the *difference* between the two countries' real money stocks. Let $1^d \equiv l_1 - l_2, \dot{m}^d \equiv \dot{m}_1 - \dot{m}_1; \eta^d \equiv \eta_1 - \eta_2,$ $f^d \equiv f_1 - f_2, \tau^d \equiv \tau_1 - \tau_2,$ and $\bar{y}^d \equiv \bar{y}_1 - \bar{y}_2.$

$$(14a) \quad \begin{bmatrix} \dot{l}^d \\ \dot{c} \end{bmatrix} = \begin{bmatrix} a_{11} & a_{12} \\ a_{21} & a_{22} \end{bmatrix} \begin{bmatrix} l^d \\ c \end{bmatrix} + \begin{bmatrix} b_{11} & b_{12} & b_{13} & b_{14} & b_{15} \\ b_{21} & b_{22} & b_{23} & b_{24} & b_{25} \end{bmatrix} \begin{bmatrix} \dot{m}^d \\ \eta^d \\ f^d \\ \tau^d \\ \bar{y}^d \end{bmatrix},$$

where

$a_{11} = -\psi\lambda^{-1} \gamma(\Omega + \epsilon)^{-1}; a_{12} = - 2\psi\delta(\Omega + \epsilon)^{-1},$
$a_{21} = -\lambda^{-1}(1 + \epsilon)(\Omega + \epsilon)^{-1}; a_{22} = 2\Gamma\delta(\Omega + \epsilon)^{-1},$
$b_{11} = -\psi\gamma(\Omega + \epsilon)^{-1}; b_{12} = \psi\lambda^{-1} \gamma(\Omega + \epsilon)^{-1}; b_{13} = -\psi(\Omega + \epsilon)^{-1}$
$\quad\quad b_{14} = 0; b_{15} = \psi(1 + \gamma\psi(\Omega + \epsilon)^{-1}),$
$b_{21} = (1 + \epsilon) (\Omega + \epsilon)^{-1}; b_{22} = \lambda^{-1}(1 +\epsilon) (\Omega+\epsilon)^{-1};$
$\quad\quad b_{23} = \Gamma (\Omega + \epsilon)^{-1}; b_{24} = 1;$
$\quad\quad b_{25} = \psi(1 - \Gamma \gamma(1 - \Gamma\gamma(\Omega + \epsilon)^{-1}),$

and

$$\Omega \equiv 1 + \gamma\Gamma,$$
$$\Gamma \equiv \gamma^{-1}k - \psi.$$

A one-dimensional system involves only *averages* or global magnitudes.

Let $l^a \equiv \dfrac{l_1 + l_2}{2}; \dot{m}^a \equiv \dfrac{\dot{m}_1 + \dot{m}_2}{2}; f^a \equiv \dfrac{f_1 + f_2}{2};$

$\eta^a \equiv \dfrac{\eta_1 + \eta_2}{2}; \tau^a \equiv \dfrac{\tau_1 + \tau_2}{2}$

and $\bar{y}^a \equiv \dfrac{\bar{y}_1 + \bar{y}_2}{2}.$

We have

(14b) $\quad \dot{l}^a = -\psi\lambda^{-1}(\Omega - \epsilon)^{-1}\gamma l^a + [-\psi\gamma(\Omega - \epsilon)^{-1}$

$$\psi\lambda^{-1}\gamma(\Omega - \epsilon)^{-1} - \psi(\Omega - \epsilon)^{-1}$$

$$o\ \psi(1 + (\Omega - \epsilon)^{-1}\gamma\psi)] \begin{bmatrix} \dot{m}^a \\ \eta^a \\ f^a \\ \tau^a \\ \bar{y}^a \end{bmatrix}.$$

The "output equations," the equations giving the short-run endogenous variables as functions of the state variables and the exogenous variables are (using self-explanatory notation):

(15a) $\quad \begin{bmatrix} y^d \\ i^d \\ \dot{p}^d \end{bmatrix} = \begin{bmatrix} (\Omega + \epsilon)^{-1}\gamma\lambda^{-1} \\ -\lambda^{-1}(1 - \gamma\psi + \epsilon)(\Omega + \epsilon)^{-1} \\ (\Omega + \epsilon)^{-1}\psi\gamma\lambda^{-1} \end{bmatrix}$

$$\begin{matrix} 2(\Omega + \epsilon)^{-1}\delta \\ 2\lambda^{-1}k(\Omega + \epsilon)^{-1}\delta \\ 2\psi\delta(\Omega + \epsilon)^{-1} \end{matrix} \end{bmatrix} \begin{bmatrix} l^d \\ c \end{bmatrix}$$

$$+ \begin{bmatrix} (\Omega + \epsilon)^{-1}\gamma & -(\Omega + \epsilon)^{-1}\gamma\lambda^{-1} \\ (\Omega + \epsilon)^{-1}\lambda^{-1}k\gamma & \lambda^{-1}(1 - \gamma\psi - \epsilon)^{-1} \\ 1 + (\Omega + \epsilon)^{-1}\psi\gamma & -(\Omega + \epsilon)^{-1}\psi\gamma\lambda^{-1} \end{bmatrix}$$

$$\begin{matrix} (\Omega + \epsilon)^{-1} & 0 & -(\Omega + \epsilon)^{-1}\gamma\psi \\ (\Omega + \epsilon)^{-1}\lambda^{-1}k & 0 & -\lambda^{-1}k\gamma\psi(\Omega + \epsilon)^{-1} \\ (\Omega + \epsilon)^{-1}\psi & 0 & -\psi(1 + (\Omega + \epsilon)^{-1}\gamma\psi) \end{matrix} \end{bmatrix} \begin{bmatrix} \dot{m}^d \\ \eta^d \\ f^d \\ \tau^d \\ \bar{y}^d \end{bmatrix} \underline{2}/$$

and

(15b) $\quad \begin{bmatrix} y^a \\ i^a \\ \dot{p}^a \\ r^a \end{bmatrix} = \begin{bmatrix} (\Omega - \epsilon)^{-1}\gamma\lambda^{-1} \\ -\lambda^{-1}(1 - \gamma\psi - \epsilon)(\Omega - \epsilon)^{-1} \\ (\Omega - \epsilon)^{-1}\psi\gamma\lambda^{-1} \\ -\lambda^{-1}(1 - \epsilon)(\Omega - \epsilon)^{-1} \end{bmatrix} [l^a]$

$$+ \begin{bmatrix} (\Omega - \epsilon)^{-1}\gamma & -(\Omega - \epsilon)^{-1}\gamma\lambda^{-1} \\ (\Omega - \epsilon)^{-1}\lambda^{-1}k\gamma & \lambda^{-1}(1 - \gamma\psi - \epsilon)(\Omega - \epsilon)^{-1} \\ 1 + (\Omega - \epsilon)^{-1}\psi\gamma & -(\Omega - \epsilon)^{-1}\psi\gamma\lambda^{-1} \\ -[1 - \epsilon](\Omega - \epsilon)^{-1} & \gamma^{-1}(1 - \epsilon)(\Omega - \epsilon)^{-1} \end{bmatrix}$$

$$\begin{matrix} (\Omega - \epsilon)^{-1} & 0 & -(\Omega - \epsilon)\gamma\psi \\ (\Omega - \epsilon)^{-1}\lambda^{-1}k & 0 & -\lambda^{-1}k\gamma\psi(\Omega - \epsilon)^{-1} \\ (\Omega - \epsilon)^{-1}\psi & 0 & -\psi(1 + (\Omega - \epsilon)^{-1}\gamma\psi) \\ (\Omega - \epsilon)^{-1}\Gamma & 0 & \psi(1 - \Gamma\gamma(\Omega - \epsilon)^{-1}) \end{matrix} \end{bmatrix} \begin{bmatrix} \dot{m}^a \\ \eta^d \\ f^a \\ \tau^d \\ \bar{y}^d \end{bmatrix}$$

The long-run comparative statics for the differences and averages can be obtained easily from equations (13a–i):

(16a) $l^d = -\lambda \dot{m}^d + \eta^d + \lambda \tau^d + k \bar{y}^d$

(16b) $c = -\dfrac{1}{2\delta} f^d - \dfrac{\gamma}{2\delta} \tau^d + \dfrac{(1 + \epsilon)}{2\delta} \bar{y}^d,$

(16c) $r^d = -\tau^d,$

(16d) $l^a = -\lambda \dot{m}^a + \eta^a - \dfrac{\lambda}{\gamma} f^a + \left(k + \dfrac{\lambda(1 - \epsilon)}{\gamma} \right) \bar{y}^a,$

(16e) $r^a = \dfrac{1}{\gamma} f^a + \dfrac{(\epsilon - 1)}{\gamma} \bar{y}^a.$

Global or average economic performance and the difference between the economic performances of the two countries are "decoupled": they can be studied independently of each other, with average outcomes a function only of current and past average policy instrument values and average exogenous shocks, while performance differences are a function only of differences in current, past, and expected future differences in policy instrument values and exogenous disturbances. The "averages" model—equations (14b) and (15b)—can indeed be viewed as a self-contained model of a single closed economy. Because the price deflators are predetermined and the real exchange rate "washes out" through the assumption of symmetrical structures, the "averages" model contains no nonpredetermined, forward-looking or jump variables. Note that after analyzing averages and differences, we can easily retrieve individual country performance, since $l_1 = \frac{1}{2} l^d + l^a$, $l_2 = -\frac{1}{2} l^d + l^a$, etc.

The "averages" economy (equation 14b) with its single predetermined state variable will be stable if and only if $-\psi\lambda^{-1}(\Omega - \epsilon)^{-1}\gamma < 0$ that is i.f.f.

(17a) $\Omega > \epsilon$

The "differences" system (equation 14a) with its predetermined variable l^d and its nonpredetermined variable c, will have a unique convergent saddlepoint equilibrium if and only if $a_{11} a_{22} - a_{21} a_{12} < 0$ that is i.f.f.

(17b) $\Omega > -\epsilon$

Since $\epsilon > 0$, (17a) implies (17b).

Equation (17b) is equivalent to the condition that an improvement in U.S. competitiveness will (given l^d, $\dot{m}^d$, η^d, f^d, and r^d) raise the effective demand for U.S. output relative to output in the rest of the world. It is a weak condition, which amounts to assuming that in a diagram with the nominal interest rate on the vertical axis and output on the horizontal axis, the IS curve (after using the Phillips curve to substitute out the [expected] rate of inflation) is either downward-sloping or upward-sloping and steeper than the LM curve. I assume that (17a) is satisfied. Given (17a) (and thereby [17b]), the saddlepoint equilibrium and the "differences" system either look like figure 4.1a (when the IS curve is downward sloping, $a_{22} > 0$ 3/ and the $\dot{c} = 0$ locus is upward-sloping) or like figure 4.1b (when the IŜ curve is upward-sloping and steeper than the LM curve, $a_{22} < 0$ and the $\dot{c} = 0$ locus is downward-sloping and cuts the $l^d = 0$ locus from above). Since the phase diagram is qualitatively similar in the two cases, I shall restrict the analysis to the case depicted in figure 4.1a. Figure 4.1c depicts the

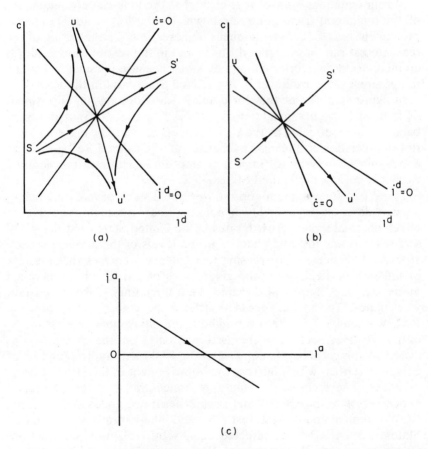

(a)

(b)

(c)

Fig. 4.1   Equilibrium and dynamic adjustment in the symmetric two-country model.

adjustment process of the single predetermined state variable for the "averages" system.

First among the policy issues to be considered now is the proper response in the ROW to a unilateral U.S. fiscal contraction.

4.3 Responses to a Tightening of U.S. Fiscal Policy

4.3.1   U.S. Fiscal Tightening without Fiscal or Monetary Response in the ROW and without Monetary Response in the U.S.A.

A fiscal tightening in the United States without any fiscal response in the ROW is, in the notation of this paper, a reduction in the average fiscal impulse (f^a) and a reduction in the difference between the two countries' fiscal impulses f^d which is twice as large as the reduction in f^a. From equations 16(a–e) it is clear that the long-run consequences of this unilateral fiscal contraction will be the following: (1) an improvement in U.S. competitiveness (c increases); (2) a lowering of the real interest rate in the United States and in the rest of the world; (3) an increase in the world real-money stock because nominal as well as real interest rates are lower in the United States and in the R.O.W.

In figure 4.2a we see that for c and l^d, the full long-run adjustment from E_1 to E_2 occurs instantaneously. Relative U.S.-ROW real-money balances are unaffected by the U.S. fiscal tightening. The required long-run depreciation in the *real* exchange rate can therefore be brought about immediately by a "jump" or step depreciation in the nominal exchange rate of the United States.

In the new long-run equilibrium, the global stock of real-money balances will be larger since lower nominal interest rates raise velocity. Given nominal money growth rates in the United States and the ROW and without any discrete changes in the levels of the nominal money stocks, the process of increasing real balances requires that the rate of inflation be held below the given rates of growth of the nominal money stocks. There will therefore be a temporary global recession: y^a declines. The global recession affects the United States and the R.O.W. equally: y^d is zero throughout the adjustment process. U.S. output declines because of the fiscal tightening but the decline is mitigated as competitiveness improves. The ROW suffers from its loss of competitiveness, which mirrors the improvement in the U.S. competitiveness. The recession is therefore concentrated in the nontraded goods sector of the United States and the traded goods sector of the ROW. Nominal and real interest rates and inflation rates in the United States and the ROW are affected equally by U.S. fiscal contraction: i^d, r^d, and $\dot{p}^d$ are zero throughout. Both nominal and real interest rates decline globally (and in each country). As in the familiar closed econ-

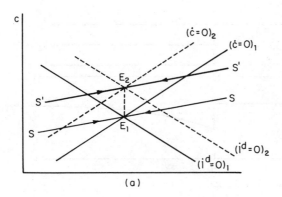

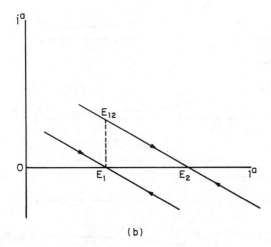

Fig. 4.2

omy IS-LM, augmented Phillips curve model, the decline in nominal
and real interest rates mitigates the contraction of aggregate demand
but does not undo it completely. There is "crowding out" (in our policy
experiment a reversal of crowding out) but less than 100%. Note that
because inflation declines during the recession, real interest rates come
down by less than nominal interest rates. Figure 4.3 summarizes the
response to the unexpected announcement at time t_0 of an immediately
implemented permanent tightening of U.S. fiscal policy.[4]

4.3.2 Monetary Policy Stabilizes the Nominal Exchange Rate

One alternative scenario often considered consists of a tightening of
U.S. fiscal policy, unaccommodating U.S. monetary policy, unchanged
fiscal policy in the ROW, and monetary policy in the ROW geared to
interest rate coupling. Given perfect international capital mobility, in-

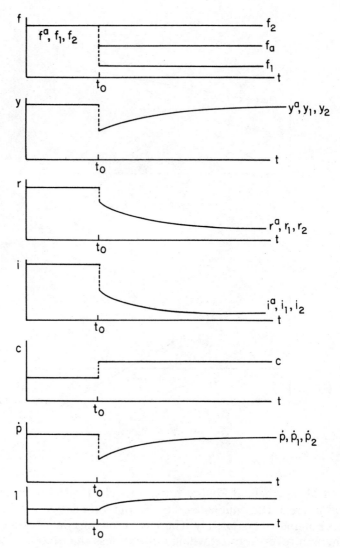

Fig. 4.3   Global and regional response to a unilateral tightening of U.S. fiscal policy.

terest rate coupling amounts to having a fixed nominal exchange rate. Under a fixed exchange rate regime, a fiscal contraction in the United States will, with perfect capital mobility, lead to a stock-shift outflow of capital from the United States, a stock-shift loss of U.S. foreign exchange reserves, and a corresponding contraction in the U.S. money stock. The ROW experiences the counterpart stock-shift inflow of capital, stock-shift gain in foreign exchange reserves, and expansion of its money stock. It is therefore arbitrary whether one assigns the stabilization of the exchange rate to the monetary policy of the ROW or to the United States. Under a fixed exchange rate regime (which is expected to be permanent), there is effectively a single global world money market or world LM schedule. Individual countries can choose their own rates of domestic credit expansion and thus collectively determine the growth of the world money stock. The distribution of this world money stock across countries is determined by the individual countries' money demand functions, with reserve flows making up the difference between changes in domestic money demand and domestic credit expansion.

The formal analysis of the fixed exchange rate regime is very simple. Let the global stock of gold and foreign exchange reserves be constant and, for notational simplicity, equal to zero. The global money stock is therefore the sum of the two countries' stocks of domestic credit. Let m be the logarithm of the global nominal money stock, D_i the logarithm of country i's stock of domestic credit, and v the share of U.S. domestic credit in total domestic credit.

(18a) $$m \equiv vD_1 + (1 - v)D_2 \qquad 0 < v < 1.$$

Setting the logarithm of the fixed nominal exchange rate equal to zero, we define the global price level, p, as follows:

(18b) $$p \equiv vp_1 + (1 - v)p_2.$$

The global money demand shock η is similarly defined as:

(18c) $$\eta = v\eta_1 + (1 - v)\eta_2.$$

and global income as

(19) $$y = vy_1 + (1 - v)y_2.$$

The proportional rate of growth of country i's domestic credit is $\mu_1 \equiv \dot{D}_i$. (Under a free-floating exchange rate regime, $\mu_i \equiv \dot{m}_i$.) The augmentation term in the Phillips curve is taken to be the policy-determined μ_i rather than the endogenously determined $\dot{m}_i$. No fixed exchange rate regime is viable unless inflation rates converge. I therefore impose $\mu_1 = \mu_2 = \mu$. This still permits short-term divergence of inflation rates. I also define $i \equiv i_1 = i_2 + \tau_2 - \tau_1$. The model consists of equations (20)–(23) and (2), (4), (7) and (9). Identical structures are again assumed.

(20) $$l = ky - \lambda i + \eta - (1 - v)\lambda(\tau_1 - \tau_2)$$

(21) $$\dot{p}_1 = \psi(y_1 - \bar{y}_1) + \mu$$

(22) $$\dot{p}_2 = \psi(y_2 - \bar{y}_2) + \mu$$

(23) $$l \equiv m - p$$

For algebraic simplicity and in order to retain comparability with the floating exchange rate case, both countries are assumed to be of equal size, so $v = \frac{1}{2}$.

The fixed exchange rate version has two state variables, l and c, which are both predetermined. The equations of motion and the determination of output in the two countries are given in equations (24) and (25) respectively.

$$(24)\quad \begin{bmatrix} \dot{l} \\ \dot{c} \end{bmatrix} = \begin{bmatrix} -\psi(K_1 + K_2)^{-1}\gamma\lambda^{-1} & 0 \\ 0 & -2\psi(K_1 - K_2)^{-1}\delta \end{bmatrix}\begin{bmatrix} l \\ c \end{bmatrix}$$

$$+ \begin{bmatrix} -\psi(K_1 + K_2)^{-1}\gamma & \psi(K_1 + K_2)^{-1}\gamma\lambda^{-1} & -\psi\dfrac{(K_1 + K_2)^{-1}}{2} \\ 0 & 0 & -\psi(K_1 - K_2)^{-1} \end{bmatrix}$$

$$\begin{array}{ccc} -\psi\dfrac{(K_1 + K_2)^{-1}}{2} & 0 & \psi\dfrac{[1 + \psi\gamma(K_1 + K_2)^{-1}]}{2} \\[2mm] \psi(K_1 - K_2)^{-1} & -\psi(K_1 - K_2)^{-1} & \psi[1 + \psi\gamma(K_1 - K_2)^{-1}] \end{array}$$

$$\begin{array}{c} \psi[1 + \psi\gamma(K_1 + K_2)^{-1}] \\[2mm] -\psi[1 + \psi\gamma(K_1 - K_2)^{-1}] \end{array} \begin{bmatrix} \mu \\ \eta \\ f_1 \\ f_2 \\ \tau_1 - \tau_2 \\ \bar{y}_1 \\ \bar{y}_2 \end{bmatrix}$$

$$(25)\quad \begin{bmatrix} y_1 \\ y_2 \end{bmatrix} = \begin{bmatrix} (K_1 + K_2)^{-1}\gamma\lambda^{-1} & (K_1 - K_2)^{-1}\delta \\ (K_1 + K_2)^{-1}\gamma\lambda^{-1} & -(K_1 - K_2)^{-1}\delta \end{bmatrix}\begin{bmatrix} l \\ c \end{bmatrix}$$

$$+ \begin{bmatrix} (K_1 + K_2)^{-1}\gamma & -(K_1 + K_2)^{-1}\gamma\lambda^{-1} & K_1\Delta^{-1} & -K_2\Delta^{-1} \\ (K_1 + K_2)^{-1}\gamma & -(K_1 + K_2)^{-1}\gamma\lambda^{-1} & -K_2\Delta^{-1} & K_1\Delta^{-1} \end{bmatrix}$$

$$\begin{array}{ccc} K_1\Delta^{-1}\gamma - (K_1 + K_2)^{-1}\gamma\frac{1}{2} & -K_1\Delta^{-1}\gamma\psi & K_2\Delta^{-1}\gamma\psi \\[2mm] -[K_2\Delta^{-1}\gamma + (K_1 + K_2)^{-1}\gamma\frac{1}{2}] & K_2\Delta^{-1}\gamma\psi & -K_1\Delta^{-1}\gamma\psi \end{array}\begin{bmatrix} \mu \\ \eta \\ f_1 \\ f_2 \\ \tau_1 - \tau_2 \\ \bar{y}_1 \\ \bar{y}_2] \end{bmatrix}$$

(26a) $$K_1 = 1 + \gamma\left(\frac{1}{2} k\lambda^{-1} - \psi\right)$$

(26b) $$K_2 = \frac{1}{2}\gamma\, k\lambda^{-1} - \epsilon$$

(26c) $$\Delta = K_1^2 - K_2^2 = (K_1 + K_2)(K_1 - K_2)$$

Several points can be made about the fixed exchange rate system. First, stability requires that $K_1 + K_2 > 0$ and that $K_1 - K_2 > 0$. This is equivalent to requiring that $K_1 > 0$ and $\Delta > 0$. Hoever, K_2 could be either positive or negative. With a fixed exchange rate, fiscal contraction in the United States will therefore definitely lower U.S. real output—

from (25) $\frac{\partial y_1}{\partial f_1} = K_1\Delta^{-1} > 0$—but it may either raise or lower real output

in the ROW—$\frac{\partial y_2}{\partial f_1} = -K_2\Delta^{-1}$. If $K_2 < 0$, the depressing effect on the

ROW's export sector of a decline in U.S. demand outweighs the beneficial effect of lower worldwide interest rates—$\epsilon > \frac{1}{2}\gamma k\lambda^{-1}$ in (26b)— and the ROW experiences a slump. If the "crowding in" effect is stronger than the direct demand effect, $K_2 > 0$, then the ROW expands while the United States contracts. Even if output in both countries declines, the decline will be steeper in the United States.

It is easily checked that, if the United States and the ROW are of similar size, total world output always contracts, even in the case where output in the ROW is stimulated by lower interest rates:

(27) $$y^a = (K_1 + K_2)^{-1}\gamma\lambda^{-1}\frac{l}{2}$$
$$+ (K_1 + K_2)^{-1}\gamma\mu - (K_1 + K_2)^{-1}\gamma\lambda^{-1}\eta$$
$$+ (K_1 + K_2)^{-1} f^a - (K_1 + K_2)^{-1}\gamma\psi\, \bar{y}^a.$$

Note that average global real liquidity under the fixed exchange rate regime—$\frac{1}{2}\, l$ given in equation (24)—behaves identically to average global real liquidity under the freely floating exchange rate regime—l^a given in equation (14b).[5] The same holds for average world output— compare equation (27) with y^a from equation (15b). That the long-run, steady-state effects of fiscal policy (or other real shocks) are the same under fixed and floating rates is also easy to check.

When therefore we compare the consequences of a tightening of U.S. fiscal policy under a floating exchange rate with that under a fixed exchange rate, holding global monetary policy constant in the sense that the growth rates of domestic credit (and therefore the growth rate of the global stock of nominal money) are the same in the two regimes, the *recession* in the United States following the fiscal contraction will be smaller under a floating exchange rate while in the ROW the recession will be deeper with a floating rate.

The global loss of output is the same under the two exchange rate regimes, but while under a floating rate the recessions in the U.S. and the ROW are identical in magnitude (although in the United States the nontraded goods sector will be hit while in the ROW it will be the traded goods sector), under a fixed rate the United States will always experience a deeper recession. It is even possible that under a fixed rate the ROW would experience a net boost to output.

The short-run behavior of the real exchange rate is quite different under the two regimes. As shown in figure 4.3, under a floating exchange rate U.S. competitiveness, which is a nonpredetermined variable in this case, sharply improves on impact to its new equilibrium level. This jump-depreciation of c reflects a jump-depreciation of e, the nominal exchange rate. While this clearly represents a hard landing for the U.S. dollar, it represents a much softer landing for the U.S. real economy than the alternative scenario in which the nominal exchange rate is kept constant throughout. In the latter case U.S. competitiveness improves gradually after the U.S. fiscal contraction and converges asymptotically to the same level achieved immediately with a freely floating exchange rate. The improvement in competitiveness is due to the U.S. rate of cost inflation falling below that in the ROW because of the relatively deeper recession in the U.S.

An alternative fixed nominal exchange rate scenario that is sometimes considered more likely is the following, which can be called the "non-McKinnon variant." The United States, instead of accepting the stock-shift contraction in its domestic money stock associated with the stock-shift outflow of capital and loss of reserves, engages in domestic open market purchases to maintain the initial level of the money stock, i.e., it sterilizes the stock-shift loss of reserves by a stock-shift expansion of domestic credit. The ROW does not sterilize. This means that the global money stock expands (through a stock-shift U.S. domestic credit expansion) until the now endogenously determined U.S. money stock again assumes its pre–fiscal contraction value.

In contrast with the first analysis of the fixed exchange rate case, there now is a once-off increase in the level of the global nominal money stock path (relative to what happens under a floating rate) accompanying the U.S. fiscal contraction. Global nominal and real interest rates will decline by more than they do both in the fixed exchange rate case without U.S. sterilization and in the floating exchange rate case. It is clear that the recession in the United States will be less deep with sterilization than without and that for the ROW the recession will be less deep or the expansion larger. It is easily checked that with a fixed exchange rate and sterilization in the United States, the impact effects of a fiscal change in the United States on output in the United States and in the ROW is given by:

(28a)
$$\frac{\partial y_1}{\partial f_1} = \frac{1 - \gamma\psi}{(1 - \gamma\psi + \gamma k\lambda^{-1})(1 - \gamma\psi) + \epsilon(\gamma k\lambda^{-1} - \epsilon)},$$

and

(28b)
$$\frac{\partial y_2}{\partial f_1} = \frac{\epsilon - \gamma k\lambda^{-1}}{(1 - \gamma\psi + \gamma k\lambda^{-1})(1 - \gamma\psi) + \epsilon(\gamma k\lambda^{-1} - \epsilon)}.$$

Assuming that the IS curve is downward-sloping $(1 - \gamma\psi > 0)$ and that the denominators of (28a, b) are positive, U.S. output declines on impact, while the ROW has a recession if the direct activity spillover effects dominate the "crowding in" effects of lower interest rates $(\epsilon - \gamma k\lambda^{-1} > 0)$, a boom if the reverse holds true.

Global economic activity (assuming the United States and the ROW to be of equal size) can either contract (if $1 - \gamma\psi - \gamma k\lambda^{-1} + \epsilon > 0$) or expand (if $1 - \gamma\psi - \gamma k\lambda^{-1} + \epsilon < 0$). This ambiguity is to be expected since, globally, monetary and fiscal policy move in opposite directions. Strong crowding out (high γ and low λ) increases the likelihood of a net expansionary effect.

4.3.3 Policies That Achieve an Improvement in U.S. Competitiveness without a Contraction of World Demand

In this subsection I take as given the fiscal tightening in the United States as well as the achievement of a lasting improvement in U.S. external competitiveness. A floating exchange rate is again assumed.

A ROW Fiscal Expansion to Match the U.S. Fiscal Contraction

In the formal setting of our little model, the transition to improved U.S. competitiveness can be achieved instantaneously and without any contraction of effective demand at home or abroad by having the U.S. fiscal contraction matched by a corresponding ROW fiscal expansion. In terms of the dynamics of equations (14a,b) and (15a,b) and the steady-state conditions of equations (16a–e), this "package" consists of a reduction in f^d with f^a unchanged. Figure 4.4 shows the instantaneous adjustment process.

There is no change in real or nominal interest rates as the effects on the global capital market of the two opposing fiscal impulses cancel each other out. For a given U.S. fiscal contraction, the improvement in U.S. competitiveness is now doubled (in our linear model) because of the fiscal expansion in the ROW. World aggregate demand is unchanged and so is aggregate demand for each country's output.

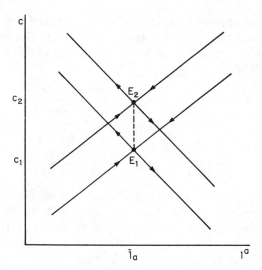

Fig. 4.4   Response to a U.S. fiscal contraction and a matching ROW
fiscal expansion.

There are several qualifications to be made before this painless adjustment package is recommended for use in the real world. First, while total output stays constant in each country, there is a shift toward the production of tradeables in the United States and toward the production of nontradeables in the ROW. Steelworkers make poor hairdressers and conversely. The problems associated with changing the sectoral composition of production, employment, and investment are ignored in our simple model.

Second, the selection of dosage and timing for the ROW fiscal expansion is made to look simpler than it is in practice because of the assumption of known, identical structures. While this in no way weakens the case for a flexible policy response *in principle,* it makes the practical task of selecting the right mix, dose, and timing a much more complicated matter than our simple model may suggest.

Third, a fiscal expansion in the ROW may be opposed for *structural* or *allocative* reasons. Increased public spending may be undesirable because of its political irreversibility and because, at full employment, the benefits from the spending are judged to be less than its cost. Lower taxes or higher transfer payments may be undesirable because of possible efficiency losses, undesirable incentive effects, or for distributional reasons.

Fourth, fiscal expansions (other than balanced-budget fiscal expansions) entail larger deficits and, in time, a larger public debt. If the real interest rate exceeds the growth rate of the real tax base, explosive debt-deficit spirals are possible unless the primary (noninterest) deficit is planned (and believed) to become a surplus in due course. If there is no reputation for fiscal rectitude, temporary (increases in) deficits will be extrapolated into the future. Fear of possible future monetization of deficits will raise long nominal interest rates. Increased uncertainty about the future course of inflation may add a further risk premium to the required rate of return on nominal government debt. In extreme circumstances, fear of partial or complete debt repudiation or of special capital levies and surcharges may build a risk premium into the rate of return on all public debt (see Blanchard and Layard eds., Dornbusch [1986] and Buiter [1985b]). A good reputation for underlying fiscal rectitude would, however, avoid the potential crowding-out resulting from such *confidence* effects. It might therefore help if such a program were supervised by or at least coordinated through an international organization or institution that has a reputation for fiscal restraint.

Finally, it may be judged that the global level of effective demand is currently excessive, and that a net deduction in global demand is in order, as well as a realignment of U.S. competitiveness. A unilateral U.S. fiscal contraction might in that case be the right policy. The point would seem to be mainly of academic interest if, as many observers argue, there remains a margin of Keynesian slack in the world economy.

A U.S. Fiscal Contraction Matched by Effective Demand-Maintaining Expansionary Monetary Policy Changes

Calls for a change in the U.S. macroeconomic policy mix, from tight money and loose fiscal policy to looser money and tighter fiscal policy, have been heard from all corners of the profession in recent years. There are two kinds of monetary policy changes that could be used in the present model: changes in level of the nominal money stock and changes in the proportional growth rate of the nominal money stock.

Money-jumps. It is clear from inspection of the steady-state conditions (16a,e) and the equations of motion (14a,b) and (15a,b) that there is only one set of discrete (discontinuous) changes in the levels of the nominal money stocks in both countries that will permit an instantaneous transition at full employment (in both countries) to the new real long-run equilibrium associated with the unilateral reduction in the U.S. fiscal impulse discussed in section 4.3.1. If $df_1 < 0$ is the size of the U.S. fiscal contraction, these nominal money-jumps in both countries are given by

$$(28) \qquad dm_1 = dm_2 = -\frac{\lambda}{2\gamma} df_1$$

At the predetermined price level, this nominal money-jump provides just the right increase in real-money balances demanded as a result of the lower nominal (and real) world interest rate associated with the lower global fiscal impulse. There is no need to force the price level path below the nominal money stock path through a policy of demand deflation and unemployment. The steady-state increase in real-money balances, which in a new-classical model with a nonpredetermined, flexible price level would be brought about by a discrete downward jump in the price level path, is achieved in the Keynesian, predetermined price-level model by a stock-shift open market purchase in each country that increases the nominal money stocks by the required amounts. It is the stickiness of *real* money balances which makes a recession inevitable when there is any exogenous shock or policy change that raises the long-run demand for money balances. This stickiness of the real money stock reflects both the stickiness of domestic costs (assumed to be a policy and exogenous shock-invariant structural property of private market behavior) and the stickiness of monetary policy. If the level of the nominal money stock is a choice variable at any given instant, policy flexibility can make up for and compensate for domestic cost inflexibility.

The great advantage of the kind of once-and-for-all nominal money-stock jumps considered here is that they don't result in any change in the rate of inflation in the short run or in the long run. They do cause the long-run level of the path of prices to be higher than it would otherwise have been, but since welfare costs are associated with the rate of inflation rather than with the level of prices,[6] this is no cause for concern. The major problem with money-jump policies is their effect on inflationary expectations. The obvious analytical distinction between a discontinuous discrete change in the level of the money stock path and a (finite) change in the instantaneous rate of change of that path may not be as obvious in practice, especially when the money stock is sampled at discrete time intervals: a once-and-for-all upward level change at a point in time in the middle of an observation interval t_0 may look much like an increase in the rate of growth between t_0 and $t_0 + 1$. If such an apparent increase in the growth rate is extrapolated into the future, serious instability may result. Governments or central banks with a reputation for monetary rectitude will be able to engineer once-off money-jumps without adverse effects on inflationary expectations. Governments or central banks with a reputation for monetary laxness will be prisoners of the markets' lack of confidence and may have to live with the adverse effects on inflation expectations of any observed increase in the money stock.

Note that if the monetary authorities had nominal income targets rather than monetary targets, there should be no credibility problems associated with a once-off increase in the nominal money stock. Nominal income targets are velocity-corrected monetary targets. They have desirable operating characteristics whenever exogenous shocks or policy changes necessitate a change in velocity.

Changes in money growth rates. The other monetary policy action (in both countries) that can achieve the transition to an improved level of U.S. competitiveness without any output or employment cost is an equal permanent increase in the rate of growth of the nominal money stock in each country. It can again be checked from the steady-state conditions (16a–e) and from the equations of motion (14a,b) and (15a,b) that the following permanent increase in $\dot{m}_1$ and $\dot{m}_2$ will achieve an instantaneous transition at full employment (in both countries) to the new real long-run equilibrium associated with the unilateral reduction in the U.S. fiscal impulse discussed in section 4.3.1.

$$(29) \qquad\qquad d\dot{m}_1 = d\dot{m}_2 = -\frac{1}{2\gamma} df^1$$

This monetary policy response would, by raising the rate of inflation in both countries, prevent the global *real* interest rate decline resulting from the U.S. fiscal contraction from being translated into a decline in *nominal* interest rates. With nominal interest rates unchanged, there is no increase in the demand for real-money balances and consequently no need for a recession to depress the general price level path below the nominal money stock path. The policy has one obvious undesirable feature: a recession is prevented at the cost of having a permanently higher rate of inflation in the world economy.

4.4   Responses to a Collapse of the U.S. Dollar

A second question addressed by economic policymakers and analysts is the proper response (in the U.S. and in the ROW) to a sudden large fall in the value of a key currency, taken here, for concreteness, to be the U.S. dollar. To determine the nature of the appropriate policy responses, we first must determine what the causes of the sudden depreciation of the currency are. There are two broad classes of possible causes: (a) the bursting of a speculative bubble that caused the dollar to be overvalued in relation to the "fundamentals"; (b) an actual or perceived change in the fundamentals driving the exchange rate. The latter category can be subdivided into a number of cases: (1) A portfolio shift against the dollar that reflects, say, greater uncertainty about the future prospects for U.S. inflation. In the simple model used here, this can be represented by a reduction in U.S. liquidity preference—a fall in η_1. (2) An increase in the *real* risk premium on foreign-owned U.S. assets. This could reflect fear of future increases in taxation of U.S. interest income and, conceivably, a greater perceived risk of repudiation or default. In the model this can be represented by an increase in $\tau_2 - \tau_1$—the real risk premium is like a net tax on U.S. interest income. (3) An unexpected increase in the level of the U.S. money stock or in the rate of U.S. monetary growth. (4) An unexpected tightening of the U.S. fiscal stance.

All four events should be thought of in relative terms, e.g., the portfolio shift against the dollar reflects an increase in uncertainty about U.S. inflation relative to uncertainty about inflation in the rest of the world. Similarly, it is looser U.S. monetary policy relative to monetary policy elsewhere or tighter U.S. fiscal policy relative to fiscal policy elsewhere that puts downward pressure on the dollar.

An important issue in determining the appropriate policy response to a sudden drop of the dollar in response to a change in private sector perceptions concerning the likely future course of the fundamentals, is whether the national authorities and the international coordinating agency share these new perceptions. A different approach will in general be called for if the authorities believe they have information superior to that used by private agents in forming expectations, but there is no way of sharing this information with private market participants or of convincing them of its relevance. In what follows, no superior public sector information is assumed.

4.4.1 A Bursting Bubble

It is well known that the solution of rational expectations models with forward-looking, nonpredetermined state variables (such as the nominal and the real exchange rate in our model) may be characterized by a *bubble;* that is, the behavior of the endogenous variables may be influenced by variables that matter only because, somehow, private agents believe that they matter. These bubble processes, which affect expectations in a self-validating manner, may be functions of the fundamental variables (i.e., those variables that enter into the structure of the model other than by merely being part of the information set used to form expectations) or of completely extraneous or spurious variables of the "sunspot" variety (Blanchard [1979]; Azariadis [1981], Obstfeld and Rogoff [1983]). In figure 4.5, it is assumed that all "fundamentals" have constant values, now and in the future, that the steady-state equilibrium corresponding to these constant values for the fundamentals is E_0 and that the associated convergent saddle path is S_0S_0. Suppose, without loss of generality, that the predetermined variable is at its steady-state value l_0^g. The nonpredetermined variable c, however, is on a bubble path EE which overvalues it relative to the path warranted by the fundamentals (S_0S_0). Its value at t_0, the time when the bubble bursts, is c_0. The bursting of the bubble moves c instantaneously to its fundamental value c^*. In a rational world, there must be uncertainty

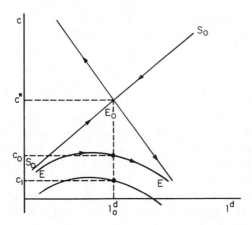

Fig. 4.5   The end of an exchange rate bubble.

about the direction of the discrete jump in the exchange rate at t_0. The instantaneous discrete upward jump in c and e would, if it were antic- ipated with certainty, promise an infinite rate of return to shorting the dollar the instant before t_0. There could, however, be a set of beliefs that at t_0 attaches some probability Π_0 to a return to the fundamental value ($\Delta c = c^* - c_0$) and some probability $1 - \Pi_0$ to a further discrete downward jump in c to c_1, which puts the exchange rate on a bubble path even further removed from its fundamental value. Provided $\Pi_0(c^* - c_0) + (1 - \Pi_0)(c_1 - c_0) = 0$, there are no expected excess returns from taking an open currency position.[7] It seems self-evident that the right thing to do for policymakers when a bubble bursts is to sit back and enjoy the sight. While we do not have a well-developed theory of the welfare economics of speculative bubbles in a world with uncertain, limited, asymmetrically distributed (insider/outsider) infor- mation, there is a strong presumption that they are costly and harmful as well as unsustainable. It may be that the fundamental valuation to which the exchange rate returns when the bubble bursts itself repre- sents an unattractive equilibrium because the fundamentals (especially current and anticipated future policy) are in a mess. That, however, is an argument for doing something about the fundamentals, when the exchange rate once again reflects those fundamentals, a course that would have been desirable even if there had been no bubble and no sudden drop in the exchange value of the dollar.

In reality, the ending of a speculative bubble is likely to be associated both with major redistributions of wealth and with short-term disrup- tion of financial markets, commerce, and production because of bank- ruptcies and insolvencies. None of these adjustment costs are included in our formal model. I would be surprised, nevertheless, if it could be shown that it is better to end a bubble with a slow puncture than with a quick burst. A hard landing of the dollar under these circumstances does not preclude a soft landing for the world economy. No policy response in the U.S. or in the ROW seems necessary.

4.4.2   A Reduction in U.S. Liquidity Preference

A downward shift in the U.S. liquidity preference schedule (a fall in η_1) has no long-run effects on competitiveness or on real or nominal interest rates. In the short run, the effects are as depicted in figure 4.6. An unexpected, immediate, permanent reduction in η_1 works just like a once-off increase in the level of the U.S. money stock. The nominal and real exchange rate jump-depreciates to E_{01} from E_0. After that the real exchange rate gradually moves back to its initial level and the system converges to E_1. In the U.S. real economic activity booms because of short-run lower nominal and real interest rates and because of the improvement in competitiveness. Average world economic activity also rises (y^a increases) because of the short-run downward pressure on nominal and real interest rates. Activity levels in the ROW are, however, depressed, as the loss of competitiveness outweighs the effect of lower interest rates. If the initial equilibrium was deemed satisfactory, the obvious policy response to the fall in liquidity preference is a matching once-off reduction in the level of the U.S. nominal money stock. This would leave all real and nominal variables (other than l_1) unchanged.

If the shift out of U.S. money represents a stock-shift currency substitution and has as its counterpart a matching stock-shift increase in foreign money demand η_2, the change in competitiveness will be twice as large. Average real-world activity (y^a, i^a, p^a and r^a) is unchanged in the short run and in the long run. The behavior of c and l^d is like that illustrated in the top diagram of figure 4.6, but with a shift up and to the left of the saddle path that is twice as large. The United States experiences a transitional boom that is matched by a transitional slump in the ROW. The obvious way to neutralize this once-off currency substitution and stabilize the exchange rate is to contract the U.S. money stock by $-\Delta\eta_1$ and expand the ROW money stock by $\Delta\eta_2$. Such monetary policy changes in addition may well have favorable effects (not formally modeled here) on the relative changes in inflation uncertainty that may have prompted the money demand shifts in the first place.

An Increase in the Real U.S. Risk Premium

An increase in the relative perceived real risk of foreign investment in the United States will in the long run raise the U.S. real and nominal interest rates and lower the ROW real and nominal interest rates, leav-

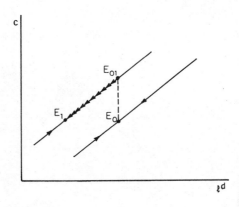

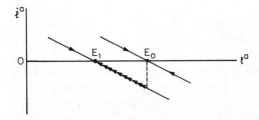

Fig. 4.6   Dollar depreciation as a result of a fall in U.S. liquidity preference.

ing the average world rates unchanged. The increase in U.S. risk and reduction in ROW risk is assumed to apply only to foreign investors, not to domestic capital formation in either country. Figure 4.7 illustrates the dynamic response pattern to this shock. Global (l^a, y^a, i^a, p^a and r^a) are not affected. The U.S. economy experiences an immediate jump-depreciation of the nominal and real exchange rate from E_0 to E_{01}.

Note that the real exchange rate overshoots its long-run equilibrium value. After the initial jump there is a gradual depreciation of the U.S. real exchange rate. The new long-run equilibrium at E_1 represents a net real depreciation relative to the initial one. The U.S. economy experiences a transitory boom which lowers its real stock of money balances. The ROW goes through a transitory slump which raises its real money balances.

One possible policy response that exactly neutralizes this increase in the U.S. foreign investment risk premium is an equal increase in $\tau_1 - \tau_2$, the excess of the U.S. tax rate on interest income accruing from abroad over the ROW's tax rate on interest income accruing from the United States. This would restore the initial equilibrium immediately. Alternatively, a once-off increase in the ROW's nominal money

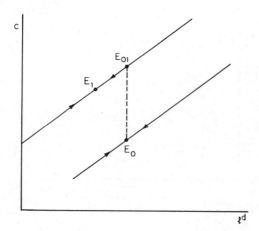

Fig. 4.7   An increase in the relative perceived risk of foreign invest-
                     ment in the United States.

stock by λ times the change in the risk premium and a reduction in the
U.S. nominal money stock by the same magnitude, would instantaneously achieve the same long-run change in the real equilibrium shown
in figure 4.7, without any transitonal U.S. inflation and ROW contraction. A permanent increase in the U.S. rate of monetary growth and
an equal reduction in the ROW rate of monetary growth with
$d\dot{m}_1 - d\dot{m}_2 \equiv d\dot{m}^d = -d$(risk premium) would, in figure 4.7, move
the economy immediately from E_0 to E_{01}, which would now be the new
long-run equilibrium.

Policy-induced Exchange Rate Collapses

    The response of the exchange rate to changes in fiscal and monetary
policy in the United States and the ROW has already been discussed
in section 4.3. The only point worth repeating here is that a hard landing
for the U.S. dollar need not represent a hard landing for the U.S.
economy or for the ROW. If the initial situation is one characterized
by current and anticipated future lax U.S. fiscal policy and tight U.S.
monetary policy, these fundamentals are likely to be reflected in a
strong (an "overvalued") U.S. real exchange rate. The first-best cooperative, coordinated global policy package to change this unfavorable
equilibrium (fiscal contraction in the United States and a once-off money
stock increase in the United States and in the ROW to meet the resulting
decrease in velocity) is accompanied by a dollar "collapse." It may
seem paradoxical that the restoration of confidence in the ability of the
U.S. to get and keep its budget under control would be accompanied
by a fall in the U.S. dollar, but such a view reflects the mistaken
identification of the exchange rate as an index of national economic
machismo.

4.5   Policy Responses to a Slowdown in Global Economic Activity

The first question that needs to be answered before one can determine the appropriate U.S. and ROW policy responses to a global economic slowdown concerns the cause(s) of this slowdown. A distinction must be made between a slowdown resulting from an adverse supply-side shock (modeled in our simple model by a temporary or permanent fall in $\bar{y}_1$ or $\bar{y}_2$) and a demand-induced slowdown. In the case of the latter we can again distinguish adverse money-demand shocks (increases in η_1 and η_2) and reductions in private U.S. or ROW demand for goods and services (which can be represented as reductions in f_1 or f_2).

4.5.1   Adverse Supply-Side Developments

Permanent reductions in productive capacity in the U.S. and the ROW raise the long-run real interest rate everywhere and thus bring down demand in line with supply. Nominal interest rates will also rise if money growth rates are unaffected and, both through real-income and interest-rate effects, the demand for real-money balances in both regions will decline in the long run. If productive capacity is affected equally in both countries ($\Delta\bar{y}_1 = \Delta\bar{y}_2 = \Delta\bar{y}$) there is no long-run change in l^d or in c. In this case, as shown in figure 4.8, the world economy

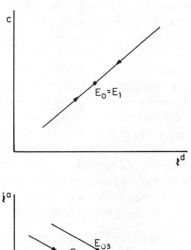

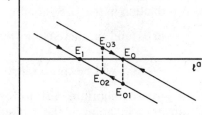

Fig. 4.8   Effects of a common permanent decline in productive capacity in both countries.

undergoes a bout of excess demand and of inflation in excess of the rate of monetary growth (affecting both regions equally) which lowers the long-run stock of money balances. In the very short run, output (which is demand-determined) actually rises because higher inflation reduces the real interest rate (nominal interest rates rise less than one-for-one with the rate of inflation because the LM curve is not vertical).

The policy response that prevents the emergence of excess demand and inflationary pressures during the transition to the lower levels of capacity output involves a contraction of demand which can be achieved either by fiscal or monetary means (or by a combination of the two). If no long-run change in competitiveness is desired, any fiscal contraction should be equal in the two countries. Probably the simplest coordinated policy action that immediately achieves the new long-run equilibrium at E_1 in figure 4.8 is a reduction in m_1 and in m_2 equal to

$$[k + \frac{\lambda(1 - \epsilon)}{\gamma}]\Delta\bar{y}.$$

If the common capacity decline at t_0 is expected to be temporary and to be reversed at t_1, there is still no action in $c - l^d$ space (the top diagram in figure 4.8). The world economy experiences a bout of excess demand between t_0 and t_1 (moving from E_{01} to E_{02}) and a bout of excess supply after t_1 (between E_{03} and E_0). The same reduction in m_1 and in m_2 at t_0 will take the world economy (without excess demand) from E_0 to E_1 where it will stay until t_1. At t_1 both nominal money stocks should be increased again by the same percentage by which they were reduced at t_0 in order to achieve a painless and instantaneous restoration of full equilibrium at E_1.

An adverse permanent supply shock in the United States alone, say, would cause a long-run worsening of U.S. competitiveness (required to choke off global demand for U.S. output), some increase in global real and nominal interest rates (but less than with a common decline in capacity output), a decline in U.S. real-money balances, and a smaller decline in the ROW real-money balances. On impact, there is likely to be a step-appreciation of the dollar. After that the real exchange rate continues to appreciate gradually towards its new long-run equilibrium. Real interest rates in the United States will be below those in the ROW during the transition. A reduction in the U.S. nominal money stock by an amount $[k + \frac{\lambda(1 - \epsilon)}{\gamma}]\Delta\bar{y}_1$, and an increase in the ROW nominal money stock by $- \frac{\lambda(1 - \epsilon)}{\gamma} \Delta\bar{y}_1$, will permit an instantaneous transition to the new, real long-run equilibrium with lower values of c, l^d, and l^a, avoiding the transitory inflation in the United States and the transitory contraction in the ROW that would otherwise occur.

4.5.2   A Demand-induced Slowdown in Economic Activity

When the cause of a disappointing level of economic activity is a decline in some component of private demand, appropriately designed demand management can minimize the damage and, in the present model, can be used to avoid it altogether. Increases in private liquidity preference (η_1 and η_2) can be met with corresponding once-off increases in the levels of the nominal money stocks—m_1 and m_2. A downward shift in the private consumption functions or a collapse of animal spirits can be offset directly by corresponding fiscal stimuli f_1 and f_2. If the balanced-budget multiplier theorem retains some validity, these fiscal stimuli can be provided without increasing the deficit. Supply-side consequences from the tax increase or transfer-payments cuts involved in a balanced-budget expansion should of course be taken into account (the behavioral links, ignored here, between f_i and $\bar{y}_i$).

Note that it is never necessary, in response to any shock, to engineer a permanent change in monetary growth rates. Once-off changes in the levels of the nominal money stocks (or temporary changes in money growth rates) are sufficient.

4.6   Conclusion

This chapter presents a rather old-fashioned study of demand management in an open, interdependent economic system. Three contingencies discussed widely during 1984 and 1985 were analyzed using an eclectic, short-run Keynesian, long-run classical, two-country model. The main conclusion is that an active monetary and/or fiscal response in both countries or regions is in general required to minimize the costs associated with the adjustment process resulting from a variety of demand-side or supply-side shocks. Only in the case of a currency collapse resulting from the bursting of an exchange market speculative bubble did a no-response policy appear desirable. A unilateral U.S. fiscal contraction will cause a temporary slowdown of world economic activity as well as a sudden drop in the nominal and real value of the dollar. Merely preventing the nominal exchange rate from changing does not reduce the magnitude of the global recession or alter the long-run real adjustment that takes place, but it would redistribute the unchanged global unemployment and excess capacity burden towards the United States and away from the ROW. A no-response policy would be appropriate if the initial situation were characterized not only by an undesirable U.S. fiscal-monetary policy mix resulting in a poor U.S. international competitive position but also by global excess demand. An expansionary fiscal move in the ROW or a combined expansionary monetary policy move in both the United States and the ROW could achieve the desired traverse to a better level of U.S. competitiveness without a global slump. These monetary stimuli need not be permanent increases in the rate of money growth. Once-off credible open market purchases raising the levels of the nominal money stocks suffice.

The proper response to a sudden drop in the value of the dollar depends crucially on the reason(s) for this drop. The bursting of a speculative bubble has no obvious monetary or fiscal policy implication. Downward pressure on the value of the dollar resulting from a once-off fall in U.S. liquidity preference calls for a matching once-off reduction in the U.S. nominal money stock. Direct currency substitution away from the dollar calls for open market sales in the United States and open market purchases in the ROW. The consequences of the emergence of a real risk premium on the return from foreign investment in the United States can be neutralized by a matching increase in the difference between the U.S. tax rate on interest income from the ROW and the ROW's tax rate on interest income from the United States. Alternatively, one might accept the depreciation of the nominal and real U.S. exchange rates but avoid the transitional U.S. inflation and ROW contraction by expanding the money stock in the ROW and reducing it in the United States.

The appropriate policy response to a slowdown in global economic activity depends on whether this slowdown reflects a deterioration of the supply side or deficient aggregate demand. To avoid the stagflation that would otherwise result from a global adverse supply shock, demand-reducing measures are called for in both countries. If the supply shock is temporary, the restrictive measures should be reversed when capacity output recovers. The appropriate response to a fall in private demand for goods and services is a fiscal stimulus. The contractionary effects of an increase in liquidity preference can be avoided by an accommodating (noninflationary) increase in the level of the money stock.

The fiscal stimuli discussed in this paper are to be interpreted as "discretionary" changes over and above the automatic changes in tax receipts and transfer payments that reflect the workings of existing tax and benefit laws, rules, and regulations as the level of economic activity varies, and that may dampen but never eliminate such fluctuations.

To provide truly satisfactory answers to the questions raised here the model would have to be extended in a number of directions. Even an analysis that focuses on the industrial world alone, would benefit from a three-region setting: the United States (plus Canada), Europe, and Japan. The complexity entailed in going to three regions virtually obliges one to use numerical rather than analytical methods. The model here ignores all stock-flow asset dynamics, those coming from the government budget identities, those coming from the current account of the balance of payments, and those resulting from real capital accumulation.[8] Again, their incorporation requires the use of numerical methods. Finally, it would be extremely desirable to allow explicitly for uncertainty. Adding some linear stochastic processes with known coefficients to the deterministic model is feasible but does not constitute much of an advance. Anything more complicated, even linear models with stochastic coefficients, let alone nonlinear stochastic models, means that we enter the mathematical or computational stratosphere. The modeling language we would like to use just does not exist yet.

The logic of the model used here, and indeed of any model that permits persistent disequilibrium or non-Walrasian equilibrium, implies that monetary and fiscal policy instruments can be used actively to stabilize output, employment, and the price level in response to a whole range of demand or supply shocks. To argue against such active policy responses, or against the adoption of explicit policy rules that would, for example, make monetary growth (or the deviation of actual monetary growth from its expected value) a function of observable contingencies, one would have to make a case for the technical, political, or institutional impossibility of an active stabilization policy.

The technical impossibility of stabilization policy has been argued on two grounds. There is the Lucas-Sargent-Wallace-Barro argument that in properly specified macroeconomic models only unperceived or unanticipated monetary policy can affect the deviations of actual real variables from their "natural" or full information values. Fiscal policy obviously has allocative effects both in the short run and in the long run, but it too cannot systematically affect the deviation of real output and employment from their capacity, full employment, or natural levels. If debt neutrality prevails, the substitution of lump-sum taxes for current borrowing has no real effects in the short run or in the long run. These policy ineffectiveness propositions for a while engaged the interest of a significant part of the macroeconomics profession but are now generally viewed as theoretical curiosa without empirical relevance.

The second technical argument against the active use of stabilization policy is much older (it goes back at least to Milton Friedman's work in the fifties and sixties) but more relevant. It is a generalization of the "long and variable lags" argument used by Friedman to make the case against active countercyclical use of monetary policy. Clearly, the length of the lag between the policy response and its impact on the variable(s) of interest (the "outside" lag) is irrelevant per se. It is uncertainty about the coefficients in the model, about the order of the lags, and indeed about the total specification of the appropriate model of the economy that forces one to qualify the confident policy prescriptives that emerge from the manipulation of models such as the one advanced here. The length of the "inside lag," the lag between the identification of the need to respond and the moment the policy handle can finally be cranked, puts further constraints on our ability to stabilize the economy through active demand management. Estimates of the "inside lag" for U.S. fiscal policy range from a few years to infinity.

It should be recognized that uncertainty about the way in which the economy works not only renders the consequences of policy activism harder to predict. It also increases uncertainty about the consequences of refraining from policy activism and sticking to preannounced, unconditional (noncontingent or open-loop) rules. It seems highly unlikely that a cautious, safety-first policy of hedging one's bets in the face of great uncertainty would ever involve the economic equivalent of locking the steering wheel and closing one's eyes.

The political or institutional case against active demand management relies in part on alleged observed asymmetries or irreversibilities in monetary and fiscal policy design. Policymakers, according to this view, are happy to cut taxes and raise spending for cyclical reasons during a slump but are reluctant to raise taxes and cut spending when the economy is overheating and a countercyclical quid pro quo is needed. While there is some informal evidence supporting this view, there are counterexamples too (e.g., the increase in the overall British tax burden by 4% of GDP during Prime Minister Thatcher's first term). It would be very valuable to have more systematic evidence on this important issue of political economy.

The conditions under which optimal, conditional stabilization policy rules would be credible (or time-consistent) also are only just beginning to be studied. The study of post–World War II economic history suggests that "stabilizing" monetary and fiscal policy actions have their desired effects only if the monetary or fiscal authorities have "conservative" reputations for underlying monetary soundness and fiscal responsibility and rectitude. Without such reputations, temporary and reversible changes in money growth, tax rates, or spending schedules are likely to be perceived as permanent. Such adverse expectations or confidence-effects may lead to inflation premiums in nominal interest rates, and even to "super-crowding out" or negative multipliers as a result of increased long real rates (see Buiter [1985b]). The coordination of international stabilization policies through international agencies with reputations for monetary and fiscal conservatism could therefore be especially effective.

One set of "cautious" global macroeconomic policy recommendations popular among international officials (see, e.g., International Monetary Fund [1985]) can be summarized as: (1) adherence to unconditional medium-term monetary growth targets; (2) continued downward pressure on structural fiscal deficits; and (3) limited countercyclical responsiveness of actual deficits reflecting the (partial) operation of the automatic fiscal stabilizers. According to the analysis of this chapter, such a policy package will not prevent a global recession if and when the United States tightens its budgetary stance. It is not even sufficient to prevent the slowdown that appears to be underway already. The risks associated with this strategy are very high. Even in the current state of the art it is not impossible to design a more flexible and a superior set of policy recommendations. Not for the first (or the last) time, caution demands, if not action now, then certainly preparation for action should the need arise.

Notes

1. We could specify the demand for real-money balances as a demand for money balances in terms of the country's consumption bundle. Let country 1's consumer price index $\bar{p}_1$ be a weighted average of the domestic value-added deflator and the domestic currency value of the foreign value-added deflator, i.e. $\bar{p}_1 = \alpha_1 p_1 + (1 - \alpha_1)(e + p_2)\ 0 < \alpha_1 < 1$. Money demand is a function of real income $y_1 + p_1 - \bar{p}_1 = y_1 + (\alpha_1 - 1)c$ and the nominal interest rate, i.e.,

$$m_1 - \bar{p}_1 = k_1 (y_1 + p_1 - \bar{p}_1) - \lambda_1 i_1, \text{ or}$$

$$l_1 = k_1 \gamma_1 - \lambda_1 i_1 + (k_1 - 1)(\alpha_1 - 1)c.$$

This equals our equation (1) when $k_1 = 1$ or when $\alpha_1 = 1$. The superior alterative specification results in slightly greater algebraic complexity.

2. Adding this would not alter the results qualitatively. Let the money demand functions including direct currency substitution be given by $m_1 - p_1 = \beta_1 \dot{e} - \lambda_1 i_1 + k_1 y_1 + \eta_1$ and $m_2 - p_2 = \beta_2 \dot{e} - \lambda_2 i_2 + k_2 y_2 + \eta_2$. In the "symmetric" case considered below, $\beta_1 = \beta_2 = \beta$; $\lambda_1 = \lambda_2 = \lambda$ and $k_1 = k_2 = k$. For any variable x let $x^d = x_1 - x_2$ and $x^a = \dfrac{x_1 + x_2}{2}$. It follows that $l^d = -(\lambda + 2\beta)i^d + ky^d - 2\beta(\tau_1 - \tau_2)$ and $l^a = -\lambda i^a + ky^a$. The behavior of "global averages" is completely unaffected by direct currency substitution. "Country differences" are affected through an increased "interest-sensitivity" of l^d, i.e., the coefficient of i^d now is $-(\lambda + 2\beta)$ instead of $-\lambda$. In addition, the last term on the r.h.s. of the l^d equation is absent without direct currency substitution. If we ignore this second (minor) difference, the analysis that follows can be applied to the case of direct currency substitution by replacing λ (in the "differences" model only) by $\lambda + 2\beta$. In the limiting case where the currencies are perfect substitutes ($\beta = +\infty$) only an ex-ante fixed exchange rate regime is viable.

3. This result is quite robust and does not depend on the assumption of a fixed level of capacity output. In Buiter (1984b) I consider the case where capacity output is given by a neoclassical production function with exogenous labor supply and a long-run endogenous capital stock. In the perfectly integrated financial markets, an increase in public spending raises the global real interest rate and thus lowers the steady-state capital stocks at home and abroad and with them domestic and foreign capacity output. If the contraction in capacity output is not biased toward the foreign country and if the increase in public spending is biased toward home goods, then higher public spending still

raises the long-run relative price of home goods. If public debt is not neutral, a lower level of domestic taxes will also (if domestic private spending is, at the margin, biased toward home goods) be associated with an increase in the relative price of home goods.

4. For i^a to decline less on impact than in the long run, we must assume that $1 - \gamma\psi - \epsilon > 0$. For r^a to decline less on impact than in the long run, we must asume that $\epsilon < 1$.

5. Since $K_1 + K_2 = \Omega - \epsilon$.

6. The statement is meant to apply only to a world without uncertainty.

7. The behavior of l^d and c given in equation (14a) can be summarized as

$$\begin{bmatrix} \dot{l}^d \\ E_t\dot{c} \end{bmatrix} = \mathbf{A} \begin{bmatrix} l^d \\ c \end{bmatrix} + \mathbf{B}z,$$

where $\mathbf{A} = (a_{ij})$, $\mathbf{B} = (b_{ij})$, and z is the vector of exogenous variables. The general solution for c and l can be shown to be (Buiter [1984a])

$$c(t) = -W_{22}^{-1}W_{21}l^d(t) - W_{22}^{-1}\int_t^\infty e^{\lambda_2(t-\tau)}\mathbf{D}E_t z(\tau)d\tau + W_{22}^{-1}F(t)$$

$$l^d(t) = e^{\lambda_1(t-t_0)}l^d(t_0) + \int_{t_0}^t e^{\lambda_1(t-s)}b_1 z(s)ds$$

$$- \int_{t_0}^t e^{\lambda_1(t-s)}a_{12}W_{22}^{-1}\int_s^\infty e^{\lambda_2(s-\tau)}\mathbf{D}E_s z(\tau)d\tau ds$$

$$+ \int_{t_0}^t e^{\lambda_1(t-s)}a_{12}W_{22}^{-1}F(s)ds.$$

λ_1 is the stable eigenvalue of $\mathbf{A}$ and λ_2 the unstable eigenvalue. $\begin{bmatrix} W_{11}W_{12} \\ W_{21}W_{22} \end{bmatrix} = \mathbf{W} = \mathbf{V}^{-1}$ where $\mathbf{V}$ is the matrix whose columns are the right eigenvectors of $\mathbf{A}$. $\mathbf{D} = [W_{21}b_1 + W_{22}b_2]$.

$\begin{bmatrix} b_1 \\ b_2 \end{bmatrix} = \mathbf{B}$. F is the bubble component. It satisfies $E_t\dot{F}(t) = \lambda_2 F(t)$ but is otherwise arbitrary.

8. For a numerical simulation model which incorporates all three sources of asset dynamics in a two-country, full-employment setting, see Buiter (1984b).

References

Aoki, M. 1981. *Dynamic analysis of open economies.* New York: Academic Press.

Azariadis, C. 1981. Self-fulfilling prophecies. *Journal of Economic Theory* 25 (December): 380–96.

Blanchard, O. J. 1979. Speculative bubbles, crashes and rational expectations. *Economics Letters* 3: 387–89.

Blanchard, O. J., R. Dornbusch, and R. Layard, eds. 1986. *Restoring Europe's Prosperity*. Cambridge, Mass.: MIT Press.

Buiter, W. H. 1984a. Saddlepoint problems in continuous time rational expectations models: A general method and some macroeconomic examples. *Econometrica* 52 (May): 665–79.

———. 1984b. Fiscal policy in open, interdependent economies. NBER Working Paper no. 1429 (August).

———. 1985a. International monetary policy to promote economic recovery. In C. van Ewijk and J. J. Klant, eds., *Monetary Conditions for Economic Recovery*, pp. 129–60. Martinus Nijhoff.

———. 1985b. A guide to public sector debt and deficits. In *Economic Policy* 1 (November): 14–79.

Buiter, W. H., and M. H. Miller. 1982. Real exchange rate overshooting and the output cost of bringing down inflation. *European Economic Review* 18 (May/June): 85–123.

———. 1983. Real exchange rate overshooting and the output cost of bringing down inflation; Some further results. In *Exchange Rates and International Macroeconomics*, ed. J. Frenkel. Chicago: University of Chicago Press.

———. 1985. Costs and benefits of an anti-inflationary policy: Questions and issues. In V. Argy and J. Nevile, eds., *Inflation and unemployment; theory, experience and policy making*. London: Allen & Unwin, pp. 11–38.

Dornbusch, R. 1976. Exchange rate dynamics. *Journal of Political Economy* 84 (December): 1161–76.

International Monetary Fund. 1985. *World economic outlook*. Washington: International Monetary Fund.

Miller, M. H. 1982. Differences in the policy mix and consequences for the real exchange rate. Mimeographed.

Mundell, R. A. 1968. *International Economics*. New York: Macmillan.

Obstfeld, M., and K. Rogoff. 1983. Speculative hyperinflations in maximizing models: Can we rule them out? *Journal of Political Economy* 31 (August): 675–87.

Sachs, J. 1985. The dollar and the policy mix: 1985. Forthcoming in *Brookings Papers on Economic Activity*.

Sachs, J., and W. McKibbon. 1985. Macroeconomic policies in the OECD and LDC external adjustment. *Centre for Economic Policy Research Discussion Paper*, no. 56 (March).

Turnovsky, S. J. 1985. Monetary and fiscal policy under perfect foresight: A symmetric two-country analysis. NBER Working Paper no. 1699 (September).

Comment   Maurice Obstfeld

Willem Buiter's chapter extends the literature on international policy coordination by showing how countries can cooperatively manage their monetary and fiscal policies to offset the effects of certain macroeco-

Maurice Obstfeld is professor of economics at the University of Pennsylvania and a research associate of the National Bureau of Economic Research. Financial support from the National Science Foundation and the Alfred P. Sloan Foundation is gratefully acknowledged.

nomic disturbances. The analytical framework is the celebrated two-country model of Mundell (1968, chap. 18), updated to include gradual price-level adjustment and rational expectations of the economy's transition path. Since its development more than two decades ago, Mundell's model has proven to be one of the most useful tools of descriptive, medium-term, macroeconomic analysis. Buiter carefully notes some important limitations of the model, for example, its failure to follow up the dynamic effects on public- and private-sector debt stocks of sustained international shifts in fiscal stance. The problem of cumulating public debt lies at the heart of the current U.S. macroeconomic problem, and further analysis must recognize that policies designed to offset the short-run effects of shocks may be unsustainable over a longer horizon.

If we leave these long-run issues aside, there is still the question of how best to use Mundell's model as a tool of policy analysis rather than as a purely descriptive framework. Buiter makes two key assumptions in his analysis of optimal policy responses. First, policymakers are assumed to know quite precisely the nature of the disturbance to world equilibrium. Second, there is an assumption that the effects of policy actions can be reliably predicted. Both these assumptions are very strong, and ignore the uncertain environment in which actual policy decisions must be made.

In the short term, policymakers observe asset prices such as exchange rates on a daily basis, but they observe data on trade flows, industrial production, price levels, employment, and other variables with much less frequency. Preliminary estimates of these numbers can be unreliable; the United States government's preliminary "flash" forecasts of quarterly GNP have been so misleading recently that they have been discontinued. Policymakers are always in the position of inferring from available data the causes of economic changes. Does a particular exchange-rate movement reflect a disturbance in asset markets, in goods markets, or in both? As Buiter demonstrates, the appropriate policy response to the exchange-rate movement depends on the nature of the underlying shock.

The second difficulty facing policymakers is uncertainty about how policies will affect the economy. Lucas's (1976) famous critique of econometric policy evaluation highlights the practical difficulties in forecasting the effects of macroeconomic policies when private decisions are based on rational expectations. In extreme cases, policies may become ineffective. I think Buiter goes too far in dismissing policy-ineffectiveness propositions as "theoretical curiosa without empirical relevance," and I am unaware of an empirical basis for this dismissal. While it is implausible that the strongest of the policy-ineffectiveness results are literally applicable to reality, the results do warn us that policy actions may have unexpected and unwanted consequences.

Uncertainty about the nature of shocks and the effects of policies places the policymaker in the type of world studied by Brainard (1967) and by Poole (1970). In that world, sophisticated fine-tuning of the sort Buiter analyzes is impossible, so authorities are likely to focus instead on some class of simple policy rules, choosing the one that tends to yield the best macroeconomic outcomes on average. Here I want to discuss aspects of the comparison between two much-analyzed policy rules: a purely floating exchange rate and an exchange rate fixed by countries' monetary authorities. The analytical literature on which my discussion builds is surveyed by Henderson (1984) and Marston (1985). My 1985 paper contains a more comprehensive comparative examination of exchange-rate regimes.

Small-Country Analysis and International Risk Sharing

The first shock analyzed by Buiter, an unexpected fiscal tightening in the United States, illustrates a central proposition of the literature on fixed versus floating exchange rates: When most shocks to the economy represent aggregate demand movements (shifts in the IS curve), floating exchange rates minimize the conditional variance of output and thus serve as automatic stabilizers. In the presence of some form of wage-price inflexibility, an unforeseen decline in aggregate demand leads to a fall in employment. But if the exchange rate is flexible, the currency will adjust instantly, falling in value against foreign currencies and shifting world demand in favor of domestic products. Compared to a fixed exchange rate, a floating rate results in a smaller decline in employment in the short run because it facilitates a rapid short-run change in relative prices. Under a fixed rate, home unemployment would persist until slowly adjusting home wages and prices had moved downward.

As Mundell (1968) recognized, the foregoing argument in favor of floating rates is primarily distributional. Under fixed rates an adverse aggregate demand shift results in a sharp fall in output. Under floating rates the output decline is dampened, but the deterioration in the terms of trade is sharper than with a fixed rate. When most shocks are to the goods market, the choice of exchange-rate system involves a short-run tradeoff between variability in employment and variability in the terms of trade. Because the incidence of unemployment is presumably less even than that of an adverse terms-of-trade shift, distributional considerations favor currency depreciation.

If most disturbances to the economy originate in asset markets, however, a fixed exchange rate minimizes the variance of output. Changes in money demand, for example, are accommodated entirely through the capital account under a fixed rate, and have no effect on output.

A major shortcoming of these results is that they answer a question posed primarily in the context of a single small country whose choice of an exchange-rate system does not affect the rest of the world's economic performance. But Buiter's analysis of a U.S. fiscal contraction makes clear why the small country's decision problem may be the wrong problem to analyze in a framework that recognizes international policy interactions. The dollar's depreciation softens the effect of the blow to U.S. output and employment. But at the same time the corresponding *appreciation* of foreign currencies against the dollar worsens the situation abroad compared to the fixed exchange rate case. By allowing the U.S. to export some of its unemployment, the dollar's depreciation has a beggar-thy-neighbor effect. The U.S. decision on an exchange-rate regime will clearly affect foreign economies, and it is not clear that what is best for America will be best for the rest of the world. To discuss the "best" exchange-rate system for the world economy, we must reformulate our notion of how a good exchange-rate system performs.

In my 1985 paper I suggest that a global perspective on exchange-rate regime choice must recognize that different exchange-rate systems have different implications for the allocation of macroeconomic risks among the participating countries. In the example discussed above, dollar depreciation shields the U.S. economy from an adverse IS shift but has the opposite effect on U.S. trading partners. In compensation, when IS shifts occur abroad, floating dollar rates allow foreign countries to export some of their own macro instability to the United States. There is a suggestive analogy to markets for insurance. The beggar-thy-neighbor effect of a dollar depreciation can be thought of as a "payment" made by the foreign country to the United States in states of the world where U.S. aggregate demand is relatively low. In the opposite situation, the United States, by allowing its currency to appreciate, compensates foreign countries. It is conceivable that both countries can simultaneously reduce output variability by sharing macroeconomic risks through a floating exchange rate.

In the balance of this discussion, I will therefore concentrate on the following question: Are there conditions under which all countries can simultaneously improve their average macroeconomic performance through the adoption of a particular exchange-rate system? Using an illustrative model, I will show that such conditions can be found, and that they result in criteria of regime choice similar to those that govern an individual country's decision. As in many similar contexts, the implementation of Pareto-improving risk-sharing arrangements may encounter problems of moral hazard and enforcement. These problems are of central importance to our understanding of how actual exchange-rate systems work, but to illustrate the exchange rate's potential role in risk allocation among countries, I will simply assume that individual governments are bound to the policy regime in place.

A Simple Model

To illustrate results, I use a log-linear version of Mundell's two-country model. Even as a medium-term framework, this model is severely limited in its omission of dynamics and expectations. Further, it makes no allowance for the important possibility that the choice of an exchange-rate system may itself lead to changes in institutional aspects of the economy. Nonetheless, the model is useful as an intuition-building device, and as a first step toward more complex analyses.

Like Buiter, I work with a model in which equation parameters are identical across countries. Under a floating exchange rate, the model is described by the equations:

$y = \delta e - \theta i + u$ (home output determination),

$y^* = -\delta e - \theta i^* + u^*$ (foreign output determination),

$m = \phi y - \lambda i$ (home money-market equilibrium),

$m^* = \phi y^* - \lambda i^*$ (foreign money-market equilibrium),

$i = i^*$ (perfect international asset substitution).

Above, variables have the same meaning as in the Buiter model, except that m and m^* are interpreted as random variables reflecting shocks to money supply net of shocks to money demand. The variances of these two monetary disturbances are denoted σ_m^2 and $\sigma_{m^*}^2$, respectively, and their covariance is σ_{mm^*}. The random variables u and u^* are shocks to the aggregate demand functions. The relevant characteristics of their joint distribution are summarized by the variances σ_u^2 and $\sigma_{u^*}^2$ and the covariance σ_{uu^*}. The model reflects the Mundell assumptions of static expectations and rigid nominal output prices, fixed at $p = p^* = 0$. For simplicity, I have also ignored direct spillover effects from one country's output to the other's aggregate demand.

Define

$$\eta \equiv \theta\phi/(\lambda + \theta\phi) < 1.$$

Then the floating-rate output levels in the two countries are

(1) $\quad y|_{\text{FLOAT}} = [(1 - \eta)(u + u^*)$
$\quad\quad\quad\quad + (1 + \eta)\,(m/\phi) - (1 - \eta)(m^*/\phi)]/2,$

(2) $\quad y^*|_{\text{FLOAT}} = [(1 - \eta)(u + u^*)$
$\quad\quad\quad\quad + (1 + \eta)(m^*/\phi) - (1 - \eta)(m/\phi)]/2.$

Different fixed exchange rate models result from different assumptions about the settlement of payments imbalances by central banks.

To be concrete, I will analyze a "dollar standard" (see my 1985 paper), a system also discussed by Buiter as the "non-McKinnon variant" of a fixed-rate regime. In this system, the foreign central bank intervenes to peg the exchange rate, holding its foreign reserves in the form of interest-bearing home-currency claims on the home treasury or private sector. Official settlements balances affect the foreign money supply but not the home money supply. The model's equations are

$$y = \delta e^f - \theta i + u \text{ (home output determination)},$$

$$y^* = -\delta e^f - \theta i^* + u^* \text{ (foreign output determination)},$$

$$m = \phi y - \lambda i \text{ (home money-market equilibrium)},$$

$$i = i^* \text{ (perfect international asset substitution)},$$

where e^f is the fixed level of the exchange rate.

Because m is not endogenous, the four equations above determine the four unknowns y, y^*, i, and i^*. The foreign money supply, m^*, is determined recursively by y^*, i, and the resulting demand for money in the foreign country.

Output levels under a fixed exchange rate are

(3) $$y|_{\text{FIX}} = (1 - \eta)u + (1 - \eta)\delta e^f + \eta(m/\phi),$$

(4) $$y^*|_{\text{FIX}} = u^* - \eta u - (1 + \eta)\,\delta e^f + \eta(m/\phi).$$

World output depends only on the reserve country's monetary conditions and on the aggregate-demand shocks u and u^*. The latter disturbance does not influence home output in this model because I have assumed away any direct spillover effect from foreign output to home demand.

In each country, policymakers are concerned with minimizing the conditional variance of output. Equations (1) through (4) imply that output variances are complicated functions of the variances of the underlying real and monetary shocks and these shocks' covariances. To illustrate how the joint distribution of shocks determines policymakers' preferences over exchange-rate regimes, I follow a practice common in the literature and look at two extreme cases, the case in which all shocks are real and the case in which all shocks are monetary.

Real Disturbances

Small-country analysis typically yields the result that when all disturbances are real (that is, shifts in u or u^*), a floating-rate regime is preferred. In a two-country setting, we need to ask whether the absence of monetary shocks implies that *both* countries gain from a float, in the sense that the variances of their outputs are lower than under a fixed rate.

Assume that monetary conditions are nonstochastic. Equations (1) and (2) imply that output variances under a floating exchange rate are

$$\sigma_y^2|_{\text{FLOAT}} = (1 - \eta)^2(\sigma_u^2 + \sigma_{u*}^2 + 2\sigma_{uu*})/4,$$

$$\sigma_{y*}^2|_{\text{FLOAT}} = (1 - \eta)^2(\sigma_u^2 + \sigma_{u*}^2 + 2\sigma_{uu*})/4.$$

Under a fixed rate, the corresponding variances, implied by (3) and (4), are

$$\sigma_y^2|_{\text{FIX}} = (1 - \eta)^2\sigma_u^2 ,$$

$$\sigma_{y*}^2|_{\text{FIX}} = \sigma_{u*}^2 + \eta^2\sigma_u^2 - 2\eta\sigma_{uu*}.$$

A first implication of these formulas is that policymakers in the two countries may prefer different exchange-rate regimes; it is therefore possible that exchange-rate regimes can not be unambiguously ranked in terms of the Pareto criterion. Imagine, for example, that $\sigma_{uu*} = 0$ and that σ_{u*}^2 is much higher than σ_u^2. In this case the home country may lose by importing macroeconomic stability from abroad through a floating exchange rate; it would prefer a fixed rate that insulates it completely from foreign aggregate-demand shocks. For the same reason, foreign policymakers would prefer a floating rate. A floating rate allows them to export some of their severe macroeconomic instability to the home country while importing relatively little instability from the home country in return.

To obtain clear-cut results, it is useful to impose an additional symmetry condition on the model, the condition that

$$\sigma_{u*}^2 = \sigma_u^2.$$

Under this additional assumption, the variability disadvantage of a fixed rate for the home country is

$$\sigma_y^2|_{\text{FIX}} - \sigma_y^2|_{\text{FLOAT}} = (1 - \eta)^2\sigma_u^2(1 - \rho_{uu*})/2,$$

where ρ_{uu*} is the coefficient of correlation between u and u^*. Notice that the above difference is positive unless u and u^* are *perfectly* correlated. Short of such perfect correlation, therefore, a floating rate, compared to a fixed rate, lowers the variance of the home country's output.

For the foreign country, the corresponding variability difference is

$$\sigma_{y*}^2|_{\text{FIX}} - \sigma_{y*}^2|_{\text{FLOAT}} = (1 + \eta)^2\sigma_u^2(1 - \rho_{uu*})/2.$$

This difference is a strictly positive number if $\rho_{uu*} < 1$. Thus, the foreign country also gains by moving to a floating exchange rate under the conditions assumed in this section.

The intuition behind these results is that sketched above. Provided aggregate-demand shocks are not perfectly correlated internationally, a floating rate enables each country to avoid more effectively some of the output risk posed by its own demand disturbance. Each country must also increase its exposure to demand shocks that occur abroad. But both countries can gain from this trade of risks when the average magnitudes of home and foreign shocks are similar; and the extent of gains from trade is greater the more highly negative is the correlation between the two countries' demand shocks. This result is the global extension of the proposition that a small country gains from floating when economic fluctuations are mostly due to shifts in aggregate demand.

Monetary Disturbances

Turn next to the second extreme case, that in which all disturbances are monetary (that is, shifts in m or m^*). Small-country analysis indicates that fixed rates are preferable when monetary shocks dominate. Can this result, too, be extended to a global setting?

Equations (1) and (2) imply that when all shocks are monetary, output variances under floating are given by

$$\sigma_y^2|_{\text{FLOAT}} = [(1 + \eta)^2\sigma_m^2 + (1 - \eta)^2\sigma_{m*}^2 - 2(1 - \eta^2)\sigma_{mm*}]/4\phi^2,$$
$$\sigma_{y*}^2|_{\text{FLOAT}} = [(1 + \eta)^2\sigma_{m*}^2 + (1 - \eta)^2\sigma_m^2 - 2(1 - \eta^2)\sigma_{mm*}]/4\phi^2.$$

Equations (3) and (4) lead to the corresponding fixed-rate variances

$$\sigma_y^2|_{\text{FIX}} = (\eta/\phi)^2\sigma_m^2,$$
$$\sigma_{y*}^2|_{\text{FIX}} = (\eta/\phi)^2\sigma_m^2.$$

For the home country, the variability disadvantage of a floating rate is

$$\sigma_y^2|_{\text{FLOAT}} - \sigma_y^2|_{\text{FIX}}$$
$$= [(1 + 2\eta - 3\eta^2)\sigma_m^2 + (1 - \eta)^2\sigma_{m*}^2 - 2(1 - \eta^2)\sigma_{mm*}]/4\phi^2.$$

Because $\eta < 1$, this difference is always positive (so that the home country prefers a fixed rate) when the correlation between m and m^* is negative. Under the symmetry assumption

$$\sigma_{m*}^2 = \sigma_m^2,$$

the variance difference above becomes

$$\sigma_y^2|_{\text{FLOAT}} - \sigma_y^2|_{\text{FIX}} = (1 - \eta^2)\sigma_m^2(1 - \rho_{mm*})/2\phi^2,$$

where ρ_{mm*} is the coefficient of correlation between m and m^*. This difference is strictly positive if $\rho_{mm*} < 1$. So if monetary shocks are of similar average magnitude across countries and imperfectly correlated, home policymakers will prefer a fixed exchange rate.

Foreign policymakers also prefer to peg under these conditions. In general,

$$\sigma_{y*}^2|_{\text{FLOAT}} - \sigma_{y*}^2|_{\text{FIX}}$$
$$= [(1 - 2\eta - 3\eta^2)\sigma_m^2$$
$$+ (1 + \eta)^2\sigma_{m*}^2 - 2(1 - \eta^2)\sigma_{mm*}]/4\phi^2.$$

Notice that if $1 - 2\eta - 3\eta^2 < 0$ and σ_m^2 is large relative to σ_{m*}^2, the foreign country may well prefer to float its currency to avoid importing too much monetary instability from abroad. But if the variances of the monetary shocks are equal,

$$\sigma_{y*}^2|_{\text{FLOAT}} - \sigma_{y*}^2|_{\text{FIX}} = (1 - \eta^2)\sigma_m^2(1 - \rho_{mm*})/2\phi^2,$$

a strictly positive number when $\rho_{mm*} < 1$.

When monetary shocks dominate and are of similar average magnitude across countries, fixed exchange rates produce the better international allocation of macroeconomic risk. Once again, the gains from trading macroeconomic risk through fixing rather than floating are greater the more highly negative is ρ_{mm*}. These findings generalize, to a global setting, the usual small-country result.

Some Qualifications

My discussion has so far been based on the assumption that, all else being equal, policymakers prefer an exchange-rate regime that dampens fluctuations in output. The justification for this assumption is largely distributional: the incidence of a change in real income caused by a terms-of-trade movement is presumably more even than that of a real-income change taking the form of a change in output and employment.

The models analyzed here and in Buiter's discussion, however, assume that each country is specialized in producing a single homogeneous good. This simplification obscures some important distributional problems that a floating rate can cause even when nonmonetary shocks are dominant. Aggregate-demand disturbances need not fall proportionally on all of the economy's products; so while the exchange-rate's response will cushion overall output, it may worsen the employment imbalance in some sectors compared to the outcome under a fixed rate. At several points, Buiter describes the sectoral implications of the shocks he considers.

Like risk pooling between countries, risk pooling within countries is limited, so any aggregate benefits of a floating exchange rate may be unevenly distributed. Therefore, when real disturbances to the economy are transitory, there is a case for resisting the exchange-rate changes that would otherwise occur. In these circumstances, a fixed exchange rate reduces relocation costs that might be needlessly incurred as factors move between sectors. Pegging may also help reduce political pressure in favor of protectionist trade legislation.

There is no case, however, for pegging in the face of a permanent real disturbance. Monetary intervention cannot prevent eventual adjustment on the real side of the economy. Defending a fixed exchange rate despite a permanent structural shock would only weaken macroeconomic performance while failing to eliminate relocation costs or protectionist pressures.

The case for fixing the exchange rate in response to temporary goods-market disturbances requires an additional premise. Either firms and individuals must be unable to borrow to "ride out" temporary negative shocks, or the market must be unable to distinguish short-lived from long-lived disturbances. Both of these problems arise in practice; and they leave the government with the job of distinguishing permanent from transitory shocks. It is hard to believe that the government can make this distinction more reliably than the private sector.

References

Brainard, William C. 1967. Uncertainty and the effectiveness of policy. *American Economic Review* 57 (May): 411–25.

Henderson, Dale W. 1984. Exchange market intervention operations: Their role in financial policy and their effects. In *Exchange rate theory and practice,* ed. John F. O. Bilson and Richard C. Marston. Chicago: University of Chicago Press (for the National Bureau of Economic Research).

Lucas, Robert E., Jr. 1976. Econometric policy evaluation: A critique. In *The Phillips curve and labor markets,* ed. Karl Brunner and Allan H. Meltzer. Carnegie-Rochester Conference Series on Public Policy, a supplement to the *Journal of Monetary Economics,* vol. 1: 19–46.

Marston, Richard C. 1985. Stabilization policies in open economies. In *Handbook of international economics,* vol. 2, ed. Ronald W. Jones and Peter B. Kenen. Amsterdam: North-Holland.

Mundell, Robert A. 1968. *International economics.* New York: Macmillan.

Obstfeld, Maurice. 1985. Floating exchange rates: Experience and prospects. *Brookings Papers on Economic Activity* 16, no. 2: 369–450.

Poole, William. 1970. Optimal choice of monetary policy instruments in a simple stochastic macro model. *Quarterly Journal of Economics* 84 (May): 197–216.

Comment   Stephen J. Turnovsky

The three questions motivating Willem Buiter's discussion are all important and highlight the growing interdependence between Western economies. Buiter presents a careful analysis of these issues within the

Stephen J. Turnovsky is professor of economics at the University of Illinois at Urbana-Champaign and a research associate of the National Bureau of Economic Research.

framework of a two-country Dornbusch model. The basic structure of this model is by now standard. Specifically, two key features are: continuous equilibrium in the money market (the exchange rate being a "jump" variable); disequilibrium in the goods market (prices being "sluggish"). This model has served the profession well for almost a decade now, in analyzing various macroshocks. I am not sure, however, that as it stands the model is the optimal vehicle for addressing all of the issues raised in this paper.

I shall structure my remarks about several issues: the specifics of the model; future anticipated shocks; strategic aspects; an alternative optimizing model.

The Model

As noted, the model is in the Dornbusch tradition and I have little to say about its specification. Like most of the current work being done on two-country models, Buiter's discussion assumes the two economies to be symmetric. This is convenient and not an unreasonable first approximation, since there is no a priori reason for, say, the United States and Europe to differ in terms of their aggregate behavior in any systematic way. The assumption has the enormous advantage of allowing one to exploit Aoki's (1981) technique of the representation of the dynamics in terms of sums and differences of the underlying variables. In the present context, this causes the dynamics of the third-order system to decompose into two subsystems involving: average variables, which follow a stable first-order adjustment; differences and the exchange rate, which follow a second-order system, having a saddlepoint. Not only does this decomposition increase the tractability of the analysis, but it also helps provide economic insight into the dynamic adjustments.

A key feature of the model is that the exchange rate responds only to differences in the variables and that averages are independent of the exchange rate. An important consequence is that averages are independent of anticipation of future shocks. They respond only to the actual shocks, when they occur. The reason for this is simply that all anticipations of future disturbances impact on the present state of the two economies through the current exchange rate. But this does not affect the averages. For the same reason, anticipated future worldwide shocks, which leave differences and therefore the exchange rate unchanged, also have no effect on the economies until the anticipated changes actually take place.

I would like to comment on one specific assumption, which has a more critical bearing on the behavior of the model than is perhaps suggested by Buiter. This concerns the deflation of money balances by the price of domestic output, p_1, rather than by the domestic cost of living, $\bar{p}_1$. As Buiter notes (n.1), the more desirable specification of monetary equilibrium is (for country 1, say)

$$m_1 - \bar{p}_1 = k_1(y_1 + p_1 - \bar{p}_1) - \lambda_1 i_1,$$

or equivalently,

$$l_1 - (1 - \alpha_1)(1 - k_1)c = k_1 y_1 - \lambda_1 i_1.$$

If either $\alpha_1 = 1$ or $k_1 = 1$, this reduces to the equation in the text. If not, there is a relative price effect in the money market, through c, and this gives rise to differences in behavior. While one does not want to quibble over details of specification, in this case the differences in behavior are of sufficient qualitative significance to merit further discussion.

First, the result of section 4.3.1, that a U.S. fiscal tightening without fiscal or monetary response in the ROW and without monetary response in the U.S. leads to an *instantaneous* long-run adjustment in the exchange rate, does not hold with this alternative specification. In general, it can be shown that we can specify the stable locus in $l^d - e$ space by a positively sloped linear equation of the form

$$(1) \qquad\qquad e - \tilde{e} = \phi(l^d - \tilde{l}^d)$$

where tildes denote steady states and $\phi > 0$. Differentiating this equation at time 0, with respect to the domestic fiscal instrument f_1, and recognizing that because of sluggish prices, l_1, l_2, and hence l^d is predetermined, yields

$$(2) \qquad\qquad \frac{de(0)}{df_1} - \frac{d\tilde{e}}{df_1} = - \phi \frac{d\tilde{l}^d}{df_1}$$

If we take $0 < \alpha_1 < 1$, it can be shown that

$$(3) \qquad\qquad \frac{d\tilde{l}^d}{df_1} \lessgtr 0 \text{ according to whether } k_1 \lessgtr 1$$

Under the assumption considered by Buiter, $d\tilde{l}^d/df_1 = 0$, and hence $de(0)/df_1 = d\tilde{e}/df_1$, implying complete instantaneous adjustment of the exchange rate. If $k_1 < 1$, then $d\tilde{l}^d/df_1 < 0$, so that on impact

$$0 > \frac{de(0)}{df_1} > \frac{d\tilde{e}}{df_1}$$

and we get only partial adjustment to the domestic fiscal contraction. On the other hand, if $k_1 > 1$, then $d\tilde{l}^d/df_1 > 0$, so

$$0 > \frac{d\tilde{e}}{df_1} > \frac{de(0)}{df_1}$$

and we get overshooting of the exchange rate to the fiscal disturbance.

Second, under the alternative monetary specification, the domestic fiscal contraction does not in general cause equal recessions in the U.S. and abroad, in contrast to Buiter's case. The reason is that the fiscal contraction leads to a depreciation of the domestic currency in both nomimal and real terms. This means that c rises to that if $k_1 < 1$, $l_1 - (1 - \alpha_1)(1 - k_1)c$ falls. This puts a squeeze on domestic real-money balances, thereby accentuating the recession in the domestic economy. By the same token, real-money balances abroad increase, thereby moderating the recession and, indeed, it is even possible for foreign output to rise. If $k_1 > 1$, these relative price effects are reversed.

A third result, that a domestic fiscal contraction matched by a foreign fiscal expression enables the improvement in U.S. competitiveness to be achieved without a contraction in output in either country, also depends upon the chosen form of monetary specification. With the alternative specification, we can easily show that while this matched policy will leave total world output unchanged, outputs in the two countries will be affected in exactly offsetting ways; the specific responses will depend upon whether $k_1 \lesseqgtr 1$.

By contrast, the result that employment and output can be maintained in response to a domestic fiscal contraction, by the appropriate balanced increases in the respective money stocks of the two economies, remains true. Again, the relative adjustments in the two economies depends upon whether $k_1 \lesseqgtr 1$.

The difference between these last two results is due to the familiar relationship between instruments and targets. Buiter's discussion focuses (implicitly) on two objectives, the stabilization of domestic and foreign output levels in the face of a domestic fiscal contraction. In general, the foreign fiscal instrument alone cannot stabilize both outputs simultaneously at their respective target levels. On the other hand, the two output objectives can be achieved by the appropriate choice of the two monetary instruments.

I now wish to comment on the application of the analysis to the "collapsing" U.S. dollar. I am not sure that the analysis is appropriate for this, but perhaps my reservation is really in part a semantic one. The analysis deals with two aspects: the bursting bubble; shifts in various kinds.

Buiter considers a situation in which the economy is following an unstable path (a bubble path), which, if pursued forever, will eventually lead to an infinitely overvalued dollar. At some point, t_0, the market recognizes the nature of the bubble path, at which time the exchange rate jumps onto the appropriate stable locus (in this case, straight to the new equilibrium point). While this may characterize a bursting of the bubble, to my mind it does not describe a "collapse" of the dollar. Rather, it represents a realignment of the currency which needs to take place. For example, suppose that the domestic money supply has been increased but that the exchange rate did not undertake the necessary jump immediately at the time the monetary increase occurred. It is clear that the increase in real-money balances will lower the domestic interest rate, which, given interest-rate parity, causes a continuous appreciation of the domestic currency. This adjustment is perverse and the jump in the exchange rate—the bursting of the bubble—is needed to get the exchange rate back on track.

The second aspect Buiter considers is the effects of various shifts in the underlying structural relationships which give rise to a depreciation of the dollar. These all strike me as being very gentle and do not capture the notion of a collapse. Indeed, I am unclear about how, precisely, one can have a collapse of a currency in a perfectly flexible exchange rate regime. The idea of a collapsing currency implies a regime which is no longer sustainable. I think that the kind of analysis first undertaken by Flood and Garber (1984), in which pressures are brought to bear on the exchange rate, bringing about an eventual breakdown of the regime, may be more appropriate for addressing this issue.

Finally, the slowdown of economic activity is also captured by shifts. Here, Buiter distinguishes between shifts on the supply side ($\bar{y}_1$, $\bar{y}_2$) and on the demand side (f_1, η_1). Since the model is dynamic, it would seem more appropriate to capture the notion of a slowdown in terms of a reduction in some underlying growth rate, rather than in terms of once-and-for-all shifts. It should be reasonably straightforward to extend the model to accommodate this.

Anticipations Effects

The shocks in the model are all unanticipated. Models of this structure lend themselves to the analysis of anticipated future shocks on the current state of the economy—so-called announcement effects. These analyses have become standard in rational-expectations models, particularly in the analysis of monetary policy, which has received most of the attention in the literature. While such exercises can always be justified in terms of their intrinsic interest, one can argue that expectational effects are of much more practical relevance in the present context, where the primary focus is on fiscal policy. Cuts in government expenditure programs require legislation and these can take years to be enacted. Yet it is clear, for example, from discussions surrounding current proposals to cut the deficit, that anticipations of their ultimate introduction will have significant immediate effects on the economy.

Under the assumption of symmetry introduced by Buiter, anticipations effects impinge on the economy in a particularly simple way. By operating through the exchange rate, they have no effects on the average variables, as I noted earlier. This means that following an announcement, but before the implementation of a specific change, the domestic and foreign economies move in precisely offsetting ways. For example, suppose that at time 0, the fiscal authorities in country 1 announce a fiscal contraction to take effect at time T. The time paths for y_1, y_2, the outputs in the two economies, are as illustrated in figure 4.9 where for convenience the equilibrium levels are set at zero.

The anticipation of the future fiscal contraction leads to an immediate depreciation of the domestic currency (appreciation of the foreign currency). With sluggish output prices, this leads to a real depreciation of the domestic currency, causing the demand for domestic output, and hence domestic output itself, to increase. This increase in activity causes the price of domestic output to begin rising. The domestic currency continues to depreciate following the announcement. This further increases the demand for the domestic good, thereby continuing to increase domestic output and the domestic rate of inflation.

This pattern continues until time T, when the anticipated contraction occurs. This reduces domestic output to a level below its long-run equilibrium. The short-run inflation is reversed and the price of domestic output starts to fall. This in turn means that the real stock of domestic money starts to rise, thereby providing an offsetting expansionary effect to output, which then gradually rises back to its equilibrium level. As this occurs, the deflation is moderated and the price of domestic output gradually approaches its new, lower equilibrium level.

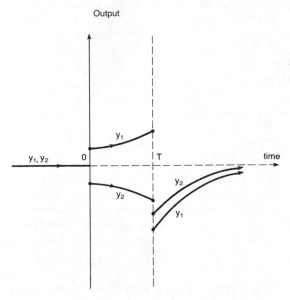

Fig. 4.9   Time paths for output in response to announced domestic fiscal contraction.

We now turn to the foreign economy. As already noted, the aggregate world economy remains stationary until time T, when the fiscal contraction actually takes place. During the period $0 < t \le T$, the averages of the domestic and foreign variables all remain fixed at their initial equilibrium levels. Since all adjustments during this phase stem directly from the initial announcement and the jump in the exchange rate this generates, it follows that, given the symmetry of the two economies, the adjustment in the rest of the world is a mirror image of that in the domestic economy.

Thus during the period following the announcement, but prior to the fiscal contraction, the initial rise in domestic output, together with the subsequent continuous rise, is matched by an equivalent initial decrease and continued fall abroad, stemming from the appreciation of the foreign currency. The falling foreign output causes the price of foreign output to begin falling at an increasing rate. At the time of the fiscal contraction, the decrease in domestic activity generates some negative spillover effects onto demand and output in the foreign economy. Output abroad therefore undergoes a modest decrease at time T, decreasing the foreign rate of inflation at that time. The falling foreign price level causes the relative price of foreign goods to decrease, causing foreign output to begin rising.

The interesting point to observe from this figure is that, in the short run, the announcement of the domestic fiscal contraction has a stimulating effect domestically but generates a recession abroad. And although after the implementation of the contraction, the domestic economy is more adversely affected than is the foreign economy, it is quite likely that the accumulated output losses resulting from the domestic fiscal contraction will be greater abroad than in the domestic economy. The appropriate policy responses which the foreign economy might undertake to mitigate these adverse effects is an interesting issue, similar to those discussed by Buiter.

Strategic Aspects

Buiter deals with policy responses to various disturbances. Much of the discussion has tended to focus on, if only implicitly, output stabilization as being the objective. With more than one target in the policymaker's objective, and with fewer policy instruments available than targets, the international stabilization problem introduces questions of strategic behavior. These have been getting increasing attention; see, e.g., Hamada (1976), Canzoneri and Gray (1985), and the papers in Buiter and Marston (1985).

The emphasis in much of this literature has been on the appropriate strategic responses to demand and supply shocks. Most of this discussion has been conducted in terms of monetary policy instruments, where the objective is to stabilize some objective, typically specified as a quadratic loss function in terms of output and price stability. This literature is very closely related to the present analysis and it is therefore of interest to summarize some of the findings; see, e.g., Turnovsky and d'Orey (1986).

1. A negative demand shock in one country (corresponding to a fiscal contraction in that country) calls for a monetary expansion in both countries. The relative amounts by which the adjustments should be borne depends upon the strategic equilibrium.

2. A negative supply shock in one country (corresponding to a reduction in activity in that country) calls for a monetary expansion in that country and probably a monetary contraction abroad.

3. From a welfare point of view, demand shocks are typically less problematical than supply disturbances. Country-specific demand disturbances of a given magnitude give rise to smaller aggregate welfare costs than do supply disturbances of equal magnitude.

4. The welfare costs of a country-specific demand disturbance (for two symmetric economies) are borne equally by the two countries. The welfare costs of a country-specific supply disturbance, on the other hand, are borne primarily by the country in which they occur.

5. The gains from cooperation are relatively small. They are, however, somewhat larger for supply shocks.

Buiter's paper discusses the monetary and fiscal policy responses as alternatives to stabilizing for the various disturbances. This raises an important issue. Most of the existing work on strategic policymaking deals with monetary policy. But an important result in game theory is that in general, even under certainty, the choice of instruments by the agents is important and will affect the equilibrium outcome. This is in contrast to optimal policymaking by a single agent, where under certainty such a choice is unimportant. The reason for the difference is that the policymakers' reaction-functions, which condition the optimization of each of the agents, depend upon the choice of policy instrument. Thus the choice of monetary or fiscal policy is not a matter of indifference in a (deterministic) strategic environment. Which is better? What if one country uses a fiscal instrument, while the other uses a monetary instrument? Does indeed an equilibrium strategy exist in these cases? These are some of the issues that are raised.

Optimizing Models

Without doubt, the Dornbusch framework is a very tractable and attractive one. But it does suffer from one serious limitation. Because it is an ad hoc model, it does not introduce welfare considerations in any explicit way. Yet welfare considerations are presumably what should guide the kinds of policy responses being discussed here.

In response to the limitations of ad hoc models, there is a growing trend to ensure that macromodels are based on some kind of underlying private-agent optimization. The extent to which this removes the arbitrariness of macroeconomic models is questionable, since the nature of the objective function and the precise constraints confronting the agents are themselves arbitrary.

In the area of international macroeconomics, the development of optimization models has been restricted to small open economies. Here a further difficulty is encountered. If one adopts the usual assumptions of uncovered interest parity and a constant rate of time discount, β say, for a steady-state equilibrium to exist, these models require that we choose $\beta = r^*$, the exogenously given foreign real interest rate. Although this restriction is not unreasonable, it typically means that the *only* sustainable equilibrium is the steady state. In other words, the economy must *always* be in steady-state equilibrium, thereby implying instantaneous adjustment to all exogenous shocks. This elimination of all transitional dynamics is obviously a severe shortcoming. There are ways of restoring the transitional dynamics, such as endogenizing the discount rate, but these are somewhat arbitrary.

In a two-country world, this last limitation does not occur. While in steady state, the equality of the world real-interest rate and the rate of time discount must hold, in the short run these rates may diverge. This permits the system to be out of steady-state equilibrium and allows for transitional dynamics. Such a framework provides an interesting line for further research into the kinds of issues analyzed by Buiter. It has the important advantage of providing a natural criterion for evaluating the welfare consequences of the various disturbances and the appropriate policy responses.

References

Aoki, M. 1981. *Dynamic analysis of open economies.* New York: Academic Press.

Buiter, W. H., and R. C. Marston, eds. 1985. *International economic policy coordination.* Cambridge: Cambridge University Press.

Canzoneri, M., and J. A. Gray. 1985. Monetary policy games and the consequences of noncooperative behavior. *International Economic Review* 26: 547–64.

Flood, R. P., and P. M. Garber. 1984. Collapsing exchange-rate regimes: Some linear examples. *Journal of International Economics* 17: 1–13.

Hamada, K. 1976. A strategic analysis of monetary interdependence. *Journal of Political Economy* 84: 677–700.

Turnovsky, S. J., and V. d'Orey. 1986. Monetary policies in interdependent economies with stochastic disturbances: A strategic approach. *Economic Journal* 96: 696–721.

5   A Positive Theory of Fiscal Policy in Open Economies

David Backus, Michael Devereux,
and Douglas Purvis

5.1 Introduction

One of the principal effects of government policy is redistribution of the social product. To some extent this is accidental, the result of policies designed to achieve other goals. But there are also systematic attempts in most developed countries to influence the distribution of income. In this paper we present a model that uses the government's penchant for redistribution to explain the intertemporal behavior of government deficits, trade deficits, and capital formation. The argument is couched in terms of an overlapping-generations economy in which the endowments of generations differ and fiscal policy consists of intergenerational transfers. The emphasis on redistribution distinguishes the analysis from the efficiency-based theories of Barro (1979) and Kydland and Prescott (1980), who postulate that tax policy is designed to minimize the welfare losses associated with distortionary taxation. To emphasize this difference, we assume instead that taxes are lump sum and explain their configuration entirely in terms of redistributive goals.

Taken at face value, the goal of government policy in our model is to maximize a welfare function which depends on generational utilities. Interpreted more broadly, the theory suggests that when capital markets are incomplete, the government can increase aggregate welfare by using

David Backus is associate professor of economics at Queen's University. Michael Devereux is assistant professor of economics at the University of Toronto. Douglas Purvis is professor of economics at Queen's University and a director of the National Bureau of Economic Research.

We are pleased to thank Dan Bernhardt, Robin Boadway, David Levine ("Go Cobb-Douglas, it's easier") and our discussants, Stanley Fischer and Kenneth Rogoff, for useful advice, and the SSHRC of Canada for financial support.

its own borrowing and lending opportunities to expand consumers' opportunity sets. The overlapping-generations framework is simply a metaphor for these capital market imperfections. the result is essentially a theory of "income-smoothing": the government, in an attempt to moderate differences in utility between generations, taxes the rich and gives to the poor.

Within this framework we show the following: First, the government in a small, open, pure-exchange economy can exploit its access to long-term capital markets to smooth fluctuations in private agents' income streams. In this case government deficits coincide exactly with deficits in the balance of trade. Second, when goods are storable, they provide an alternative method of smoothing income. In an open economy, however, consumption and investment decisions are separable; the exact identity between government deficits and trade deficits is broken, although they remain correlated. Third, in a world composed of many economies there are no policy conflicts if all countries are small in the sense of being price-takers. The equilibrium resulting from each country's smoothing its own income stream is efficient from a global viewpoint. Finally, the theory implies that tests of the Ricardian equivalence theorem based on aggregate time series have no power: if the government redistributes income optimally, aggregate consumption behaves exactly as if it were chosen by a single, infinitely-lived household.

These points are developed in sections 5.3–5.6. Section 5.2 is devoted to a brief look at the data. In the final section we comment on the strengths and weaknesses of the model and suggest extensions that seem particularly useful.

5.2 Some Stylized Facts

We start with the fact that government tax revenues in most developed countries are strongly procyclical. The top panels of figures 5.1–5.5 illustrate this for the United States, Canada, the United Kingdom, Germany, and Japan. Recent work by Sahasakul (1983) on U.S. personal income tax reveals that both average and marginal tax *rates* are procyclical as well, probably reflecting the automatic response of a progressive income tax. We plan further work to examine this contention more closely.

Since government spending on goods and services varies little over the business cycle, consumers' consumption of the public good exhibits almost no cyclical tendency despite large variations in payment for these services. The implication is that government deficits are countercyclical. This is easily verified using the bottom panels of the figures, where government deficits (excluding interest payments) for the same

billions of constant US $

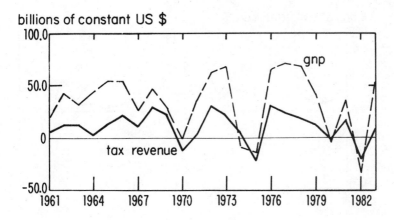

billions of constant US $

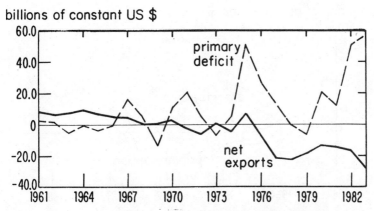

Fig. 5.1   United States real GNP and tax revenue (first difference)(*top*),
                      United States primary deficit and net exports (*bottom*)

five countries are shown. The bottom panels also show the behavior
of net exports. The strong but imperfect negative correlation between
the two predicted above is apparent in most of the countries. For
example, the sharp fiscal expansions in the United Kingdom in the
early 1970s and in Canada in 1974–75 both were accompanied by sharp
declines in net exports. The behavior of the two deficits during the last
couple of years in the charts is of particular interest. The U.S. data
show clearly the inverse correlation between the government deficit
and the trade surplus, while for some of the other countries net exports
have grown over the past few years, regardless of the behavior of their
own government deficits. The suggestion is that their net exports are
influenced significantly by U.S. policy. Similar remarks can be made

millions of constant cdn $

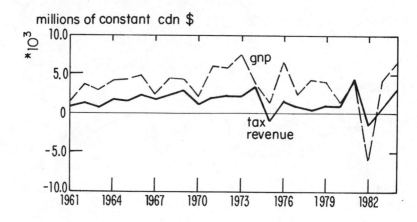

millions of constant cdn $

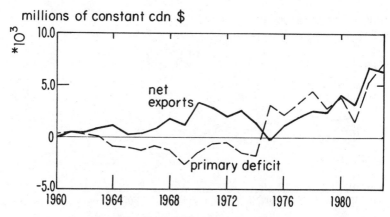

Fig. 5.2   Canada real GNP and tax revenue (first differences) (*top*),
                     Canada primary deficit and net exports (*bottom*)

about other episodes where the two series are positively correlated in various countries, including the United States. This underscores the need for a multicountry framework like that begun in section 5.4.

5.3 Optimal Fiscal Policy in a Pure Exchange Economy

We make the case for income-smoothing in an overlapping-generations economy with identical two-period consumers who have log-linear preferences and make no bequests. As in Levine (1983), population is constant and there is a single commodity available each period. The absence of bequest motives is clearly important in providing an incentive for public income-smoothing (Barro, 1974). None of the other elements is necessary, but they make the analysis simpler.

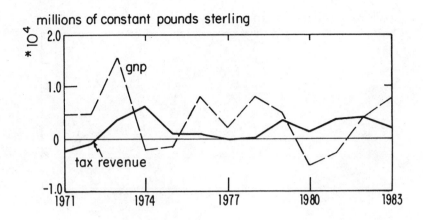

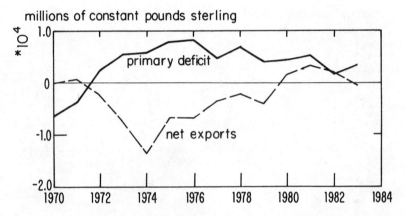

Fig. 5.3   United Kingdom real GNP and tax revenue (first differences) (*top*),
United Kingdom primary deficit and net exports (*bottom*)

The object is to compare two types of equilibria: a competitive equilibrium with no government and a welfare optimum supported by lump-sum taxes and transfers. Each is examined in both a closed economy, in which prices clear markets, and in an open economy facing prices fixed in world markets. We view the welfare optimization as an approximation to actual government behavior and as the basis for a positive theory of fiscal policy.

The fundamental building blocks of the model are the consumers. The representative of generation t is alive in periods t and $t + 1$ and is endowed with amounts (a_t, b_{t+1}) of the commodity in each of these two periods. The aggregate endowment of commodity t is therefore

(1) $$e_t = a_t + b_t.$$

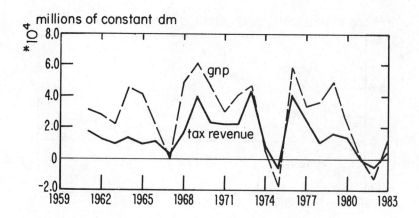

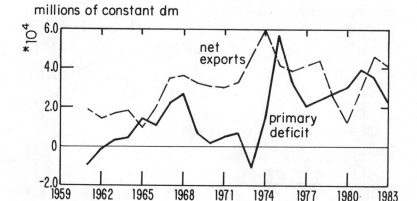

Fig. 5.4   Germany real GNP and tax revenue (first differences) (*top*), Germany primary deficit and net exports (*bottom*)

Preferences over consumption in the two periods, denoted c_t and d_{t+1}, are characterized by the utility function

(2) $$u(c_t, d_{t+1}) = \log c_t + \alpha \log d_{t+1}.$$

If the price of commodity t is p_t, then consumers choose c_t and d_{t+1} to maximize utility, subject to the budget constraint

(3) $$p_t c_t + p_{t+1} d_{t+1} \leq p_t a_t + p_{t+1} b_{t+1},$$

where p_{t+1} is the perfectly anticipated price in the second period of generation t's life. The demand functions are

(4) $$c_t = (1 + \alpha)^{-1}(p_t a_t + p_{t+1} b_{t+1})/p_t$$

$$d_{t+1} = \alpha(1 + \alpha)^{-1}(p_t a_t + p_{t+1} b_{t+1})/p_{t+1}.$$

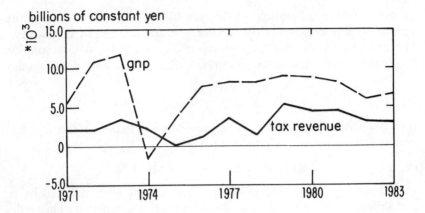

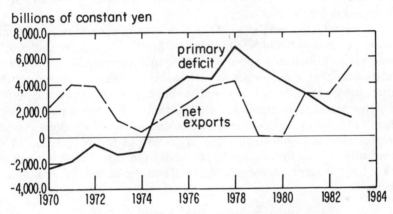

Fig. 5.5   Japan real GNP and tax revenue (first differences) (*top*),
Japan primary deficit and net exports (*bottom*)

In the closed economy a competitive equilibrium is characterized by
a sequence of prices, $\{p_1, p_2, \ldots\}$, or one-period rates of interest, $r_t = p_t/p_{t+1} - 1$, satisfying the equilibrium conditions

(5) $c_t + d_t = e_t, t = 1,2, \ldots$.

In period 2 and after this implies that prices satisfy the difference
equation

(6) $b_{t+1}p_{t+1} - (\alpha a_t + b_t)p_t + \alpha a_{t-1}p_{t-1} = 0.$

But in period 1 generation 0 has, in addition to its endowment, some
savings from the previous period, which it spends in period 1. With
only one good per period this expenditure cannot depend on relative
prices. We introduce some price sensitivity with a now familiar device

by representing generation 0's savings by a fixed, arbitrary quantity denominated in period 0 prices, denoted M, and referred to as "money." The old generation now has a trivial choice problem, whose solution involves consuming its endowment plus whatever its holdings of money will buy:

(7) $$d_1 = b_1 + M/p_1.$$

A competitive equilibrium is therefore a solution to the difference equation satisfying the initial condition,

(8) $$\alpha a_1 p_1 + b_2 p_2 + (1 + \alpha)M = 0.$$

In fact there is a continuum of equilibria of this sort, indexed by p_1 and differing in the level of consumption of generation 0. This indeterminacy does not appear in the welfare-maximizing solution so we disregard it for the moment.

The model is a special case of the overlapping-generations economies studied by Balasko and Shell (1980; 1981a, b). They prove under more general conditions than those used here that a competitive equilibrium exists and that the competitive allocation is weakly Pareto-optimal (there are no Pareto-improving redistributions involving a finite number of consumers). The equilibrium allocation is Pareto-optimal if prices shrink at least as fast as the aggregate endowment (the interest rate is greater than or equal to the rate of growth of the economy). To see what this implies for our model, consider the case where each generation has the same endowment (a,b). Then the difference equation for prices is

(9) $$bp_{t+1} - (\alpha a + b)p_t + \alpha a p_{t-1} = 0.$$

Its characteristic equation has two roots, 1 and $\alpha a/b$. The first stems from the homogeneity of demand functions; the second tells us that the rate of interest approaches $(\alpha a/b) - 1$. If this is positive, as it will be if young consumers save, then the equilibrium is Pareto-efficient. In fact this condition suffices even if the endowment is bounded but varies over time.

Even if the equilibrium is Pareto-optimal, the government may prefer transfer schemes that help some generations at the expense of others. Another theorem from Balasko and Shell (1980) assures us that any efficient allocation can be supported as a competitive equilibrium by a system of lump-sum transfers. The question is which allocations the government is likely to prefer. One useful welfare function treats generations similarly, but places greater weight on those closest to the present:

(10) $$W = \Sigma \beta^t u_t,$$

where $0 < \beta < 1$ is a discount factor, u_t is the utility of generation t, and the sum is over current and future generations. The welfare function is utilitarian with the exception of the discount factor, which is needed to ensure a solution to the infinite-horizon programming problem. In the present case W is given by

$$(11) \qquad W = \sum_{t=0}^{\infty} \beta^t [\log c_t + \alpha \log d_{t+1}].$$

Because utility is additively separable, the value of c_0 does not affect the optimal plan.

In a closed economy the welfare optimum is obtained by maximizing W subject to the aggregate resource constraints,

$$(12) \qquad c_t + d_t \le e_t, \qquad t = 1,2, \ldots .$$

The solution to the problem involves

$$(13) \qquad \begin{aligned} c_t &= \theta \, e_t \\ d_t &= (1 - \theta)e_t \qquad t = 1,2, \ldots , \end{aligned}$$

where $\theta = \beta/(\alpha + \beta)$. Note in particular that the allocation to generation 0, d_1, is determined by the condition that its marginal utility equal the discounted marginal utility of c_1. The shadow prices associated with the constraints are

$$(14) \qquad p_t = (\alpha + \beta)\beta^{t-1}/e_t.$$

With a constant endowment stream this implies an interest rate of $(1 - \beta)/\beta > 0$. More generally the rate of interest is determined by the ratio of next period's endowment to this period's:

$$(15) \qquad 1 + r_t = e_{t+1}/\beta e_t.$$

Supporting this allocation as a competitive equilibrium requires the government to redistribute income, and there are a number of ways to do this. Basically the government must shift the budget constraints of consumers so that their after-tax incomes equal the values of their expenditures:

$$(16) \qquad y_t = p_t c_t + p_{t+1} d_{t+1}.$$

Clearly there is no unique way to accomplish this. The government can, with the same effect, transfer purchasing power to a generation when its members are young or when its members are old. For simplicity, we adopt the convention that the government transfers credits to each generation equal to the difference between its current endowment and its consumption at the welfare optimum. This involves real transfers of, say, g_t to the young and h_t to the old given by

(17)
$$g_t = \theta e_t - a_t$$

$$h_t = (1 - \theta)e_t - b_t.$$

It should be clear from the resource constraint that the government's budget is always balanced:

(18)
$$g_t + h_t = 0.$$

As a result, only limited smoothing is possible: the only feasible transfer schemes in this economy involve redistribution of the endowment between generations in the same period.

Let us turn now to an open economy facing fixed world prices. The possibility of trading with the rest of the world means that aggregate consumption need no longer equal the economy's endowment every period. In an economy with no government, the competitive allocation is given by the demand functions of the various consumers evaluated at world prices. The trade balance, tb_t, is defined by

(19)
$$t\,b_t = e_t - (c_t + d_t)$$

$$= (a_t - c_t) + (b_t - d_t).$$

Since the budget of any generation is balanced, a trade deficit is simply the result of less saving by the young than dissaving by the old.

The open economy also gives rise to additional possibilities for policy. The government can effectively transfer purchasing power from one generation to another by borrowing and lending in world capital markets. If prices converge to zero and the aggregate endowment is bounded, then the government's constraint can be expressed as a present value:

(20)
$$\sum_{t=1}^{\infty} p_t(c_t + d_t) \le \sum_{t=1}^{\infty} p_t e_t + p_0 F_0,$$

where F_0 is the net foreign asset position of the economy, measured in units of commodity 0. The solution to this problem involves demands of

(21)
$$c_t = \beta^t\,[(1 - \beta)/(\alpha + \beta)]Y/p_t$$

$$d_t = \alpha\beta^{t-1}\,[(1 - \beta)/(\alpha + \beta)]Y/p_t,$$

where Y is the value of the economy's endowment:

(22)
$$Y = \sum_{t=1}^{\infty} p_t e_t + P_0 F_0.$$

If prices in the world economy decline at rate β, as they would if the world had a constant endowment and were managed as the closed economy above was, then c and d would be constant. Otherwise the plan will respond to fluctuations in prices, which we can think of as arising from fluctuations in the world endowment. As with the allocation of risk, idiosyncratic variations can be eliminated by the market, but aggregate variations cannot.

The implied tax policy again has the ambiguity noted earlier. If we retain the convention that transfers are made when they are consumed, the government runs a deficit when its country's endowment is small, relative to the norm, and a surplus when its endowment is large. The fluctuations in the government deficit are matched exactly by the trade balance. In a sense consumers, taken as a group, use the government's ability to borrow and lend to expand their opportunity set. Since the constraints for the closed economy are more restrictive than those for the open economy, the latter always achieves at least as high a level of welfare; the gains from intertemporal trade are nonnegative.

The following examples illustrate the salient features of the open economy under laissez-faire and the optimal tax policy.

Example 5.3.1. Consider an economy with $\alpha = 1$, $\beta = 0.9$, and an endowment (a_t, b_{t+1}) that alternates between $(3,1)$ (t odd) and $(3,2)$ (t even). The aggregate endowment thus varies between 4 (t even) and 5 (t odd). With $p_t = \beta^t$ the competitive allocation alternates between $(c_t, d_t) = (1.95, 2.67)$ (t odd) and $(2.40, 2.17)$ (t even), the trade balance between 0.38 (t odd) and -0.43 (t even). If generation 0 is treated the same way (it consumes 2.40 and 2.67), the value of the welfare function is 16.60. The welfare optimum, on the other hand, involves constant levels of consumption: $c = 2.18$ and $d = 2.42$. The trade balance and government deficit alternate between 0.32 (t odd) and -0.60 (t even). The value of the welfare function is 16.70. (This uses the same net foreign asset position as the competitive equilibrium, namely, the difference between generation 0's first-period endowment, 3, and its first-period consumption, 2.4. Y is then 41.34.)

Example 5.3.2. Suppose that in example 5.3.1 the world endowment is perfectly correlated with the domestic endowment and that prices are given by $p_t = (1/5)\beta^t$ (t odd) and $p_t = (1/4)\beta^t$ (t even). Then there are no opportunities for improving on the competitive equilibrium. The competitive equilibrium and the welfare optimum are identical. The analogy with risk-sharing should be obvious. If we view this as a proposition in trade theory, we see that there are no gains from trade when countries have the same preferences and endowments.

Example 5.3.3. With $\alpha = 1$ and $\beta = 0.9$, let the endowment of generation t be $(2, 1 + \delta^{t+1})$, with $\delta = 0.7$. The aggregate endowment in

Table 5.1   Competitive Equilibrium for Example 5.3.3

t	c_t	d_t	u_t	e_t	tb_t	p_t
1	1.670	1.961	1.132	3.700	0.068	0.900
2	1.604	1.856	1.051	3.490	0.030	0.810
3	1.558	1.783	0.992	3.343	0.002	0.729
4	1.526	1.731	0.950	3.240	−0.017	0.656
5	1.503	1.695	0.920	3.168	−0.030	0.590
6	1.487	1.670	0.899	3.118	−0.039	0.531
7	1.476	1.652	0.884	3.082	−0.046	0.478
8	1.468	1.640	0.873	3.058	−0.050	0.430
9	1.463	1.631	0.866	3.040	−0.054	0.387
10	1.459	1.625	0.861	3.028	−0.056	0.349

period t is therefore $3 + \delta^t$. Assume again that world prices are given by $p_t = \beta^t$. Since the endowment is shrinking, the competitive equilibrium has consumption declining over time, as shown in table 5.1. Treating generation 0 the same way gives us an initial foreign asset position of 0.24 and a welfare value of 9.58.

The value of the economy's endowment, including $F_0 = 0.24$, is 28.94, which corresponds to a "permanent" aggregate consumption level of 3.21. Equating the marginal utilities of young and old allows us to divide this into $c = 1.52$ and $d = 1.69$. With the endowment shrinking, the trade balance is initially positive, declines gradually, and reaches a lower asymptote of −0.06. The value of the welfare function is 9.62.

5.4   Implications for International Policy Coordination

The world economy is a closed system, so we might expect the closed-economy theory of the previous section to describe the optimal world equilibrium. We show that decentralized policymaking replicates the efficient world allocation if individual countries are too small to affect world prices by their own actions. Large countries, however, may want to exploit their ability to influence prices to raise domestic welfare at the expense of the rest of the world. As in Frenkel and Razin (1984), the world economy has a fixed endowment, so policies designed to change consumption in one country must change consumption in the rest of the world by an equal and opposite amount. Our guess is that optimal fiscal policy by a large economy is "beggar thy neighbor," but developing this argument remains a task for the future.

We begin by deriving efficient worldwide tax policies. We say that an allocation is *policy-efficient* if (i) it is Pareto-efficient, in the sense that welfare in any particular country cannot be raised without lowering welfare in at least one other country, and (ii) the value of an economy's consumption equals, at equilibrium prices, the value of its endowment. Note that condition (i) defines Pareto–optimality in terms of welfare functions of countries, rather than utilities of individual consumers. Condition (ii) guarantees that the allocation can be supported as a competitive equilibrium without net transfer payments between countries. The two suffice to determine a unique allocation, which can be supported as a competitive equilibrium with the appropriate choice of lump-sum taxes.

We derive the policy-efficient allocation by looking first at Pareto-efficient allocations. If there are n countries, indexed by i, then any efficient allocation is the solution to a problem of the form,

$$(23) \qquad \max W = \sum_i \pi_i W_i, \; \Sigma \pi_i = 1,$$

subject to the world resource constraints, for some choice of the welfare weights π_i. To make this tractable, assume that countries have identical preferences but different endowments. As in section 5.3, the welfare of an individual country is given by

$$(24) \qquad W_i = \sum_{t=0}^{\infty} \beta^t [\log c_{i,t} + \alpha \log d_{i,t+1}],$$

where we have introduced additional subscripts to distinguish countries. The world resource constraint is

$$(25) \qquad \sum_i (c_{i,t} + d_{i,t}) \le \sum_i e_{i,t}, \; t = 1, 2, \ldots \; .$$

If the world endowment, e_t, is bounded, so that a solution to the global welfare problem exists, and if p_t are the shadow prices associated with the constraints, then the first-order conditions are

$$(26) \qquad \pi_i \beta^t / c_{i,t} = p_t$$

$$\pi_i \, \beta^{t-1} \alpha / d_{i,t} = p_t,$$

$$i = 1, 2, \ldots, n, \qquad t = 1, 2, \ldots \; .$$

The shadow prices, which give the market prices of the competitive equilibrium that supports this allocation, are

$$(27) \qquad p_t = (\alpha + \beta)\beta^{t-1}/e_t.$$

(The fact that these are independent of the π_is is an artifact of the countries' having identical, homothetic preferences.)

Now let us compute the welfare weights. If we impose condition (ii), then for each country

$$(28) \qquad \sum_{t=1}^{\infty} p_t(c_{i,t} + d_{i,t}) = \sum_{t=1}^{\infty} p_t e_{i,t} + p_0 F_{i,0} = Y_i.$$

In the present case this implies that the welfare weight is

(29) $$\pi_i = Y_i/[(1 + \alpha/\beta)\Sigma\beta^t]$$

$$= (1 - \beta)\Sigma\beta^{t-1}(e_{i,t}/e_t) + p_0 F_{i,0}.$$

In short, the weight varies inversely with the country's wealth relative to the world as a whole.

The question is whether this policy-efficient allocation can be attained by decentralized policymaking. Will the Nash solution—in which each country chooses taxes to maximize its own welfare, given its budget constraint, the taxes of other countries, and the world equilibrium condition—be policy-efficient? The answer depends upon how governments view prices. At one extreme we might consider small economies, whose decisions have no influence on world prices. It should be clear by analogy with the second welfare theorem that the policy-efficient allocation is the best any such country can attain. Decentralized policymaking is efficient.

The question is whether this decentralization result extends to policy coordination between large countries. Our intuition is that it does not, but we have yet to specify a model in which policy conflicts lead to suboptimal allocations.

5.5 Fiscal Policy in a Model with Capital

We saw in section 5.2 that while government deficits and trade balances are positively correlated, the correlation is hardly as close as predicted by the pure-exchange model. One reason might be physical capital, which provides an alternative method of transferring goods between periods and which is, as an empirical matter, closely related to both national income and the balance of trade.

We examine the interplay of trade deficits, capital formation, and fiscal policy in a variant of the Diamond (1965) debt model, used recently in a similar context by Persson (1985). We add to the model of section 5.3 the possibility of using some or all of the current endowment, which we now refer to as "labor," to produce output next period. In the simplest model each unit of labor produces one unit of "output," which is divided between consumption and capital. Capital is converted into next-period output by the production process Ak^γ, with $0 < \gamma < 1$.

The representative of generation t therefore consumes c_t and invests k_{t+1} in period t. In period $t + 1$ it consumes d_{t+1}, financed by its endowment, production, and saving from period t. The overall constraint is

(30) $p_t(c_t + k_{t+1}) + p_{t+1}d_{t+1} \leq p_t a_t + p_{t+1}[b_{t+1} + A_{t+1}k_{t+1}^\gamma].$

Utility maximization yields the demand functions

(31) $$c_t = (1 + \alpha)^{-1} y_t / p_t$$

$$d_{t+1} = \alpha(1 + \alpha)^{-1} y_t / p_{t+1}$$

$$k_{t+1} = (\gamma A_{t+1} p_{t+1} / p_t)^{\sigma},$$

where $\sigma = 1/(1 - \gamma)$ and

(32) $$y_t = p_t a_t + p_{t+1} b_{t+1} + (\gamma / p_t)^{\sigma} (A_{t+1} p_{t+1})^{1+\sigma}.$$

A competitive equilibrium in a closed economy is a sequence of prices satisfying the equilibrium conditions.

(33) $$c_t + d_t + k_{t+1} = e_t + A_t k_t^{\gamma}, \qquad t = 1, 2, \ldots .$$

As before we can express this as a difference equation in prices, but unlike the pure-exchange model it is highly nonlinear. The welfare optimum is derived by maximizing W, given in section 5.3, subject to the resource constraints.

(34) $$c_t + d_t + k_{t+1} \le e_t + A_t k_t^{\gamma}, \qquad t = 1, 2, \ldots .$$

The optimal policy is essentially the solution to an optimal growth problem. One of its interesting features is that the steady-state rate of interest, $(1 - \beta)/\beta > 0$, does not depend on how individual agents discount the future (the parameter α). This characteristic and others are described by Samuelson (1967) and Calvo and Obstfeld (1985).

Our interest, however, lies in the small, open economy, which is considerably easier to study because prices are exogenous and demand decisions are completely separate from investment decisions. In the laissez-faire equilibrium, the competitive allocation is described fully by the demand functions stated earlier. The capital stock is determined solely by prices, and the returns to capital and labor are then consumed and saved as prescribed by the demand functions and the distribution of income. Generations with larger endowments and higher profits from capital consume more than others.

The welfare optimum is computed much as before. If prices converge to zero and the endowment is bounded, then we can again express the government's constraint as an infinite sum:

(35) $$\sum_{t=1}^{\infty} p_t(c_t + d_t + k_{t+1}) \le \sum_{t=1}^{\infty} p_t(e_t + A_t k_t^{\gamma}) + p_0 F_0.$$

The problem is recursive: the capital stock is determined by

(36) $$k_{t+1} = (\gamma A_{t+1} p_{t+1} / p_t)^{\sigma},$$

as before. From this we define the economy's wealth as

(37) $$Y = \sum_{t=0}^{\infty} p_t(e_t + A_t k_t^\gamma - k_{t+1}) + p_0 F_0,$$

and consume

(38) $$c_t = \beta^t[(1 - \beta)/(\alpha + \beta)] \, Y/p_t$$

$$d_t = \alpha\beta^{t-1}[(1 - \beta)/(\alpha + \beta)]Y/p_t.$$

The interest derives from the interaction between capital formation and trade. Consider, for example, an economy with constant endowment, e, and productivity, A. If the world rate of interest is constant at $(1 - \beta)/\beta$, then consumption is constant and the capital stock approaches its steady-state value,

(39) $$k^* = (\gamma A \beta)^\sigma.$$

A positive shock to the endowment simply raises Y, which increases consumption in all periods. As in section 5.3, this raises the trade balance in the period of the shock and lowers it in other periods since domestic consumption is higher. Alternatively, consider a temporary rise in the productivity parameter, A. This raises the demand for capital that period and also raises the economy's wealth, which raises consumption slightly in every period. The trade balance, given by

(40) $$tb_t = (e_t + A_t k_t^\gamma) - (c_t + d_t + k_{t+1}),$$

will fall when the capital is imported, rise the next period when the capital is used in production, and fall slightly in other periods because the economy now consumes more each period. Both of these features are illustrated in the following examples.

Example 5.5.1. Let $\alpha = 1$, $\beta = \gamma = .8$, $A = a = e = 1$, and $b = 0$, and consider the behavior of the economy when world prices oscillate, as they would if the world endowment were oscillating. To make this concrete, let $p_t = \beta^t$ when t is even, and $2\beta^t$ when t is odd. In both the competitive and optimal equilibria the capital stock, k_t, is 3.436 when t is even, 0.0034 when t is odd. These fluctuations in the capital stock, which make even generations much richer, lead to a competitive equilibrium in which the utilities of the two generations fluctuate along with prices. Consumption, production, and the trade balance are given by

c_t	d_t	tb_t	u_t	
2.684	1.251	−6.361	1.281	t even
0.500	1.342	2.591	−0.468	t odd

The value of the welfare function is 2.28.

The welfare optimum smooths these fluctuations somewhat, although the government's budget constraint ensures that even generations still do better since they face a lower rate of interest. We start with $F_0 = -5.12$, the dissaving of generation 0 in its first period of life and compute the optimal allocation of total income, $Y = 15.18$. Quantities are

c_t	d_t	tb_t	u_t	
1.687	2.107	-6.220	0.575	t even
0.843	1.054	2.536	0.575	t odd

which imply a welfare value of 2.30.

Example 5.5.2. With the same parameter values and $p_t = \beta^t$, we examine an economy in which the productivity parameter, A_t, oscillates between 1 (t odd) and 2 (t even). The capital stock therefore oscillates between 0.107 and 3.436. The trade balance is driven by the need to import capital goods in odd periods, and the output from those capital goods in even periods, and alternates between -3.84 and 4.587. The discrepancy in utility between generations brought about by this variation in the productivity of capital is eliminated completely in the welfare solution, which raises W from -1.80 to -0.72.

5.6   On Testing the Ricardian Equivalence Theorem

One of the consequences of the government's income-smoothing is that the aggregate economy behaves like a single infinite-horizon consumer. If government policy is approximately as we have modeled it, then tests of debt neutrality based on aggregate time series data have very little power. The result is based on the following idea: the essential difference between an overlapping-generations economy and an economy with infinitely-lived agents is that the latter can redistribute purchasing power across time without restraint, but the former cannot. But suppose that the government performs this redistribution as we have described. Then there is no longer any need for further redistribution and the two models are observationally equivalent.

The argument is quite general, but a statement based on log-linear preferences should suffice to communicate its essential elements.

Proposition. Consider the model of section 5.3. The demand for aggregate consumption, $C_t = c_t + d_t$, associated with the welfare problem is identical to that of a single infinitely-lived consumer with endowment $\{e_1, e_2, \ldots\}$ and utility function

(41) $$U = \Sigma \beta^t \log C_t.$$

The proof is straightforward. We know that the welfare optimum involves equating the discounted marginal utilities of the young and old:

(42) $$\beta^t / c_t = \beta^{t-1} \alpha / d_t.$$

Since the utility functions are homothetic this implies that the ratio of c_t to d_t is a fixed number independent of t, in this case

(43) $c_t/d_t = \beta/\alpha.$

Now aggregate consumption can be expressed

(44) $C_t = (1 + \alpha/\beta)c_t,$

and the utility function, U, and welfare function, W, are equivalent.

Now consider tests of the neutrality proposition, of which Aschauer (1985) is a nice example (and a good source of other references). The standard approach is to assume that aggregate consumption is the outcome of an infinite-horizon optimization. The optimization has the property that the timing of taxes, and therefore the value of currently outstanding debt, is irrelevant—the Ricardian equivalence theorem. It also imposes testable restrictions on the behavior of aggregate consumption, taxes, and debt. Aschauer, for one, finds that the data cannot reject the restrictions and therefore support the theorem. Our proposition, however, says that if the government manipulates taxes to smooth income, then our model, in which the timing of taxes is central, cannot be distinguished empirically from his. His test has no power and provides as much support for our model as for his.

5.7   Final Remarks

We have argued that distributional objectives provide an incentive for fiscal authorities to smooth the incomes of private agents. The details were developed in a model with two-period agents, overlapping lives and log-linear preferences, but we think its main features are considerably more general. A quick look at some data suggests that the theory agrees, at least roughly, with observed variations in aggregate income, government deficits, and trade balances.

Despite this somewhat cursory empirical verification, there are a number of theoretical extensions that appear to us worth pursuing. First, we would like to extend the theory to scholastic environments, in which fluctuations in the endowment stream are to some degree unpredictable. In these environments income-smoothing amounts to risk-sharing. Gordon and Varian (1985) have taken this route in a model with a similar structure, and their insights would be useful here as well. Second, and perhaps more important to the open economy issues, we would like to introduce a nontraded good, so that some of the impact of changes in the intertemporal pattern of consumption opportunities can be taken in the form of changes in the domestic relative price. Third, the conditions on the decentralization result of section 5.4 might be examined more closely. We argued, in short, that there are costs of uncoordinated policies only if some countries are large, in the sense of being able to influence world prices by their own actions. Kehoe (1987) presents a counterexample, in which the global costs of decentralized fiscal policy rise as the number of countries grows. Finally, the model could be made richer by allowing for generational heterogeneity, so that fiscal policy might involve redistribution both within and across generations. In fact, the procyclical nature of tax rates in developed countries may simply be the accidental consequence of progressive taxation within generations.

References

Aschauer, D. 1985. Fiscal policy and aggregate demand. *American Economic Review* 75 (March): 117–27.

Balasko, Y., and K. Shell. 1980. The overlapping generations model, I: The case of pure exchange without money. *Journal of Economic Theory* 23: 281–306.

———. 1981a. The overlapping generations model, II: The case of pure exchange with money. *Journal of Economic Theory* 24: 112–42.

———. 1981b. The overlapping generations model, III: The case of log-linear utility functions. *Journal of Economic Theory* 24: 143–52.

Barro, R. 1974. Are government bonds net wealth? *Journal of Political Economy* 82 (November-December, no. 6): 1095–1117.

———. 1979. On the determination of the public debt. *Journal of Political Economy* 87 (October): 940–71.

Bruce, N., and D. Purvis. 1984. Consequences of government budget deficits. *Royal Commission on the Economic Union and Development Prospects for Canada.*

Calvo, G., and M. Obstfeld. 1985. Optimal time-consistent fiscal policy with uncertain lifetimes. NBER Working Paper no. 1593.

Diamond, P. 1965. National debt in a neoclassical growth model. *American Economic Review* 55 (December): 1126–50.

Frenkel, J., and A. Razin. 1984. Budget deficits and rates of interest in the world economy. NBER Working Paper no. 1354.

Gordon, R., and H. Varian. 1985. Intergenerational risk sharing. NBER Working Paper no. 1730.

Kehoe, P. 1987. Coordination of fiscal policies in a world economy. *Journal of Monetary Economics* 19 (May): 349–76.

Kydland, F., and E. Prescott. 1980. A competitive theory of fluctuations and the feasibility and desirability of stabilization policy. In *Rational expectations and economic policy,* ed. S. Fischer. Chicago: University of Chicago Press.

Levine, D. 1983. The overlapping generations model. UCLA. November.

Persson, T. 1985. Deficits and intergenerational welfare in open economies. *Journal of International Economics* 19 (August): 67–84.

Sahasakul, C. 1983. Are marginal tax-rate changes predictable? University of Rochester. (December).

Samuelson, P. 1967. A turnpike refutation of the golden rule in a welfare-maximizing many-year plan. In *Essays on the theory of optimal economic growth,* ed. K. Shell. Cambridge: MIT Press.

Comment   Stanley Fischer

Backus, Devereux, and Purvis (BDP) present a very clean theoretical paper that explains its assumptions and conclusions and leaves little for the discussant to do except to provide an intuitive explanation of the results and to talk about their relevance to real world fiscal policy.

The facts that the positive theory is called upon to explain are that budget deficits are countercyclical and net exports are procyclical—sometimes. Thus there is a "strong but imperfect" negative correlation between them. Theory tells us the negative relationship should indeed be imperfect. The cyclical character of net exports depends on the disturbances moving the economy.

First consider aggregate demand policy disturbances. In the floating exchange rate Mundell-Fleming model, with a given level of government spending and fixed tax rates, monetary expansion causes both the budget deficit and net exports to decrease. The association will be positive in that case. Fiscal expansion causes the budget deficit to increase and net exports to decrease. There will be a negative correlation between the budget deficit and net exports, but the budget deficit will be procyclical and net exports countercyclical.

Neither of these cases corresponds to the BDP reading of their charts. Their case is rather one of aggregate supply or productivity disturbances. Their positive theory is that when output is high because of a productivity shock, countries both lend abroad and raise taxes on the current generation for the benefit of later poorer generations. Thus in the presence of a favorable shock, a country will run a current account surplus to effect the lending, and a budget surplus because taxation is high.

BDP's underlying consumers are finite-lived finite-horizon maximizers. The fiscal authority, however, takes the long view, maximizing a discounted weighted sum of generational utility levels. The fiscal authority's actions effectively make the economy behave like one in which individuals have infinite horizons. Hence the interesting BDP argument that the economy behaves as if Ricardian equivalence holds even though it is thoroughly non-Ricardian.

That result seems close to a general result that in cases where stabilization policy can achieve first best solutions, the reduced form fails to show any effects of the policy. The general result goes back at least to Kareken and Solow,[1] who gave the example of a situation in which

Stanley Fischer is professor of economics at the Massachusetts Institute of Technology and a research associate of the National Bureau of Economic Research.

1. Robert M. Solow and John Kareken, Lags in monetary policy, part 1 of Lags in fiscal and monetary policy, by Albert Ando et al., in *Commission on money and credit, stabilization policies* (Englewood Cliffs, NJ: Prentice-Hall, 1963), 14–96.

active anticipatory monetary policy succeeds in stabilizing output to the extent of reducing GNP to a white noise process. Then there will be no correlation between output and previous monetary policy. Of course, if policy is not absolutely perfect, it will be possible to detect some of its effects. In the BDP model, if the fiscal authority makes mistakes, it will be possible to see individuals adjusting their lifetime consumption patterns to the debt-tax mix.

Shocks in BDP are transitory. Consider a small country starting with a balanced budget and zero net exports that suffers a permanent favorable productivity shock that affects the endowment of the young. What will happen to net exports and the budget? The first reaction is that consumption and output should rise by the same amount so there is no effect on net exports or the budget deficit. The presence of old people makes a difference though. The social welfare function requires them to share the bonanza. It also requires the burden of their increased consumption to be shared with future generations. The government will issue some debt, appearing initially to run a procyclical budget deficit. The result for the balance of payments is not obvious.

BDP have isolated one particular type of disturbance—transitory productivity shocks—for which their analysis applies. Saudi Arabia in the first post-oil shock period fits such a case well. But there are many other types of disturbance for which other correlations would be expected. Printed on the side of their paper should be the following notice. Warning: Correlations among endogenous variables are not independent of the shocks that move them.

Comment   Kenneth Rogoff

There are any number of plausible reasons why Ricardian equivalence may not hold: finite lives, tax distortions, imperfect capital markets, uncertain fertility, etc. However, as Barro (1974) points out, although many different reasons will imply that the timing of taxes "matters," they do not all suggest the same positive or normative conclusions. Backus, Devereux, and Purvis (BDP) posit that deficits are important because individuals do not leave bequests,[1] and they obtain some interesting results. Ideally, however, one would eventually like to see how their main conclusions hold up in models where deficits matter

Kenneth Rogoff is an associate professor at the University of Wisconsin, and a research associate of the National Bureau of Economic Research.

1. Frankel and Razin (1986) present an open-economy model of budget deficits based on individual utility maximization. The absence of bequests is also important in their framework.

because taxes are distorting, or because of capital market imperfections. The issue of robustness would be less important, of course, if one could amass empirical evidence showing that absence of bequests is by far the most important reason for the failure of Ricardian equivalence. (Barro [1979] argues that tax distortions are more important.)

The BDP model is closed by the assumption that governments smooth consumption across generations.[2] Interestingly, their paradigm suggests the possible importance of certain shocks that have not been conventionally recognized as major factors in the determination of government budget deficits. For example, suppose there is an unanticipated positive shock to the rate of technological progress. The BDP model would predict an increase in the budget deficit, as future generations are now expected to be better off. There are, of course, other ways for society to transfer income across generations besides government debt. The current generation can also transfer income to future generations by increasing expenditure on education or by reducing pollution. Clearly, the existence of these other margins of substitution does not imply that the deficits channel is insignificant.

It is superficially anomalous that voters are willing to elect governments that care about future generations and yet are not willing to leave bequests themselves. This is internally consistent, however, if the trend rate of growth of productivity is high and if there are legal restrictions on leaving private debt to one's heirs. Hence agents are at a corner solution in terms of private bequests and use government debt to achieve an interior maximum. Thus it is perfectly possible to observe symmetric responses of deficits to temporary positive and negative productivity shocks, as in the BDP model. (Symmetric, in terms of deviations from trend. It might require a very large positive shock to observe an actual surplus.)

The BDP model, interpreted literally, captures the effects of government consumption smoothing across generations. Can it be interpreted more broadly to explain what happens when the government smooths consumption on a very short-term basis? The answer to this question is not immediately obvious. If individuals can borrow and lend at the same rate as the government, there would be no need for the government to run deficits. Again, it would be interesting to ask what types of capital market imperfections yield the same conclusions as the BDP's no-bequests assumption.

In section 5.4, BDP show that the gains from policy cooperation among governments become small as the number of countries grows

2. BDP's analysis is related to some analyses found in the social security literature; see, for example, Samuelson (1975) or Feldstein (1985). Both of these papers employ an OG model with no bequests and examine how income should be distributed across generations to maximize social welfare.

large. With an infinite number of countries, decentralized decision making yields a Pareto-optimal allocation. This is a model-specific result. Chari and Kehoe (1987) provide a natural example (in a model with distorting taxes) in which the cooperative equilibrium remains significantly better than the noncooperative equilibrium, even as the number of countries grows large. Incidentally, there is no theoretical presumption that governments can always better attain their objectives by cooperating. Rogoff (1985) provides an example in which the inflation credibility problems of governments vis-à-vis their own citizens are exacerbated when sovereign governments coordinate their monetary policy decisions.

References

Barro, Robert. 1974. Are government bonds net wealth? *Journal of Political Economy* 82: 1095–1117.
———. 1979. On the determination of public debt. *Journal of Political Economy* 87: 940–71.
Calvo, Guillermo A., and Maurice Obstfeld. 1985. Optimal time-consistent fiscal policy with uncertain lifetimes. NBER Working Paper no. 1593.
Chari, V. V., and Patrick J. Kehoe. 1987. International coordination of fiscal policies in limiting economies. Federal Reserve Bank of Minneapolis, Research Department Working Paper 317.
Feldstein, Martin. 1985. The optimal level of social security benefits, *Quarterly Journal of Economics* 100: 303–20.
Frenkel, Jacob A., and Assaf Razin. 1986. Budget deficits and rates of interest in the world economy. *Journal of Political Economy* 94: 564–94.
Rogoff, Kenneth. 1985. Can international monetary cooperation be counterproductive? *Journal of International Economics* 18: 199–217.
Samuelson, Paul A. 1975. Social security in a life-cycle growth model. *International Economic Review* 16: 539–44.

6 Fiscal Policies and International Financial Markets

Alan C. Stockman

6.1 Introduction

The development of international financial markets over the past several years (like the development of domestic markets in the United States) is proceeding at a record pace. Trade in foreign stocks has risen dramatically in the United States and other countries, as have trades in foreign corporate and government bonds; domestic corporations issue debt denominated in foreign currencies and sold on foreign markets. Trade in forward and futures markets has risen and the markets have proliferated. Futures markets on indexes of assets have been formed; options trade has skyrocketed. Finally, currency swaps (and interest rate swaps), which permit virtually any state-contingent arrangements, have become commonplace.

These developments raise many questions. What is the source of demand for these assets? Why have these markets developed now and not earlier? What new opportunities for corporations and individuals do these markets offer? This paper discusses one major issue raised by these developments: the impact of sophisticated international financial markets on the effects of government policy. Specifically, this paper concentrates on the international effects of fiscal policies. One important question the paper does *not* address is the nature of the transition from a world with less developed to one with more developed international financial markets. Instead, the paper compares two worlds: one with and one without sophisticated international asset markets.

Alan C. Stockman is associate professor of economics at the University of Rochester and a research associate of the National Bureau of Economic Research.

I have benefited by comments from Andrew Abel, Patrick Kehoe, and Jacob Frenkel. This research was supported by National Science Foundation Grant SES-8309576.

The paper employs several models to make this comparison; the conclusion that these markets affect the results does not depend on a specific model of fiscal policy.

International financial markets permit individuals to trade over time and across prospective states of the world. By borrowing or lending with their counterparts in other countries, individuals can, for example, try to eliminate fluctuations in consumption caused by seasonal or cyclical variations in domestic output. The extent of their success in this endeavor depends, in equilibrium, on the timing of similar output fluctuations in other countries. Intertemporal trade is one function of asset markets. In a world of uncertainty, they have a second function: asset markets permit individuals to hedge against unwanted risk. If domestic output is low in one state of the world and high in another, individuals can choose a portfolio of assets with a positive return in the former state and a negative return in the latter state. Future states of the world can be treated analogously to future periods of time. The extent to which domestic individuals can succeed in smoothing their consumption across states depends, in equilibrium, on the pattern of output across states in other countries.

Consider a world with two countries that are identical except for endowments. Country A receives an endowment of a perishable good X and country B receives a perishable good Y. Identical, infinite-lived, risk-adverse individuals inhabit these countries. Each has an instantaneous utility function $U(x) + U(y)$, where x and y are consumptions of goods X and Y. In a stationary equilibrium, country A exports to B half of its endowment of X and imports half of country B's endowment of Y. Now introduce a simple government policy: the government of the domestic country imposes a lump-sum tax on domestic residents and uses the proceeds to make lump-sum ("foreign aid") transfer payments to residents of the other country. The results of this policy, according to the method of comparative statics on the model's equilibrium, would be that wealth is redistributed. Domestic wealth falls and foreign wealth rises, so domestic consumption of each good falls and foreign consumption rises. Had this government policy been perfectly anticipated, the results would have been the same in the absence of international financial markets. The results would also be the same, in the absence of international financial markets, if individuals had been *uncertain* about future government policies. Because everyone in the domestic country is identical by assumption, it is impossible to sell on domestic markets the risk inherent in uncertainty about future policy.

Suppose that, in this example, there are international financial markets in noncontingent claims, that is, simple borrowing and lending are allowed. Uncertainty about future government policy in the domestic country will induce risk-averse, expected-utility-maximizing domestic individuals to self-insure by saving. Suppose the policy is imposed, randomly, in some periods and not in others. Individuals will consume less X and Y and save more in periods without the policy, that is, in periods when the government does not tax them to provide foreign aid. They will dissave in periods with the policy in order to mitigate its effects. Foreigners will consume more in periods without the policy, in anticipation of possible foreign-aid receipts in some future period, and save in periods with the foreign aid. The size of the change in consumption immediately following the imposition of the government policy is smaller in the presence of borrowing and lending because loan markets permit consumption smoothing. The magnitude of these changes in saving and consumption, and of any associated change in interest rates, depends on how expectations of future policy change over time (which in turn depends on the stochastic process governing the policy), the curvature of the utility function, and so forth. Clearly, some self-insurance possibilities are present because of international capital markets, though noncontingent claims are inferior to contingent claims for this purpose.

Complete contingent claims would eliminate the effect of the actual policy on consumption in this example. Because all individuals have the same information and agree upon the relevant probability distributions in this example, they will choose to trade in claims, prior to the realization of the policy, that "undo" the income transfer from any potential policy. Because only the domestic government may impose this policy, foreigners are wealthier than domestic residents and will consume more every period, regardless of whether the domestic government actually makes the transfers. Given the initial probabilities (at date 0) that the government will make transfers of particular sizes in various time periods, actual imposition of a transfer has no effects whatsoever. Introduction of complete international financial markets, therefore, has major implications regarding the effects of this policy.

The treatment of government policy as uncertain and exogenous deserves some comment. The assumption of exogeneity is inessential, though it corresponds to questions economists frequently ask, such as, "What would be the effects of a rise in taxes?" Government policy might well be the outcome of a political equilibrium with inputs such as lobbying, voting, and exogenous shifts in opportunities, which operate through political institutions that constrain bureaucrats, politicians, lobbyists, and voters. Generally, such a model will have elements of randomness attached to its inputs, so that resulting policies will be stochastic. Policy can then be treated as a stochastic process (that might be correlated with stochastic processes on other disturbances to the economy). Lucas (1976) and Cooley, LeRoy, and Raymon (1984a,b) have argued that the assumption of rational expectations requires the stochastic process on policy to be specified as part of the environment of constraints under which individuals maximize utility.[1] Lucas applied this argument to the investment tax credit and other policies; Cooley, LeRoy, and Raymon have applied the argument to policy on the growth rate of the money supply; Stockman and Dellas (1986) have applied it to tariffs; and Stockman and Hernandez (1987) have applied it to exchange controls. Rather than changing government policy in a way that individuals thought was impossible when they maximized utility, the economist is constrained to consider changes in policies that correspond to the probability distributions that are part of a fully specified economic environment that is known to individuals when they make their choices.[2]

Without international financial markets (and abstracting from differences across individuals within a country), the treatment of government policies as outcomes of a stochastic process has no effect on equilibrium allocations (though it may affect prices). Given the treatment of future government policy as part of the stochastic environment facing individuals when they make choices, the availability of international financial markets in state-contingent claims can have major effects on the results of policies.

When government policies are not simply redistributions, financial markets will not simply "undo" the policies. Generally, pure social gains and losses from policies will be shared among participants in financial markets. Distortions introduced by policies, however, cannot be eliminated by financial markets: the substitution effects of policies will continue to operate. In Stockman and Dellas (1986), for example, the effects of tariffs are examined in a world with complete international asset markets. In a two-country, two-good world with trade due to differing endowments, a small tariff raises consumption of the exportable good and improves welfare in the absence of financial markets. With these markets, however, a tariff reduces consumption: consumption of both goods is lower with a domestic tariff and no foreign tariff than with a foreign tariff and no domestic tariff. The existence of contingent assets, therefore, has a major impact on the positive implications of the theory. The results obtain from the ability of these assets to eliminate income effects of changes in policy (as individuals spread wealth optimally across prospective states of the world), leaving substitution effects in place. Rosen's (1985) survey of implicit contracts in labor economics makes a similar point about optimal contractual arrangements.

The following sections of this paper present these examples in which the effects of fixed policy in an open economy are altered by the existence of sophisticated international financial markets. Section 6.2 examines a change in government spending under the assumptions that this spending is productive and that nondistorting taxes are varied to maintain a balanced budget. Section 6.3 examines changes in distorting taxes holding fixed the government's budget deficit. Finally, section 6.4 examines changes in the budget deficit in an overlapping-generation model without Ricardian equivalence.

6.2   Government Spending and International Financial Markets

This section discusses the effects of increases in domestic government expenditures, financed by increases in lump-sum taxes on domestic residents, in a two-country world with complete contingent international asset markets, and contrasts the results with those in the absence of these markets.

Government spending can serve a variety of roles. The effects of fiscal policy differ depending upon the type of government expenditures analyzed. This section develops a simple illustrative model of the international effects of changes in productive government expenditure (e.g., on infrastructure). A key element of the model is that this productive expenditure does not affect all goods in the same way. The effects of a change in government spending are shown to depend on the availability of international asset markets.

Consider a two-country world in which the domestic country is endowed with a tradeable good X and the foreign country is endowed with a tradeable good Y. There is a representative, risk-averse, expected-utility-maximizing individual in each country who has instantaneous utility function $U(x) + V(y)$. Purchases or consumption of X require(s) a productive input to reduce "transactions costs" that use up real resources. They may include costs of shipping the good to its location of consumption, costs of consuming the good, or costs of household production such as preparation, and so forth. It is simplest to assume that X, besides being a consumption good, is a productive input into this "transactions" activity. X can be used privately by an individual to produce transactions services, or it can be used by the government to produce a public good that has a positive marginal product for transactions services. One might think of X as a system of roads and bridges, police and security services, courts to enforce criminal law, or other productive public goods. These public goods interact with private production of transactions services and lower private costs of a given volume of transactions. Let g be the level of government expenditure on these items (and neglect all other government spending). Individuals who wish to consume x_0 units of X must purchase $x_0\theta(g)$ units of X, where $\theta - 1 > 0$ of the goods are used for transactions services and the rest are consumed. The productivity of government expenditures motivates the conditions $\theta' < 0$ and $\theta'' > 0$.

The representative individual in the domestic country maximizes expected utility of consumption of X and Y in each state of the world z, $x(z)$, and $y(z)$, given the exogenous probability distribution $F(z)$ on states. So he maximizes

(1) $$\sum_{t=0}^{\infty} \beta^t \int U[x(z_t)] + V[y(z_t)] \, dF(z_t).$$

subject to the budget constraint,

(2) $$\sum_{t=0}^{\infty} \int p(z)\bar{X} - p(z)\theta(z)x(z) - q(z)y(z) - p(z)g \, dz_t,$$

where $\bar{X}$ is the (state-independent) endowment of good X, and $p(z_t)$ and $q(z_t)$ are domestic present-value state prices of X and Y at date t. For example, if z_{0t} is a possible value of z at date t, then $p(z_{0t})$ is the present-value (period zero) price of X in state z_0 at date t in the domestic country. The time subscripts on the functions inside the integral have been suppressed. This formulation permits complete markets within the country. In the absence of complete international financial markets, state prices may differ across countries. For simplicity, I abstract from all uncertainty except that which enters through future government policy. The state vector can be written as

(3) $$z = (g, g^*),$$

where g and g^* are the levels of government expenditure in the two countries. The public-good aspects of government spending do not extend outside national boundaries, by assumption, so θ depends only on g, and θ^* depends only on g^*; these functions will be written $\theta(g)$ and $\theta^*(g^*)$.

The representative individual in the foreign country has a similar maximization problem, though his utility function may be different and his budget constraint is different. He maximizes

(4) $$\sum_{t=0}^{\infty} \beta^t \int U^*[x^*(z_t)] + V^*[y^*(z_t)] \, dF(z_t),$$

subject to

(5) $$\sum_{t=0}^{\infty} \int q^*(z_t)\bar{Y} - p^*(z_t)\theta^*(z_t)x^*(z_t) - q^*(z_t)y^*(z_t) - p^* (z_t)g^* \, dz_t,$$

where asterisks denote foreign variables. While foreign and domestic state prices may differ in the absence of complete international financial markets, arbitrage in the goods market on a state-by-state basis guarantees that the relative price of X in terms of Y in each state is equal across countries, that is, $p(z)/q(z) = p^*(z)/q^*(z)$ for every z.

In the absence of international financial markets, equilibrium requires that in whatever state materializes, world supply and demand are equated for each good, that is,

(6) $$\bar{X} = \theta(g)x + \theta^*(g^*)x^* + g + g^*,$$

$$\bar{Y} = y + y^*.$$

In addition, equilibrium in domestic asset markets (and similarly in foreign asset markets) requires that demands and supplies of state-contingent assets are equal. Because everyone is alike within a country, there are no net trades on these domestic asset markets. However, the equilibrium conditions can be used to price assets, that is, to find the prices at which individuals are satisfied with zero net trades. If asset prices differ across countries so that for some z, $p(z) \neq p^*(z)$ or $q(z) \neq q^*(z)$, then there are private gains from trade on international asset markets.

Necessary conditions for utility maximization in each country and equilibrium conditions in the goods markets give three equations, for each date t, in domestic consumption of each good and, with the normalization $q = 1$, the relative price p. These are (with time subscripts suppressed):

(7a) $$U'(x) = p\theta V'(y),$$

(7b) $$U^{*'}[(\bar{X} - \theta x - g - g^*)/\theta^*] = p\theta^* V^{*'} (\bar{Y} - y),$$

(7c) $$p\bar{X} = p\theta x + y + pg.$$

Foreign allocations can then be determined from equilibrium conditions.

Using the last equation to eliminate the price, the system reduces to two equations in two unknowns. Comparative statics can be used to determine the effects of changes in government spending in either country. An increase in government spending may move the economy toward or away from the socially efficient level of spending. An increase in government spending in the domestic country raises domestic consumption of X by $|x\theta' dg|$ for any given gross domestic purchases of X; the cost is dg units of X. The socially optimal level of X is, therefore, implicitly given by $x\theta' = -1$. Similarly, the socially optimal level of foreign government spending is given implicitly by $x^*\theta^{*'} = -1$. The analysis of changes in government spending is simplified by consideration of changes in g or g^* around the socially optimal points.[3] The results of total differentiation[4] are then

(8a) $$dx = [1/\pi 1\pi 5 - \pi 2\pi 4)] (\pi 3\pi 5 \, dg - \pi 2\pi 6 \, dg^*),$$

(8b) $$dy = [1/(\pi 1\pi 5 - \pi 2\pi 4)] (\pi 1\pi 6 \, dg^* - \pi 3\pi 4 \, dg),$$

where

(9) $\pi 1 \equiv (\bar{X} - \theta x - g)U''(x) - \theta U(x) < 0,$

$\pi 2 \equiv -y\theta V''(y) - \theta V'(y) \gtrless 0,$

$\pi 3 \equiv y\theta' V'(y) < 0,$

$\pi 4 \equiv -\theta(\bar{X} - \theta x - g)U^{*\prime\prime}(x^*)/\theta^* - \theta U^{*\prime}(x^*) \gtrless 0,$

$\pi 5 \equiv y\theta^* V^{*\prime\prime}(y^*) - \theta^* V^{*\prime}(y^*) < 0,$

$\pi 6 \equiv y\theta^{*\prime} V^{*\prime}(y^*) < 0.$

The sign of $\pi 2$ depends on the elasticity of the domestic marginal utility of consumption of imports. If $r_y \equiv -yV''/V' = 1$, then $\pi 2 = 0$. In that case, a rise in domestic government expenditures unambiguously increases domestic consumption of exportables and reduces the foreign consumption of that good. Even with a separable utility function $(U + V)$, the increase in domestic government spending may affect domestic imports. For example, if r_y and $r_x^* \equiv -x^* U^{*\prime\prime}/U^{*\prime}$ are both equal to one, then $\pi 2 = 0$ but $\pi 4 > 0$, so a rise in domestic government spending increases domestic imports as well as consumption of exportables. For small enough r_x^*, imports will fall with an increase in government spending. A rise in foreign government spending leaves domestic consumption of exportables unchanged if $r_y = 1$, and increases or decreases x as r_y is greater than or less than 1. If r_y is close to 1, then an increase in foreign government spending unambiguously raises domestic imports. The effects of changes in government spending frequently depend on the curvature of the utility functions, even when the utility functions are separable. As I will show below, these ambiguities in the theory are removed once complete international financial markets are introduced.

With complete international financial markets, state prices are equated across countries and equilibrium conditions for assets help determine allocations in goods markets as well as asset prices. World supply of each good in each state (and time) must equal demand, so the previously stated equilibrium conditions must hold for each z (and t). The equilibrium conditions, together with the necessary conditions for utility maximization, imply that, for every z,

(10) $V^{*\prime}[\bar{Y} - y(z)] = \phi V'[y(z)],$

(11) $U^{*\prime}\{[\bar{X} - x(z)\theta(g) - g - g^*]/\theta^*(g^*)\}$

$= \phi U'[x(z)]\, \theta^*(g^*)/\theta(g),$

where ϕ is the ratio of the marginal utility of wealth of the representative foreign individual to the marginal utility of wealth of the representative domestic individual, i.e., the multiplier on equation (5) divided by the multiplier on equation (2).[5] Note that ϕ is a function of the probability distribution $F(z)$, but it does not depend on realized values of g or g^*. Equations (10) and (11) imply that, with complete international asset markets, consumption of y is independent of realizations of z. An econometrician examining time-series or cross-sectional data would see no response of y to observed changes in z. This contrasts with the ambiguous conclusions in the absence of any international asset markets.

To determine the relation between increases in government spending and allocations, the second equation can be totally differentiated (with ϕ held fixed). Letting $\gamma(z) = 1 + x(g)\theta'(g)$ and $\gamma^*(z) = 1 + x^*(z)\theta^{*\prime}(g^*)$, the result is:

$$(12) \quad (-U''\theta/\theta^* - U''\phi\theta^*\theta)\,dx(z) = (-\theta'U'\theta^*\,\phi/\theta^2 + \gamma U^{*\prime\prime}/\theta^*)dg$$
$$+ (U'\theta^{*\prime}\phi/\theta + \gamma^* U^{*\prime\prime}/\theta^*)\,dg^*.$$

The coefficient on $dx(z)$ is positive. At the socially optimal g and g^*, $\gamma = \gamma^* = 0$. In that case, small changes in g or g^* have no first-order effects on economic efficiency, the coefficient on dg is positive, and the coefficient on dg^* is negative. An increase in domestic government spending raises domestic consumption of exportables, while an increase in foreign government spending reduces it. Because these results are obtained in the neighborhood of the social optimum, changes in g and g^* have no income effects. Therefore, an increase in domestic government spending reduces foreign imports, while an increase in foreign government spending raises them.[6] These results on the effects of changes in productive government expenditure in the presence of sophisticated international financial markets contrast with the ambiguous effects obtained in their absence.

6.3. Distorting Taxes

Section 6.2 assumed that taxes were lump sum. This section examines the effects of changes in distorting taxes with and without sophisticated international financial markets. As in section 6.2, the results illustrate that any effects of policy that operate through redistribution of wealth are eliminated by complete international financial markets. This section applies that principle to a tax on consumption. The tax might take the form of value-added tax or an income tax with various effective deductions or credits for saving. This section uses a two-country model similar to the one in section 6.2, but simplified to include only two time periods (the extension to more is straightforward) and a single consumption good that is endowed to both countries. When the timing of endowments differs across countries, there is an obvious role for financial markets: borrowing and lending will facilitate intertemporal smoothing of consumption. Suppose that in the first period the home endowment is small and the foreign endowment is large and that this is reversed in the second period. Then the home country will borrow from the foreign country in the first period and repay its loans in the second period.

This section will examine the effects of a temporary increase in domestic consumption taxes in the first period under several assumptions about accompanying changes required by the government's budget constraint. In the absence of international financial markets other than those for simple, noncontingent loans, a tax increase has a substitution effect and an income effect. Starting from a situation of equal taxation in the two periods, a rise in first-period domestic taxes, with a lump-sum refund of the tax revenue, reduces the domestic demand for loans and lowers the interest rate at which the domestic country borrows. A small increase in taxes reduces first-period consumption and raises second-period consumption. These results are changed in the presence of complete international financial markets.

Assume the representative individual in the domestic country maximizes

$$(13) \qquad E[U(c,\ 1\ -\ L)\ +\ \beta U(c',1\ -\ L')],$$

where c and L are consumption and leisure, one unit of time is available each period, and primes denote second-period variables. For simplicity, it will be assumed that $U_{12} = 0$ (which does not affect the main results but reduces the algebra involved). Output, y, is a stochastic function of labor inputs: $y = \alpha L$, where α is a positive random variable. Similarly, second-period output is $y' = \alpha' L'$. The government taxes consumption at a rate τ. Define $T \equiv 1 + \tau$. Denote the present value of the state price of goods in state z by $p(z)$. Initially, assume that changes in government spending accompany changes in taxes and that such spending is neutral (it is useless or it affects utility in a separable way). Changes in g and tax revenue are equal. Then the budget constraint facing the representative domestic individual is:

$$(14) \qquad \int \alpha L\ -\ Tc\ +\ p(\alpha' L'\ -\ T'c')\ dz\ =\ 0,$$

where

$$(15) \qquad z \equiv (\alpha, \alpha^*, T, T^*, \alpha', \alpha^{*\prime}, T', T^{*\prime})$$

indexes states of the world, with asterisks denoting foreign variables. Implicitly, c, L, c', L', and p are functions of z.

The foreign country has an analogous description that will not be repeated here. In the absence of state-contingent international assets, but with noncontingent international loan markets, the budget constraint can be simplified, reflecting the zero net trades on internal asset markets due to the representative agent assumption. The budget constraint with only noncontingent international loans is effectively

(16) $$\alpha L - Tc + p(\alpha'L' - T'c') = 0,$$

where $p \equiv R^{-1}$ is the inverse of 1 plus the interest rate on default-free loans.

Equilibrium conditions are:

(17a) $$\alpha L + \alpha^* L^* = c + c^* + g + g^*,$$

(17b) $$\alpha'L' + \alpha^{*'}L^{*'} = c' + c^{*'} + g' + g^{*'}.$$

Together with the necessary conditions for utility maximization by individuals in each country who choose consumption and leisure in each period, this generates a set of equations with a solution that depends on the concavity of utility and the relative sizes of various exogenous terms. The main elements of the solution for this case (with only noncontingent international loans) can be illustrated by assuming that labor supplies are fixed at unity, so countries receive stochastic endowments, α and α^*. Then the model reduces to two equations in c and R:

(18) $$U_1(c) = TR\beta E(U_1\{[\alpha' + R(\alpha - Tc)]/T'\}/T'),$$

(19) $$U^*_1(\alpha + \alpha^* - g - g^* - c)$$
$$= T^*R\beta E(U^*_1\{[\alpha^{*'} - R(\alpha - Tc)]/T^{*'}\}/T^{*'}).$$

Equation (18) follows from maximization of equation (13) subject to equation (16), and equation (19) follows from the analogous foreign maximization problem along with equation (17) and the balanced-budget assumption. Recall that government spending varies with tax revenue: $dg = cdT + (T - 1)dc$.

Consider a realization of α and α' for which $c + g < \alpha$ in equilibrium. This would happen if, for example, the countries are identical *ex ante*, if (α, α^*) and $(\alpha', \alpha^{*'})$ are independently drawn, $g = g^*$, and the realized value of α^* exceeds that of α. Then the domestic country is a net borrower in the first period. Differentiation of equations (18)–(19) shows that (as long as $c - \alpha$ is not too large) an increase in first-period domestic taxes reduces private consumption but has an indeterminate effect on aggregate demand and the interest rate because of the increase in government purchases. Second-period consumption,

(20) $$c' = [\alpha' + R(\alpha - Tc)]/T',$$

is also indeterminate. It depends on the direction of the interest rate change and the magnitudes of the substitution and wealth effects.

The effects of a consumption tax are changed when individuals have access to complete international financial markets. Then the equilibrium conditions (17) must hold on a state-by-state basis. These conditions, and the necessary conditions for utility maximization in each country, imply

(21) $U^*_1[\alpha L(z) + \alpha^* L^*(z) - g - g^* - c(z)]$

        $= \phi U_1[c(z)] \, T^*/T,$

(22) $U_1[c(z)]/U_2[1 - L(z)] = T/\alpha,$

(23) $U^*_1[\alpha L(z) + \alpha^* L^*(z) - g - g^* - c(z)]/$

        $U_2^*[1 - L^*(z)] = T^*/\alpha^*,$

and

(24) $\pi(z)U_1[c(z)]/p(z)T$ = arbitrary constant

for all z. In these equations, ϕ is the ratio of the foreign marginal utility of wealth to the domestic marginal utility of wealth (a ratio of multipliers on the wealth constraints), and the constant in equation (24) is arbitrary because one of the state prices can be normalized without loss of generality. The first three sets of equations (for each z), (21)–(23), determine production, trade, and consumption, and equation (24) then determines state prices. Another set of equations, identical in form to these, describes the solution for equilibrium in the second period.

Total differentiation of equations (21)–(24) yields the effects of a high realization of domestic taxes in the first period, compared to another state with a lower realization of domestic taxes. This comparison, across alternative realizations of taxes, requires that ϕ be held fixed, because ϕ is a function only of the probability distributions and other parameters of the model, not of subsequent realizations of random variables. Note that if L and L^* are fixed, so that the model is one with endowments, then equation (21) alone, along with the government budget constraint, determines the effect of a change in taxes on consumption. In that case, an increase in T lowers domestic consumption and may raise or lower foreign consumption depending on the magnitude of the substitution effect in the domestic country from the tax. The change in T, however, leaves second-period consumption *unaffected* in each country. This result contrasts with the implication of the model without state-contingent international asset markets.

With endogenous production, domestic and foreign output move in the same direction, regardless of whether output rises because of the increased demand by the government or falls because of the reduced demand by domestic individuals.[7] (This result is, however, sensitive to the assumption that utility is separable in goods and leisure.) Unlike the case in which international financial markets are limited to non-contingent bonds, a change in taxes and government spending in the first period leaves output in each country unaffected in the second period.

The assumption that government spending has no effect on marginal utilities of other goods is extreme. Kormendi (1983) and Aschauer

(1985) have estimated that roughly one-third of government consumption can be treated as if it were private consumption. It is straightforward to examine the implications of the model of government spending is a direct substitute for private spending. Consider the extreme case in which instantaneous utility depends on leisure and on $c + g$, the sum of private and government consumption. As long as g is below the level of consumption that would be chosen privately, this is equivalent to a lump-sum transfer to the public of the revenue obtained from the consumption tax. (Individuals effectively obtain this transfer by reducing private expenditure on the good as government expenditure rises.) Assume also that the countries are identical *ex ante*. In this case, an increase in first-period domestic taxes unambiguously reduces output in each country, reduces domestic consumption, and raises foreign consumption.[8] Intuitively, complete international capital markets eliminate the direct income effects of the policy but leave the substitution effect. Higher consumption taxes reduce domestic demand in the first period. If world output were unchanged, as in the endowment model, then consumption in the foreign country would unambiguously rise. Foreign individuals attempt to spread this gain to current leisure as well as to future consumption and leisure. Asset trades have previously guaranteed that any increase in consumption of goods or leisure, not due to a substitution effect, will be shared by foreign and domestic individuals. The net results are an increase in foreign consumption and decreases in output in each country associated with the fall in domestic consumption. In this case, an increase in government spending and taxes has a contractionary effect on output in each country, a contractionary effect on domestic consumption, and an expansionary effect on foreign consumption.

6.4   Budget Deficits without Debt Neutrality

In this section I build upon the work by Frenkel and Razin (1986) on the international transmission of budget deficits. Frenkel and Razin apply Blanchard's (1985) model of uncertain lifetimes to analyze the international implications of fiscal policies, and they demonstrate that, in the absence of Ricardian equivalence, government budget deficits may increase domestic aggregate demand but can be transmitted *negatively* to the rest of the world, decreasing foreign aggregate demand. This section takes the Frenkel-Razin model as a point of departure and introduces complete international financial markets, subject to the natural limitation that the unborn cannot trade in these markets. The results indicate that in the presence of these asset markets, the effects of deficits on the current account and other variables is very different than in their absence.

I follow the setup of Frenkel and Razin. There are two countries with representative individual consumers (in equal numbers) and two governments. A single good is endowed to these two countries, and the endowments follow an exogenous stochastic process. The description of the two countries is identical: each country is essentially described by Blanchard's model. Foreign variables are denoted with an asterisk. Individuals face a fixed probability of death in each period, regardless of age, denoted $(1 - \sigma)$, where σ is the survival probability. They contract with life insurance companies that collect an individual's assets and liabilities upon his death. Yaari (1965) discusses the equivalence between these companies and a set of annuity and bond markets. A transversality condition requires that the limit (as the length of life goes to infinity) of the present value of net assets is nonnegative, so an individual does not borrow an unrestricted amount in the expectation that the life insurance company will bail him out when he dies. Insurance companies are perfectly competitive and operate costlessly so that insurance premiums are proportional factors equal to the probability of death. Under these assumptions, and with α_t denoting the present value price of a good at date t, α_{t-1}/α_t is 1 plus the one-period interest rate at $t - 1$; σ^{t-1}/σ^t is 1 plus the life insurance premium at $t - 1$; and the gross interest rate (including the insurance premium) faced by an individual is $(\alpha_{t-1}\sigma^{t-1}/\alpha_t\sigma^t)^{-1}$. The discount factor is fixed at δ, and utility is time separable and instantaneously logarithmic; individuals maximize expected utility. Following Blanchard (1985), aggregate consumption is then

$$(25) \qquad C_t = (1 - \sigma\delta) \, W_t,$$

where W_t is aggregate wealth, which equals discounted disposable personal income (discounted with the gross interest rate) minus private debt. In general, in the Frenkel-Razin analysis, the probabilities of death, discount rates, and so forth may differ across countries. It will be convenient here, though, to focus on the simplest case in which all these parameters are equal across countries.

Governments in each country finance an exogenous stochastic process of spending, which has no effect on production or any marginal rates of substitution or marginal utilities, with either taxes or debt. The government, which lives forever, discounts at a rate that does not incorporate an insurance premium. The present value of spending plus initial government debt equals the present value of taxes.

The equilibrium condition in the world goods market at $t = 0$ is

$$(26) \quad (1 - \alpha\sigma) \, W_0 + (1 - \alpha^*\sigma^*) \, W_0^* + g_0 + g_0^* = y_0 + y_0^*.$$

Domestic and foreign wealth at date zero are, in the Frenkel-Razin model,

(27) $W_0 = y_0 - \tau_0 + PV_0 (y - \tau) + B_{g0} - B_0,$

(28) $W_0 = y_0^* - \tau_0^* + PV_0(y^* - \tau^*) + B_{g0}^* + B_0,$

where $PV_0 (x)$ denotes the present value at date 0 of subsequent values of x, using the gross private discount factor, B_g is government debt at date 0 (so that future tax liabilities and government debt are both included in wealth), and B_0 is net indebtedness at $t = 0$ of the domestic consumers to foreign consumers. To keep matters as simple as possible, assume that this initial private indebtedness is zero, that government debt is equal in each country, that current government spending is equal in each country, and that the probability distribution of future government spending is the same in the two countries.

Following Frenkel and Razin, dates after $t = 0$ are assumed to have, with probability 1, some constant levels of government spending, taxes, and outputs (which, while they are constant for $t = 1, 2, 3, \ldots$, may differ from the values at $t = 0$). Then the present value function is $PV_0(x) = x_1 \sigma R/(1 - \sigma R)$, where x is the future $(t = 1, 2, \ldots)$ value of x and R is an average present-value price. Equations (26)–(28) then determine R and wealth in each country for given values in each country of government spending, initial government debt, taxes, output, and initial private indebtedness.

Now consider a tax cut financed by increased government borrowing in the domestic country at $t = 0$. Assume that the foreign government has a balanced budget and that the domestic government budget was balanced prior to the tax cut. The government budget constraint implies that $d\tau_0 + Rd\tau_1/(1 - R) = 0$, because taxes are raised in all future periods (equally) to offset the current tax cut. Using this fact, differentiation of equations (26)–(28) implies that the tax cut reduces R, that is, raises the interest rate, raises domestic wealth, and lowers foreign wealth (see Frenkel and Razin 1986).

Consider now an extension of this analysis to incorporate complete international financial markets. The results above apply to a world in which individuals can trade on annuity markets with other residents of the same country (recall that the "insurance companies" are essentially annuity and bond markets), but they are unable to trade in contingent *international* financial markets.[9] In particular, suppose that it is possible to trade assets whose returns are contingent on the level of domestic taxes, and other assets whose returns are contingent on foreign taxes. Then the risk of tax changes in either country can be shared internationally. Generations who are not yet born are unable to trade on these markets. In the absence of state-contingent international financial markets, domestic wealth (of currently living individuals) rises and foreign wealth falls from a cut in domestic taxes, while the reverse results from a cut in foreign taxes. In either case, the wealth of the unborn in the country with the tax cut also falls. Starting from this situation, domestic and foreign individuals can agree on mutually beneficial exchanges in which domestic individuals make payments if there is a cut in domestic taxes and receive payments if there is a cut in foreign taxes. For simplicity, assume that the probability distributions of future taxes are identical in the two countries. Because it is also assumed that tastes, horizons, government spending, and wealth are the same in the two countries, this makes the two countries symmetric *ex ante,* and these payments will equal exactly half of the tax cuts. Similarly, individuals in each country gain expected utility from sharing the risk of the subsequent tax increases associated with a current tax cut. With the symmetry assumptions, all individuals, regardless of nationality, will share in the higher future domestic taxes associated with a tax cut; this occurs through liabilities that will be exchanged prior to the realization of policy. Domestic and foreign individuals can share the risks by exchanging obligations so that half of any tax cut (or increase) gets paid to (by) individuals in the other country (who, like domestic individuals, are liable for taxes for each year they are alive, but only those years).

Given these financial trades that result in asset market equilibrium, a tax cut in either country increases wealth of currently living individuals in both countries. Their wealth can be expressed as

$$(29) \quad W_0 = W_0^* = y_0 - (\tau_0 + \tau_0^*)/2 + PV_0[y - (\tau + \tau^*)/2] + B_{g0},$$

where $y = y^*$ in each period and $B_{g0} = B_{g0}^*$. All individuals currently alive gain equally from a domestic tax cut. With the symmetry assumptions, the tax cut has no effect on the current account, though the interest rate rises due to the increase in aggregate demand. The rise in the interest rate reduces the quantity demanded to the level of the fixed supply of goods and, in equilibrium, the current consumption of each individual is unaffected.

The currently unborn in the domestic country suffer a fall in wealth from a domestic tax cut at date zero. The loss cannot be shared with the currently unborn in the foreign country because none can participate in financial markets. The increased debt sold by the domestic government at date zero, when it cut taxes, was purchased in equal amounts by both foreign and domestic individuals. Therefore, the increased domestic government debt is distributed throughout the world. As currently living individuals age and die, they sell debt to new generations. As older individuals sell debt to younger ones, the life-cycle path of consumption is tilted: the young consume less and the old consume more. This tilting is permanent and raises the real interest rate. The higher real interest rate, in turn, lowers the present value of future labor income and tends to reduce wealth. On the other hand, the additional government debt enters positively into wealth. Domestic individuals who were born after the tax cut differ from foreign individuals born after the tax cut in one respect: the former must pay the higher domestic taxes. Consequently, whether foreign wealth rises or falls in the new steady state, domestic wealth is smaller than foreign wealth. Essentially, world wealth includes government bonds but does not include the full present value of the taxes associated with those bonds. This, alone, raises world wealth. But although the bonds are held by foreign as well as domestic individuals, only the latter pay the higher taxes in the future. Therefore, at the original interest rate, foreign wealth rises and domestic wealth may rise or fall. The tilting of consumption as the additional debt is passed across generations raises the interest rate and lowers the present value of any given income stream, so the higher interest rate reduces wealth in each country. Combining these two effects, a domestic tax cut has an indeterminate effect on steady-state wealth in each country, though foreign wealth rises by more (or falls by less) than domestic wealth.

The international impact of a domestic tax cut in the short run and during the transition to a new steady state is markedly different in the presence of complete international financial markets, though the steady-state effects are not altered in kind. Although this example has assumed complete markets, one may expect that similar results apply to a world in which asset markets are more limited but still offer some opportunities for state-contingent trade. The presence of money and nominal bonds, for example, would introduce an asset with a state-contingent real return.

6.5 Conclusions

This paper has presented examples of changes in the international effects of fiscal policies that can result from the existence of sophisticated international financial markets. The examples have assumed complete markets. In many historical circumstances, it would be unrealistic to assume that these markets were available to individuals either directly or indirectly through multinational corporations or financial intermediaries. However, the rapid development of these markets makes it useful to examine their effects. The proper model for any empirical application would depend upon whether those markets are available in that time period or set of countries. The complete markets framework is a useful benchmark case. While the assumption of complete markets is unrealistic, so is the more common assumption that there are no markets for contingent claims. For many purposes, it is not clear that economists should have much confidence in the implications of theoretical models, or interpretations of economic statistics, that ignore these markets.

International financial markets remove some of the ambiguities associated with opposing income and substitution effects, lead to models with stronger predictions, and in some cases reverse the effects of policies. These markets also tend to eliminate intrinsic dynamics that would otherwise occur through asset accumulation. (Dynamics could still be extrinsic or occur through other channels.) This is probably desirable, given that variations in real exchange rates exhibit very little dynamics and, instead, seem to be associated with "news."

The examples in this paper have treated policy as exogenous. A model that explains why particular economic policies are chosen by the political process could be incorporated into the examples. Because gainers and losers from economic policies are affected by financial markets, the model of policy formulation will also be affected.

There are many other fiscal policies, besides those examined above, whose effects would be altered by the ability of households to trade in financial markets. Personal and corporate income taxes, with provisions for miscellaneous deductions, credits, and exclusions, may have very different effects in the presence of financial markets than without them. The effects of increased uncertainty about future taxes—overall levels, the cross-sectional distribution of taxes, and the timing of taxation—will be affected by the ability of individuals to use financial markets to hedge this risk. The issue of changes in uncertainty raises an important question: Which variations in government policy can be hedged by financial markets and which cannot? With rational expectations and complete markets, individuals could hedge against *all* changes in future policies—including changes in "policy regimes." Which, if any, changes in policy (or "rules" or "regimes") are individuals *un*able to insure against? For example, could a decision maker in government choose to make policy decisions diverge systematically from the probability distribution governing these policies that is implicit in financial markets? Or would these implicit probability distributions always incorporate the possibility that the decision maker would attempt to make decisions in this way? These are not academic, metaphysical issues, but substantive questions that are directly related to the effects of fiscal (and other) policies in the presence of contingent international financial markets.

Notes

1. I do not want to take a stand on whether Cooley, LeRoy, and Raymon are expanding on Lucas's point or are, as they believe, in disagreement with some of what Lucas says.

2. This does not imply that individuals have perfect knowledge of all parameters in the model. It does imply, though, that individuals "know that they don't know" certain things.

3. Given foreign consumption of X and foreign government spending, domestic consumption is maximized by g such that $x\theta' = $ minus 1. Andrew Abel has correctly pointed out in his comments to this paper that while the world social optimum is characterized by $x\theta' = x^*\theta^{*'} = $ minus 1, this may not be the optimum for either country individually. Changes in g or g^* around some other value that might describe the equilibrium of a policy game between the two countries involve additional ambiguities in the results. The additional terms reflect changes in the distortion caused by not having government spending at the optimal level for the world.

4. Substitution of equation (7c) into equations (7a) and (7b) gives:

$$(\bar{X} - \theta x - g) \, U'\,(x) = \theta V'\,(y)y,$$

$$(\bar{X} - \theta x - g) \, U^{*'} \, [(\bar{X} - \theta x - g - g^*)/\theta^*]$$
$$= y \, \theta^* V^{*'}(\bar{Y} - y).$$

Recall that $\theta = \theta(g)$ and $\theta^* = \theta^*(g^*)$. Total differentiation gives:

$$\begin{bmatrix} \bar{X} - \theta x - g)U'' - \theta U' & - \theta(yV'' + V') \\ (\bar{X} - \theta x - g)\dfrac{\theta}{\theta^*} V^{*''} - \theta U^* & -\theta^*(V^{*'} - yV^{*''}) \end{bmatrix} \begin{bmatrix} dx \\ dy \end{bmatrix}$$

$$= \begin{bmatrix} \theta'yV' + (x\theta' + 1)V' \\ (x\theta' + 1)V^{*'} + (\bar{X} - \theta x - g)\dfrac{x\theta' + 1}{\theta^*} V^{*''} \end{bmatrix}$$

$$\begin{bmatrix} 0 \\ y\theta^* V^{*'} + \dfrac{V^{*''}}{\theta^*} (\bar{X} - \theta x - g)(1 + \theta^{*'}x^*) \end{bmatrix} \begin{bmatrix} dg \\ dg^* \end{bmatrix},$$

which reduces to equations (8) and (9) if $x\theta' = X^*\theta^{*'} = 1$.

5. Letting λ and λ^* be the domestic and foreign marginal utilities of wealth, necessary conditions for maximization of equation (1) subject to equation (2) include, for every z and t,

$$\beta^* U'[x(z)] = \lambda \, p(z) \, \theta(g),$$
$$\beta^* V'[y(z)] = \lambda \, q(z).$$

Similarly, the foreign maximization problem yields necessary conditions

$$\beta^* U^{*'}[x^*(z)] = \lambda^* \, p^*(z) \, \theta^*(g^*),$$
$$\beta^* V^{*'}[y^*(z)] = \lambda^* \, q^*(z).$$

Dividing these equations, noting that state prices are equated internationally so $p(z) = p^*(z)$ and $q(z) = q^*(z)$, and using equilibrium conditions to eliminate $x^*(z)$ and $y^*(z)$, yields equations (10) and (11), where $\phi \equiv \lambda^*/\lambda$.

6. If $\gamma \neq 0$ then the coefficient on dg includes an additional term. This term is negative if $\gamma > 0$, reflecting an inefficiently large g, or positive if $\gamma < 0$, reflecting a suboptimal g. A change in g away from the social optimum increases the magnitude of the inefficiency and lowers consumption of X in both countries. Similarly, a change in g toward the optimum reduces the inefficiency and raises consumption of X in both countries. This is evident from the fact that

the coefficients on dg and dg^* in equation (12) have terms involving γ or γ^* with signs opposite to those of γ and γ^*. These results illustrate that any income effects from efficiency gains or losses are shared internationally.

7. This result follows directly from equations (21)–(23), which imply that

$$\phi U_2(1 - L)/\alpha = U_2^*(1 - L^*)/\alpha^*.$$

Given α and α^* (and ϕ), L and L^* move together.

8. Modifying the model so that utility depends on $c + g$, necessary conditions for utility maximization, equilibrium conditions, and government budget constraints $g = (T - 1)c$ and $g^* = (T^* - 1)c^*$ imply, in the case with (*ex ante*) identical countries.

$$\alpha U_{11}(Tdc + cdT) = -TU_{22}dL + U_2dT,$$
$$\alpha U_{11}(Tdc^* + cdT^*) = -TU_{22}dL^* + U_2dT^*,$$
$$\alpha(dL + dL^*) = T(dc + dc^*) + c(dT + dT^*),$$
$$T^*U_{11}(Tdc + cdT) + U_1dT^* = TU_{11}(Tdc^* + cdT^*) + U_1dT.$$

Using the first two equations to eliminate dc and dc^* and solving for dL and dL^* gives

$$\frac{dL}{dT} = \frac{dL^*}{dT} = \frac{U_2}{2\alpha^2 U_{11} + 2TU_{22}} < 0,$$

$$\frac{dc}{dT} = \left[\frac{U_2}{\alpha TU_{11}}\right]\left[\frac{2\alpha^2 U_{11} + TU_{22}}{2\alpha^2 U_{11} + 2TU_{22}}\right] - \frac{c}{T} < 0,$$

$$\frac{dc^*}{dT} = \left[\frac{-U_2}{\alpha U_{11}}\right]\frac{U_{22}}{2\alpha^2 U_{11} + 2TU_{22}} > 0.$$

9. An alternative story consistent with the previous analysis is that individuals do not have rational expectations about possible changes in policy, instead attributing zero probability to a tax cut.

References

Aschauer, David. 1985. Fiscal policy and aggregate demand. *American Economic Review,* 75 no. 1 (March): 117–27.

Blanchard, Olivier. 1985. Debt, deficits, and finite horizons. *Journal of Political Economy* 93, no. 21 (April): 223–51.

Cooley, Thomas F., Stephen Leroy, and Neil Raymon. 1984a. Econometric policy evaluation: Note. *American Economic Review,* 74 no. 3:467–70.

———. 1984b. Modeling policy interventions. University of California, Santa Barbara. Mimeo.

Frenkel, Jacob A., and Assaf Razin. 1986. Fiscal policies in the world economy. *Journal of Political Economy* 94, no. 3 (June). 564–94.

Kormendi, Roger. 1983. Government debt, government spending, and private sector behavior. *American Economic Review,* 73, no. 5 (December): 994–1010.

Lucas, Robert E. 1976. Econometric policy evaluation: A critique. In *The Phillips curve and labor markets,* ed. K. Brunner and A. H. Meltzer. Carnegie-Rochester Conference Series on Public Policy, a supplement to the *Journal of Monetary Economics,* vol. 1: 19–46.

Rosen, Sherwin. 1985. Implicit contracts: A survey. *Journal of Economic Literature,* (September): 1144–76.

Stockman, Alan C., and Harris Dellas. 1986. Asset markets, tariffs, and political risk. *Journal of International Economics* 21, no. 3–4 (November): 199–214.

Stockman, Alan C., and Alejandro Hernandez D. 1987. Exchange controls, capital controls, and international financial markets. *American Economic Review* (forthcoming).

Yaari, Menahem E., 1965, Uncertain lifetime, life insurance, and the theory of the consumer. *Review of Economic Studies* 32 (April): 137–50.

Comment   Andrew B. Abel

Alan Stockman's paper presents a few simple models to illustrate the important insight that the effects of fiscal policy depend very much on the nature of international financial markets. This general and powerful insight has a long tradition in the international economics literature based on the Mundell-Fleming model and the scores of papers which have extended and refined the original analysis of fiscal policy under fixed and flexible exchange rates. Stockman's paper differs from this tradition both in its mode of analysis and in the economic phenomena on which it focuses. Stockman analyzes the aggregate effects of tax policy in a rational expectations model with maximizing consumers and flexible prices. Rather than focusing on the implications of alternative exchange rate regimes, he focuses on the implications of the degree to which tax liability risk can be diversified internationally.

Fiscal Policy in the Absence of International Insurance

Stockman presents three models in his paper to demonstrate that his general conclusions are robust with respect to various changes in the model. My discussion will focus only on the first of the three models. Furthermore, to make the discussion simple, I will analyze a very special case of this model. Since the intertemporal aspects of the model do not drive the results, I will dispense with them and analyze a one-period world economy. The representative domestic consumer has the utility function

$$(1) \qquad\qquad \ln x(z) + \ln y(z),$$

where $x(z)$ is the domestic consumption of the domestic endowment good (say good X) in state z and $y(z)$ is the domestic consumption of the foreign endowment good (say good Y) in state z. In order to consume

Andrew B. Abel is Amoco Foundation Term Professor of Finance at the Wharton School, University of Pennsylvania, and a research associate of the National Bureau of Economic Research.

one unit of good X, a domestic consumer must purchase θ units of good X; a foreign consumer must purchase θ^* units of good X to consume one unit of this good.

The domestic government purchases $g \geq 0$ units of good X, and the foreign government purchases $g^* \geq 0$ units of good X. Each government finances its purchases by lump-sum taxes on its own residents. Government purchases are useful in allowing consumers to transform expenditure on good X into consumption of good X. In particular, $\theta = \theta(g)$, $\theta' < 0$, $\theta'' > 0$, and $\theta^* = \theta^*(g^*)$, $\theta^{*'} < 0$, $\theta^{*''} > 0$. Stockman's major conclusion continues to hold if θ and θ^* are invariant to g and g^*, respectively, but I retain his assumption that government spending is useful in order to comment on Stockman's presentation of the socially optimal fiscal policy.

Let $p(z)$ be the domestic country's terms of trade in state z. More precisely, $p(z)$ is the price of good X in terms of good Y. Finally, let $\bar{X}$ and $\bar{Y}$ be the endowments of the representative domestic and foreign consumers, respectively.

The assumption of logarithmic utility implies that domestic consumers will allocate their disposable income $p(z)(\bar{X} - g)$ to equate the expenditure on good X, $p(z)\theta(g)x(z)$, to the expenditure on good Y, $y(z)$. Therefore,

(2) $$x(z) = (\bar{X} - g)/(2\theta),$$

(3) $$y(z) = p(z)\theta(g)x(z).$$

Since the residents of each country equate the expenditure on good X and the expenditure on good Y, it must be the case that worldwide private expenditure on X, $p(z)(\bar{X} - g - g^*)$ is equal to worldwide private expenditure on Y, $\bar{Y}$. Therefore, we obtain

(4) $$p(z) = \bar{Y}/(\bar{X} - g - g^*).$$

Substituting equation (4) into equation (3), and the resulting equation into equation (2), yields

(5) $$y(z) = (\bar{Y}/2)[1 + g^*/(\bar{X} - g - g^*)].$$

Now consider an increase in g. Domestic (real) private expenditure on good X, θx, falls in response to the increase in g. In addition, the terms of trade improves ($p(z)$ increases), and, if $g^* > 0$, domestic consumption of good Y increases.

Fiscal Policy in the Presence of International Insurance

Now we consider a world economy with well-developed international financial markets. In this one-period world, there is no scope for international borrowing or lending. The only scope for international financial transactions is the international diversification of fiscal policy risk. A representative domestic consumer will choose state-contingent consumptions $x(z)$ and $y(z)$ to maximize expected utility. The associated Lagrangian is:

(6) $L = E\{\ln x(z) + \ln y(z) - \mu\,[p(z)\theta(g)x(z)$
$$+ y(z) - p(z)(\bar{X} - g)]\}.$$

The first-order conditions can be written as

(7) $$p(z)\theta(g)x(z) = \mu^{-1} = y(z).$$

Recalling the budget constraint $E\{p(z)\theta(g)x(z) + y(z)\} = E\{p(z)(\bar{X} - g)\}$, we can use equation (7) to obtain

(8) $$\mu^{-1} = E\{p(z)(\bar{X} - g)\}/2.$$

The terms of trade are the same as in equation (4) so that using equations (4), (7), and (8) we obtain

(9) $$x(z) = E\{1 + g^*/(\bar{X} - g - g^*)\}\,(\bar{X} - g - g^*)/2\theta,$$

(10) $$y(z) = E\{1 + g^*/(\bar{X} - g - g^*)\}\,\bar{Y}/2.$$

Now consider a large realization of g. As in the absence of international financial markets, real private domestic expenditure on good X, θx, is reduced by an increase in g. However, contrary to the result in the absence of international financial markets, the domestic consumption of good Y is invariant to the realization of g. This example illustrates Stockman's main point. More generally, Stockman's result may be described as follows: International financial markets permit risk sharing of country-specific risks. If (a) the marginal utility of good Y is independent of the consumption of good X, (b) fiscal policy does not drive a wedge between the domestic and foreign prices of good Y, and (c) fiscal policy does not affect the supply of good Y available to the worldwide private sector, then optimal risk sharing implies that domestic and foreign consumption of good Y are each invariant to the realization of fiscal policy.

Regime Changes

Although the fundamental logic of Stockman's result is sound, one might argue with his interpretation of fiscal policy. In Stockman's model, the observed time series of fiscal policy is a sequence of realizations of an exogenous stochastic process. In this view the "policymaker" is extremely ineffectual. Even if we were to untie the policymaker's hands and let him choose the realization of g, his freedom of choice is still limited in the long run. If we are to plausibly maintain the assumption of rational expectations, then the frequency distribution of his choices for g must match the *ex ante* distribution specified in the consumer's maximization problem.

An alternative analysis of fiscal policy using Stockman's model would begin by defining a regime as a stochastic process for g and g^*. A policy regime change would be a change in the stochastic process governing g and g^*. Of course, this merely shifts the problem back one step in a way that I will elaborate below. First, however, I will briefly discuss the effects of a regime change. A change in the stochastic process for g and g^* changes the marginal utility of income. The effects on domestic consumption would appear in equations (9) and (10) by changing $E\{1 + g^*/(\bar{X} - g - g^*)\}$. As an example, suppose that the density function of g depends on the parameter α. In particular, let the density function be written as $f(g - \alpha)$, so that α is simply a location parameter; an increase in α shifts the density function of g to the right by an equal amount. With this specification, an increase in α increases the mean value of g and, since it increases the value of $E\{1 + g^*/(\bar{X} - g - g^*)\}$, it also raises domestic consumption of good Y. This result is qualitatively the same as in the absence of international financial markets, despite the availability of insurance against the realization of fiscal policy. The obvious counterpoint to this is, of course, that if international capital markets provided insurance against regime changes (i.e., changes in α) as well as against realizations under a particular regime, then the international pattern of consumption of good Y would be invariant to fiscal policy. This example underscores Stockman's concluding observation that the effectiveness of fiscal policy depends on the degree of availability of insurance against various changes in policy and/or policy regimes.

A Counterexample

Although the analysis of a regime change in the preceding section seems to illustrate Stockman's main point, it can also be used to construct a counterexample to Stockman's finding that under complete insurance, "[a]n econometrician examining time-series or cross-sectional data would see no response of y to observed changes in z." Consider an economy inhabited by a sequence of one-period-lived cohorts. Each period is described by the model above. In period t, the density functions of g_t and g^*_t are given by $f(g_t - \alpha_t)$ and $f^*(g^*_t - \alpha^*_t)$. The location parameters α_t and α^*_t are deterministic but time varying. Thus, the distributions of g_t and g^*_t change deterministically over time, and the movements in this distribution (i.e., the policy regime changes) are not insurable. If there are international financial markets to share fiscal risk, then, as shown above, periods with a high value of α_t will be periods with a high value of domestic consumption of good Y. In addition, periods with a high value of α_t will on average have high values of g_t so that the covariance of g_t and y_t will be positive rather zero, even though there are perfect international insurance markets.

Optimal Domestic Fiscal Policy

My comments above concern the effects of international risk-sharing on the efficacy of fiscal policy and address the main point of Stockman's paper. I would also like to discuss the question of the optimal level of g in the absence of international financial markets. Stockman states that the socially optimal level of domestic fiscal policy satisfies $x\theta' = -1$. When this condition is satisfied, a one unit increase in g reduces worldwide private expenditure on good X but raises domestic consumption of good X by one unit, for a given level of domestic expenditure on good X, thereby leaving worldwide private consumption of X unchanged. While this condition characterizes the worldwide social optimum, it does not characterize the level of domestic fiscal policy which maximizes domestic welfare. The reason that the domestic welfare-maximizing level of g differs from the level which maximizes worldwide welfare is that an increase in g improves the domestic economy's terms of trade. Substituting equations (2) and (5) into the utility function (1), differentiating with respect to g (assuming that g^* is sufficiently small so that the second-order conditions are satisfied), and using the goods market equilibrium condition $\theta x + \theta^* x^* + g + g^* = \bar{X}$, we obtain the following characterization of optimal domestic fiscal policy from the point of view of the domestic economy:

(11) $$\theta' x = -\theta^* x^*/(\theta x + \theta^* x^*).$$

As the share of the domestic economy in the world economy approaches zero, the right-hand side of equation (11) approaches -1, and hence the characterization of domestically optimal fiscal policy in equation (11) approaches the characterization of socially optimal fiscal policy given by Stockman. To the extent that one would argue that political forces might lead to optimal fiscal policy, the domestically optimal policy described in equation (11) would appear to be the outcome rather than the policy described by Stockman.

Comment   Patrick J. Kehoe

The purpose of Stockman's paper is twofold: First, it promotes a type of stochastic comparative statics (SCS) as an alternative to standard

Patrick J. Kehoe is an assistant professor in the Department of Economics at the University of Minnesota, and is affiliated with the Federal Reserve Bank of Minneapolis.

deterministic comparative statics (DCS). Second, it shows how the degree of completeness of markets, here international financial markets, may be crucial for the SCS results. Stockman accomplishes this through a series of examples that clearly illustrate his points, and I have nothing to add to them. Instead I will expand on his two main themes.

Comparative Statics: Deterministic Versus Stochastic

When we study a dynamic economy, we are often concerned with how the economy will respond to various types of shocks. We would like to perform experiments in which these shocks can be interpreted as taking place in a single economy in real time, that is, calendar time. I argue that there is no logically consistent way to carry out such experiments in a deterministic setting. However, in a stochastic setting such experiments are straightforward.

In a deterministic setting, shocks are classified as either "unanticipated" or "anticipated." With unanticipated shocks we consider an economy in which agents are assumed to know the future with certainty and then we ask what happens if some event unexpectedly occurs. This question is ill-posed, since we solve for an equilibrium conditional on certain assumptions which we then violate in our thought experiment. This makes our experiment internally inconsistent and, hence, nonsensical.

A simple example should make this clear. Consider a world in which Stockman knows that his house will never burn down. Now suppose that it does. What happens? This question is ill-posed because if Stockman knew his house could burn down, he would have had enough sense to have already bought some insurance—or at least a fire extinguisher.

More generally, the logical problem is the following. We start by assuming there is, using Arrow's terminology, a single possible state of the world. Part of this state includes Stockman's house sitting there in fine condition. Given this state we define the natural commodity space and we define preferences over this space. We can then compute equilibrium allocations and welfare for this economy. However, serious problems arise if we attempt to evaluate equilibrium allocations and welfare in some "unexpected" state of the world in which Stockman's house has burned down. Since these allocations are not contained in our original commodity space and our preference order is not even defined over such a point, I have no idea what the word *welfare* means in this context.

In order to avoid a possible misunderstanding, I should expand on one small point. If we simply ignore these logical difficulties and interpret such experiments as if they were conducted in a truly stochastic world, then there are special cases in which we may get the "right" answer. In particular, if in the stochastic world either there is no possibility for sharing risk—because of the market structure or the physical environment—or there is no value in sharing risk—because agents are risk neutral—then we will get the right answer in the analogue deterministic environment in the sense that we will obtain the same numerical values for the consumption allocations either way.

An example of such a stochastic environment is a representative agent Lucas-tree economy, that is, a pure exchange economy populated by agents who have identical preferences and who, for every possible realization of uncertainty, have identical endowments. In such a model, no matter how we conduct our experiments, and no matter what we assume about markets, the equilibrium will always be ''don't trade and eat your own fruit.'' This may be a useful model for studying asset prices, but it is not very useful for studying trade. As soon as we add a little heterogeneity to this environment—either in preferences or in endowments—how we conduct our thought experiments and what we assume about market structure become crucial. (For an analysis of how such experiments work in a Lucas model with heterogenous agents, see Backus and Kehoe [1987].)

Finally, some may attempt to salvage DCS experiments as reasonable approximations to SCS experiments in which the shocks under consideration occur ''rarely.'' However, they cannot be salvaged. For example, an SCS experiment in an economy where there is a small positive probability of a house burning down will typically be vastly different from a DCS experiment in an economy where there is a zero probability of a house burning down.

With the other type of deterministic shocks—the anticipated shocks—we consider two distinct settings for some economically exogenous variable. For each setting, we solve for a separate perfect foresight equilibrium and then compare the endogenous variables, prices, and allocations across the equilibria. From this description it is clear that these comparisons cannot be interpreted as taking place in a single economy in real time. Rather, for economies specified at the country level, they should be interpreted as cross-country experiments. Thus, even though they are internally consistent, they are useless for many of the thought experiments we want to consider.

In a stochastic setting, it is straightforward to model shocks that take place in real time. The basic algorithm for conducting consistent experiments involving a shock to an exogenous variable is the following:

1. Consider an economy in which agents place a positive probability on at least two values of this variable.
2. Compute one equilibrium in which agents engage in all mutually beneficial trades and in which their expectations are confirmed.

3. Draw different time paths of realizations of the exogenous stochastic variables.

4. Compare equilibrium prices and allocations across these realizations.

In this setup we can compute cross-moments between any variables of interest. (For interesting examples of this algorithm, see Svensson [1985] and Stockman and Svensson [1985].)

For some variables, such as endowments or productivity, these experiments have a straightforward interpretation. However, for government policy variables the interpretation is less clear. In his paper, Stockman models government policies as exogenous stochastic variables. The policy experiments he considers are comparisons across realizations of these processes. How should we interpret such experiments? That depends on the underlying model of government behavior.

Suppose that we assume a government is a single administration that chooses a policy function to maximize its objectives. This function will have as arguments the state variables of the economy which include, among other things, all exogenous stochastic variables. As in Stockman's model, government policy will follow a stochastic process. However, there are some differences. Basically, we have pushed the exogenous uncertainty back to a deeper level: back from the level of an institution called the government to the more primitive level of agents' tastes and technology. As a result, policy introduces no new randomness into the economy. Of course, if we introduce shocks into the government objective function, government policy will add to the randomness. However, if we start building a model of these shocks, we will end up with them being functions of the original primitive shocks. Government policy will again introduce no new randomness. I will discuss the implication of this in a moment. For now, simply realize that in this interpretation we are investigating the operating characteristics of the economy under a single policy regime, where I define a *regime* to be a particular policy function of the government. Note that although we can give the word *regime* many reasonable definitions, I will use it in the concrete sense just described.

Suppose now, however, that we are interested in comparing outcomes across regimes. One way to do this is to specify two different objective functions for the government and then solve for two equilibria. In the first equilibrium, agents correctly believe that with probability 1 the government maximizes the first objective function; in the second equilibrium, agents correctly believe that with probability 1 the government maximizes the second objective function. Although we can compare the operating characteristics of these two regimes, we cannot interpret comparisons across these equilibria as real-time experiments for the same reasons as before.

There is, however, an alternative to this type of experiment. Suppose that the government is composed of a sequence of administrations with possibly differing objective functions. Suppose, for simplicity, that there are only two possible administrations and that for some as-yet-to-be-specified process the government switches randomly between them. Then, for each administration we can solve for a policy function, and we can solve for a single equilibrium and consistently compare across these regimes. As far as I know, this is the *only* way to compare regimes consistently in a way that can be interpreted as taking place in a single economy in real time. (For a good exposition of these ideas, see Cooley, LeRoy, and Raymon [1984].)

Since the main point of Stockman's paper is to show how the degree of completeness of markets can affect SCS results, he does not need to develop a deep model of government behavior. However, the nature of the underlying model is important for two reasons: it clarifies the possible interpretations of Stockman's experiments, and it helps us think about what financial markets we need in order to have complete markets.

In Stockman's model, the fundamental uncertainty is in government policy itself. In this setup, to have complete markets Stockman needs securities that pay off as functions of government policy. With casual reading, we may leave Stockman's paper with the mistaken impression that if we do not see securities that explicitly depend on government policies, then we necessarily have incomplete markets. With more careful reading, however, we realize that this is simply because Stockman took a useful shortcut in modeling government behavior. With a deeper model of government behavior, government policy will itself be a function of other stochastic variables, such as productivity. In this case, to have complete markets we do not need securities that depend on government policy directly; we only need to have enough securities that are correlated with the primitive stochastic elements.

Market Completeness and Stochastic Comparative Statics

Stockman's second purpose is to investigate how the degree of completeness of international financial markets affects the results of SCS. To show this, Stockman conducts experiments in two polar regimes: one with complete international financial markets and another with no international financial markets. The punchline of these examples is that the results may differ widely across the regimes.

Loosely speaking, the intuition for these examples is as follows. With complete markets, optimal behavior by agents involves eliminating all diversifiable income effects, while with incomplete markets, agents are artificially constrained so that they cannot eliminate all of these effects. In both cases, however, substitution effects remain. Then for a given

SCS experiment, if the substitution effects go in the opposite direction of the income effects, it is possible to have experiments that have opposite signs in the two cases. Basically, the income effects due to incomplete markets need to swamp the substitution effects.

Since Stockman's examples illustrate these points clearly, I will concentrate on answering this question: Why should we be interested in knowing how the completeness of markets affects SCS results?

A reason Stockman seems to favor is that the increasing sophistication of financial markets in countries like the United States means that we are moving from a regime of less complete markets to one of more complete markets. Thus, wisdom gleaned from the earlier stages of market development may soon prove faulty. I am not that comfortable with this motivation.

Another reason, which I find more appealing, is that this analysis may give us insight into which traditional trade theory results obtained using deterministic models will be overturned once we switch to stochastic models. This is because DCS results often are very similar to SCS results with incomplete markets. Basically, both get the income effects wrong in the same direction. Thus, if the completeness of markets overturns an SCS experiment under incomplete markets, it may also overturn the analogous DCS experiment.

A final reason is that Stockman's paper is the beginning of a research project that investigates the effects of incomplete markets more broadly. If this is true, then I would like to add a word of caution. We have learned from Harris and Townsend (1981) that in terms of thinking about what it means for government policy to be optimal, there is a world of difference between an environment in which incomplete markets are simply imposed and one in which markets are as complete as they can be, given the informational-spatial-communication structure.

If we are not careful, we may end up analyzing what Ed Prescott calls a "chicken model." The analysis of such a model goes something like this: First, assume that the private sector wants chickens but can't make them. Next, assume that governments can make chickens. The amazing policy result is that in equilibrium the government should make chickens and supply them to the private sector. I hope we have more exciting things to work on than this.

Of course, Stockman has not fallen into the chicken coop. Rather, he has provided us with a series of thought-provoking examples.

References

Backus, David K., and Patrick J. Kehoe. 1987. Trade and exchange rates in a dynamic competitive economy. Federal Reserve Bank of Minneapolis, Research Department working paper 348.

Cooley, Thomas F., Stephen LeRoy, and Neil Raymon. 1984. Modeling policy interventions. University of California, Santa Barbara. Mimeo.

Harris, Milton, and Robert M. Townsend. 1981. Resource allocation under asymmetric information. *Econometrica* 49:33–64.

Stockman, Alan C., and Lars E. O. Svensson. 1985. Capital flows, investment, and exchange rates. National Bureau of Economic Research, working paper 1598.

Svensson, Lars E. O. 1985. Money and asset prices in a cash-in-advance economy. *Journal of Political Economy* 93 (October): 919–44.

7   Expansionary Fiscal Policy and International Interdependence

Linda S. Kole

7.1 Introduction

In the 1980s, the large magnitude of current and expected U.S. budget deficits has led to renewed interest in the effects of fiscal expansion in an open, macroeconomic environment. We have witnessed a fascinating episode of real dollar appreciation, high real interest rates, and growing U.S. current account deficits. Many elements of this experience are well-explained by economic theory. For instance, the classic Mundell-Fleming analysis of fiscal expansion in a large country leads one to the conclusion that the exchange rate will appreciate while the trade balance deteriorates and world real interest rates rise. Given the size of the U.S. fiscal expansion, it is not particularly surprising that we have observed these effects. What is difficult to explain is the precise magnitude of the changes and the pattern of events that occurred.

The steady rise in the dollar and the serious deterioration of the trade balance from 1980 to 1985 prompted many observers to assert that the dollar had become overvalued. If the dollar was indeed overvalued, it is important to gauge how much of its overvaluation stemmed from the expansionary fiscal stance in the United States. Another related question is: How much of the rise in real interest rates, at home and abroad, resulted from the increase in government borrowing? The fact

Linda S. Kole is an economist in the Division of International Finance, Board of Governors of the Federal Reserve System. This chapter was prepared while the author was an assistant professor of economics at the University of Maryland.

Financial support from the University of Maryland General Research Board is gratefully acknowledged. Also, the author thanks Margarida Mateus for excellent research assistance. This work represents the views of the author, and should not be interpreted as representing the views of the Board of Governors of the Federal Reserve System.

that the United States has become the largest net international debtor in the world indicates the large volume of capital inflows occurring in recent years. Can fiscal policy explain the U.S. experience of steady appreciation along with a massive decumulation of net foreign assets? This chapter approaches these questions by examining both the domestic and foreign effects of a large country's fiscal expansion.

We focus here on the real exchange rate and real interest rates as the major economic mechanisms that transmit easy U.S. fiscal policy to the other developed nations of the world. To the extent that a fiscal expansion induces dollar appreciation, foreign countries will benefit from increased trade competitiveness. Also, as expansionary fiscal policy affects U.S. aggregate demand, a portion of the change in domestic absorption will spill over abroad. Asset markets represent another important channel through which the foreign economic outlook is dependent on U.S. fiscal policy. If assets are good substitutes, much of an increase in domestic real interest rates caused by a fiscal expansion will eventually show up abroad, leading to some degree of foreign crowding out. Furthermore, because international capital flows respond to both current and future expected events, even anticipated changes in U.S. fiscal policy may cause economic ripples abroad.

The future economic prospects of many developing nations, especially those with huge dollar-denominated debts, are also crucially affected by U.S. fiscal policy. Although appreciation of the dollar from 1980 to 1985 may have improved the competitiveness of some developing countries whose currencies were not pegged to the dollar, it had adverse effects as well. The high value of the dollar caused an increase in the real debt burden during a period in which the prices of many of the primary commodities exported by debtor nations were falling in real and dollar terms. Compounding this problem was the fact that higher world real interest rates, due in part to large U.S. budget deficits, considerably bloated the debt service payments these countries had to make. The combination of these unhappy events virtually guaranteed that debt problems would be recurrent.

Most economic analyses of fiscal policy are performed in a small country framework that takes foreign prices and interest rates as exogenous.[1] Models that assume that foreign variables are fixed are clearly inappropriate for the examination of a large country's fiscal expansion. This chapter examines the repercussion effects caused by a large country that embarks on a fiscal expansion. It is shown that the impact effect, dynamics, and the new long-run steady state equilibrium can be substantially different when one relaxes the assumption that the country undergoing expansion is small.

The conventional small country analysis of expansionary fiscal policy, where an initial appreciation is followed by a period of depreciation and net foreign asset decumulation, is contrasted with the two-country case, in which the subsequent dynamics are not as clear-cut. It is shown that if assets are imperfect substitutes, or if there exists a large degree of initial capital market integration, then an increase in government spending can lead to quite a different path of dynamic adjustment. After the initial appreciation at the moment of the fiscal expansion, the exchange rate may continue to appreciate while current account surpluses cause accumulation of net foreign assets. This type of adjustment path is consistent with the current account being primarily determined by the service account instead of by the conventional predominance of the trade balance.

The next section of this chapter develops a two-counry model tailored to accentuate some of the channels through which a fiscal expansion in a large, open nation can affect the rest of the developed world (here proxied by the second country). The major focus of the analysis is the effects of fiscal policy on the real exchange rate, real interest rates, and the balance of payments. The results of both an unanticipated and an anticipated balanced budget expansion are discussed in section 7.3. In section 7.4, a bond-financed fiscal expansion is analyzed by presenting simulation results. Finally, in sections 7.5 and 7.6 we comment on the recent experience of the United States and draw some tentative conclusions.

7.2   The Model

The model developed below is quite similar to that of Sachs and Wyplosz (1984). However, their model was specific to the small country case, so it did not provide a mechanism for analyzing the international effects we are interested in. We consider two countries which produce distinct composite goods. Output is assumed to be fixed in each country in order to abstract from cyclical phenomena, and for increased tractability. This assumption allows us to highlight the interdependent nature of world interest rates and the exchange rate, leaving other repercussion effects aside. The model is a fairly standard macro model of goods markets; it is simplified considerably by omitting the money market. For analytical convenience, we impose symmetry on many parameters of the model across countries.

Table 7.1 presents the model in its simplest form. Equation (1) is the national income identity which states that domestic real income, y, equals private absorption, a, plus government spending on goods and services, g, plus the trade balance, T. The trade balance has been defined as the domestic country's exports less its imports, in domestic real terms, and thus T appears negatively in the foreign equation and is deflated by the real exchange rate, $X = eP^*/P$.

Table 7.1   **The Model**

(1) $y = a + g + T = \bar{y}$ $y^* = a^* + g^* - T/X = \bar{y}^*$

(2) $a = (1 - \sigma)y_d + \delta w - \phi r$ $a^* = (1 - \sigma)y_d^* + \delta w^* - \phi r^*$

(3) $y_d = rb_d + r^*Xb_d^* + \bar{y} - z$ $y_d^* = rb_f/X + r^*b_f^* + \bar{y}^* - z^*$

(4) $w = \bar{m} + b_d + Xb_d^*$ $w^* = \bar{m}^* + b_f^* + b_f/X$

(5) $T = -\epsilon a + X\epsilon^*a^* + \eta X$

(6) $b = b_d + b_f = b_d^q(r - (\dot{X}/X)^e - r^*)w + Xb_f^d(r - (\dot{X}/X)^e - r^*)w^*$

(7) $\dot{X} = \bar{r} - \bar{r}^* + \Omega[\Theta \bar{b}_d^* + \Theta^* \bar{b}_f^* - (1 - \Theta)\bar{b}_d - (1 - \Theta^*)\bar{b}_f + (\Theta b_{d0}^* + \Theta^* b_{f0}^*)\bar{X}]$

where $\Theta = b_{d0}/w_0 = b_d^q(0)$ $\Theta^* = b_{f0}/w_0^* = b_f^d(0)$

$0 \le \Omega = [b_d^{q'}w_0 + b_f^{d'}w_0^*]^{-1} < \infty$

(8) $\dot{b} = \dot{b}_d + \dot{b}_f = rb + g - z$ $\dot{b}^* = \dot{b}_d^* + \dot{b}_f^* = r^*b^* + g^* - z^*$

(9) $\bar{z} = \bar{g} + b_0\bar{r}$ $(\dot{b} = 0)$ $\bar{z} = b_0^*\bar{r}^*$ $(\dot{b}^* = 0)$

(10a) $\dot{b} = \mu(\bar{b} - b)$

(10b) $\tilde{b}_t = (\bar{b} - b_0)(1 - e^{-\mu t})$ $\tilde{g}_t = \mu(\bar{b} - b_0)$ $\tilde{z}_t = b_0\tilde{r}_t + (\mu + r_0)\bar{b}_t$

(11) $(X\dot{b}_d^*) - \dot{b}_f = T + Xr^*b_d^* - rb_f$

(11′) $n\dot{f}a = \dot{b}_d^* - \dot{b}_f = \tilde{T} + r_0^*b_{d0}^*\bar{X} + r_0^*\bar{b}_d^* + b_{d0}^*\bar{r}^* - r_0\bar{b}_f - b_{f0}\bar{r} - b_{d0}^*\dot{X}$

Note: All starred variables are in foreign currency terms. Variables with a tilde, $\tilde{x}$, represent deviations from the initial steady state, so that $\tilde{x} = x - x_0$. Variables with a bar, $\bar{x}$, represent constants while a variable $\dot{x}$, represents the time derivative, dx/dt. The first derivative of a function $f(x)$ with respect to x is denoted as f'.

Private absorption in each country is defined in equation (2), where y_d is real disposable income, w is real wealth, and r is the real interest rate. The inclusion of disposable income in the absorption equations introduces the implicit assumption that some agents in the economy are liquidity-constrained, so that a unit increase in current disposable income will be met by an increase in consumption of $(1 - \sigma)$. Equation (3) defines disposable real income as real income plus interest earnings less taxes, where b_d (b_f) represent real domestic (foreign) holdings of domestic bonds, and b_d^* (b_f^*) are real domestic (foreign) holdings of foreign bonds. For simplicity, taxes, z, are represented as a lump sum.

Absorption is specified as a negative function of the real interest rate. The implicit assumption is that savings respond positively to an increase in the real interest rate. Physical capital investment was excluded from the model to decrease the dimensionality of the dynamic system. However, a part of absorption in this model could be thought of as investment, in the form of inventory or durable goods investment. Private absorption in each country is also a positive function of real wealth. The marginal propensity to consume out of wealth, δ, can be thought of as a discount rate.[2] Wealth is defined in equation (4) as real money balances, $\bar{m}$, plus the real value of domestic and foreign bonds.

Two crucial assumptions are embedded in this definition of wealth. The inclusion of domestic bonds as a component of domestic wealth involves the assumption that households are not effectively immortal and/or do not discount the future tax liabilities associated with domestic bonds.[3] Secondly, we assume that the demand for real balances depends only on real income, which in this model implies that the real stock of money remains constant in each country. In essence, this assumption allows us to ignore the effects of changing price levels on real wealth and the real exchange rate. Although the joint assumption of output and price fixity is unrealistic, it accentuates the role of interest rate and exchange rate interaction in response to fiscal policy. A fuller model which allowed both price and output flexibility was developed in Kole (1984), and it was shown that the results were not crucially dependent on the stringency of the assumptions. Later, we will discuss how relaxing these assumptions alters the results.

The domestic trade balance is specified in equation (5) to depend negatively on domestic absorption and positively on foreign absorption and the real exchange rate. For simplicity, ϵ and ϵ^* are assumed to be constant so that, ceteris paribus, a constant share of absorption in each country is devoted to imports. The substitution effect is thus entirely contained in the parameter η. Also, in equation (5) it is assumed that neither government spends on imports.

Equations (1) through (5) describe the markets for the domestic and foreign composite goods. One can see on inspection that the short-run response to an increase in government spending will be a combination of an increase in r to crowd out domestic absorption and a decrease in X to crowd out foreign demand through the trade balance. In this fixed price version of the model, an appreciation has another side effect: it increases real foreign wealth while decreasing real domestic wealth, helping to crowd out domestic demand.[4]

Asset markets are described by a simple portfolio balance model in which residents of each country hold two assets: domestic and foreign bonds. Walras's Law allows us to ignore one of these markets, so we'll concentrate on the equilibrium condition in the domestic bonds market, given by equation (6). For asset market equilibrium, the total outstanding real stock of domestic bonds must be equal to the amount demanded by domestic investors, $b_d^d(\cdot)w$, plus the amount demanded by foreign investors, $Xb_d^f(\cdot)w^*$. The demand for domestic bonds in each country depends positively on the real return on domestic bonds relative to foreign bonds, $(r - (\dot{X}/X)^e - r^*)$, where $(\dot{X}/X)^e$ is the expected rate of real depreciation, hereafter assumed to be identical to the actual rate of depreciation.[5]

Linearizing equation (6) around the initial steady state and doing a bit of rearranging brings us to equation (7), the portfolio balance condition which governs the dynamic behavior of the real exchange rate given perfect foresight. In this equation, X_0 has been set equal to one for convenience. The parameters θ and θ^* represent the initial share of domestic bonds in domestic and foreign wealth respectively. Ω is the inverse of a wealth-weighted measure of the degree of asset substitutability. Note that as assets approach perfect substitutability Ω approaches zero, and equation (7) becomes a statement of real interest parity. However, as assets become less substitutable and $\Omega > 0$, their relative supplies start to matter.[6] For instance, an increase in the stock of domestic bonds at home must, ceteris paribus, cause an appreciation $(\dot{X} < 0)$ to decrease the real domestic return on foreign bonds and eliminate excess supply in the domestic bond market.

Next, we consider the public sector in each country by examining the governments' budget constraints given by equation (8). Government spending and interest payments on outstanding bonds is financed by taxes or by issuing new bonds. In equation (9), we assume that the foreign country pursues a passive fiscal policy and does not change government spending ($\dot{g}^* = 0$). Foreign taxes are always adjusted to cover the government's interest burden on outstanding bonds, so that the stock of foreign bonds remains constant. In contrast, we assume that the domestic government engineers a fiscal expansion. The evolution of taxes in the case of a balanced budget expansion is given by equation (9).

On the other hand, suppose that the government undertakes a fiscal expansion without initially raising taxes. Then the ensuing deficit will be financed by bond creation. However, the government cannot increase the bond supply forever or the model would be unstable.[7] To rule out this possibility, we need a terminal condition to guarantee that eventually the government's budget will be balanced. We adopt the condition proposed by Sachs and Wyplosz, equation (10a). This bond supply rule is convenient because it means that the domestic stock of bonds evolves independently of the other dynamic variables in the system. Equation (10a) implies that there is some target stock of outstanding bonds, $\bar{b}$, which the government shoots for. If this target exceeds the existing stock of bonds, the government will continue to increase the supply of bonds up to $\bar{b}$. However, if $\bar{b} < b$, the government will retire the debt at the rate μ. Under this rule, a permanent fiscal expansion will lead to the evolution of bonds, government spending, and taxes described by equation (10b).

When government spending increases, it is initially financed solely by bond creation. By assumption, taxes also increase automatically to cover the increase in debt service stemming from the fiscally induced increase in the real interest rate.[8] Over time, less of the increase in g is financed by bond creation and more is financed by raising taxes. By the time the stock of outstanding bonds reaches its target level, taxes will have risen enough to cover both the increased government spending and the larger service on outstanding debt. Note that given rule (10) and the government budget constraint (8), the government's choice of $\bar{g}$ and $\bar{b}$ will determine μ. For a given fiscal expansion, the higher $\bar{b}$, the lower μ, the rate of adjustment to the new steady state level of domestic bonds.

Finally, the third dynamic relationship, the balance of payments in real domestic currency terms, is presented in equation (11). The left hand side of equation (11) is the change in net foreign assets held domestically. Under a perfectly flexible exchange rate regime, this capital account deficit must match the current account surplus, which is the trade balance plus the service account on the right hand side of equation (11). The linearized version of equation (11) is given by equation (11′). Note that the last term on the right hand side of equation (11′) represents capital gains on initial domestic holdings of foreign bonds. A real depreciation causes domestic residents to reap a capital gain of $\dot{X}b^*_{d0}$. If we assume that these gains are capitalized at each instant of time, then real depreciation will lead to a decumulation of net foreign assets as domestic investors cash in foreign bonds to realize their capital gains. It is difficult to know how one should treat capital gains because in actuality, they are not continuously capitalized and, in the short run may be more important to central banks' accounting balances than to the balance of payments. In small country models capital gains are usually left out by defining the balance of payments and its components in foreign currency terms. However, in a two-country model, capital gains are difficult to ignore, except in the special case where initial holdings of foreign assets are nonexistent. A capital gain for one country represents a capital loss for the other; a capital gain in domestic currency terms is a capital loss in foreign currency terms. In the analysis that follows, we ignore the capital gains term because of the uncertainty involved with its treatment, but we do comment on how its inclusion would affect the results.

Short-run goods market equilibrium of the system is described by solving equations (1) through (5) for r and r^* as a function of X, g, and all asset stocks. Explicit algebraic treatment is given in the Appendix. We have assumed that initially the current account is in balance and that $r_0 = r^*_0$, $b^*_{d0} = b_{f0}$, $T_0 = 0$, and $X_0 = 1$ to further simplify the analysis. Equilibrium is then described by:

$$
\begin{array}{ll}
(+)(+)\,(+)\,(+) & (-)(?)\,(-)\,(+) \\
(12) \qquad r = r(X,\ g,\ nfa,\ b) & r^* = r^*(X,\ g,\ nfa,\ b).
\end{array}
$$

A real depreciation improves the domestic trade balance and increases domestic real wealth so that with fixed output, it must be crowded out by an increase in the domestic interest rate. The exact opposite results obtain abroad; real depreciation causes a fall in the foreign real interest rate to eliminate excess foreign supply. An increase in government spending raises the domestic real interest rate to crowd out domestic demand, whereas the effects of a domestic fiscal expansion abroad are ambiguous. The condition that a fiscal expansion has a net expansionary effect abroad which causes a short-run increase in r^* is: $\sigma(1 - \sigma)b_{f0} > \phi\epsilon'$.[9] If this condition holds, the increase in foreign demand due to the fiscal expansion outweighs the negative effect of the direct crowding out of the domestic trade balance. An increase in net foreign assets increases domestic wealth (decreases foreign wealth), which increases domestic demand (decreases foreign demand) and causes an increase in r (decrease in r^*). Because an increase in domestic bonds increases domestic wealth and exerts upward pressure on r, it will also increase foreign interest income and thereby foreign demand and r^*.

The short run effects of a fiscal expansion on the endogenous variables of the system: r, r^*, and X, are well known. When assets are perfect substitutes, an increase in government spending causes an excess demand for domestic goods, and thus an increase in the real interest rate and/or an appreciation is required to clear the domestic goods market. The relative magnitudes of the decrease in X and the increase in r and r^* depend on the net effect of domestic fiscal policy on foreign absorption. A foreign expansion requires less of an appreciation and more of an increase in r^* than a foreign contraction. Excess supply in the foreign goods market puts downward pressure on r^*, and thus r, so the real exchange rate must crowd out more of the domestic excess demand.

These short-run results hold in either the balanced budget expansion or the bond-financed case. Increased government spending must cause appreciation and increased interest rates. However, short-run equilibrium tells us little about the new long-run steady state associated with higher domestic government spending, or about the dynamic path by which we arrive there. To analyze the dynamics of the system, we'll start by considering a balanced budget expansion, thus setting $\dot{b} = \dot{b}^* = 0$. In this case, equations (7) and (11') reduce to:

$$
(7a) \qquad \dot{X} = \bar{r} - \bar{r}^* + \Omega[(\theta - \theta^*)n\tilde{f}a + (1 + \theta - \theta^*)b^*_{d0}\bar{X}], \text{ and}
$$

$$
(11a) \qquad n\dot{f}a = (\eta' + r_0^* b^*_{d0})\bar{X} + r_0^* n\tilde{f}a + b^*_{d0}(\bar{r}^* - \bar{r}) + \epsilon'\bar{g}.
$$

Below we present the system in abbreviated matrix form. The values of all of the coefficients in terms of the parameters of the system can be found in the Appendix; here we will only concern ourselves with the signs.

$$
(13) \quad
\begin{bmatrix} \dot{X} \\ \dot{nfa} \end{bmatrix}
=
\overset{\displaystyle (A)}{\begin{bmatrix} \overset{(+)}{a_{11}} & \overset{(+)}{a_{12}} \\ \underset{a_{21}}{(?)} & \underset{a_{22}}{(?)} \end{bmatrix}}
\begin{bmatrix} \tilde{X} \\ \tilde{nfa} \end{bmatrix}
+
\underset{\displaystyle (\gamma)}{\begin{bmatrix} \overset{(+)}{a_{13}} \\ \underset{a_{23}}{(?)} \end{bmatrix}}
\tilde{g}.
$$

Because we have one jump variable, X, and one predetermined variable, nfa, we need the determinant of A to be negative for stability. If assets are perfect substitutes, the condition for a negative determinant reduces to: $\sigma r_0^* < \delta$.[10] This is likely to hold because $\sigma < 1$ and in equilibrium, $r^* = d$.[11] In the case of imperfect substitutability with $b_{d0}^* = 0$, we have a condition which is even more likely to be satisfied: $\sigma r_0^* < \delta + \Omega(\theta - \theta^*)\phi/2$. As long as the domestic investors hold more domestic bonds than foreigners do as a share in wealth, the second term on the right hand side of the inequality is positive. The general condition for a negative determinant can be found in the Appendix. As is noted in system (13), the signs of the coefficients in the equation describing net foreign asset accumulation are ambiguous. To better understand the dynamics of the system, it is useful to examine how the signs of a_{21}, a_{22}, and a_{23} depend on the values or the model's parameters. One crucial parameter in the dynamic system is the amount of foreign bonds held domestically (and vice versa—they are assumed to be equal here).

In figure 7.1, we present a hypothetical example of how the magnitude of initial cross-country asset holdings affects the phase diagram of the system. The other parameter values used for this example are the same ones that will later be used for the simulations.[12] For simplicity, we analyze the perfect substitutes case so that equation (7a) collapses to $\dot{X} = \tilde{r} - \tilde{r}^*$. Figure 7.1a presents the dynamic phase diagram for the small country case that obtains when initial domestic holdings of foreign bonds are small or nonexistent. The $\dot{X} = 0$ schedule describes asset market equilibrium when there is no expected appreciation or depreciation. The schedule slopes down because a depreciation raises the rate of return differential and must be accompanied by a decrease in net foreign assets to decrease $r - r^*$ and maintain $\dot{X} = 0$. Above the schedule, $r > r^*$, so there is portfolio imbalance unless depreciation prevails. Below the schedule, appreciation is necessary for asset market equilibrium. The $\dot{nfa} = 0$ schedule is the locus of points for which the current account is balanced. This schedule slopes

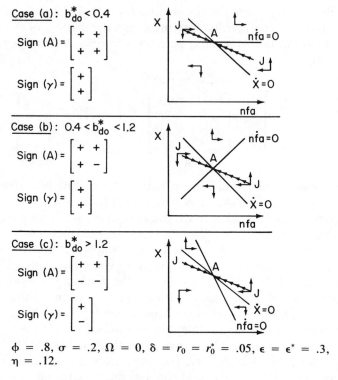

Case (a): $b_{do}^* < 0.4$

Sign (A) = $\begin{bmatrix} + & + \\ + & + \end{bmatrix}$

Sign (γ) = $\begin{bmatrix} + \\ + \end{bmatrix}$

Case (b): $0.4 < b_{do}^* < 1.2$

Sign (A) = $\begin{bmatrix} + & + \\ + & - \end{bmatrix}$

Sign (γ) = $\begin{bmatrix} + \\ + \end{bmatrix}$

Case (c): $b_{do}^* > 1.2$

Sign (A) = $\begin{bmatrix} + & + \\ - & - \end{bmatrix}$

Sign (γ) = $\begin{bmatrix} + \\ - \end{bmatrix}$

$\phi = .8$, $\sigma = .2$, $\Omega = 0$, $\delta = r_0 = r_0^* = .05$, $\epsilon = \epsilon^* = .3$, $\eta = .12$.

Fig. 7.1   Examples of possible phase diagrams

down because a depreciation which improves the trade balance requires a decrease in net foreign assets and thus the service account to eliminate the current account surplus. To the right of the schedule, we have accumulation of net foreign assets through the service account, and to the left, we have decumulation. Here the stability condition of a negative determinant implies that the $\dot{X} = 0$ schedule must be steeper than the $n\dot{fa} = 0$ schedule with the stable trajectory JJ between them.

In the second panel of figure 7.1, we illustrate the dynamics of the system for a slightly higher range of initial foreign bond holdings. For this intermediate range of b_{do}^*, the $n\dot{fa} = 0$ schedule is positively sloped. A depreciation still has a positive effect on the current account, but now the net effect of an increase in net foreign assets on the current account is negative. As b_{do}^* rises, the interest component of the current account becomes more important; the increase in the service account caused by $r_0 n\dot{fa}$ is more than compensated for by the decrease due to $-b_{do}^*(\bar{r} - \bar{r}^*)$. Over the range applicable to case (b), when b_{do}^* is higher, the slope of the $n\dot{fa} = 0$ schedule is steeper.

The third case shown is for relatively large initial asset holdings. When $b_{d0}^* > 1.2$, the slope of the $nfa = 0$ schedule again becomes negative, but becomes steeper than the $\dot{X} = 0$ schedule. Now a depreciation actually worsens the current account; the trade balance improvement caused by depreciation is swamped by the service account deterioration associated with the increase in $(r - r^*)$.[13] Is case (c) simply a theoretical curiosity or is it a real possibility? The service account is often ignored in international models, but here it plays the overwhelming role in dynamic adjustment. The lower η, or the less responsive the trade balance to a change in the real exchange rate, the likelier it is that this case will obtain. When the trade balance is inelastic with respect to the real exchange rate, the service account may become the dominant determinant of the current account.

The predominant influence of the service account may be a short-run phenomena in many developed nations. Any country confronting a J curve may experience periods in which a depreciation initially worsens the balance of payments by deteriorating the service account without appreciably improving the trade balance. Eventually, one would expect the trade balance to improve enough to outweigh the negative service account and improve the overall balance of payments.[14] In contrast, in less-developed debtor nations which export primary commodities with low demand elasticities, a depreciation may deteriorate the current account for a longer period of time.

At this point we should comment on the impact of capital gains. If capital gains are continuously capitalized, then the likelihood that the economy is characterized by case (b) or (c) increases. Given the parameter values used in figure 7.1, in order for case (a) to be relevant b_{d0}^* must be less than .143, while case (b) obtains when initial domestic holdings of foreign bonds are in the range: $.143 < b_{d0}^* < .625$. Therefore, the more important the capital gains in the balance of payments, the less likely it is that the dynamics of the system will parallel the small country case.

7.3 A Balanced Budget Expansion

The dynamic behavior of the economy in response to a balanced budget expansion depends on the degree of asset substitutability, the responsiveness of trade to changes in absorption and the real exchange rate, and on the initial degree of capital market integration. We will start with the standard case; assets are assumed to be perfect substitutes, and initially residents of each country hold only assets denominated in their own currency ($b_{d0}^* = b_{f0} = 0$). Figure 7.2a depicts the dynamic path of the economy following a permanent balanced budget expansion. Both the $\dot{X} = 0$ and the $nfa = 0$ schedules shift inward;

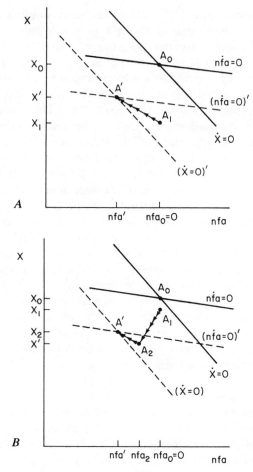

Fig. 7.2   Balanced budget expansion (BBE) when assets are perfect substitutes ($\Omega = 0$) and $b_{d0}^* = b_{f0} = 0$. *A*, an unanticipated BBE. *B*, an anticipated BBE

the former because the increase in government spending causes an increase in the real rate of return differential, requiring an appreciation and/or a decrease in net foreign assets to restore steady state portfolio equilibrium. The current account schedule shifts inward because an increase in *g* directly improves the trade balance by shifting domestic demand from foreign to domestic goods, so either an appreciation or a decumulation of net foreign assets is necessary to restore current account balance. The instantaneous effect is an appreciation to clear the home goods market by choking off foreign demand. The exchange rate jumps from A_0 to A_1, a point which is located on the trajectory to the new steady state equilibrium, A'. From that point on, the domestic country runs a current account deficit and undergoes depreciation until arriving at A'. In the long run, the expanding country experiences a loss in net foreign assets and probably an appreciation. The long-run changes in the level of net foreign assets and the real exchange rate are:

(14a) $\overline{nfa} - nfa_0 = -[\sigma/2(\delta - \sigma r_0^*)]\overline{g}$, and

(14b) $\overline{X} - X_0 = [(\sigma r_0^* - 2\delta\epsilon)/2\eta(\delta - \sigma r_0^*)]\overline{g}.$

Given that $\delta = r_0^*$, the condition for long-run real depreciation is $\sigma > 2\epsilon$. If this condition holds, the net effect of the increase in government spending on the current account is negative and a long-run real depreciation is necessary. This condition is unlikely to hold unless a country has quite a high propensity to save and a low marginal propensity to import out of absorption.[15]

When $b_{d0}^* = b_{f0} = 0$, the portfolio balance schedule becomes steeper as assets become less perfect substitutes. A given balanced budget expansion will cause less loss of net foreign assets and more appreciation. The higher the Ω, the higher the risk premium, $\overline{r} - \overline{r}^*$, needed to induce foreign investors to hold more domestic bonds. At the same time, the current account requires more appreciation because an appreciation only affects the trade balance; with initial asset stocks equal to zero, there are no service account effects generated by a change in the real exchange rate.

Figure 7.2b illustrates the effects of a balanced budget expansion that is anticipated several periods before its occurrence. As soon as the expansion is foreseen, the exchange rate appreciates to X_1, as investors expecting future increases in the domestic real interest rate raise their demands for domestic assets. Since the expansion has yet to materialize, the system follows the dynamics dictated by the original dynamic schedules and further appreciation occurs. In this region there is a current account deficit due to the appreciation, so net foreign assets decumulate over this period. The appreciation has a contractionary effect on the domestic economy, while demand increases abroad. To clear both goods markets, r declines while r^* increases so that $\overline{r} - \overline{r}^*$ is negative and equal to the expected appreciation over the period. By the time of the implementation of the fiscal expansion, the economy has arrived at A_2 on the stable trajectory to the new equilibrium. From then on the economy evolves as in the unanticipated case described above. With the fiscal expansion in place, r increases so that it exceeds r^* until the new equilibrium is reached.

When initial asset holdings are large enough to ensure that the current account balance schedule is upward-sloping, a balanced budget expansion will again shift the portfolio balance schedule down and to the left, but will shift the current account schedule down and to the right. Higher government spending crowds out domestic demand for foreign goods. To keep the current account in balance, there must be an appreciation to depress the trade balance and/or a higher level of net foreign assets to worsen the service account.

If assets are perfect substitutes, the dynamics of the system are similar to those shown in figure 7.2. At the new steady state equilibrium, we again have an appreciated exchange rate, as long as condition (14b) holds, and a lower level of net foreign asset holdings than in the initial steady state. The model yields the familiar result that the steady state real exchange rate does not depend on initial asset stocks in a world of perfect capital mobility. Also, it can be shown that the new level of net foreign asset holdings is positively associated with the initial stock of foreign bonds held domestically because of the service account benefits derived from them.

If assets are less than perfect substitutes, then we may end up with the different dynamics shown in figure 7.3. As before, an unanticipated balanced budget expansion causes a jump appreciation to clear goods markets. However, the magnitude of the initial appreciation is less than in the perfect substitutes case. Initially, the domestic interest rate increases, but unlike the perfect substitutes case, the foreign interest rate decreases. The net effect of the increase in government spending and the appreciation on the current account is positive, resulting in foreign excess supply that causes r^* to fall. After the initial appreciation, the economy undergoes steady appreciation and accumulation of net foreign assets until the new equilibrium is reached. During the adjustment period, there is a current account surplus along with an excess demand for foreign assets at the prevailing interest rate differential. Even though $r - r^*$ increases, which in itself raises the demand for domestic assets, this effect is overwhelmed by the wealth effect caused by appreciation. The initial decrease in X causes portfolio disequilibrium by decreasing (increasing) the proportion of foreign (domestic) bonds in the domestic (foreign) portfolio below (above) desired levels. To eliminate the net excess demand for foreign assets, appreciation must be expected.

The dynamic effects of an anticipated balanced budget expansion for this case are shown in figure 7.3b. The jump appreciation caused by the anticipation of expansion and higher returns on domestic bonds engenders a current account deficit by worsening the trade account. Initially, r decreases and r^* increases to clear both the domestic and foreign goods markets, which experience a decrease and increase in demand respectively. Appreciation and decumulation of net foreign assets occur until the day of the expansion, at which point the economy arrives at the stable trajectory to the new long-run equilibrium.

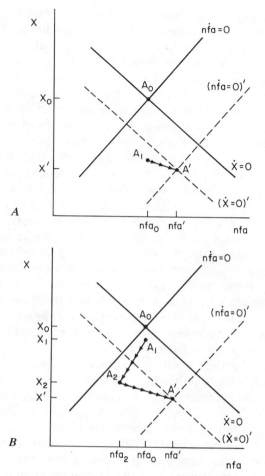

Fig. 7.3   BBE when $\Omega > 0$ and $.4 < b_{d0}^{*} < 1.2$. *A*, an unanticipated BBE. *B*, an anticipated BBE

Here, the new steady state is characterized by an appreciated real exchange rate and a *higher* level of net foreign assets. The new steady state exchange rate is higher when assets are less substitutable due to the familiar result that $\partial(\bar{r} - \bar{r}^{*})/\partial\Omega > 0$. As assets become less substitutable, the interest rates in each country are freer to diverge from each other, so that they can bear more of the burden of equilibrating both goods markets. Given some degree of imperfect asset substitutability, the exchange rate is also higher when initial holdings of foreign assets are higher. In the new steady state, a positive relative return differential will have a negative impact on the service account because more debt service must be paid abroad, while less interest is received domestically. Therefore, for a given increase in g, less appreciation is necessary to eliminate the current account surplus due to crowding out of private domestic demand. In the long run, the trade balance suffers less deterioration, whereas the service account deteriorates by more as $b_{d0}^* = b_{f0}$ are increased.

When $.4 < b_{d0}^* < 1.2$, the level of net foreign assets in the new steady state is positively related to the degree of imperfect asset substitutability. As assets become less substitutable, the portfolio disequilibrium caused by a given change in the exchange rate grows larger. The fiscally induced appreciation causes investors to reshuffle their portfolios toward foreign bonds. Finally, the new steady state level of net foreign assets is negatively related to the initial foreign position of domestic investors. The higher b_{d0}^*, the more net debt service will flow abroad, increasing the tendency to decumulate net foreign assets.

Next, we examine possible dynamic responses to a balanced budget expansion when initial foreign asset holdings are relatively large. Under this scenario, a balanced budget expansion shifts both schedules down and to the left. Here, the increase in government spending has a negative impact on the current account; although the trade balance improves, the service account deteriorates by a larger amount. Therefore, either a decrease in net foreign assets and/or an appreciation is needed to restore current account balance.

If domestic and foreign assets are perfect substitutes, the new long-run steady state is likely to be characterized by a lower real exchange rate as well as an increase in net foreign assets held domestically.[16] The dynamic path to the new equilibrium is quite similar to that of figure 7.3a and is thus not shown here. However, the underlying dynamics of the economy are quite different. The impact effect of the fiscal expansion is appreciation and an increase in interest rates, but the foreign interest rate increases by more than the domestic rate does. This increase in the relative return to foreign bonds improves the service account, and along with the direct crowding out due to the increase in g, outweighs the deterioration of the current account due to appreciation. Persistent current account surpluses generate net foreign asset accumulation for the domestic country while appreciation matching $\bar{r} - \bar{r}^*$ maintains portfolio equilibrium. The domestic country ends up with a higher level of net foreign assets in the new steady state because of the service account surpluses experienced in the adjustment period. This result is in contrast to the usual loss of net foreign assets through persistent trade balance deficits following a permanent fiscal stimulus.

The dynamics of an anticipated fiscal expansion in this case are shown in figure 7.4a. After a small appreciation of the exchange rate as soon as the expansionary policy is expected, the exchange rate appreciates while capital flows abroad. Initially, the domestic real in-

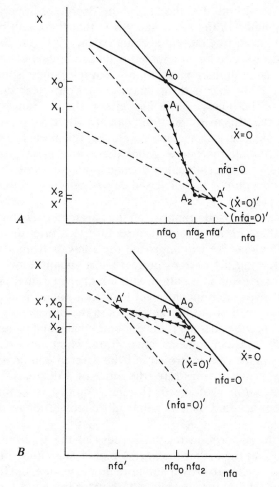

Fig. 7.4   Anticipated BBE when $b_{d0}^* = b_{f0} > 1.2$. *A*, perfect substitutes case. *B*, imperfect substitutes case

terest rate declines while the foreign real rate rises, so $\dot{X} < 0$ is essential for portfolio balance. Meanwhile, a current account surplus, primarily caused by a service account surplus, guarantees net foreign asset accumulation. On the day of the expansion, the economy arrives at A_2 on the stable path to a new steady state.

When assets are imperfect substitutes and investors initially hold relatively large amounts of international assets, it is possible that the dynamic and long-run results of the small country case are restored. The larger the Ω, the larger the $\tilde{r} - \tilde{r}^*$, so the greater the cumulative losses in net foreign assets through the service account over the transition period. Also, note that the higher the degree of imperfect asset substitutability and b_{d0}^*, the more likely it is that there will be a long-run depreciation to restore current account balance.[17] Figure 7.4b shows the dynamic response to an anticipated balanced budget expansion for this case. The usual initial appreciation when the policy is announced coincides with a fall in r and an increase in r^* to clear both goods markets. Before the policy comes into effect, the exchange rate continues to appreciate to ensure portfolio balance while net foreign assets accumulate through service account surpluses. When the fiscal impetus occurs, the economy reaches A_2, and there is a large jump in the domestic interest rate to eliminate excess demand at home. From then on, the current account is in deficit and depreciation accompanies capital inflows.

Above, we have focused primarily on the parameters Ω and b_{d0}^* while ignoring the others in the system. Let us turn to a brief discussion of the other parameters. We will approach the analysis from a simplified angle by considering the case of perfect asset substitutability. A balanced budget expansion in a nation with a higher marginal propensity to save out of disposable income will lead to a higher real exchange rate and a lower level of net foreign assets in the new steady state. In the long run, disposable income is lower domestically and higher abroad. This causes a decrease in domestic absorption, which relieves pressure on the real exchange rate to crowd out the foreign component of demand. The higher the savings rate, the more of a decrease (increase) in savings will occur in the domestic (foreign) country. Over time, larger domestic current account deficits will lead to a lower long-run level of net foreign assets.

The higher the absorption responsiveness of the trade balance, ϵ, the lower the $\bar{X}$ and the higher the $\overline{nfa}$. A higher magnitude of ϵ causes a given fiscal expansion to crowd out more domestic demand for foreign goods, and thus the real exchange rate must appreciate by more to ensure current account balance. The larger improvement in the trade balance also engenders a long-run gain in the net foreign asset position. The more elastic the trade balance with respect to the real exchange rate (the higher η), the less the real appreciation needed for current account balance. In the long run, the terms-of-trade elasticity is also positively related to the level of net foreign assets.

An increase in the initial level of the real interest rate leads to a higher $\bar{X}$ and a lower $\overline{nfa}$. Due to the fiscally induced loss of service account income, there will be more of a tendency for net foreign asset decumulation, and current account balance will require a more competitive level of the real exchange rate. Finally, increases in δ will be associated with further appreciation and more capital outflows in response to the increase in g. If absorption is more elastic with respect to wealth, long-run real appreciation has a more negative (positive) effect on domestic (foreign) absorption.[18] Therefore, a lower $\overline{X}$ and higher $\overline{nfa}$ will be necessary to equilibrate the current account.

At this point, a comment on the simplifying assumptions employed above is in order. In Kole (1984), the model was revised to account for output and price flexibility by including standard money demand equations and allowing price changes based on excess supply or demand. These changes resulted in a four by four dynamic model upon which simulations were performed. When output is allowed to deviate from its full employment level, the impact of fiscal expansion on the exchange rate and interest rates is reduced in magnitude, but the basic direction of movement remains the same. The adjustment process takes longer in the fuller model, probably because of the less dramatic nature of the events occurring in the initial periods following an expansion.

Also, the assumption that the expanding country was initially neither a net debtor nor creditor was relaxed. It was shown that the debt situation is likely to deteriorate following a fiscal stimulus in a lender country if the initial level of debt is large and/or domestic and foreign bonds are imperfect substitutes. Under these conditions, the negative impact of increased world interest rates on a debtor nation's service account far outweighs any trade balance improvement derived from the real depreciation of its currency.

7.4 A Bond-Financed Increase in Government Spending

Next, we analyze the dynamic adjustment to a permanent increase in government spending which is originally financed by bond creation. For any given spending increase, there are unlimited combinations of $\overline{b}$, the target stock of outstanding bonds, and μ, the rate of adjustment to that target, that are consistent with equation (10). We will look at two cases to examine what different dynamic and long-run effects can be expected as the rate of adjustment increases and the amount of bonds created decreases.

The short-run effect of a bond financed fiscal expansion will be an increase in the domestic real interest rate and a discrete appreciation, both occurring to clear the home goods market. In general, the initial amount of appreciation and increase in the interest rate will be larger in magnitude than in the balanced budget case. In the initial period, domestic taxes increase to cover higher debt service, but the increase in government sending is entirely financed by the issuance of new domestic bonds. The budget deficit creates a larger initial boom in demand than that caused by a balanced budget expansion. Because more crowding out is needed in the first period, X and r must move by more.

In the long run, the results of a bond-financed increase in government spending are similar to those of a balanced budget expansion with some qualifications. In the new steady state, the larger the increase in the stock of domestic bonds created to temporarily finance budget deficits, the higher the steady state real exchange rate and the domestic real interest rate.[19] In the case of perfect asset substitutability, an increase in the stock of bonds boosts world interest rates by raising world wealth. The higher supply of domestic bonds must be matched by an increase in world saving which can only be accomplished through a higher equilibrium interest rate.

When assets are imperfect substitutes, the steady state real interest rate differential is positively related to the amount of bond creation. Because the relative supply of domestic bonds is higher in the new steady state, they must carry a permanently higher return to induce investors to hold them. As before, there is a negative relationship between the amount of long-run real interest rate adjustment and real exchange rate adjustment. Therefore, the real exchange rate will be higher, when $\bar{b} - b_0$ is higher. Another reason for the positive association between the long-run real exchange rate and the amount of bond creation is that eventually government debt service has a negative impact on disposable income. With a higher long-run stock of bonds, more taxes will have to be levied to cover the government's debt service. If there were no capital mobility, the increase in the domestic government's debt service would not affect disposable income; all of the interest payments on the increased stock of bonds would be received and taxed away domestically. However, as long as foreigners hold some of the increased stock of domestic bonds, domestic residents will suffer a long-run real income loss. This result contrasts with the classic Diamond model (1965), in which swapping external for internal debt raises utility in the efficient case.[20]

When assets are close or perfect substitutes, the steady state level of net foreign assets resulting from a bond-financed increase in g will be lower, the higher the degree of bond creation. The larger initial appreciation and rise in r associated with bond finance increase the likelihood that the current account will be in deficit during the transition to a new equilibrium. The cumulative effect of the current account deficits is a lower domestic net foreign asset position. If instead domestic and foreign bonds are poor substitutes and b_{d0}^* is small, then it is possible that bond creation will enhance the ultimate external position. The larger the increase in the stock of bonds, the larger the equilibrium increase in the domestic real interest rate. When initial cross-country bond holdings are small, the negative service account effect of an increase in r will also be small. Consequently, the major effect associated with the large increase in r will be a decrease in domestic absorption and a current account improvement.

The dynamic adjustment to a bond-financed increase in government spending cannot be represented diagrammatically because both of the schedules shift each period due to the changing stock of government bonds. The equations of motion in the bond financed case are:

(7b) $\dot{X} = \bar{r} - \bar{r}^* + \Omega[(\theta - \theta^*)n\bar{f}a - (1 - \theta)\bar{b}$

$\qquad\qquad + (1 + \theta - \theta^*)b_{d0}^*\bar{X}]$, and

(11b) $n\dot{f}a = (\eta' + r_0^* b_{d0}^*)\bar{X} + r_0^* n\bar{f}a + b_{d0}^*(\bar{r}^* - \bar{r}) + \epsilon'\bar{g}$.

During the adjustment period, $\bar{r} - \bar{r}^*$ depends positive on $\bar{b}$. Also, when $\Omega \neq 0$, progressive increases in the stock of domestic bonds have the additional effect of raising the steady state risk premium associated with them.

Simulations were performed to analyze the dynamic paths of the forcing variables on the way to the new equilibrium. We focus on a 10% rise in government expenditures and examine two combinations of μ and $(\bar{b} - b_0)$:

Case (a) $\mu = .1$ $(\bar{b} - b_0) = 1$ Slow adjustment, high bond target
Case (b) $\mu = .5$ $(\bar{b} - b_0) = .2$ Fast adjustment, low bond target.

The other parameter values assumed for the simulations are: $X_0 = 1$, $nfa_0 = 0$, $\phi = .8$, $\sigma = .2$, $\delta = r_0^* = r_0 = .05$, $\theta = .7$, $\theta^* = .3$, $\epsilon = \epsilon^* = .3$, $\eta = .12$, and $T_0 = 0$. We consider the cases of perfect asset substitutability ($\Omega = 0$) and mild imperfect asset substitutability ($\Omega = .2$). For now we leave aside the case of strong imperfect asset substitutability, because these simulations implicitly assume that the two countries are of roughly equal size. Modern experience between large developed countries suggests that strong imperfect asset substitutability is unlikely to hold. We also look at various different values for initial international bond holdings: $b_{d0}^* = b_{f0} = .3, .8$, and 2.0. Table 7.2 summarizes the results of the simulations.

With perfect asset substitutability, the adjustment paths with low or medium initial cross-country bond holdings are fairly similar to each other. After an initial appreciation, depreciation and decumulation of net foreign assets take place until the new equilibrium is reached. Figure 7.5 depicts the paths of the real exchange rate, the real return differential, and the level of net foreign assets following a domestic fiscal expansion at time $t = 15$, for the case where $b_{d0}^* = .3$ and $\Omega = 0$. For reference, the paths of the variables for both cases (a) and (b) are compared to the paths which result from a balanced budget expansion of equal magnitude.

One can see from figure 7.5 that the initial jump appreciation and increase in the real return differential is larger in both bond-financed cases due to the higher domestic demand pressure caused by a gov-

Table 7.2 Simulation Results for a Bond-Financed Fiscal Expansion

	$\Omega = 0$					
	$b^*_{d0} = .3$		$b^*_{f0} = .8$		$b^*_{d0} = 2.0$	
	$\mu = .1$	$\mu = .5$	$\mu = .1$	$\mu = .5$	$\mu = .1$	$\mu = .5$
$X(0)$	.645	.682	.694	.731	.768	.797
$r(0)$	.119	.129	.118	.124	.116	.119
$nfa(1)$	−.041	−.035	−.038	−.036	−.031	−.034
$\bar{X}$	.896	.813	.896	.813	.896	.813
$\bar{r} - \bar{r}^*$	.094	.069	.094	.064	.094	.064
$\overline{nfa}$	0	0	0	0	0	0
	−.845	−.319	−.792	−.225	−.667	0
Adjustment	$\dot{X}>0$	$\dot{X}>0$	$\dot{X}>0$	$\dot{X}>0$	$\dot{X}>0$	$\dot{X}>0$[a]
Path	$nfa<0$	$nfa<0$	$nfa<0$	$nfa<0$	$nfa<0$	$nfa<0$
						for $t<21$,
						$nfa<0$
						for $t<20$.

	$\Omega = .2$					
	$b^*_{d0} = .3$		$b^*_{d0} = .8$		$b^*_{d0} = 2.0$	
	$\mu = .1$	$\mu = .5$	$\mu = .1$	$\mu = .5$	$\mu = .1$	$\mu = .5$
$X(0)$	.708	.732	.825	.837	.940	.942
$r(0)$	.135	.142	.141	.144	.137	.137
$nfa(1)$	-.031	-.027	-.031	-.030	-.045	-.045
$\bar{X}$	.862	.799	1.036	.881	1.208	1.025
$\bar{r}$	.135	.085	.136	.089	.117	.085
$\bar{r} - \bar{r}^*$	.082	.032	.084	.041	.047	.032
$\overline{nfa}$	-.134	-.041	-.400	-.033	-1.291	-.425
Adjustment Path	$\dot{X}>0^a$ for $t<21$, $nfa<0$ for $t<35$.	$\dot{X}>0^a$ for $t<44$, $nfa<0$ for $t<21$.	$\dot{X}>0$ $nfa<0$	$\dot{X}>0^a$ for $t<22$ $nfa<0$ for $t<21$.	$\dot{X}>0$ $nfa<0$	$\dot{X}>0$ $nfa<0$

[a]After an initial period of depreciation and decumulation of net foreign assets, the adjustment path to steady state is characterized by $\dot{X}<0$ and $nfa>0$.

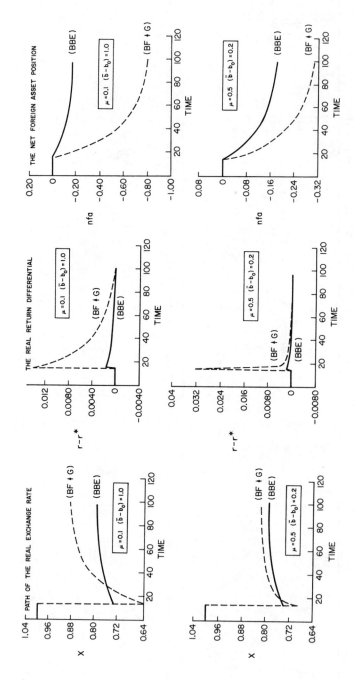

Fig. 7.5 Dynamic adjustment to a balanced budget expansion (BBE) vs. a bond-financed expansion (BF ↑ G) when $\Omega = 0$ and $b_{d0}^{*} = .3$

ernment deficit. Comparing case (a) and (b), we can see that the initial appreciation is larger for the slow adjustment case. In contrast, the initial jump in $r - r^*$ is larger for the fast adjustment case. Even though the long-run stock of domestic bonds is lower in case (b), the initial increase in r is greater because the bonds are expected to arrive in the economy sooner.

Figure 7.5 also shows that after the initial period, the rates of net foreign asset decumulation and depreciation are higher for bond-financed expansions. This result indicates that the current account deficits induced by the initial appreciation are much larger than in the case of a balanced budget expansion. As the level of domestic bonds approaches its target level and we near a balanced budget position, the rates of depreciation and net foreign asset decumulation slow down. The faster the rate of adjustment (μ) or the lower the change in the supply of government bonds due to the expansion, the more quickly the system returns to the dynamics associated with a balanced budget expansion.

If initial international bond holdings are large, then a bond-financed expansion may yield more interesting dynamics, especially in the high adjustment case. Figure 7.6 shows that in both cases a jump appreciation is initially followed by depreciation and net capital inflows. However, in case (b) the situation shortly changes, and appreciation and accumulation of net foreign assets occur until the new equilibrium. What causes the real exchange rate to initially move away from its long-run equilibrium value? The deficit financed increase in government spending has its most expansionary effect in the initial period. Because of short-run demand pressure, both the real exchange rate and the real interest rate overshoot their long-run levels. A current account deficit is inevitable in the short run; the trade balance deteriorates in response to the appreciation while the service account worsens as higher interest payments are sent abroad.

The large increases in the stock of domestic bonds which occur in the periods immediately succeeding the increase in g contribute to the high level of the domestic interest rate and the negative service account. Eventually, as the domestic stock of bonds approaches its target level, taxes increase and the budget deficit is reduced. The corresponding decrease in demand pressure allows r to fall. Subsequent adjustment is then characterized by gradual appreciation and capital outflows. In contrast, in the slow adjustment case, by the time the stock of domestic bonds is near $\bar{b}$ and the increase in taxes has relieved demand pressure on the interest rate, the stock of domestic bonds has grown enough to keep interest rates from falling. Thus, the entire path to equilibrium is characterized by $r > r^*$ and depreciation.

If assets are less than perfect substitutes, then the dynamic paths are more likely to be characterized by smooth adjustment when initial

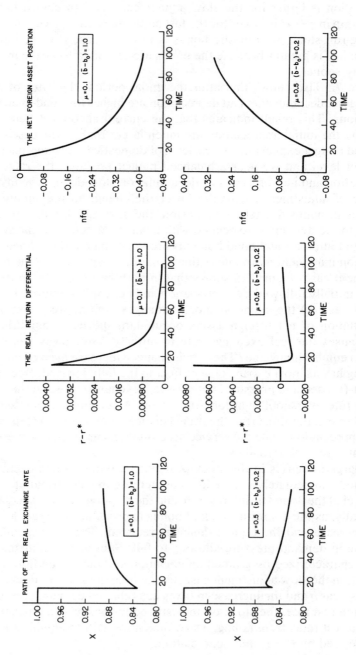

Fig. 7.6   Dynamic adjustment to a bond-financed expansion when $\Omega = 0$ and $b_{d0}^* = 4.0$

cross-country asset holdings are high. Imperfect asset substitutability allows a much larger jump in the domestic real interest rate, so the service account will play a more dominant role. The initial negative impact of the service account on the balance of payments will be larger when b_{d0}^* is larger. Consequently, the likelihood that net foreign asset decumulation accompanies depreciation along the adjustment path increases with initial domestic holdings of foreign bonds. If instead b_{d0}^* is small, the initial deficit in the current account is eventually replaced by a surplus as interest rates moderate and the exchange rate depreciates.

The differences between a balanced budget and a bond-financed fiscal expansion can be summarized as follows. On impact, the exchange rate appreciates and the domestic interest rate shoots up, both changes being larger in the case of temporary bond finance of government spending. In cases where a balanced budget expansion leads to depreciation and current account deficits, subsequent dynamics are characterized initially by a higher rate of net foreign asset decumulation and depreciation when bond finance is employed. When a balanced budget expansion is instead associated with appreciation and the accumulation of net foreign assets on the path to the new steady state, using bond finance initially causes the opposite dynamics, but may eventually be associated with similar dynamics as long as the increase in the stocks of bonds occurring over the period is not too large. And finally, for a given fiscal stimulus, the new steady state levels of the domestic real interest rate and the exchange rate will be higher and the level of net foreign assets lower when bond finance is initially used instead of taxes.

7.5 Comments on Recent U.S. Experience

What can be said about the recent U.S. experience of large bond-financed deficits and steady real appreciation in light of the above theoretical framework? A thorough empirical investigation of the impact of the domestic fiscal expansion on the international economy is beyond the scope of this study. However, we can take a brief look at the data to try and determine whether or not the above model helps explain the course of events. In the following discussion, we will focus on the United States and the other major countries, Japan, Germany, France, and the United Kingdom.

The U.S. fiscal expansion of the 1980s occurred in conjunction with fiscal contractions of varying magnitudes in the other major developed nations. Organization for Economic Cooperation and Development (OECD) estimates of general government structural budget balances indicate that between 1981 and 1985, the U.S. structural balance deteriorated by approximately 2.9% of nominal GNP. In contrast, over this period, the structural budget balances of most of the other nations improved: Japan's by 2.7%, Germany's by 3.1%, and France's by 3% of nominal GNP or GDP. The United Kingdom's structural budget balance is estimated to have worsened by about .2% of GDP from 1981 to 1985. Changes in inflation-adjusted structural budget balances show similar trends.[21]

Both the nominal and real value of the U.S. dollar rose in the early 1980s. If one measures the real exchange rate as an index of U.S. manufacturing wholesale prices relative to those of other industrial nations, adjusted for nominal exchange rates, then by the third quarter of 1981 the United States experienced 22.1% real appreciation over the 1980 average.[22] After a brief respite in late 1981 real appreciation continued steadily, but at a slower rate, through 1982 and 1983. By the end of 1982, the index of relative wholesale prices had risen 28.1% from its 1980 average; by the end of 1983 this index had risen by 32.0%. After the second quarter of 1984, both nominal and real dollar appreciation sped up again, so that by the end of 1984 U.S. manufacturing wholesale prices relative to other industrial countries had increased 44.2% from the 1980 average. By the end of the second quarter of 1985, this index had declined slightly to 43.9% above the 1980 level.

Figure 7.7 shows the U.S. *ex post* real interest rate on 3-month Treasury bills. We use *ex post* real rates as a very rough proxy for short-term *ex ante* real rates. Note that the U.S. real interest rate reached its highest levels in 1981 and 1982, declined during the recession, and rebounded strongly in 1984. Also, notice that between the first quarter of 1981 and that of 1985, the real interest rate was above, and often substantially above 4%. Figure 7.7 also shows that *ex post* short-term real interest differentials $r - r^*$ between the United States and the four other countries under consideration have usually been positive since 1980. When the differentials are averaged over each year, the years 1981 and 1984 stand out as being the periods of the largest real interest rate discrepancies.[23] These years both correspond to large increases in U.S. real interest rates as well as considerable real appreciation of the dollar.

High real interest rate differentials and real appreciation can be explained by a bond-financed fiscal expansion in the context of our model. However, there were undoubtedly other important factors at play. The course of monetary policy in the United States vis-à-vis the other major countries, portfolio, savings, and investment shifts, and the different speed and strength of recovery from the last recession between nations also influenced the path of the real exchange rate and real interest rates.[24] It is also possible that during some periods the dollar was on a bubble path. We leave to future research the difficult problem of empirically separating all of these diverse effects.

Let us now consider U.S. current account developments in the 1980s. Figure 7.8 depicts the current account along with the trade balance and

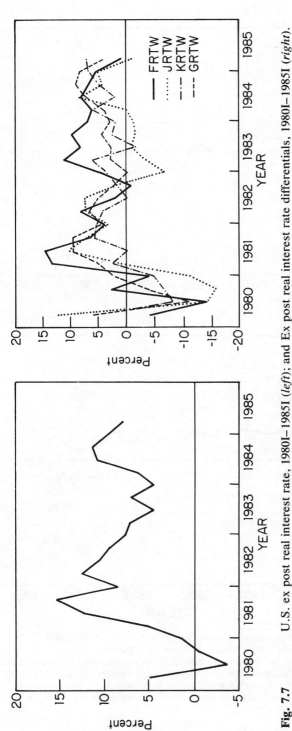

Fig. 7.7   U.S. ex post real interest rate, 1980I–1985I (*left*); and Ex post real interest rate differentials, 1980I–1985I (*right*).

Source: All data is from the IMF International Financial Statistics.

Note: The short-term ex post real interest rates were calculated as follows: 3-month nominal interest rates for each country were adjusted by subtracting the wholesale or industrial price inflation occurring over the subsequent quarter. The nominal rates used were the U.S. Treasury Bill rate, the West German, Japanese, and French call money rates, and the Eurodollar rate in London. The wholesale price index was used to calculate inflation in the U.S. and Japan. For Germany and France, industrial goods price indexes were used, and the manufacturing output price index was used for the U.K.

Ex post real interest rate differentials are the U.S. rate minus the foreign rate or, $r - r^*$. FRTW, JRTW, KRTW, and GRTW denote the U.S.–French, U.S.–Japanese, U.S.–U.K., and U.S.–West German real interest rate differentials, respectively.

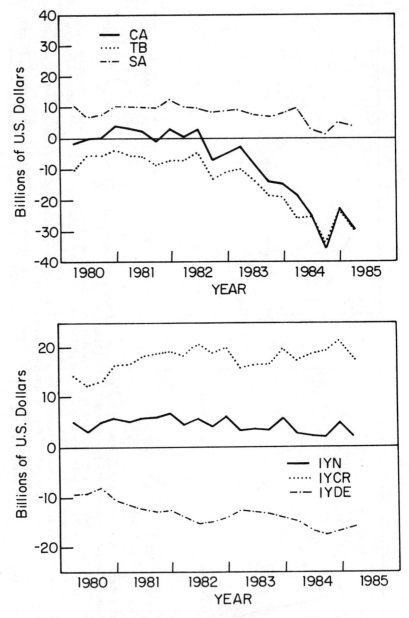

Fig. 7.8   U.S. current account developments, 1980I–1985I
Source: IMF Balance of Payments Statistics.
Note: Top panel represents U.S. current account (CA), trade balance
(TB), and service account, excluding transfers (SA) for 1980I–1985I.
Bottom panel represents other U.S. investment income—net (IYN),
credit (IYCR), and debit (IYDE) transactions for 1980I–1985I.

the service account excluding transfers. In addition, the lower panel of Figure 7.8 shows the component of the service account which reflects dividends, interest, and other investment income; this part of the service account is the most relevant in terms of the model described above. The current account was either positive or roughly in balance until the third quarter of 1982, when it began its steady decline to substantial deficit levels. It is interesting to note that the large real appreciation of 1981 did not considerably worsen the current account; the service account improvement more than compensated for the mild deterioration of the trade balance. The 1981 experience of real appreciation accompanied by current account surpluses is a pattern which could be predicted by the above model. One might expect a fiscal expansion to improve the current account through the service account, especially if one included a mechanism which allowed a gradual response of the trade balance to real exchange rates.

After 1982, however, this pattern clearly broke down. The dramatic decline of the trade balance was accompanied by a gradual worsening of the service account. Net investment earnings (excluding reinvested earnings) have fallen every year since 1981, reflecting to some extent the loss of net foreign assets held in the United States. While U.S. current account deficits grew to unprecedented levels, real appreciation of the dollar continued. This pattern of events can only be described well in the above framework with an anticipated future fiscal expansion beyond the expansion that was already in place. Although in the early 1980s future U.S. budget deficits were expected to remain high throughout the rest of the decade, it is unlikely that in 1984 or 1985 economic agents anticipated an expansion of a magnitude large enough to explain the behavior of the dollar. Therefore, it is safe to conclude that fiscal policy was not the only culprit behind the evolution of the current account, real interest rates, and dollar exchange rates that the United States witnessed in the first half of the 1980s.

7.6 Concluding Remarks

Expansionary fiscal policy in an open economy can have dramatically different results depending on whether the expanding country is large or small. Within a simple two-country framework, this chapter has demonstrated that the initial amount of international capital market integration is a crucial factor in the dynamic adjustment path and the long-run steady state associated with a permanent increase in government spending. The high degree of capital mobility in the world today suggests that the initial asset market conditions explored above may be quite important.

As countries hold more of each other's assets, the service account and capital gains become more important in the adjustment process.

A balanced budget expansion in a small country leads to an appreciation on impact followed by steady depreciation and decumulation of net foreign assets through trade balance deficits. However, under certain circumstances this standard result is modified. A large country that increases its government spending has the ability to raise world interest rates. When initial cross-country bond holdings or the degree of imperfect asset substitutability are relatively large, dynamic responses to a fiscal expansion may be characterized by appreciation and accumulation of net foreign assets. This result pertains to both a balanced budget expansion and a bond-financed expansion that eliminates budget deficits over time. However, if deficit finance is resorted to for too long of a period, or if the increase in the stock of domestic bonds associated with a given increase in government spending is too large, then the standard dynamics are restored.

Several extensions of the analysis presented above would improve our understanding of the international effects of a large country's policies. The model lends itself nicely to the analysis of the presence of a "safe haven" in international asset markets. Also, a comparison of various tax policies such as an increase in income taxes or the imposition of an import tax surcharge could be considered in a similar framework. Finally, the addition of a physical investment sector could shed light on the extent of international crowding out associated with expansionary fiscal policy.

The international interdependence of the world's economies has increased markedly in recent decades. Many repercussive effects of a large country's stabilization policies are often ignored. This chapter has analyzed just a few of the channels through which one nation's fiscal expansion spill over abroad. Further theoretical work and empirical investigation in this area is crucial to both economists and policymakers.

Appendix

The linearized version of equations (1) to (5) is:

(1') $\quad \tilde{y} = \tilde{a} + \tilde{g} + \tilde{T} = 0 \qquad\qquad \tilde{y}^* = \tilde{a}^* - \tilde{T} = 0;$

(2') $\quad \tilde{a} = (1 - \sigma)\tilde{y}_d + \delta\tilde{w} - \phi\tilde{r} \qquad \tilde{a}^* = (1 - \sigma)\tilde{y}_d^* + \delta\tilde{w}^* - \phi\tilde{r}^*;$

(3') $\quad \tilde{y}_d = r_0^*\tilde{b} + r_0^*\tilde{nfa} + b_0\tilde{r} + b_{d0}^*(\tilde{r}^* - \tilde{r}) + r_0^*b_{d0}^*\tilde{X} - \tilde{z};$

$\qquad \tilde{y}_d^* = b_{d0}^*(\tilde{r} - \tilde{r}^*) - r_0\tilde{nfa} - r_0b_{f0}\tilde{X};$

(4') $\quad \tilde{w} = \tilde{b} + \tilde{nfa} + b_{d0}^*\tilde{X} \qquad\qquad \tilde{w}^* = -\tilde{nfa} - b_{f0}\tilde{X};$ and

$(5')$ $\tilde{T} = \epsilon'\tilde{g} + \eta'\tilde{X}$ where $\epsilon' = \epsilon/(1 - \epsilon - \epsilon^*)$ and
$$\eta' = \eta/(1 - \epsilon - \epsilon^*).$$

Here we present the algebra for the balanced budget case. As in the text, we assume an initial curent account balance and that $r_0 = r_0^*$, $b_{d0}^* = b_{f0}$, $T_0 = 0$, and $X_0 = 1$. For convenience, we define two parameters: $\phi' = \phi + (1 - \sigma)b_{d0}^*$ and $\delta' = \delta + (1 - \sigma)r_0$. Using equations $(1')$ through $(5')$, we can express short-run equilibrium as a system in r and r^*:

$$\begin{bmatrix} \phi' & -b_{d0}^*(1 - \sigma) \\ -b_{d0}^*(1 - \sigma) & \phi' \end{bmatrix}\begin{bmatrix} \tilde{r} \\ \tilde{r}^* \end{bmatrix} = \begin{bmatrix} \eta' + \delta'b_{d0}^* & \sigma + \epsilon' & \delta' \\ -(\eta' + \delta'b_{d0}^*) & -\epsilon' & -\delta' \end{bmatrix}\begin{bmatrix} \tilde{X} \\ \tilde{g} \\ \tilde{nfa} \end{bmatrix}.$$
$$(A')$$

Solving this system, we have:

$\mathrm{Det}(A') = |A'| = \phi^2 + 2(1 - \sigma)\phi b_{d0}^*$ and
$\tilde{A} = |A'|/\phi = \phi + 2(1 - \sigma)b_{d0}^*;$

$\tilde{r} = (\eta' + \delta'b_{d0}^*)\tilde{X}/\tilde{A} + [\phi(\sigma + \epsilon') + \sigma(1 - \sigma)b_{d0}^*]\tilde{g}/|A'| + \delta'\tilde{nfa}/\tilde{A};$

$\tilde{r}^* = -(\eta' + \delta' b_{d0}^*)\tilde{X}/\tilde{A} + [\sigma(1 - \sigma)b_{d0}^* - \phi\epsilon']\tilde{g}/|A'| - \delta'\tilde{nfa}/\tilde{A};$ and

$\tilde{r} - \tilde{r}^* = 2(\eta' + \delta'b_{d0}^*)\tilde{X}/\tilde{A} + (\sigma + 2\epsilon')\tilde{g}/\tilde{A} + 2\delta'\tilde{nfa}/\tilde{A}.$

In the case where the fiscal expansion is initially bond-financed, the equilibrium rate of return differential evolves as follows:

$\tilde{r} - \tilde{r}^* = 2(\eta' + \delta'b_{d0}^*)\tilde{X}/\tilde{A} + (1 + 2\epsilon')\tilde{g}/\tilde{A}$
$$+ 2\delta'\tilde{nfa}/\tilde{A} + [\delta - (1 - \sigma)\mu]\tilde{b}/\tilde{A}.$$

The dynamic system described by equations (7a) and (11a) in the text is:

$$(13) \quad \begin{bmatrix} \dot{X} \\ \dot{nfa} \end{bmatrix} = \begin{bmatrix} \overset{(+)}{a_{11}} & \overset{(+)}{a_{12}} \\ (?) & (?) \\ a_{21} & a_{22} \end{bmatrix}\begin{bmatrix} \tilde{X} \\ \tilde{nfa} \end{bmatrix} + \begin{bmatrix} \overset{(+)}{a_{13}} \\ (?) \\ a_{23} \end{bmatrix}\tilde{g};$$
$$\qquad\qquad\qquad (A) \qquad\qquad\qquad (\gamma)$$

$a_{11} = \Omega(1 + \theta - \theta^*)b_{d0}^* + 2(\eta' + \delta'b_{d0}^*)/\tilde{A}$; $a_{12} = \Omega(\theta - \theta^*) + 2\delta'/\tilde{A}$;

$a_{21} = \eta' + r_0 b_{d0}^* - 2b_{d0}^*(\eta' + \delta'b_{d0}^*)/\tilde{A}$; $a_{22} = r_0 - 2\delta'b_{d0}^*/\tilde{A}$;

$a_{13} = (\sigma + 2\epsilon')/\tilde{A}$; and $a_{23} = \epsilon' - 2b_{d0}^*(\sigma + 2\epsilon')/\tilde{A}$.

Note that the inclusion of capital gains causes the second row of the system to be more likely to be negative. Denoting the coefficients of the system with capital gains as a_{ij}', we have:

$a_{21}' = a_{21} - b_{d0}^* a_{11}$; $a_{22}' = a_{22} - b_{d0}^* a_{12}$; and $a_{23}' = a_{23} - b_{d0}^* a_{13}$.

The determinant of the system is clearly the same, with or without capital gains:

$$\text{Det}(A) = |A| = 2\eta'(\sigma r_0^* - \delta)/\bar{A} + \Omega b_{d0}^*(\phi r_0^* - 2\delta b_{d0}^*)/\bar{A}$$
$$+ \Omega\eta'(\theta - \theta^*)(2\sigma b_{d0}^* - \phi)/\bar{A}.$$

For stability, a sufficient condition is that $|A| < 0$.

Notes

1. For an excellent review of the literature on the effects of expansionary fiscal policy in an open economy, the interested reader is referred to Penati 1983. Dornbusch 1984 also provides a good summary of various models of exchange rate determination, with a particular emphasis on disentangling the various causes of the overvaluation of the dollar in the early eighties.

2. As Sachs and Wyplosz point out, the analysis in Blanchard 1985 indicates that with finite-lived consumers, δ is likely to be more than r. In steady state equilibrium, with infinitely-lived agents, δ must be equal to r. Note that these results apply when taxes are a lump sum; if instead one introduced a more sophisticated method of taxation, then the relevant interest rate would be the after-tax real rate of return.

3. Blanchard 1985 formalizes this assumption by introducing individuals who are devoid of a bequest motive and face a given probability of death. Recent work by Buiter 1984 and Frenkel and Razin 1984 has incorporated this departure from Ricardian equivalence into the analysis of fiscal policy.

4. In general, this wealth effect is ambiguous; while an appreciation decreases the value of domestically held foreign bonds, it also decreases the home consumer price index. The net wealth effect will then depend on the relative share of foreign bonds in the domestic portfolio vis-à-vis the relative share of imports in domestic absorption.

5. Since there is no stochastic uncertainty in the model, the assumption of rational expectations is equivalent to perfect foresight.

6. See Dornbusch 1982 for a capital asset pricing model in a utility-maximizing framework which nicely demonstrates this result.

7. A good discussion of this instability problem can be found in Blinder and Solow 1973. Also, see Blanchard 1984.

8. This assumption seems reasonable given that in many developed countries interest income is part of taxable income.

9. This condition is equivalent to the condition: $(\partial a^*/\partial r)(\partial r/\partial g) > \partial T/\partial g$. Foreign absorption increases because of the increase in foreign interest income earned on domestic bonds $(\partial a^*/\partial g = (1-\sigma)b_{f0}\partial r/\partial g)$, while the foreign trade balance deteriorates by ϵ' due to the crowding out of domestic absorption to the magnitude of ϕ. See the Appendix for the algebra underlying this result.

10. This condition guarantees that the system evolves along a unique saddle path which converges to the steady state. Holding r and r^* constant, the condition implies that $\partial nfa/\partial nfa < 0$ or that the state variable evolves according

to the unique stable root of the system. This can be seen by setting $g = 0$ in equation (1). An increase in net foreign assets causes an increase in absorption of $(1-\sigma)r_0 + \delta$, meaning that the trade balance must decline by this amount for goods market equilibrium. If we also look at equation (11), we see that an increase in net foreign assets increases the service account by r_0. Thus, $\partial nfa/\partial nfa = r_0 + \partial T/\partial nfa = r_0 - (1-\sigma)r_0 - \delta = (\sigma r_0 - \delta) < 0$.

11. Again, if one believes that an equilibrium is characterized by $\delta > r$, as in Blanchard 1985, the condition for a negative determinant is even more likely to hold.

12. For the most part, the parameter values chosen are the same as those used by Sachs and Wyplosz. However, they assumed that domestic residents of a small country held one-half of its assets in foreign bonds ($\theta = .5$), which is probably too high for the large country case. Also, because they neglected to include interest income in disposable income, their stability condition in the case of perfect asset substitutability required that $\delta > r_0$; thus they assumed $\delta = .1$ and $r_0 = .05$.

13. The intuition behind the relative slopes of the schedules is as follows. An increase in net foreign assets leads to excess demand, and as the real exchange rate and the real return differential decrease to clear the goods market there is a magnified effect on the current account. Note that $(\bar{r} - \bar{r}^*)$ appears with a multiple of $-b_{d0}^*$ in equation (11a); thus we need more appreciation to clear the current account than to maintain portfolio balance.

14. An interesting extension of the model would include dynamic adjustment in the trade balance. For instance, it would be interesting to consider the case in which the coefficient η was actually a distributed lag, with η growing over time.

15. It would be interesting to do an empirical analysis which focused on this condition. One country in which the condition may actually apply is Japan, which has a fairly high savings rate and a low proportion of imports in consumption.

16. The condition for long-run appreciation (14b) remains the same, but now equation (14a) becomes:

(14a') $$\overline{nfa} - nfa_0 = [b_{d0}^*(2\epsilon\delta - \sigma r_0^*) - \sigma\eta]\bar{g}/2\eta(\delta - \sigma r_0^*).$$

17. When net capital inflows occur between the two steady states, domestic wealth decreases while foreign wealth rises. In addition, r unambiguously increases from r_0, while r^* can go either way. These two effects may depress domestic demand and cancel out the positive effect of the balanced budget expansion. Furthermore, both of these effects have a negative impact on the current account. Therefore, a long-run depreciation is necessary to eliminate excess supply (demand) at home (abroad) by restoring current account balance. The dynamics of this case can be quite similar to those of figure 7.2a, except that in the long run the new equilibrium may be at a point such that a real depreciation has occurred.

18. The higher δ, the more important the effect of the redistribution of assets between countries through the current account.

19. In other words,

$$\partial\bar{X}/\partial(\bar{b} - b_0) > 0, \quad \partial\bar{r}/\partial(\bar{b} - b_0)\Big|_{\Omega=0} = \partial\bar{r}^*/\partial(\bar{b} - b_0)\Big|_{\Omega=0} > 0, \text{ and}$$

$$\partial(\bar{r} - \bar{r}^*)/\partial(\bar{b} - b_0)\Big|_{\Omega\neq0} > 0.$$

20. Diamond's result is due to the fact that when debt is issued externally there is no displacement of capital domestically, so there is less of a loss in efficiency associated with issuing government debt. Because capital accumulation is not considered in this model, we capture only the negative effect of interest payments flowing abroad.

21. Cumulative changes in inflation-adjusted structural budget deficits as a percent of nominal GNP or GDP between 1981 and 1985 are estimated by the OECD to be as follows: U.S., -3.6%; Japan, 2.4%; Germany, 2.7%; France, 1%; and the United Kingdom, -2.5%. The source of these data is the *OECD Economic Outlook,* issues 38 through 41.

22. The exchange rate adjusted index of manufacturing wholesale prices for the United States relative to other major industrial countries is from the *IMF International Financial Statistics,* series 63ey 110.

23. For instance, the U.S.–German average real interest differential was 7.08% in 1981, 3.30% in 1982, 3.08% in 1983, and 6.98% in 1984. The pattern is similar for the U.S.–U.K. and the U.S.–Japan differential. The U.S.–French differential was quite high in 1981 and 1984 but was also relatively high in 1983.

24. See Blanchard and Summers 1984 for an excellent discussion of the various economic factors contributing to high U.S. and world real interest rates.

References

Basevi, G., O. J. Blanchard, W. H. Buiter, R. Dornbusch, and R. Layard. 1983. Macroeconomic prospects and policies for the European community. CEPS Paper no. 1.

Blanchard, O. J. 1984. Current and anticipated deficits, interest rates, and economic activity. NBER Working Paper no. 1265.

———. 1985. Debt, deficits and finite horizons. *Journal of Political Economy* 93 (April): 223–47.

Blanchard, O. J., and R. Dornbusch. 1984. U.S. deficits, the dollar and Europe. *Banca Nazionale del Lavora Quarterly Review* 148: 89–113.

Blanchard, O. J., and L. H. Summers. 1984. Perspectives on high world real interest rates. *Brookings Papers on Economic Activity* 2: 273–334.

Blinder, A. S., and R. M. Solow. 1973. Does fiscal policy matter? *Journal of Public Economics* 2: 319–338.

Boyer, R. S., and R. J. Hodrick. 1982. Perfect foresight, financial policies and exchange rate dynamics. *Canadian Journal of Economics* 15 (1): 143–164.

Branson, W. H., and W. H. Buiter. 1983. Monetary and fiscal policy with flexible exchange rates. In *Economic interdependence and flexible exchange rates,* ed. J. S. Bhandari and B. H. Putnam. Cambridge: M.I.T. Press, 303–24.

Buiter, W. H. 1984. Fiscal policy in open interdependent economies. NBER Working Paper no. 1429.

Diamond, P. A. 1965. National debt in a neoclassical growth model. *American Economic Review* 55 (5): 1126–50.

Dornbusch, R. 1982. Exchange rate risk and the macroeconomics of exchange rate determination. In *International financial markets,* ed. R. G. Hawkins and R. M. Levich. Greenwich, Conn.: JAI Press.

————. 1983. The overvalued dollar and the international monetary system. Unpublished manuscript.

————. 1984. External debt, budget deficits and disequilibrium exchange rates. Unpublished manuscript.

Dornbusch, R., and S. Fischer. 1980. Exchange rates and the current account. *American Economic Review* 70 (5): 960–71.

Frenkel, J. A., and A. Razin. 1984a. Budget deficits and rates of interest in the world economy. NBER Working Paper no. 1354.

————. 1984b. The international transmission of fiscal expenditures and budget deficits in the world economy. NBER Working Paper no. 1527.

Giovannini, A. 1983. *Essays on flexible exchange rates*. Unpublished Ph.D. dissertation, M.I.T.

International Monetary Fund. *International financial statistics*, selected issues. Washington, D.C.

Kole, L. S. 1984. *Essays on stabilization policies under flexible exchange rates*. Unpublished Ph.D. dissertation, M.I.T.

Krugman, P. R. 1983. International aspects of U.S. monetary and fiscal policy. In *The economics of large government budget deficits*. Federal Reserve Bank of Boston Conference Series 27: 112–40.

Mundell, R. 1968. *International economics*. New York: Macmillan.

Obstfeld, M., and A. C. Stockman. 1983. Exchange rate dynamics. NBER Working Paper no. 1230.

Organization for Economic Cooperation and Development. 1985. *OECD Economic Outlook,* various issues. Paris.

Penati, A. 1983. Expansionary fiscal policy and the exchange rate: A review. *IMF Staff Papers* (September): 542–69.

Sachs, J. D., and C. Wyplosz. 1984. Real exchange rate effects of fiscal policy. NBER Working Paper no. 1255.

Turnovsky, S. J. 1976. The dynamics of fiscal policy in an open economy. *Journal of International Economics* 6: 115–142.

Comment   Robert J. Hodrick

The large real appreciation of the dollar during the 1980s is surely one of the most surprising economic events of the decade. How much of the appreciation is attributable to the change in government fiscal policy in the United States? Is there a role for monetary explanations?

There are difficult questions to address because the United States is so large. Analysis of the issues therefore requires some type of two-country model, but these models are notoriously difficult to solve because they are analytically complex. Also, where explicit models have been done, it is often found that the results are not terribly different from the analysis of the small country case. Linda Kole has made some

Robert J. Hodrick is professor of finance in the J. L. Kellogg Graduate School of Management at Northwestern University and is a research associate of the National Bureau of Economic Research.

progress in understanding these issues with a two-country framework by making a number of simplifying assumptions. Her results are interesting because they are quite different from the results of small country analyses of these issues.

Unfortunately, I find some of the simplifying features of the Kole model to be less desirable than others. In order to set the stage for these criticisms, I want to discuss how the model differs from the results of the small country model developed in Boyer and Hodrick (1982). After this discussion, I explain how a monetary sector could be added to the Kole model, and I conclude by suggesting some features of the real world that ought to be modeled in developing a deeper understanding of the questions posed above.

A Small Country Model

The small country model of Boyer and Hodrick (1982) can be presented in two equations. The first is an expression of money and international capital market equilibrium given by

$$(1) \qquad m_t - s_t = -\alpha(r_t^* + \dot{s}_t) + b_t,$$

where m_t is the logarithm of the nominal money supply, s_t is the logarithm of the exchange rate of domestic currency for foreign currency, r_t^* is the foreign nominal interest rate, and b_t is the logarithm of net foreign assets. A dot over a variable indicates its time derivative, and all Greek letters are constant positive parameters. The specification of (1) assumes purchasing power parity with a normalized foreign price level set equal to one, and uncovered interest rate parity with the domestic nominal interest rate equal to the foreign nominal interest rate plus the expected rate of change of the exchange rate. The second equation provides the evolution of the net foreign assets of the country, which reflects a Metzleric savings function with a target real wealth that depends on the disposable income of the country. The specification is

$$(2) \qquad \dot{b}_t = \gamma_0 - \gamma_1 g_t - \gamma_2 \mu_t - \beta_1(m_t - s_t) - \beta_2 b_t,$$

where g_t is the logarithm of government expenditure, and μ_t is the rate of growth of the nominal money supply.

The general solution for the exchange rate for arbitrary time paths of the exogenous processes is

$$(3) \quad s_t = \int_t^\infty [r_\tau^* + \lambda_1 m_\tau + q_2(\gamma_0 - \gamma_1 g_\tau - \gamma_2 \mu_\tau)]e^{-\lambda_1(\tau - t)}d\tau + q_2 b_t,$$

where λ_1 is the positive root of the system and q_2 is a negative normalized eigenvalue. Expression (3) is particularly convenient for analyzing the initial effects of a change in policy. Since q_2 is negative, the coefficients of current and future government spending and the rate of money growth are both positive. Consequently, an unexpected increase in the profile of government spending depreciates the domestic currency.

For constant values of the government policies and the foreign interest rate a steady state exists. A permanent increase in the level of government spending causes inflation and a decumulation of foreign assets as the new steady state is approached. Agents attempt to smooth their consumption streams in the face of higher taxes to finance the expenditures. This causes a current account deficit and the loss of foreign assets. If the economy has time to prepare for the increase in government spending, there will be foreign asset accumulation accompanying the depreciation of the currency. Agents know that they will be poorer in the long run, and they attempt to save today to offset the decrease in wealth in the future.

How does the Kole analysis differ from these results? Consider her figure 7.2. An unanticipated permanent increase in government spending that is financed by taxes causes a real exchange rate appreciation and a current account deficit. During the transition to the new steady state, the real exchange rate depreciates. Does the nominal exchange rate also appreciate?

To address this question I added a monetary sector to the Kole model. The logarithm of the real exchange rate can be written as

$$(4) \qquad x_t = s_t + p_t^* - p_t,$$

where p_t^* is the logarithm of the foreign currency price of the foreign good and p_t is the logarithm of the domestic currency price of the domestic good.[1] Define the logarithms of the domestic and foreign price levels as π and π^*, where

$$(5a) \qquad \pi_t = (1 - \theta)(s_t + p_t^*) + \theta p_t = s_t + p_t^* - \theta x_t, \text{ and}$$

$$(5b) \qquad \pi_t^* = (1 - \theta^*)p_t^* + \theta^*(p_t - s_t) = p_t^* - \theta^* x_t,$$

where θ and θ^* are the consumption shares of the domestic good in the home and foreign countries. Assume that the money market equilibrium in the home and the foreign countries depends only on the nominal interest rate of the country, as in

$$(6a) \qquad m_t - \pi_t = -\alpha i_t; \text{ and}$$

$$(6b) \qquad m_t^* - \pi_t^* = -\alpha i_t^*.$$

---

1. In the Kole model there is no difference between the real exchange rate and the terms of trade. Such distinctions arise when there are nontraded goods and the real exchange rate is defined in terms of price levels of the foreign and domestic countries.

The monetary sector of the model is completed by defining the nominal interest rate in each country to be a weighted average of the real interest rates on the two goods plus the expected rate of change of the price level, as in

(7a) $$i_t = (1 - \theta)r_t^* + \theta r_t + \dot{\pi}_t, \text{ and}$$

(7b) $$i_t^* = (1 - \theta^*)r_t^* + \theta r_t + \dot{\pi}_t^*.$$

Taking the difference of the money market equilibriums in (6) and substituting for the nominal interest differential from (7) and the price level differential from (5) gives

(8) $$(m_t - m_t^*) - [s_t - (\theta - \theta^*)x_t]$$

$$= - \alpha[\dot{s}_t + (\theta - \theta^*)(r_t - r_t^* - \dot{x}_t)].$$

In (8) the real interest differential is equal to the expected rate of change of the real exchange rate if the assets are perfect substitutes, hence the solution for the nominal exchange rate can be found to be

(9) $$s_t = \int_t^\infty (1/\alpha)[(m_t - m_t^*) + (\theta - \theta^*)x_t]e^{-(1/\alpha)(\tau - t)}d\tau,$$

which indicates that a nominal appreciation coincides with a real appreciation when $\theta > \theta^*$. The decrease in the real exchange rate in response to a balanced budget increase in government spending found above translates into a permanent appreciation of the domestic currency, even in nominal terms.

Kole also analyzes the general case in which assets are not perfect substitutes. In this case the level of net foreign assets also enters the determination of the nominal exchange rate, as would be true if expenditures were included in the money market equilibriums in (6). Since this variable is predetermined, the prediction of an initial nominal appreciation still holds, but the fall in net foreign assets along the approach to the new equilibrium opens up the possibility that the domestic currency may depreciate in the new steady state.

At a casual empirical level, Kole's model seems to capture the major features of the current real appreciation of the dollar. Massive federal budget deficits have been accompanied by a real appreciation and a large current account deficit. But can a nonstochastic model really match the stylized facts?

Mussa (1985) documents that real exchange rates have been near random walks under flexible exchange rates. If the real exchange rate were a random walk, its expected rate of change would be zero, and the expected rate of change of the nominal exchange rate would be the expected inflation differential. Cumby and Obstfeld (1984) investigate this latter proposition empirically and find strong evidence against it.

The hypothesis really makes little sense economically since it implies that one country's output can become infinitely valuable in terms of the other country's output. The point is that we really have very little experience with the flexible rate regimes, and the near random walk nature may reflect more about price stickiness that is absent from the Kole model and those discussed above, than it does about underlying dynamic processes.

Another feature of the world that is missing from the Kole model is investment in physical assets. It is hard to explain the strong performance of the U.S. economy in recent years, in spite of high real interest rates, without some discussion of good investment possibilities and changes in the tax treatment of depreciation. Making the real output of the economy endogenous raises the issue of tractability of the model, but it would be much more interesting if there were international business cycles and growth.

Finally, I would be negligent in my duty as a discussant if I did not raise the issue of Ricardian equivalence. Much more work must be done in order to determine the extent to which future taxes are reflected in the current behavior of the agents in the economy. Outstanding quantities of government bonds are almost surely not fully regarded as wealth by the population as they are in the Kole model. Yet what fraction of the bonds is considered wealth? This is certainly an area where much interesting work remains.

References

Boyer, R. S., and R. J. Hodrick. 1982. Perfect foresight, financial policies, and exchange rate dynamics. *Canadian Journal of Economics* 15: 143–64.

Cumby, R., and M. Obstfeld, 1984. International interest rate and price level linkages under flexible exchange rates: A review of recent evidence. In J. Bilson and R. Marston, eds., *Exchange Rate Theory and Practice,* 121–51. Chicago: University of Chicago Press.

Mussa, M. 1985. Nominal exchange rate regimes and the behavior of real exchange rates: Evidence and implications. Paper read at the Carnegie-Rochester Conference on Public Policy, Carnegie-Mellon University (November).

Comment   Alessandro Penati

A stylized result of open economy macromodels is that an expansionary fiscal policy causes an instantaneous appreciation of the real exchange rate, which is then followed by a steady real depreciation

Alessandro Penati is assistant professor of finance at the Wharton School of the University of Pennsylvania.

and a current account deficit. The predictions of these models, however, seem at variance with the U.S. experience between 1981 and 1985, when a sharp initial real appreciation of the dollar was followed by further appreciations. Can standard portfolio models account for the recent dynamics of the dollar real exchange rate? Linda Kole's analysis shows that the answer is yes, provided that a two-country model is used instead of the more common small open economy framework.

The particular model utilized to study the impact of fiscal shocks on the real exchange rate is a two-country extension of the portfolio model developed by Sachs and Wyplosz (1984). In the model, the demand for real cash balances is always constant, given that it depends only on full employment output. The increase in real interest rates following the fiscal expansion is thus determined by the desired proportion between domestic and foreign bonds and by the crowding out of private domestic absorption, which is equal to consumption in the model. I have some queries about the specification of the consumption function that plays a key role in the transmission of fiscal shocks to the real exchange rate. Consumption is assumed to be linear in income, wealth, and the real rate of interest: income appears because of the liquidity constraints faced by consumers, while a constant relative risk-aversion utility function is all that is needed to include wealth and the real interest rate (Merton 1971). With this utility function, however, these two last variables would be highly nonlinear in the consumption function. The function's linearization around steady state values would make it difficult to carry out comparative static exercises between steady states. In addition, the coefficient of wealth is set equal to the rate of time preference in the numerical simulations, a condition that would result from a logarithmic utility function. In such a case, however, the real interest rate would drop out of the consumption function. Finally, the numerical value chosen for the coefficient of the real interest rate, .8, equal to that of disposable income, seems to me unreasonably high in view of the available empirical evidence.

The model is used to investigate the trajectory of the real exchange rate when one country adopts an expansionary fiscal policy. Several cases are considered: a balanced budget and a debt-financed fiscal expansion, an anticipated and an unanticipated expansion, perfect and imperfect substitution between domestic and foreign bonds, zero and large holdings of foreign currency denominated bonds, and fast-growing and slow-growing government debt—perhaps too many cases, as a reader may forget the main objective of the analysis in a myriad of phase diagrams and simulations.

One may recall that the purpose of the study is to find the conditions under which a fiscal expansion causes a steady appreciation of exchange rate determination in portfolio models. The key element turns out to be the wealth effect of the capital gains and losses due to exchange rate movements. Panel 'a' in figure 7.3 illustrates this point well. In the model represented by that figure, domestic residents hold a large fraction of their wealth in the form of foreign bonds, while foreigners hold only bonds denominated in their currencies. A domestic balanced budget fiscal expansion increases the real interest rate to crowd out domestic demand and appreciates the real exchange rate to crowd out foreign demand; the appreciation, in turn, reduces domestic wealth by imposing capital losses on domestic investors. If the wealth effect of capital losses outweighs the relative price effect due to the increase in the real interest rate, there will be an excess demand for foreign bonds immediately after the fiscal expansion so that an expected appreciation will be needed to achieve bond market equilibrium. With perfect foresight, the real rate will actually appreciate in the transition to the new steady state, along with the desired accumulation of net foreign assets that originates from a stable current account surplus.

Theoretically, therefore, a fiscal expansion can result in a steady appreciation of the real exchange rate in portfolio models. I do not think, however, that the model can help us to understand the recent U.S. experience. On empirical grounds, the wealth effect of exchange rate capital gains and losses must be minimal given the industrial countries' propensity to invest the vast majority of their wealth within national boundaries (Penati and Dooley 1984). On theoretical grounds, stability conditions in portfolio models generally impose that appreciations be accompanied by a current account surplus in the transition to the steady state. Indeed, portfolio models owe part of their popularity to this characteristic, which can account for the steady appreciations experienced by the surplus countries in the second half of the seventies. In the recent case of the dollar, however, the puzzle is precisely the opposite; namely, why did the dollar appreciate in real terms for five consecutive years when the U.S. current account was increasingly moving into deficit? I doubt that the solution to this puzzle can be found in traditional portfolio models.

References

Merton, R. 1971. Optimum consumption and portfolio rules in a continuous-time model. *Journal of Economic Theory* 3: 373–413.

Penati, A., and M. Dooley. 1984. Current account imbalances and capital formation in industrial countries, 1949–81. *IMF Staff Papers* 31: 1–24.

Sachs, J., and C. Wyplosz. 1984. Real exchange rate effects of fiscal policy. NBER Working Paper no. 1255.

8 Fiscal Policy, Trade Intervention, and World Interest Rates: An Empirical Analysis

Sweder van Wijnbergen

8.1 Introduction

The past five years have witnessed a revival of interest in the relation between public sector deficits and the real rate of interest, spawning a literature that is already too large to adequately discuss it here. Much of the renewed interest was triggered by the striking differences in real interest rate response after the oil price shocks in 1973–74 (OPEC = 1) and those in 1979–80 (OPEC = 2). The question addressed in this paper is whether real interest patterns since 1979 can be explained by the changes in fiscal policy in the major industrial countries since 1979.

After OPEC-1, real interest rates fell dramatically and remained low, often even negative, until the end of the 1970s (see fig. 8.1 in sec. 8.5). Many observers see OPEC-1 as a major explanatory factor behind this period of low real interest rates (see, e.g., Bruno and Sachs 1985). The oil price shock in 1973–74, so this argument goes, effected a huge transfer of real income from low-saving oil-exporting countries in the Middle East. This increased world savings and led to an *ex ante* world current account surplus. To restore global equilibrium and bring the world current account to zero, real interest rates fell.

Sweder van Wijnbergen is a senior economist in the Trade and Adjustment Policy Division of the Country Policy Department of the World Bank, and a research fellow of the Centre for Economic Policy Research in London.

Part of this paper was written while I was a visitor at the Institute for International Economics Studies in Stockholm. This paper also draws on background work for the World Bank's World Development Report 1985. I am indebted to my colleagues on the WDR-1985 team for many helpful discussions. Robert Price of the OECD provided invaluable help with data collection, and Tina Jacobson and Nadeem Burney gave me much appreciated research assistance. Section 8.2 and 8.4 draw extensively on my paper in *Economic Policy* (van Wijnbergen 1985a).

This paper does not necessarily reflect the views of the World Bank or its affiliated institutions.

Such a fall in real interest rates did not materialize after the second series of oil price shocks in 1979–80. Instead, real interest rates reached historical highs right through 1984, as nominal rates failed to decline in line with the substantial decline in inflation. Much of the subsequent discussion has focused on whether the monetary and fiscal policies followed in the major industrial countries were to blame for this failure of real interest rates to decline after OPEC-2 the way they did after OPEC-1.

We will not be concerned with monetary policy; while some of the developments since 1979 can be explained by the changes in monetary policy that were enacted in, mainly, the United States and Britain, it is impossible to use monetary policy as the dominant explanation of real interest rates in the 1980s. Blanchard and Dornbusch (1984) have argued this forcefully by pointing out that the steepening of the term structure and the sheer persistence of high real rates argue against such a purely monetary explanation. Fiscal deficits will need to be considered, and that is the main focus of this paper.

The theoretical literature on interest rate effects of public sector deficits and the related issue of debt neutrality goes back a long time, of course, but it received a new impetus with the influential contribution by Barro (1974). Barro pointed out that private intergenerational transfers can compensate for government-induced intergenerational transfers and so leave the welfare of current and future generations unaffected by changes in public sector deficits. Under the conditions outlined in that article, substitution between current and future taxes will leave expenditure patterns unaffected. One needs many restrictive assumptions for such savings behavior to emerge, as noted by Barro himself. The empirical evidence seems mixed at best (see Kormendi 1983, Koskela and Viren 1983, Seater and Mariano 1985, and van Wijnbergen 1985a). This paper builds on the results of van Wijnbergen (1985a) that do not support debt neutrality (see also sec. 8.3.1).

Without debt neutrality, the international repercussions of fiscal deficits cannot be ignored. The recent debt-servicing problems of many developing countries have brought home the importance of world interest rates to debtors of less developed countries (LDC): a 1 percentage point increase in world interest rates costs LDC debtors US $2.7 billion initially, an income loss that climbs to no less than 8 billion within five years. For comparison, this is almost one-third of the total OECD development aid in 1984 (van Wijnbergen 1985a).

Nevertheless, not much has been done to assess the quantitative impact of fiscal policies in the OECD on world interest rates and on the terms of trade between different regions of the world. Most of the attempts are in a closed-economy framework and take an unstructured reduced-form approach (a careful exercise along these lines is Mueller and Price 1984). However, recent theoretical literature strongly suggests that a global general-equilibrium framework is more appropriate (Buiter 1984, Frenkel and Razin 1985a,b, Persson and Svensson 1985, van Wijnbergen 1985b). This is because international asymmetries in intertemporal and intratemporal expenditure patterns and initial debt positions are important determinants of the size and direction of relative price and real interest rate response to fiscal policy changes.

In this paper I report on an attempt to apply such a framework empirically. Savings and investment, and the associated current account imbalances, are interpreted as manifestations of intertemporal trade. In the empirical analysis, I have therefore looked for responsiveness of intertemporal trade patterns to intertemporal prices (real interest rates) in addition to the more traditional intratemporal relative prices and income levels. This is a significant departure from the existing empirical literature, where current account behavior is typically analyzed as a function of intratemporal variables only. At the core of the analysis is a careful study of private and public savings interaction in the industrial countries, while the global repercussions of fiscal policies are traced using a full multicountry global general-equilibrium approach. The explicit attention to supply-side considerations, to the aggregate supply response to relative price changes and changes in factor supplies, is another major departure from the existing literature on empirical macromodels.

In many ways this attempt is as yet rudimentary. I do not attempt to estimate the structure of intertemporal preferences directly (see Mankiw, Rothenberg, and Summers 1983 for such an attempt in a closed-economy framework). Instead, I test the actual savings and current account response to changes in relative prices, real interest rates, and contemporaneous income levels directly. This procedure is, of course, open to the Lucas-critique (Lucas 1976) that such response patterns might themselves change when policy changes. Further work is obviously needed, although uncertainty about whether policy shifts are temporary or permanent surely introduces some sluggishness in such behavioral changes.

The remainder of the paper is organized as follows. The theoretical structure of the model is presented in section 8.2. In section 8.3 I discuss the empirical results of two tests for debt neutrality suggested by the theory of section 8.2. Both strongly reject debt neutrality. The empirical estimation results are discussed in section 8.4. Section 8.5 analyzes the impact of observed changes in fiscal policy on world interest rates over the period 1979–84. Finally, section 8.6 discusses a specific application of a recent proposal to close U.S. fiscal deficits through trade taxes (an across-the-board import surcharge). Here we demonstrate the empirical importance of the interactions between interventions in intratemporal trade and intertemporal relative prices: protectionism is shown to have significant consequences not only for the intratemporal terms of trade but also for the intertemporal terms of trade (real interest rates). Van Wijnbergen (1984) also raises this issue in a theoretical context; here I show its empirical relevance. Trade intervention directed against LDCs exacerbates the transfer problem they face and, the empirical analysis shows, deteriorates their external balance more than it improves the current account in the Organization for Economic Cooperation and Development (OECD). The resulting global imbalance is resolved through higher world interest rates, which puts an additional burden on LDCs. Section 8.7 concludes.

8.2   Theoretical Structure of the Model

This section presents the theoretical structure underlying the empirical model. The structure of the model is similar to the one outlined in Marion and Svensson (1983), while the treatment of the interaction between private and foreign savings follows Blanchard (1985). Several concepts from the duality theory are used; a good reference is Dixit and Norman (1980). In particular, I use the revenue function, which gives the maximum value added that can be obtained from given factor supplies at given relative prices. I denote this function by R for current and r for future revenue. (In general, I will use capital letters for current variables and lower-case letters for future variables.)

Similarly, the expenditure function E gives the minimum discounted value of expenditure E needed to achieve welfare level U at given relative prices. The derivative of E with respect to any price yields the (Hicksian) demand for the corresponding good.

P (p) is the relative price of OECD goods in terms of LDC goods today (in the future). This corresponds to RPOE (see appendix for list of variable definitions) in section 8.3. Q (q) is the current (future) oil price in terms of LDC goods; δ is the world discount factor where $\delta = 1/(1+\rho)$; ρ is the real own rate of interest on OECD goods (RROE in sec. 8.3 and 8.4); W is the real product wage in terms of LDC goods; while Π (π) is a true consumption price index. Other symbols are self-explanatory.

Finally, variables without asterisk or superscript "o" refer to the OECD (like R); asterisks refer to LDCs (like R^*), and a superscript "o" (like R^o) refers to OPEC. In the theory model, I ignore foreign assets/debt inherited from "period zero"; the empirical analysis, of course, incorporates beginning-of-period foreign debts or assets.

8.2.1   The OECD Block

Aggregate supply is derived from the revenue function:

$$(1) \qquad\qquad Y = R_P$$

$$= Y(P, Q; K, L)$$

$$= Y(1, Q/P; K, L).$$

This is the equation estimated below. Labor used (L) is determined by equalizing the real product wage to the marginal product of labor:

$$(2) \qquad\qquad R_L = W,$$

or

$$(2a) \qquad\qquad L = L(W/P, Q/P; K).$$

In a CES world it is possible to write equation (2a) as

$$(2b) \qquad\qquad L = L(W/P, Y)$$

Finally, oil demand Z can also be derived from the revenue function:

$$(3) \qquad\qquad Z = -R_Q.$$

The more interesting part is on the private consumption side. I follow Blanchard (1985) in identifying a difference between private and government discount factors as a source of breakdown for debt neutrality. This lends itself to a very simple empirical test.

First, some arithmetic: Define δ as the government's discount factor, equal to over one plus the world interest rate, and $\tilde{\delta}$ as the private discount factor. Then the perceived current and future tax burden equals

$$(4) \qquad\qquad T + \tilde{\delta}t = T + \delta t + (\tilde{\delta} - \delta)t.$$

Now the government budget constraint tells us

$$(5) \qquad\qquad G + \delta g = T + \delta t;$$

substituting equation (5) into equation (4) leads to

$$(6) \qquad\qquad T + \tilde{\delta}t = G + \delta g + (\tilde{\delta} - \delta)t$$

$$= G + \tilde{\delta}g + (\tilde{\delta} - \delta)(t - g)$$

$$= G + \tilde{\delta}g + \frac{(\tilde{\delta} - \delta)}{\delta}(G - T).$$

The private budget constraint then becomes:

$$(7) \qquad R + \tilde{\delta}r - PI - T - \tilde{\delta}t = E(\Pi, \tilde{\delta}\pi, U),$$

which, after substituting in equation (6), becomes

$$(8) \qquad R - G + \tilde{\delta}(r - g) - PI + \frac{(\tilde{\delta} - \delta)}{\delta}(G - T)$$

$$= E(\Pi, \tilde{\delta}\pi, U).$$

This has two testable implications: one for private consumption, and one for the current account. First, private consumption. Current real consumptions equals

$$(9) \quad E_{\Pi} = C_{1E}\left(\frac{\tilde{\delta}\pi}{\Pi}\right)\left[R - G + \tilde{\delta}(r - g) - PI + \left(\frac{\tilde{\delta} - \delta}{\delta}\right)(G - T)\right].$$

This is the equation in section 8.3 where we approximate $R - G + \tilde{\delta}$ $(r - g) - PI$ by applying a Koyck lag to $R - G$ in the way advocated by Friedman (1951). C_{1E} is the marginal propensity to spend out of wealth in period 1.

The second test occurs in the current account (CA) equation, which is an *alternative* for an investment equation given income and consumption. The CA equals:

$$(10) \quad CA = R - G - E_{\Pi}\Pi - PI$$

$$= (R - G)(1 - C_{1E}) - C_{1E}\tilde{\delta}(r - g)$$

$$- (1 - C_{1E})PI - C_{1E}\frac{(\delta - \tilde{\delta})}{\delta}(G - T).$$

Equation (10) shows that changes in government expenditure when considered permanent will not influence the CA if $(1 - C_{1E})dG = C_{1E}dg$, which will hold if expenditure shares per unit of time are equal over time. It also shows that a change in deficit in the CA equation therefore also allows for a test of debt neutrality. The empirical results for these two tests, both of which reject debt neutrality, are discussed in section 8.3.

In the empirical model, T is actually a function of other variables (income and consumption) in an attempt to capture both indirect and direct sources of tax revenues.

Finally, demand for OECD goods is assumed to depend on total expenditure and relative prices, in standard budget allocation fashion.

The OECD block is rounded out by the dynamic accumulation identities listed at the end of section 8.3.

8.2.2   LDC Block

Contrary to the OECD block, capital goods are imported by the LDC block (from the OECD) rather than produced at home. Also, largely because of data limitations, no distinction is made between the public and private sector.

The national budget constraint becomes:

$$(11) \quad R^*(1, Q; K, L) + \delta r^*(1, q; k) - PI^*$$

$$= E^*[\Pi(P,1)\delta\pi(p,1), U^*],$$

which yields LDC welfare U^* as a function of current and future relative prices and the world discount factor. Of special interest is the welfare effect of terms of trade changes:

$$(12) \qquad E_u^* \frac{dU^*}{dP} = -(I^* + E_p^*).$$

Note that terms involving $r_k^* I_p^*$ and I^*_p drop out via intertemporal production efficiency ($\delta r_k^* = P$).

The current account equals

$$(13) \qquad CA^* = R^* - PI^* - E_\Pi \Pi$$

plus interest payments if initial debt is not zero. The WISH utility structure (see Razin and Svensson 1983) assumed here allows us to write real consumption expenditure as a function of the LDC consumer discount factor and welfare:

$$(14) \qquad E_\Pi^* = E_\Pi \left(1, \frac{\delta \pi}{\Pi}, U^* \right).$$

Equation (14) clearly is a function of relative prices and welfare which, by substituting in the indirect utility function, can be written as a function of relative prices and wealth. In our empirical consumption function, we will proxy wealth by a Koyck-lag applied to current income to derive permanent income in the way suggested by Friedman (1951). LDC imports of final consumption goods from the OECD depend on total real consumption expenditure in the period E^*_Π and relative prices:

$$(15) \qquad E_P^* = E_\Pi \Pi_P.$$

The most interesting derivative of equation (13) concerns the terms of trade; a permanent term of trade shock $dP = \delta dp$ has the following effect on the CA:

$$(16) \quad CA_P^* \, dP + CA_p^* \, \delta dp = -(1 - C_{1E}^*) E_P^* \, dP + C_{1E}^* E_p^* \, \delta dp$$
$$- [(1 - C_{1E}^*)I + PI_P],$$

where C_{1E}^* is the share of wealth spent on period one goods. With sufficient symmetry over time, the first two terms cancel (see van Wijnbergen 1984 for a more careful statement). This opens up the possibility of a negative CA response in the LDCs to an increase in the relative price of OECD goods (dP, $dp > 0$), even though the utility structure assumed rules out Harberger-Laursen-Metzler terms of trade effects on savings. The effect comes via investment, however; if investment is sufficiently inelastic (I_p small enough), the term $(1 - C_{1E}^*)I$ will dominate and the current account will deteriorate. This effect will be even stronger if the shock is temporary, since then the positive term $(C^*_{1E}E_P\delta dp)$ will drop out. This negative effect is confirmed in the empirical analysis and drives much of the results on the real interest rate effect of protectionism. The rest of the LDC block is straightforward. Equation (14) gives real consumption, so investment can be derived from equations (14) and (16), the CA identity, and real income.

It remains to fill out the supply side of the economy. Aggregate supply of LDC goods equals the derivative of the revenue function with respect to its output price by simple property of the revenue function (Dixit and Norman 1980):

$$(17) \qquad Y^* = R^*_1 = Y(1, Q; K, L).$$

Data problems do not allow us to estimate output as a function of factor supplies K and L and relative prices; I have an estimate of K constructed from investment flows using the perpetual inventory method and a 5% depreciation rate. No observations on labor use are available, however. To get around this problem we simply assume a minimum real consumption wage, which provides a link between the terms of trade and the real product wage relevant for employment conditions:

$$(18) \qquad \frac{W^*}{\Pi(P,1)} = Y = > \hat{W}^* = -\psi\hat{P}.$$

This can be substituted into a labor demand function that is defined implicitly by the requirement that the marginal value of labor equals the real product wage: $R^*_L = W^*$. If that is inserted into equation (17), we get the aggregate supply function that I estimated empirically:

$$(17a) \qquad Y^* = Y^* (\underline{Q}, \underline{P}, \underset{+}{K})$$

The block is completed by dynamic equations linking current and future capital, depreciation and investment, and an equation linking current and future foreign debt and the current account (see sec. 8.3).

8.2.3   OPEC Block

The OPEC block is simplified a great deal by not endogenizing the process OPEC uses to set the relative price of oil in terms of OECD goods, $\bar{Q} = Q/P$ (for a similar model where the price *is* endogenized, incorporating exhaustibility of oil, see van Wijnbergen 1985c). OPEC income Y^o then is simply the oil price times OECD- and LDC-derived demand for oil, Z and Z^*, plus their income from foreign assets. Expenditure is once again summarized by an expenditure function, so the intertemporal budget constraint becomes

$$(19) \qquad (Z^* + Z)Q + (z + z^*)\delta q = E^o[\Pi(P,1), \delta\pi(p,1), U^o].$$

The current account equals

(20) $CA_1 = Y^o - E_{\Pi}^o \Pi,$

which will be a function of relative prices and current and expected oil income.

Expenditure then follows from the current account identity linking income, expenditure, and the current account. The final equation links expenditure on OECD goods to relative prices and aggregate expenditure:

(21) $E_P^o = E_{\Pi}^o \, \Pi_P^o \, .$

Finally, the current account equals changes in net foreign assets.

8.2.4   Closing the Model

What remains are the two market clearing equations tying down relative prices P and $\delta(= 1[1 + \rho])$, where δ is the own rate of interest on OECD commodities.

The first is the OECD commodity market clearing equation:

(22) $Y(Q, W/P, K) = E_P + E_P^* + E_P^o + I + I^*.$

The second is a market clearing equation for future goods which, via the intertemporal budget constraint, can be transformed into an equation requiring the world current account to be zero:

(23) $CA + CA^* + CA^o = 0.$

The empirical problems of assessing expectations of future terms of trade changes dp is resolved, following Marion and Svensson (1983), by simply assuming that future foreign and domestic goods are perfect substitutes so that p becomes exogenous and future foreign and domestic goods can be aggregated into one commodity, future goods.

8.3   Two Tests for Debt Neutrality

The theoretical structure of section 8.2 suggests two tests of nonneutrality. The first involves private savings behavior directly, the second concerns the current account (see eqs. [9] and [10] in sec. 8.2). Consider first private savings.

The theoretical analysis of section 8.2 suggests that the relevant measure of disposable income is income minus government expenditure, not income minus taxes. If private and social discount factors differ (following Blanchard 1985), fiscal deficits will have an additional influence on private consumption, the coefficient of which will be proportional to that discount factor difference. That suggests estimation of the following equation:

$$CPROE = a_o + a_1 RROE + a_2(Y - GROE)$$
$$+ a_3(GROE - TROE),$$

where Y is net national income; GROE is real government expenditure (minus inflationary erosion of the public debt and minus transfer payments that we interpret as negative taxes); and TROE is real government revenue minus transfer payments.

Debt neutrality implies $a_3 = 0$, and no debt neutrality implies $a_3 > 0$: (Note that equation [9] suggests that there is *no* presumption that $a_3 = a_2$, not even without debt neutrality; Y-TROE would, therefore, be the appropriate definition of disposable income by a fluke only.)

When I run this equation on OECD aggregates, I get:

$$CPROE = -109. + 435. RROE + 0.58 (Y - GROE)$$
$$(2.56) (0.80) \qquad (6.88)$$

$$+ 0.62 (GROE - TROE) + 0.33 \times CPROE(-1)$$
$$(6.99) \qquad\qquad\qquad (3.38)$$
$$(1966-1983, 2SLS)$$

The coefficient on the deficit is very significantly different from zero (t-statistic of 6.99!). Therefore our test strongly supports the crowding out hypothesis and rejects the no crowding out, debt neutrality hypothesis.

The second test involves the current account equation. Equation (10) in section 8.2 suggests that the CA should depend on disposable income $Y - GROE$ and various intratemporal and intertemporal relative prices (through C_{1E} and PI, cf. eq. [10]). However, government deficits, for a given level of government expenditure, enter only if debt neutrality fails to hold, if $\delta \neq \tilde{\delta}$:

$$CAROE = 63.6 \quad + \quad 375.3 RPOET - 152.9 RPOILT$$
$$(0.88) \qquad (1.92) \qquad\quad (3.36)$$

$$+ 0.045 (Y - GROE) \qquad - 0.18 (GROE - TROE)$$
$$(2.15) \qquad\qquad\qquad (2.53)$$
$$(1966-1983, 2SLS, \hat{\rho} = 0.5).$$

The empirical results for this equation also strongly reject debt neutrality. The coefficient on government deficits is highly significantly different from zero and of the "right" sign.

8.4   Estimation Results

This section reports on the results obtained when estimating the model presented in section 8.2.

8.4.1 OECD Block

Aggregate Demand

In section 8.2.1 we provided evidence against the debt neutrality hypothesis and in favor of the traditional tax-based definition of private disposable income. This leads to:

$$\text{CPROE} = -51.8 + 0.36\,(Y - \text{TROE}) + 0.59\,\text{CPROE}(-1)$$
$$\quad\quad\quad (1.30)\quad (6.33)\quad\quad\quad\quad\quad (9.04)$$

$$(R^2 = 0.99, 1966–1983, \text{2SLS}),$$

where Y equals net national income minus inflationary erosion of public debt.

The second important equation is a current account equation (we could alternatively have estimated an investment equation):

$$\text{CAROE} = -63.6 + 375.3\,\text{RROET} - 152.9\,\text{RPOILT}$$
$$\quad\quad\quad\quad (0.88)\quad (1.92)\quad\quad\quad\quad (3.36)$$

$$+ 0.045\,(Y - \text{GROE}) \quad - 0.18\,(\text{GROE} - \text{TROE})$$
$$\quad\quad (2.15)\quad\quad\quad\quad\quad\quad (2.53)$$

$$(1966–1983, \text{2SLS}, \bar{\rho} = 0.5).$$

The positive interest effect should not be surprising. Notice also the strongly significant negative effect of government deficits (GROE − TROE). This provides additional evidence against the debt neutrality hypothesis. Finally the negative oil price and positive disposable income effects also conform to prior expectations.

For given value of real GDP (GDPROE = YROE − OILROE*RPOIL, output minus imported oil), investment can be determined from the CA identity:

$$\text{IROE} = \text{GDPROE} + \text{RROE} \times \text{NFAROE}(-1)$$
$$\quad\quad\quad\quad - \text{CPROE} - \text{GRCOE} - \text{CAROE},$$

where GRCOE is real government consumption.

Aggregate expenditure ATROE (= CPROE + GRCOE + IROE) is allocated over domestic (ADROE) and LDC goods:

$$\log \text{ADROE} = 0.05 + 0.99 \log \text{ATROE} + 0.01 \log \text{RPOE}$$
$$\quad\quad\quad\quad (4.83)\quad (76.8)\quad\quad\quad\quad (4.33)$$

$$(R^2 = 0.99, 1966–1983, \text{2SLS}).$$

This equation implies a pure own price elasticity of demand of -0.99 (ADROE and ATROE are both deflated by the price of OECD goods!). Of more interest is the implied income elasticity of demand for LDC exports, which is 1.6, considerably below the value used in, for example, Cline (1984).

Aggregate Supply

First is the labor demand equation, linking changes in unemployment rates, itself expressed in percentage points, to changes in real product wages and changes in real output:

$$UOE = UOE(-1) + 0.84 + 19.3 \,[\log WROE - \log WROE(-1)]$$
$$\qquad\qquad\qquad (3.82)\quad (1.61)$$

$$\qquad\qquad - 31.5 \,[\log YROE - \log YROE(-1)]$$
$$\qquad\qquad (5.52)$$

$(R^2 = 0.96,\ 1969–1983,\ 2SLS)$.

Changes in output are linked to (percentage) changes in labor use (approximated by *minus* changes in the unemployment rate), changes in the beginning of period capital stock, and changes in the real product price of oil:

$$\log YROE = \log YROE(-1) + 0.03 - 0.03 \,[UOE - UOE(-1)$$
$$\qquad\qquad\qquad\qquad (1.45)\quad (6.08)$$

$$\qquad\qquad + 0.34 \,[\log KROE(-1) - \log KROE(-2)]$$
$$\qquad\qquad (0.50)$$

$$\qquad\qquad - 0.02[\log RPOIL - \log RPOIL(-1)]$$
$$\qquad\qquad (1.67)$$

$(R^2 = 0.99,\ 1969–1983,\ 2SLS)$.

The coefficient on unemployment changes (which is in percentage points), is clearly incompatible with the underlying production function framework. The simulations were performed using what the value theory suggests: $(1 - .34)/100$.

The within-period part of this block is rounded out by econometric equations linking capital depreciation CKPOE to the beginning of period capital stock, real tax revenues to consumption and income, and real oil imports to the real product price of oil and real output:

$$CKPOE = -201 + 0.05\, KROE(-1)$$
$$\qquad\qquad (12.2)\quad (49.3)$$

$$(R^2 = 0.99,\ 1966–1983).$$

$$TROE = 591 + 0.34\, CPROE(-1) + 0.25\, YROE$$
$$\qquad (14.3)\ (4.04)\qquad\qquad\quad (4.63)$$

$$(R^2 = 0.99,\ 1966–1983).$$

$$\log(OILROE) = \log[OILROE(-1)] - 12.1$$
$$\qquad\qquad\qquad\qquad\qquad (2.01)$$

$$- 0.06 \ T \ - \ 0.16[\log \text{RPOIL} \ - \ \log \text{RPOIL}(-1)]$$
$$\quad (2.66) \quad\quad (2.46)$$

$$+ \ 3.53 \log \text{YROE} \ - \ 2.06 \log \text{YROE}(-1)$$
$$\quad (3.93) \quad\quad\quad\quad\quad (1.80)$$

($R^2 = 0.97$, 2SLS, 1966–1983).

Finally, dynamic equations link current and future asset stocks via physical investment, current account deficits, and fiscal deficits:

$$\text{KROE} = \text{KROE}(-1) - \text{CKROE} + \text{IROE},$$
$$\text{NFAROE} = \text{NFAROE}(-1) + \text{CAROE},$$
$$\text{DBTROE} = \text{DBTROE}(-1) - \text{NLROE}.$$

8.4.2 OPEC Block

The OPEC block is very much simplified. OPEC sets the real price of oil in terms of OECD goods, RPOIL, which is therefore considered exogenous. It then supplies all the oil demanded by OECD and LDC at that price. Its total income equals oil imports times the oil price, plus earnings on foreign assets:

$$\text{YROPEC} = (\text{OILROE} + \text{OILRLDC}) \ \text{RPOIL}$$
$$+ \ \text{NFAROPEC}(-1) \ \text{RROE}.$$

For a given income we obtain expenditure via a CA equation, using the identity that income minus expenditure equals the current account. The CA equation is:

$$\text{CAROPEC} = -7.2 + 348. \ \text{RROE}$$
$$\quad\quad\quad (0.51) \ (2.84)$$
$$+ \ 0.61 \ \text{YROPEC} \ - \ 129. \ \text{RPOIL}(-1)$$
$$\quad (6.93) \quad\quad\quad\quad\quad (6.30)$$

($R^2 = 0.86$, 1966–1983, 2SLS, $\hat{\rho} = 0.58$).

Once again we get a strong positive interest rate effect; OPEC, of course, is also a net creditor. OPEC saves a very high proportion of current income, but the negative term on *lagged* oil prices indicates a strong catching-up effect on expenditure.

Total expenditure ATROPEC can be obtained from the value of income and the current account identity:

$$\text{ATROPEC} = \text{YROPEC} - \text{CAROPEC}.$$

Finally OPECs demand for OECD goods is a function of total expenditure and relative prices:

$$\log (\text{ADROPEC}) = 0.39 + 0.78 \log (\text{ATROPEC})$$
$$(1.18) \ (11.4)$$

$$- 1.71 \log (\text{RPOE})$$
$$(2.53)$$

$(R^2 = 0.91, 1969-1983, \text{2SLS}, \hat{\rho} = 0.64)$.

The only intertemporal link in this block is via the current account and the beginning and end of period net foreign assets:

$$\text{NFAROPEC} = \text{NFAROPEC}(-1) + \text{CAROPEC}.$$

8.4.3   LDC Block

Aggregate supply (total output) in LDCs is a function of real oil prices, the terms of trade, and physical capital.

$$\log (\text{YRLDC}) - \log [\text{KRLDC}(-1)] = - 1.18 + 0.016 \, t$$
$$(10.5) \quad (2.54)$$

$$- 0.10 \log [\text{RPOIL}(-1) * \text{RPOE}(-1)]$$
$$(2.47)$$

$$-0.23 \log \text{RPOE}$$
$$(1.18)$$

$(R^2 = 0.99, 1967-1983)$.

The LDC output equation works remarkably well, with strong negative effects of the (LDC) real product price of oil RPOIL * RPOE and strong positive terms of trade effects (i.e., RPOE comes in with a negative coefficient).

Aggregate expenditure can be derived from real income and the CA; the CA equations can be estimated as follows:

$$\text{CARLDC} = 377. - 237. \, \text{RRLDC} \qquad -303. \, \text{RPOE}$$
$$(2.38) \quad (2.96) \qquad\qquad\quad (2.73)$$

$$- 74.3 \, \text{RPOIL} - 0.15 \, \text{NFARLDC}(-1)$$
$$(1.24) \qquad\qquad (1.48)$$

$$- 0.36 \, \text{YRLDC}(-1) + 0.05 \, \text{YROE}$$
$$(1.79) \qquad\qquad\quad (1.16)$$

$(R^2 = 0.94, 1966-1983, \text{2SLS}, \hat{\rho} = 0.10)$.

This time, interest rate effects are negative, which is no surprise: LDCs are large debtors. Total expenditure then equals:

$$\text{ATRLDC} = \text{YRLDC} + \text{RRLDC} \times \text{NFARLDC}(-1)$$
$$- \text{OILRLDC} \times \text{RPOIL} - \text{CARLDC}.$$

LDC expenditure on OECD goods (ADRLDC) depends on total LDC expenditure (ATRLDC) and relative prices:

$$\log (ADRLDC) = -2.79 + 1.05 \log (ATRLDC) - 2.14 \log(RPOE)$$
$$ (3.58) \quad (9.60) (6.42)$$

($R^2 = 0.96$, 1967–1983, 2SLS).

Total (private and government; no breakdown is available) real consumption expenditure (CPRLDCT) depends on real output (YRLDC), the stock of debt (= minus NFARLDC), and lagged consumption:

$$CPRLDC = -134.9 + 0.58 \ YRLDCT$$
$$ (1.63) \quad (3.87)$$

$$+ \ 0.45 \ NFARLDC \ (-1) + 0.63 \ CPRLDC(-1)$$
$$(2.17) (2.88)$$

($R^2 = 0.98$, 1967–1982, 2SLS).

Gross investment then equals the difference between total expenditure and real consumption:

$$IRLDC = ATRLDC - CPRLDC.$$

Finally, the dynamic equations: future net foreign assets equal current stocks and the CA:

$$NFARLDC = NFARLDC(-1) + CARLDC.$$

Next period's capital equals today's beginning of period stock plus gross investment minus depreciation. We assumed depreciation to be equal to 5% of the capital stock each year. This leads to:

$$KRLDC = 0.95 \ KRLDC(-1) + IRLDC.$$

8.4.4 Closing the Model

The model is closed by a world CA-equals-zero equation and an OECD commodity-market-clearing condition. These jointly determine the real interest rate (RPOE) and the OECD/LDC terms of trade (RPOE). The world CA equation states that the world current account has to equal zero:

$$CAROE + CAROPEC + CARLDC/RPOE + CARDIS = 0.$$

CARDIS is the world current account discrepancy, which is entered exogenously.

OECD commodity market clearing implies:

$$YROE = ADROE + ADROPEC + ADRLDC.$$

Walras's law makes the LDC commodity-market-clearing equation redundant.

8.5   Fiscal Policy in the OECD during 1979–84

8.5.1   Historical Overview

From reading professional and journalistic commentaries alike, one gets the impression of a near-consensus characterization of fiscal policies in the first five years of this decade, with disagreements not on what happened but on what effect changes in fiscal policies had on interest rates and so on. The 1980s are seen as a period of retrenchment or at least containment of government expenditure, with imbalances triggered by the fact that tax cuts in the United States have eroded the revenue base more than warranted by the expenditure restraint actually achieved. Some observers claim that, OECD-wide, even that is not true; surpluses in Western Europe and Japan are claimed to have offset the increased deficits in the United States (Blanchard and Summers 1984). I will argue here that that view is at variance with the facts and, by its exclusive focus on public sector deficits, misleading in its emphasis.

Three measurement problems have, I think, clouded the discussion. First is, of course, the issue of inflationary erosion of public sector debt. Second comes the problem of cyclical adjustment. And finally, and most importantly since generally ignored, the distinction between government expenditure on goods and services, on the one hand, and transfer payments, on the other.

The importance of the first two issues is demonstrated in figure 8.1. When only real interest payments are included in government expend-

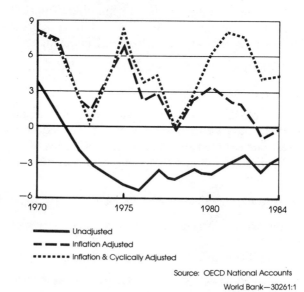

Source: OECD National Accounts
World Bank—30261:1

Fig. 8.1   Public sector surplus in the United Kingdom as a percentage of national income, 1970–84.

iture, the United Kingdom turns out to have run a public sector surplus throughout most of the past 15 years. Table 8.1 presents inflation-adjusted government balances as a share of national income for the major industrial countries. The figures confirm that the United States has seen by far the largest shift in public sector deficits, from a 3.6% surplus to a 2.7% deficit (all as a percentage of national income). However, table 8.1 also documents an increase in public sector deficits in the other eight major industrial economies, with reductions in Japan and West Germany too small to offset increases in Italy, France, the United Kingdom, and, to a lesser extent, the smaller countries like Holland and Belgium. Overall the public sector deficit increased by 3 percentage points of aggregate national income when the United States is included, and between 0.6 and 1.7 percentage points (depending on whether one starts from 1979 or 1980) when the United States is excluded. Anyhow, there were no major fiscal improvements in the non-U.S. industrial countries.

Cyclical correction presents a much more contentious issue. Cyclical correction is not really a problem in the United States or Japan, since unemployment in 1979 and 1984 was not that different in each country. It is, however, a major issue in Western Europe as figure 8.1 demonstrates for the United Kingdom. Cyclical corrections like the one in figure 8.1 are behind the Blanchard-Summers claim that fiscal contraction in Western Europe has more or less offset fiscal expansion in the United States.

However, in this paper I argue that fiscal deficits drive up real interest rates because imperfect private savings offsets would trigger an incipient, global, current account deficit at unchanged real interest rates. In that case, cyclically adjusted deficits are not a relevant measure. It is actual government dissaving that needs to be matched, not what government dissavings would have been had other policies allowed a return to 1979 levels of unemployment.

Finally, transfer payments. From a macroeconomic point of view, these are better seen as negative taxes rather than as a component of government expenditure. If one rearranges the numbers along those lines, a surprising picture emerges (fig. 8.2). In the nine major industrial economies, government revenues net of outlays on Social Security (OECD national account definitions) have remained constant as a share of national income throughout the past 20 years right up to 1984, at around 22%. The big increase in deficits is due to a substantial increase in government expenditure on goods and services; as a share of national income, government expenditure on goods and services increased by a full 3 percentage points. To put that in perspective, to restore the 1979 ratio in 1984, actual expenditure would need to be cut by no less than $220 billion; this corresponds to, for example, reducing the entire U.S. defense budget to zero in 1984.

Table 8.1. Inflation-Adjusted Government Budget Balance as a Percentage of National Income in Selected Industrial Countries, 1965–84

Year	United Kingdom	Germany	Italy	France	Japan	United States	Nine large industrial countries	
							Including United States	Excluding United States
1965–73	3.8	1.0	-3.6	1.8	1.8	1.6	1.5	1.4
1974–78	2.7	-2.4	0.3	0.5	2.4	1.0	0.1	-0.6
1979	2.1	-1.9	-0.7	0.8	-4.4	3.6	0.7	-1.3
1980	3.4	-2.1	4.5	2.2	-3.6	2.0	0.7	-0.2
1981	2.2	-2.5	2.0	0.5	-3.3	2.4	0.6	-0.8
1982	1.5	-1.9	-0.3	-0.4	-2.8	-2.0	-1.6	-1.3
1983	-1.1	-1.7	-0.4	-1.5	-3.4	-3.0	-2.7	-2.4
1984	-0.3	-0.4	-4.7	-1.9	-1.7	-2.7	-2.3	-1.9

Note: Negative sign indicates deficit.

Source: OECD National Accounts; national sources.

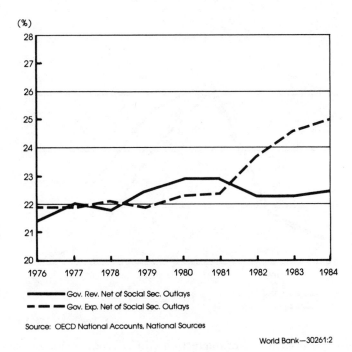

Source: OECD National Accounts, National Sources

World Bank—30261:2

Fig. 8.2   Government expenditure on goods and services, an revenues net of Social Security outlays as a percentage of national income.

In section 8.5.2, I will use the model outlined in sections 8.2 and 8.4 to trace the consequences for global equilibrium of a counterfactual slowdown of government expenditure to half its historically observed pace. Section 8.6 is forward looking and deals with different ways of reducing existing fiscal deficits and their implications for world interest rates and terms of trade between different regions of the world.

8.5.2 Looking Back: Global Economic Effects of a Slowdown in Government Expenditure

The experiment performed is a slowdown in government consumption that would half the increase in the share of total government expenditure in national income between 1979 and 1984. This is, in fact, quite a dramatic cutback in real government expenditure starting at US$13.5 billion in 1980 and climbing to a cut of no less than US$109.5 billion in 1984. Not surprisingly, a real shock of that magnitude has major implications for world interest rates and the distribution of current account imbalances. Figure 8.3 compares actual real interest rates with what the model predicts would have happened if government

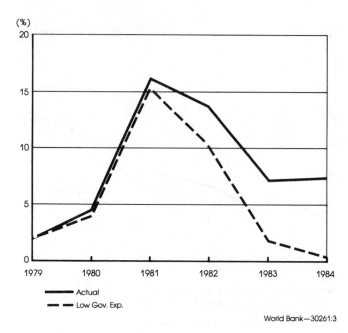

Fig. 8.3   Own rate of interest on OECD goods (real). Actual (solid line) and simulated (dotted line) real interest rate; the simulation assumes reduced real government expenditure (see text).

expenditure would have gone up only 1.5% of base run national income. The real rate concept used is the own rate of interest on OECD goods, here defined as LIBOR minus the GNP-weighted inflation rate in the dollar GNP deflator for the nine major OECD countries.

Two things stand out in figure 8.3. First, it seems clear that fiscal policy changes and their impact on global current account equilibrium explain a negligible fraction of the rapid increase in real interest rates in 1979–82. However, and this is the second point, from 1982 onward, almost all of the increase in real rates can be ascribed to the pressure on world savings exerted by increased fiscal expenditure and the fact that it was deficit financed. The fiscal cutback enacted in this run would have taken less than 1 percentage point out of real interest rates in 1980 and 1981, almost 3 percentage points in 1983, and 5 and almost 7 percentage points in 1983 and 1984, respectively. Total (real) interest cost on public debt throughout the OECD would have fallen by 1984. This provides additional effects on government deficits which, in the OECD as a whole, would decline by no less than US$160 billion in 1984.

Because of reduced pressure on OECD commodities markets, the relative price of OECD goods in terms of LDC goods decline by about 3 percentage points, implying a slightly larger drop in the own rate of interest on LDC goods than in the own rate of interest on OECD goods we just discussed.

The biggest current account realignment would be from OPEC toward the LDCs. The latter would run a substantially lower deficit because of the favorable terms of trade and real interest rate developments. The difference starts at a small US$2 billion in 1980 but climbs to a US$22 billion improvement in 1984. As a result, the real value of LDC debt would be at US$824 billion at the end of 1984 rather than US$884 billion as it is in the base case.

Lower real interest rates would, according to our simulation results, have increased investment in the LDCs by 13% in 1984, auguring well for future growth; in fact output in the LDCs would have been higher in 1984 already, by 3 percentage points.

Much of the current debt crisis may be due to unsustainable policies in the LDCs themselves before 1980. But these simulation results strongly suggest that the current situation would be substantially more favorable for the developing countries had the OECD practiced more fiscal restraint in the mid-1980s, with appropriate monetary policies in place to avoid Keynesian effective demand problems.

8.6   Looking Ahead: Trade Taxes to Reduce Deficits

In this section I discuss the global impact of intervention in commodity trade in order to reduce public sector deficits. There is no need to discuss more direct measures, such as a cut in government expenditure, since their effect can be deduced from the results of section 8.5.

I will discuss a flat tariff of 10% on all final goods imports into the OECD. This measure is, of course, not a good simulation of the across-the-board import tariff occasionally discussed in the United States, because intra-OECD trade is not captured in the model used here, and the volume of OECD trade with the non-oil developing countries is too small for tariffs on it to make much of a dent in overall deficits. The reason to bring it up, nevertheless, is to draw attention to important interactions between intratemporal and intertemporal trade through the global terms of the trade effects such measures would have, interactions that have completely been left out of the discussion of these measures. I will show that these interactions are, in fact, very important: the adverse terms of trade effects on the LDCs' terms of trade exacerbate the transfer problem they face to such an extent that real interest rate effects are reversed.

8.6.1   Protectionism, the Transfer Problem, and the
         Real Rate of Interest

This experiment is set up as follows: The model was first made to track a "central case" that underlies the global projections in the *World Development Report 1985* (World Bank 1985). I then superimposed on that case an additional 10% tariff on OECD imports from the LDCs and solved the model for the general equilibrium response of real interest rates, terms of trade, and so on. I ran two variants of this experiment. In the first one the tariff revenues collected by the public sector are handed out to the private sector, with no direct effect on fiscal deficits. In the second one the revenues are used to reduce public sector deficits.

This experiment would constitute a very large increase in tariffs, more than doubling the average tariff level LDCs are currently facing. On the other hand, there is congressional pressure in the United States for a 20% surcharge, while the European Economic Community would beyond doubt retaliate in kind if that would, indeed, happen. The 10% tariff is, therefore, certainly within the realm of the possible.

Consider first the case where tariff revenues are handed out again rather than used to reduce public sector deficits. The empirical results indicate that a 10% tariff would largely be shifted forward toward LDC exporters rather than backward to the OECD consumers: the LDC terms of trade with respect to the OECD deteriorate with no less than 7 percentage points, so 70% of the tariff is shifted forward. This has, of course, strong effects on LDC exports: the average export volume growth rate over the five-year period is 3 percentage points below what it would have been without the tariff. Moreover, the model clearly demonstrates the export-tax equivalence of import tariffs: OECD export growth to LDCs fails by no less than 4.6 percentage points on average over five years. This decline in OECD exports also explains the current account response patterns and real interest rate effects, to which we now turn.

The most dramatic aspect of this simulation is the interest rate effect of such an increase in protectionism. The empirical evidence (see section 8.4) indicates no significant effect of the final goods terms of trade on the CA in the OECD, but a significant final goods terms of trade effect in LDCs; therefore, a terms of trade deterioration of the LDCs with respect to the OECD leads to an *ex ante* CA deterioration in the LDCs but no symmetric improvement in the OECD. As a result, if a big increase in tariffs in the OECD leads to a deterioration of the LDC/OECD terms of trade (which it will do at anything short of 100% backward shifting), there will be an *ex ante* world current account deterioration, necessitating higher real interest rates to restore global current account balance. This shows the double perversity of trade intervention: LDCs suffer twice. First, their static, *intratemporal* terms of trade deteriorate; second, they will be hit by higher real interest rates, or, in other words, their *intertemporal* terms of trade deteriorate also.

The numbers are substantial. The experiment we performed is admittedly a rather aggressive one: an across-the-board 10% import surcharge directed against LDCs, imposed in 1985 and sustained throughout. The impact effect on real interest rates, via the asymmetry in CA response to terms of trade changes, is dramatic. Real interest rates rise no less than 2 percentage points in the first year, and are still almost 1% higher in 1989 (.7 percentage point).

Moreover, this is the real rate in terms of OECD commodities. The effect is even more dramatic when looked at in terms of the goods LDCs need to export to service their debt, because the LDC/OECD terms of trade deteriorate steadily throughout the simulation period under this high protection scenario. Their own rate of interest on LDC goods shoots up with a full 5 percentage points in the first year of the import surcharge, and in 1989 it is still 1.3 percentage point higher than what it otherwise would have been.

It should, finally, not come as a surprise that the high protectionism scenario has a major impact on LDC growth. The LDC growth rate falls to 3.5% on average over the next five years, down from a healthier 5% in the benchmark case, with more slowdown to come: LDC investment in the final year, 1989, is only 84% of its ''central case'' value.

Applying tariff revenues against public sector deficits rather than handing them out to OECD consumers moderates the upward pressure on interest rates to some extent (cf. fig. 8.4), but it does not otherwise affect the results a great deal. The tariff revenues start at about US$10 billion and increase to US$15 billion (in 1984 dollars) in 1989, reducing the increase in interest rates by about 0.5 percentage point each year, compared to the case where tariff revenues are handed out. This is not enough to reverse the increase in real interest rates. The negative terms of trade effect exacerbating the LDCs' transfer problem dominates the deficit-reducing effect of higher tariffs by a wide margin (fig. 8.4).

8.7 Conclusions

In this paper I present a simple, global, theoretical, general-equilibrium model. The model is designed to discuss the global effects on intertemporal and intratemporal trade of various fiscal policy measures and interventions in commodity trade. Moreover, it has been constructed with empirical estimation in mind, so some effort has gone into avoiding clearly unobservable variables.

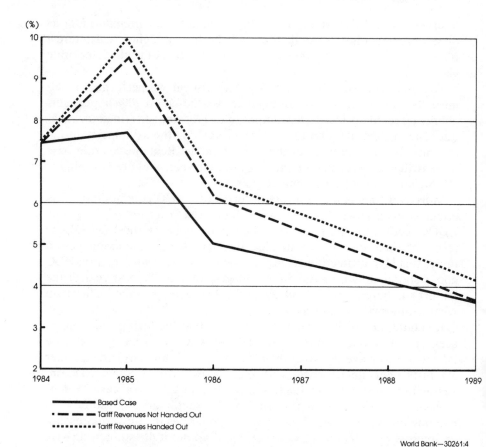

Fig. 8.4   Own rate of interest on OECD goods (real).
Effect of 10% tariff against LDC exports on world interest rates.

The theoretical structure suggests two tests of debt neutrality, both of which, when applied to OECD data, resoundingly reject debt neutrality. These two tests are then incorporated in an empirical version of the theoretical model. The empirical global model that I obtain this way is unique in several aspects.

It has a tightly focused structure, designed around questions concerning the impact of fiscal policy measures and interventions in commodity trade on intertemporal and intratemporal trade patterns and relative prices. The global general-equilibrium structure is a distinguishing feature of the model, with the real interest rate and the structure of the terms of trade resulting from global current account balance and various commodity market clearing conditions. Another feature that sets this model apart from all other empirical macromodels is its explicit incorporation of aggregate supply considerations. At the core of the industrial countries block, finally, is an explicit analysis of the interaction between private and public savings.

In the applied part of the paper, I first present data demonstrating that government revenues net of Social Security outlays have remained remarkably constant as a share of national income from 1965 right up to 1984. This suggests that the fiscal policy debate has focused too much on tax cuts and has not paid enough attention to what was really going on, a major OECD-wide, deficit-financed, increase in government expenditure. I then assess the effect of this deficit-financed increase in real government expenditure on real interest rates by running a simulation with the empirical model presented earlier, under the assumption of a halving of that increase in government expenditure.

The results show, first of all, that fiscal policy explains only a negligible fraction of the rapid increase in real interest rates between 1979 and 1982. However, from 1982 almost all of the increase in real interest rates can be ascribed to the pressure on world savings exerted by increased fiscal expenditure and the fact that that increase was deficit financed.

In section 8.6 I discuss various trade interventions designed to reduce fiscal deficits. I point out, and document empirically through simulation runs, the importance of interactions between intertemporal and intratemporal trade. A tariff directed against LDC exports (along the line of proposals currently under discussion in the U.S. Congress) is shown to significantly deteriorate the LDC terms of trade. This in turn leads to a significant *ex ante* deterioration of the LDCs' current account without an offsetting *ex ante* improvement in the OECD current account. The net result is an increase in the world interest rate to restore global current account balance, a possibility that I already pointed out in the theoretical section. The simulation exercise demonstrates the empirical importance of this mechanism: After imposition of a 10% tariff against LDC exports, real interest rates rise a full 2 percentage points initially. They are still 0.5 percentage point higher after five years. Protectionism directed against LDCs, therefore, not only shifts their intratemporal terms of trade unfavorably, but it also causes a deterioration of their intertemporal terms of trade.

Applying tariff revenues against the public sector deficit rather than handing them out to consumers is shown not to reverse these results, although there is a slight moderation in the interest rate effect (0.5 percentage point). This moderation does not affect the basic message, that trade taxes will exacerbate the LDC transfer problem to such an extent that interest rates will actually increase, the deficit reduction notwithstanding.

Appendix
List of Variables

All real variables are in terms of industrial countries' goods unless otherwise indicated. An extensive source description is available on request.

ADRLDC   Real expenditure on industrial countries' goods by developing countries.

ADROE   Real expenditure on industrial countries' goods by industrial countries.

ADROPEC   Real expenditure on industrial countries' goods by OPEC.

ATRLDC   Real total expenditure by developing countries.

ATROE   Real total expenditure by industrial countries.

ATROPEC   Real total expenditure by OPEC.

CARDIS   Real world current account discrepancy.

CARLDC   Real current account balance of developing countries, corrected for capital losses on net foreign assets, in terms of developing countries' goods.

CAROE   Real current account balance of industrial countries, corrected for capital losses on net foreign assets.

CAROPEC   Real current account balance of OPEC, corrected for capital losses on net foreign assets.

CKROE   Real consumption of physical capital in the industrial countries.

CPROE   Real private consumption expenditure in the industrial countries.

CTRLDC   Real total consumption expenditure in developing countries.

CPROE   Real private consumption expenditure in industrial countries.

DBTROE   Real total government debt

GRCOE   Real government consumption in industrial countries.

GROE   Real government expenditure on goods and services in industrial countries.

IRLDC   Real total gross fixed capital formation in developing countries.

IROE   Real total gross fixed capital formation in industrial countries.

KRLDC   Real stock of physical capital in developing countries.

KROE   Real stock of physical capital in industrial countries.

NFARLDC   Real net foreign assets of developing countries.

NFAROE	Real net foreign assets of industrial countries.
NFAROPEC	Real net foreign assets of OPEC.
NLROE	Real total government budget surplus in the OECD corrected for inflationary erosion of the public debt.
RPOE	Relative price of industrial countries' goods in terms of developing countries' goods. Base year 1980.
RPOIL	Relative price of oil in terms of industrial countries' goods.
RRLDC	Own real rate of interest on developing countries' goods.
RROE	Own real rate of interest on industrial countries' goods.
TROE	Real government revenue minus transfer payments in industrial countries.
UOE	Standardized unemployment rate in industrial countries (OECD definition).
WROE	Real wage in terms of industrial countries' goods in industrial countries.
Y	Real net national income in industrial countries.
YRLDC	Real gross domestic product in developing countries.
YROE	Real gross domestic product in industrial countries.
YROPEC	Real gross domestic product in OPEC.

References

Barro, R. 1974. Are government bonds net wealth? *Journal of Political Economy* 82, no. 6 (November-December): 1095–1117.

Blanchard, O. 1985. Debt, deficits, and finite horizons. *Journal of Political Economy* 93 (April): 223–51.

Blanchard, O., and R. Dornbusch. 1984. U.S. deficits, the dollar and Europe. *Banca Nazionale del Lavoro Quarterly Review* 48:89–113.

Blanchard, O., and L. Summers. 1984. Perspectives on high world real interest rates. *Brookings Papers on Economic Activity* 2:273–334.

Bruno, M., and J. Sachs. 1985. *The economics of worldwide stagflation.* Cambridge, Mass.: Harvard University Press.

Buiter, W. 1984. Fiscal policy in open interdependent economies. NBER Working Paper no. 1429.

Cline, W. 1984. *International debt.* Cambridge, Mass.: MIT Press.

Colaco, F., and S. van Wijnbergen, eds. 1986. *International capital flows and the developing countries.* In preparation.

Dixit, A., and V. Norman. 1980. *The theory of international trade.* Cambridge University Press.

Dornbusch, R. 1985. The effects of OECD macroeconomic policies on non-oil developing countries: A review. World Bank, WDR-1985 Background Paper. Forthcoming in Colaco, F. and S. van Wijnbergen, eds. *International capital flows and the developing countries.*

Frenkel, J., and A. Razin. 1985a. Government spending, debt and international economic interdependence. *Economic Journal*, 619–36.

————. 1985b. Fiscal expenditures and international economic interdependence. In W. Buiter and R. Marston. *International economic policy coordination,* Cambridge: Cambridge University.

Friedman, M. 1951. *A theory of the consumption function.* Princeton, N.J.: Princeton University Press.

Kormendi, R. 1983. Government debt, government spending and private sector behavior. *American Economic Review* 994–1010.

Kosuela and Viren. 1983. National debt neutrality: Some international evidence. *Kyklos.*

Lucas, Robert E., Jr. 1976. Econometric policy evaluation: A critique. In *The Phillips curve and labor markets,* ed. Karl Brunner and Allan H. Meltzer. Carnegie-Rochester Conference Series on Public Policy, a supplement to the *Journal of Monetary Economics,* vol. 1:19–46.

Mankiw, G., J. Rothenberg, and L. Summers. 1983. Intertemporal substitution in macroeconomics. NBER Working Paper no. 000.

Marion, N., and L. Svensson. 1983. Structural Differences and macroeconomic adjustment to oil price changes: A three-country approach. Stockholm: Institute for International Economic Studies. Seminar paper no. 248.

Mueller, P., and R. Price. 1985. Public sector indebtedness and long-term interest rates. World Bank, WDR-1985 Background Paper.

Persson, T., and L. Svensson. 1985. Current account dynamics and the terms of trade: Harberger-Laursen-Metzler two generations later. *Journal of Political Economy.*

Razin, A., and L. Svensson. 1983. The terms of trade and the current account: The Harberger-Laursen-Metzler effect. *Journal of Political Economy.*

Seater, J., and R. Mariano. 1985. New tests of the life cycle and tax discounting hypothesis. *Journal of Monetary Economics.*

Svensson, L. 1984. Oil prices, welfare and the trade balance. *Quarterly Journal of Economics.*

van Wijnbergen, S. 1984. Tariffs, employment and the current account: Real wage resistance and the macroeconomics of protectionism. CEPR Discussion Paper no. 30.

————. 1985a. Interdependence revisited: A developing countries' perspective on macroeconomic management and trade intervention in the industrial world. *Economic Policy* 1, no. 1.

————. 1985b. On fiscal deficits, the real exchange rate and the world interest rate. *European Economic Review,,* forthcoming.

————. 1985c. Taxation of international capital flows, the intertemporal terms of trade and the real price of oil. *Oxford Economic Papers.*

————. 1987. Fiscal deficits, investment and the current account: An intertemporal disequilibrium analysis. World Bank. *Economic Journal.*

World Bank. 1985. *World development report 1985.* Oxford: Oxford University Press.

Comment   Guillermo A. Calvo

This paper provides a framework for the analysis of the impact of certain key macro policy measures on world equilibrium. In contrast with much of the earlier work in this area, an attempt is made to ground some of the equations on standard micro theory. I think we should be

Guillermo A. Calvo is professor of economics at the University of Pennsylvania.

thankful to the author for undertaking such an ambitious and coura-
geous enterprise.

From the point of view of economic substance, the paper tackles
two sets of problems that turn out to be rather independent from one
another. In the first part of the paper, a great deal of emphasis is put
on disproving the empirical significance of the Ricardian equivalence
proposition. The last part of the paper, on the other hand, focuses on
simulations where government expenditure, not deficit, takes center
stage.

The test of Ricardian equivalence is based on a model where such
an equivalence would fail if and only if the government faces a different
"discount rate" than the public. In the formal presentation of the
model, the analysis proceeds along the purest canons of micro-perfect-
foresight analysis. However, the empirical implementation assumes
that future expected government expenditure, for example, is a weighted
average of present and past levels of government expenditure. Thus,
in the paper's notation, g is determined by G (including its past history).
Since individuals are assumed to be keenly aware of the government's
budget constraint, we have

(1) $$T + \delta t = G + \delta g.$$

Hence, given G, a fall in T, say, is expected to give rise to a future
rise in t of an exactly equal (present value) magnitude. In other words,
the paper assumes that all changes in taxes are transitory, unless they
are accompanied by a contemporaneous change in G. This assumption
will certainly sound extreme to some advocates of the Reagan "tax
cuts," since some of them viewed these cuts as a way to induce Congress to put a lid on government expenditure. (Judd 1985 studies the
effect of this sequence of events.)

Let us consider a slight generalization of the paper's assumption in
which changes in expected future (present value) taxes per unit change
of present taxes is > -1. This means, by equation (1), that, given G,
expected government expenditure, g, is an increasing function of $(T-G)$,
implying that a test like the one in this paper, where expected government expenditure is a function of its lagged values, and not of present
taxes, will show a positive response of consumption to a fiscal deficit.
The reason is simple: lower taxes today are a signal that future government expenditure will be lower. In this context, therefore, the finding that aggregate consumption responds to taxes could not be claimed
to be a "proof" that there is a discrepancy between the discount rates
faced by the government and the private sectors.

In sum, the paper presents a test of the Ricardian proposition conditional on the assumption that changes in taxes are purely transitory.
Any departure from this rather extreme case would put the paper's
results into question. In this respect, it would perhaps be instructive

to allow for the possibility that expected government expenditure be a function of current taxes, and then carry out a test similar to that in the paper. If it is shown that taxes play a role in determining consumption, independent of the one they may have in forecasting future government expenditure, then the kind of doubts raised by my previous comments could be put to rest very quickly.

I think the paper would be greatly improved by being more explicit about the underlying theoretical apparatus. I found it particularly annoying that there is no reference to capital-mobility assumptions, not even a cursory remark on the type of assets available to the different agents around the world. I tried to infer the financial structure from the other assumptions of the model, but that turns out to be also very confusing. For example, van Wijnbergen's equation (14) implies that the OECD's "rate of interest" is also relevant for consumption decisions in the LDCs; does this imply perfect capital mobility? If so, what determines the geographical allocation of physical capital? Adjustment costs? If so, there will normally be cross-equation restrictions between the consumption and investment equations, or between the consumption and current account equations, and so forth. However, the paper imposes no cross-equation restriction in this respect, so we are back to square one.

In addition, some of the parts which are more explicitly modeled would benefit from a more thorough discussion. For example, it would be useful to know the theory behind the assumption that the consumption function contains lagged consumption as an explanatory variable in the empirical implementation of the model (e.g., sec. 8.4.1). This is so, because not every justification for such an assumption is going to imply structural stability to regime changes. Hall (1978) is an example of a theory that would rationalize the presence of lagged consumption, but which will not support the hypothesis that the equation's parameters are invariant to regime changes.

To summarize, I think the paper is useful in that it attempts to explain the facts from a true general equilibrium perspective. From this point of view, keeping good track of accounting identities is already an important step forward. I am much less certain, however, that—beyond making use of those identities—the paper exploits the constraints of the theory. This is not necessarily a reprehensible feature of the paper, but it suggests that the credibility of the results would be enhanced if the simulations were carried out in terms of several alternative empirical models.

References

Hall, Robert. 1978. Stochastic implications of the life cycle—Permanent income hypothesis: Theory and evidence. *Journal of Political Economy* 86:6.

Judd, Kenneth L. 1985. Short-run analysis of fiscal policy in a simple perfect foresight model. *Journal of Political Economy* 93, no. 2, (April): 298–319.

Comment   John T. Cuddington

The objective of Sweder van Wijnbergen's paper (henceforth Sweder), like the Knight and Masson (KM) paper (chap. 2, this volume), is to determine the extent to which the very high real interest rates since 1979 can be explained by expansionary fiscal policies in the major industrial countries. The empirical models in the two papers differ in perhaps predictable ways, given the authors' respective employers. Sweder's model disaggregates the world into three regions: OECD, OPEC, and LDCs, whereas the KM model adopts a four-region breakdown into the United States, Germany, Japan, and the rest of the world. The appropriateness of the two disaggregations, of course, depends on the purpose to which the models will be put. For some purposes, the KM approach of lumping together the world's biggest debtor countries—the non-oil LDCs—and the oil exporters, which have at times during in the 1970s been large international creditor countries, may be misleading. Similarly, aggregating all of OECD together, as Sweder does, has the disadvantage of implying that the United States and Japan can be treated as a single economic entity.

It seems unlikely that income redistribution among the OECD countries can be ignored, and many important policy problems in recent years have involved the mix of monetary and fiscal policies *among* the OECD nations. The last section of Sweder's paper, for example, considers a recent proposal to reduce the U.S. fiscal deficit by imposing an across-the-board import surcharge. This policy cannot really be satisfactorily analyzed in a model that lumps all of the OECD together, for this implies that the import surcharge is really a uniform surcharge levied by all of OECD against all imports from OPEC and the developing countries. Presumably this is far from what proponents of an import surcharge to reduce the U.S. fiscal deficit had in mind. Some advocate a tax on total imports of oil, or total domestic consumption of oil (whether produced in the United States or abroad). Others seem to have in mind a U.S. import surcharge on imports from other industrial countries, especially Japan in light of its large bilateral surplus vis-à-vis the United States. In any event, a tariff on imports from LDCs is (hopefully) a nonstarter, given their need to increase imports in order to service their large foreign debts.

John T. Cuddington is an associate professor of economics at the Edmund A. Walsh School of Foreign Service, Georgetown University.

Due to the degree of aggregation employed, therefore, I interpret Sweder's analysis in section 8.6 as an empirical demonstration and assessment of the general principle that there can be important interactions between interventions in intratemporal trade (via tariffs, quotas, etc.) and intertemporal trade. Specifically, trade taxes can have important effects on the real interest rate. In Sweder's model, OECD tariffs on LDC and OPEC imports drive up the world interest rate, thereby inflicting a double "whammy" on LDCs: Not only does this policy turn the intratemporal terms of trade against them, it also worsens their intertemporal terms of trade (i.e., drives up world interest rates thereby worsening their debt burden). I think this lesson is an important one, and one that would be robust to more country-disaggregation in the model.

An important contribution in Sweder's paper is an interesting discussion of the *facts* regarding the stance of fiscal policy in the OECD countries in the early 1980s. He claims that the fiscal deficit of OECD "correctly measured" has increased sharply since 1981. Three measurement issues are addressed. The first involves the importance of correcting the deficit for the effect of inflation on the real value of the outstanding public debt. The second is the appropriateness of cyclically adjusting the deficit. The third is the importance of compositional effects, that is, whether expenditure or revenue changes are most important when analyzing changes in the fiscal deficit.

Regarding the first point, the data in table 8.1 show the inflation-adjusted budget surplus/deficit for the nine large industrial countries. Their combined fiscal position moved from a small surplus of 0.6% of national income in 1981 to a deficit that peaked at 2.7% in 1983. Contrary to widespread opinion, the growing deficit in the United States has not been "more or less" offset by surpluses in the remaining industrial countries. Hence, the hypothesis that large fiscal deficits in the OECD countries was a major cause of the high real interest rates cannot—on the basis of this evidence, at least—be rejected out of hand.

While I have no argument with inflation-adjusted measures of the fiscal deficit when trying to assess the macroeconomic effects of deficits, it is difficult to say much about the *causal* link between fiscal deficits and real interest rates by just comparing the two time series. Thus, it is essential to go beyond causal empiricism to a model-based analysis of the sort undertaken by Sweder or KM. One of the main reasons for the fiscal deterioration in the early 1980s, shown in table 8.1, was the disinflationary policy being pursued, especially in the United States. Although inflation came down, nominal interest rates fell only slowly; hence, real rates rose sharply. This causes real interest payments on government long-term (fixed nominal interest rate) debt obligations to rise. The resulting deterioration in the inflation-adjusted fiscal deficit is, at least to some extent, just an *endogenous* response of the deficit to fluctuations in the real interest rate. It need not reflect a change in the tightness or looseness of fiscal policy.

This leads to a second point about the appropriateness of using a cyclically adjusted or "full employment" measure of the deficit. Sweder rejects the use of cyclically adjusted measures on the grounds that it is the *actual* deficit, not the level of the deficit would have prevailed had the economy been at full employment, that determines the pressure that fiscal deficits exert in the credit markets. I do not find this argument convincing. The importance of cyclical adjustment is to get a measure of *policy-induced* changes in fiscal stance, rather than endogenous changes that result from business cycle fluctuations. Many analysts use cyclically adjusted deficits as a shortcut, rather than undertaking a general equilibrium analysis. The simulation part of Sweder's paper is an example of this more complete approach. It models the effect of government *spending*, not the endogenous fiscal deficit, on private saving and investment behavior (with the latter two depending on income, if not the cyclical position of the economy).

The final measurement issue involves the different components of the government budget that give rise to the deficit. Sweder argues that transfer payments are, from a macroeconomic point of view, more appropriately treated as negative taxes than expenditures. When outlays on Social Security are netted out against taxes, he finds that net taxes remained remarkably stable over the last 20 years right up to 1984. "The big increase in deficits is due to a substantial increase in government expenditure on goods and services; as a share of national income, government expenditure on goods and services increased by a full 3 percentage points" (section 8.5.1). This fact is important when trying to understand the role of growing OECD fiscal deficits in the macroeconomy of the early 1980s. More importantly, it brings out a point that all economists know but frequently ignore, namely the macroeconomic effects of deficits depend critically on how they arise. Increases in government spending and reductions in tax revenue collections both increase the fiscal deficit, yet their macro effects can be quite different. This is true in simple textbook Keynesian models; it is also true in neoclassical models with Barro-Ricardian debt neutrality.

At the empirical level, it would be worthwhile to *test* whether transfer payments can, in fact, be treated as if they are just negative taxes. Even in the national context, the differing income distribution effects from transfers and taxes may or may not cause them to have different macro implications. In a model that nets all transfers *within the OECD* against all tax revenue, the netting of taxes and transfers is likely to be even less credible. A related issue is whether or not to treat interest payments on the public debt—either the total nominal amount or real interest payments—as transfer payments. This is, in fact, the way that they are recorded in the U.S. national income accounts, although many other countries account for them as factor payments (just as private interest payments are recorded). In sum, there are a number of neutrality or equivalence propositions involving the various components that comprise the budget deficit. A useful empirical exercise would be to test them, thereby providing some guidance regarding appropriate degrees of aggregation in medium-size, macro-simulation models.

The last half of the paper uses an empirically estimated simulation model to analyze the effect on the real interest rate of cutting the growth rate for government current expenditures in half, so that it rises from 22% to 23.5% of GDP rather than to 25%—the actual increase over the 1979–84 period. The model assumes that the real interest rate is determined in a perfectly integrated world capital market. This assumption undoubtedly overstates the extent to which developing countries could borrow during the late 1970s. Nevertheless, it is admittedly a tractable one. Each region specializes in the production of its own production good, as in the Mundell-Fleming model, and debt nonneutrality in the OECD segment of the model is motivated by a Blanchard interest wedge story, which assumes that the private rate of interest exceeds the government rate because private agents face a constant probability of death whereas the government does not.

Although the analytical model in the early sections of the paper is an excellent example of a model that pays careful attention to intertemporal considerations, the empirical model looks quite conventional (i.e., ad hoc in terms of its intertemporal underpinnings). Consumption, for example, depends on current income, future income having been solved out using the Koyck specification employed in early work by Friedman. There is no attempt to use a forward-looking rational expectations specification in order to explicitly incorporate future income or taxes into consumption decisions. In fact, no expectational variables enter the model. To some extent this reflects the nonmonetary nature of the model. In future work along these lines, a more detailed treatment of expectational and monetary factors would be worth pursuing.

How well does the model explain the sharp rise in the real interest rate between 1980 and 1981, which is shown in figure 8.3? Sweder answers this question by asking: How much lower would the time path of interest rates have been during 1979–84 if the increase in the ratio of government expenditure to GDP was cut in half (as described above)? The simulated effect on interest rates is shown as the dotted line in figure 8.3. I conclude from this figure that the rapid increase in government spending can *not* explain why real interest rates rose sharply to 15% in 1980–81. Rates are virtually unchanged in the simulation where government expenditure grows more slowly. The exercise, however, does suggest that real interest rates would have come down much more quickly in 1981–84 if government spending in the OECD, and especially in the United States, had been less expansionary.

In short, the paper seems to provide a good explanation of why real interest rates *stayed* high in the early 1980s, but not how they got there in the first place. To answer the latter question, I suspect that shifts in monetary policy in the OECD and the very rapid erosion of OPEC's current account surplus after the second oil price hike (unlike its behavior after the 1973–74 price increase) played an important role. Expectations in 1979–80 of worsening fiscal deficits in the years ahead may also be an explanation, albeit one that is difficult to put to the empirical test. Needless to say, all of this is beyond the scope of the present paper. It does an admirable job of demonstrating the importance of international repercussions of fiscal expansion in a multicountry, intertemporal, equilibrium framework.

9 Optimal Tax Policy for Balance of Payments Objectives

Kent P. Kimbrough

The proper role of tax policy in open economies has been and continues to be an area of considerable interest to economists.[1] Boadway, Maital, and Prachowny (1973) and Dasgupta and Stiglitz (1974) consider optimal tax policy in an open economy in the Ramsey sense of maximizing welfare subject to a revenue constraint. The principle result emerging from these two papers is that revenue considerations do not justify the introduction of tariffs and other barriers to international trade—the only sound welfare theoretic case for enacting trade barriers is the optimum tariff argument. Along similar lines, Razin and Svensson (1983a) study the optimal response of tax rates and budget deficits to permanent and temporary productivity shocks. They show that, starting from a stationary state, both permanent and temporary drops in productivity call for permanent increases in tax rates while only temporary declines in productivity call for any change in the government's budget (it should go into deficit when productivity is unusually low). Kimbrough (1986a) extends Razin and Svensson's setup and examines the optimal response of tax rates, government spending, and budget deficits to inflows of foreign aid to the public and private sectors. He shows that tax rates should be permanently reduced and government spending on public goods permanently increased in response to an inflow of foreign aid accruing to the public sector, while just the reverse is optimal when the increment in foreign aid accrues to the private sector. Persson and Svensson (1986) consider how the public debt can be restructured over time so that the optimal tax policy will be time consistent, paying

Kent P. Kimbrough is associate professor of economics at Duke University.

The author would like to thank Jeremy Greenwood for his extremely valuable comments on earlier drafts of the paper and to thank Phil Brock and Zvi Hercowitz for their comments also.

particular attention to the differences in the required restructuring of the debt for large and small economies.

Another major strand of the literature on the role of tax policy in open economies, in addition to studies based on the Ramsey tax problem and its open economy implications, has dealt with the optimum use of tax policy to mitigate distortions and achieve noneconomic objectives (see, for example, Johnson 1965 and Bhagwati 1968). The literature on the optimum structure of taxation for the attainment of noneconomic objectives has concentrated exclusively on microeconomic goals such as achieving a target level of output in the import-competing sector, a target level of imports, or a minimum level of employment in a given industry. However, many important policy questions concern the appropriate use of tax policy for macroeconomic objectives. For instance, one of the oldest and most pervasive arguments put forth in favor of tariffs, quotas, capital controls, and other barriers to international flows of goods and capital is that such policies are useful devices for improving a nation's trade balance and correcting balance of payments difficulties. Indeed, such sentiments were the cornerstone of the policy prescriptions of the mercantilists which Adam Smith attacked in *The Wealth of Nations*. More recently, large and rising U.S. trade deficits, about 3.4% of GNP in 1984 and up from 1.4% in 1982, have led Congress to consider enacting a 20% across-the-board tariff. Work by Mussa (1974, 1976) and Razin and Svensson (1983b) sheds considerable light on the likely impact of these and other policies. Mussa demonstrates that levying a tariff will only temporarily improve the balance of payments; the most reliable way to permanently improve the balance of payments is to reduce the rate of domestic credit creation. Razin and Svensson show that while temporary tariffs improve the current account by making current goods relatively more expensive in terms of future goods, the current account effects of permanent tariffs are ambiguous.

Given that the impact of tariffs and other taxes on the balance of payments and the trade balance are by now fairly well understood, it seems appropriate to study the optimal structure of taxation for achieving various balance of payments objectives. The purpose of this paper is to examine, from the perspective of the literature on noneconomic objectives, the optimal tax policies for achieving various balance of payments related objectives. The aim is to provide a general welfare theoretic framework for studying optimal policies concerning balance of payments and other international finance related objectives. The basic framework of analysis is the traditional two-sector model of international trade theory and public finance modified to include both monetary considerations and intertemporal decision making. To this end the cash-in-advance, exchange economy setup of Helpman (1981) is extended to a two-good, production economy setup.[2] This frame-work is used to consider four balance of payments–related objectives. First, the optimal tax policy for attaining a trade balance target is examined. Second, the closely related issue of a target level for domestic wealth is discussed. Optimal taxation for achieving a target level of international reserve holdings by some prespecified date is the third issue to be studied. Finally, the optimal tax policy for a balance of payments target is outlined.

The paper is organized as follows. Section 9.1 describes the economy. In section 9.2 the representative agent's optimization problem is discussed, and in section 9.3 the economy's general equilibrium is outlined. Sections 9.4–9.7 examine the optimal tax structure for attaining a trade balance target, a wealth target, a target level of international reserves, and a balance of payments target. Concluding remarks are presented in section 9.8.

9.1 Description of the Economy

Consider a small open economy that produces and consumes two traded goods. The economy is inhabited by an infinitely-lived representative agent whose goal is to maximize his lifetime utility, U, which is given by

$$(1) \qquad U = \sum_{t=1}^{\infty} \rho^{t-1} U(X^t, Z^t),$$

where $0 < \rho \leq 1$ is the agent's subjective discount factor and X^t and Z^t are his consumption of the two goods in period t. The pattern of international trade may vary over time; in some periods good Z may be imported and in others it may be exported, and similarly for good X. Production in each sector is subject to constant returns to scale, and it is assumed that the factors of production, labor and physical capital, are in fixed supply. In each period t the representative agent has two sources of income. First, the agent produces and sells his output of the two goods, X_s^t and Z_s^t, at the producer's relative price p_s^t. In terms of good X this provides the agent with income of $X_s^t + p_s^t Z_s^t$. Producer prices may differ from consumer prices, p^t, and the world terms of trade, p^{*t}, due to the presence of taxes and subsidies on production, consumption, and international trade. In addition to his income from goods production, the agent also receives transfer payments from the government that have a value of τ^t in terms of good X.

Domestic residents can also transact in domestic and world bond markets, although transactions in the world market may be subject to taxes, subsidies, or capital controls. In period t the representative agent can buy or sell real bonds denominated in terms of good X. On the world market one of these bonds yields $1 + r^{*t}$ units of good X in period $t + 1$, where r^{*t} is the world real interest rate. However, the return to domestic agents in period $t + 1$ is $1 + r^t$ which may differ from the world return due to the previously mentioned distortions.

The monetary mechanism of exchange dictates that agents must use domestic currency to buy domestically produced goods and foreign currency to buy foreign produced goods.[3] Agents satisfy their demand for goods by purchasing them first from domestic suppliers and then from foreign suppliers. Therefore, if good X is exported in period t and the agent purchases X^t units of the good he will use his current holdings of domestic money, M^t, to buy them. Likewise, if good Z is imported in period t, his purchases of imports $Z^t - Z_s^t$, will be financed out of his holdings of foreign money, M^{*t}.

The sequencing of transactions in the economy is the same as that adopted by Helpman (1981) in his comparison of exchange-rate regimes and by Greenwood and Kimbrough (1987) in their investigation of foreign exchange controls. For purposes of outlining the sequencing of transactions a sketch of one period of the representative agent's life will now be given. Throughout this sketch it is assumed for illustrative purposes that good X is exported and good Z is imported in period t. The agent enters period t with a certain amount of the two currencies left over from period $t - 1$. At the beginning of the period he receives domestic currency from his sales of goods in the previous period. That is, at the start of period t the agent receives $P^{t-1}(X_s^{t-1} + p_s^{t-1}Z_s^{t-1})$, where P^{t-1} is the domestic currency price of good X in period $t - 1$. At the same time the agent also receives his transfer payments from the government which have a nominal value of $P^t\tau^t$.

Next, the agent enters the bond and foreign exchange markets. He receives income from the bonds he purchased last period of $P^t(1 + r^{t-1})b^{t-1}$ units of domestic currency and buys new bonds worth P^tb^t. Having completed his bond market transactions the agent enters the foreign exchange market and allocates his cash holdings between domestic and foreign money in the amounts M^t and M^{*t}. A unit of foreign currency exchanges for e^t units of domestic money, where the exchange rate, e^t, may either be market determined or pegged by the domestic government.

During the last part of period t the agent uses the cash he has acquired to buy goods. He then enters period $t + 1$ with $M^t - P^t(X^t + p^tZ_s^t)$ units of domestic currency and $M^{*t} - P^{*t}p^t(Z^t - Z_s^t)$ units of foreign currency, where P^{*t} is the foreign currency price of good X. Arbitrage in the world market for good X guarantees that $P^t = e^tP^{*t}, t = 1,2 \ldots$. However, because of taxes and subsidies on domestic consumption and production, there are wedges between the exchange rate adjusted foreign nominal price of good Z and the domestic nominal prices facing consumers and producers.

9.2 The Agent's Optimization Problem

The representative agent makes consumption, production, and asset choices so as to maximize his lifetime utility as given by (1). This maximization is subject to the budget constraints facing the agent, the cash-in-advance constraints implied by the monetary mechanism of exchange, and the production technology and factor supplies with which the agent is endowed. Given the setup of the problem the agent's production decisions will be made so as to maximize the present value of his output. Assuming that domestic markets are perfectly competitive, the solution to this problem yields output supply functions with the standard properties:

$$(2) \qquad X_s^t = X_s^t(p_s^t), \qquad Z_s^t = Z_s^t(p_s^t), \qquad t = 1,2,\ldots,$$
$$(-) (+)$$

where the signs under the arguments of the supply functions show the signs of the partial derivatives of the supply functions. Since the supply functions in (2) maximize the value of output, $X_s^t + p_s^t Z_s^t$, the envelope theorem implies that

$$(3) \qquad \frac{-\,\partial X_s^t/\partial p_s^t}{\partial Z_s^t/\partial p_s^t} = p_s^t, \qquad t = 1,2 \ldots.$$

Given his production choices as characterized by (2) and (3), the agent chooses $X^t, Z^t, m^t = M^t/P^t, m^{*t} = M^{*t}/P^{*t}$, and b^t for $t = 1,2, \ldots$ to maximize (1) subject to the following constraints for $t = 1,2, \ldots$ (the convention here is that all period zero variables are identically zero):

$$(4) \quad m^t + m^{*t} + b^t = \frac{P^{t-1}}{P^t} [X_s^{t-1}(p_s^{t-1}) + p_s^{t-1}Z_s^{t-1}(p_s^{t-1})] + \tau^t$$

$$+ (1 + r^{t-1})b^{t-1} + \frac{P^{t-1}}{P^t} \{m^{t-1} - \omega[X^{t-1} + p^{t-1}Z_s^{t-1}(p_s^{t-1})]$$

$$- (1 - \omega)\, [X_s^{t-1}(p_s^{t-1}) + p^{t-1}Z^{t-1}]\} + \frac{P^{*t-1}}{P^{*t}} \{m^{*t-1}$$

$$- \omega p^{t-1}[Z^{t-1} - Z_s^{t-1}(p_s^{t-1})] - (1 - \omega)\, [X^{t-1} - X_s^{t-1}(p_s^{t-1})]\},$$

$$(5) \qquad \omega[X^t + p^t Z_s^t(p_s^t)] + (1 - \omega)\, [X_s^t(p_s^t) + p^t Z^t] \le m^t,$$

$$(6) \qquad \omega p^t[Z^t - Z_s^t(p_s^t)] + (1 - \omega)\, [X^t - X_s^t(p_s^t)] \le m^{*t},$$

where ω is an indicator variable that equals one when good Z is imported and zero when good Z is exported. (To keep the notation simple the possibility that both goods might be imported or exported in the same period has been ignored.) Equation (4) is the agent's period t

budget constraint while equations (5) and (6) are the cash-in-advance constraints confronting the agent in period t.

In the current framework, money is required for transactions purposes but agents choose whether or not to hold money as a store of value on the basis of wealth maximizing considerations. As discussed by Helpman (1981) and Greenwood and Kimbrough (1987), so long as domestic and foreign inflation rates, $\pi^t \equiv (P^{t+1} - P^t)/P^t$ and $\pi^{*t} \equiv (P^{*t+1} - P^{*t})/P^{*t}$, exceed the rates dictated by the optimum quantity of money rule, $-r^t/(1 + r^t)$ and $-r^{*t}/(1 + r^{*t})$, bonds will dominate money as a store of value and the cash-in-advance constraints, (5) and (6), will hold as equalities. These conditions, which imply positive nominal interest rates, are assumed to hold in the remainder of the analysis.

Treating (5) and (6) as equalities and using them in (4), it is straightforward to show that maximization of (1) subject to the resulting constraint yields, in addition to the constraint itself, the familiar first-order conditions

(7) $$U_Z^t/U_X^t = p^t, \quad t = 1,2,\ldots,$$

(8) $$\rho^{t-1}U_X^t/U_X^1 = d^t, \quad t = 1,2,\ldots,$$

where $d^t \equiv \Pi_{j=1}^{t}(1 + r^j)^{-1}$, $d^1 \equiv 1$, and $U_j^t \equiv U_j(X^t,Z^t)$ is the period t marginal utility of good $j, j = X,Z$. Within-period consumption choices are made so as to equate the marginal rate of substitution between the two goods to the consumer's relative price, p^t. The intertemporal allocation of consumption is such that the marginal rate of substitution between goods in period 1 and period t is equal to the domestic real discount factor, d^t.

9.3 General Equilibrium

In addition to the representative agent whose consumption, production, and asset plans have just been described, the economy has another actor: the government. Like the representative agent the government must satisfy a budget constraint. For the discussion of optimal tax policy that follows it is useful to artificially divide the government into two branches. One branch of the government is the fiscal authority. They finance real transfer payments of $\tau^t - \mu^t$ from the net revenues collected from the taxes and subsidies they levy on production, consumption, international trade, and international borrowing and lending. The fiscal authority's budget constraint, which is not written out formally since the distorting taxes to be levied are yet to be determined, states that the present value of their transfer payments, $\Sigma d^t(\tau^t - \mu^t)$, must equal the present value of the net revenues earned on the distorting taxes and subsidies they impose.

The other branch of government, the central bank, controls the money stock or pegs the exchange rate through the use of transfer payments, μ^t, and its holdings of interest-bearing international reserves, b_R^t.[4] The central bank's budget constraint for $t = 1,2, \ldots$ is

$$m_s^t - m_s^{t-1}/(1 + \pi^{t-1}) = \mu^t + b_R^t - (1 + r^{*t-1})b_R^{t-1},$$

which states that the excess of the central bank's transfers and reserve acquisitions, $b_R^t - b_R^{t-1}$, over its interest earnings on its previous reserve holdings, $r^{*t-1}b_R^{t-1}$, must be financed by money creation, $m_s^t - m_s^{t-1}/(1 + \pi^{t-1})$, where m_s^t is the real money supply in period t. When the central bank is pegging the exchange rate rigidly or with preannounced adjustments, it is useful to rewrite their budget constraint as

(9) $$b_R^t = (1 + r^{*t-1})b_R^{t-1} + [m_s^t - m_s^{t-1}/(1 + \pi^{t-1}) - \mu^t],$$

$$t = 1,2 \ldots .$$

Equation (9) emphasizes that the dynamic behavior of the central bank's international reserve holdings depends on the accumulation of interest on past reserve holdings and flows of reserves through the balance of payments. The balance of payments is the flow demand for real balances, $m_s^t - m_s^{t-1}/(1 + \pi^{t-1})$, less the flow supply of real balances provided by the central bank via its domestic credit operations, μ^t. (Recall that the money stock is demand determined when the central bank pegs the exchange rate.)

Equilibrium in the domestic money market requires that the demand for money equal the supply in each period. As noted earlier, with domestic and foreign inflation rates exceeding the rates dictated by the optimum quantity of money rule, the cash-in-advance constraints will hold with equality. From (5) it follows that, in real terms, the demand for domestic money by domestic residents is $\omega[X^t + p^t Z_s^t(p_s^t)] + (1 - \omega)[X_s^t(p_s^t) + p^t Z^t]$. If foreign residents are solving a similar optimization problem, then their demand for domestic money reflects their demand for imports of domestic goods. Since the goods market must clear in each period, it follows that, in equilibrium, the foreign demand for domestic money equals $\omega[X_s^t(p_s^t) - X^t] + (1 - \omega)p^t[Z_s^t (p_s^t) - Z^t]$. Therefore, the demand for domestic money in period t is simply the value of domestic output at consumer prices, and the money market equilibrium condition can be written as

(10) $$m_s^t = X_s^t(p_s^t) + p^t Z_s^t(p_s^t), \quad t = 1,2, \ldots .$$

Letting $m_s^t = M_s^t/e^t P^{*t}$, where M_s^t is the nominal money stock, it can be seen that under floating rates the money market equilibrium condition determines the equilibrium exchange rate while under a pegged-rate system it determines the equilibrium nominal money stock. From

(9) and (10) it follows that for a given exchange rate policy, $\{e^t = \bar{e}^t\}_{t=1}^{\infty}$, and nominal transfer policy, $\{T^t = \bar{e}^t P^{*t}\bar{\mu}^t\}_{t=1}^{\infty}$, the time path of the central bank's international reserves reflects movements in the balance of payments as determined by the intertemporal behavior of the demand for money.

In addition to the previously discussed budget constraints and market clearing conditions, international trade must balance intertemporally. For the distortion-free case, this can be demonstrated by multiplying the sequence of budget constraints in (4) by the discount factor $d^t = d^{*t} \equiv \Pi_{j=1}^{t} (1 + r^{*j})^{-1}$ and summing the resulting expressions. The fact that the cash-in-advance constraints hold with equality can then be used to eliminate the money terms from the resulting equation. Finally, the transfer payment terms can be eliminated by discounting and summing the central bank's budget constraint as given by (9), using (10) in the resulting expression, and noting that in the absence of distorting taxes $\tau^t = \mu^t$. This yields the desired intertemporal trade balance condition ($p_s^t = p^{*t}$ when there are no distortions)

$$(11) \qquad \sum_{t=1}^{\infty} d^{*t}(X^t + p^{*t}Z^t) = \sum_{t=1}^{\infty} d^{*t}[X_s^t(p_s^t) + p^{*t}Z_s^t(p_s^t)].$$

A similar proof, but one involving the fiscal authority's budget constraint, shows that (11) must also hold in the presence of distorting taxes and subsidies.

9.4   Trade Balance Target

Trade balance deficits are commonly viewed with alarm by policymakers and they are not long tolerated before action is taken to eliminate them. One possible explanation for such concerns may be the observed correlation between declines in income and a worsening trade balance that arises as a result of the consumption-smoothing behavior of consumers in response to temporary changes in income. Despite the fact that the resulting correlation between income and the trade balance reflects the optimal response of consumers to exogenous fluctuations in income, if policymakers mistakenly believe causation to be running from the trade balance to income they may perceive there to be some scope for activist policy to improve matters. Although it is apparent that for a distortion-free small open economy the imposition of trade balance targets by the government can only reduce welfare, it is important from an economic standpoint to consider the welfare maximizing structure of taxes and subsidies for attaining trade balance targets when the government deems them to be desirable.

Formally, suppose that the government imposes a sequence of trade balance targets, $\tilde{tb}^t$, for periods $t = 1, \ldots, k$. These constraints require that

(12) $\quad X_s^t(p_s^t) - X^t + p^{*t}[Z_s^t(p_s^t) - Z^t] \geq \tilde{tb}^t, \qquad t = 1, \ldots, k$.

The optimal policy maximizes the representative agent's lifetime utility as given by (1) subject to the economy's lifetime budget constraint (11) and the sequence of trade balance targets given by (12). Technically, the planning problem confronting the government is to choose $\{X^t\}_{t=1}^{\infty}$, $\{Z^t\}_{t=1}^{\infty}$, and $\{p_s^t\}_{t=1}^{\infty}$ to maximize

(13) $\quad \displaystyle\sum_{t=1}^{\infty} \rho^{t-1} U(X^t, Z^t) + \lambda \cdot \sum_{t=1}^{\infty} d^{*t}\{X_s^t(p_s^t) - X^t + p^{*t}[Z_s^t(p_s^t) - Z^t]\}$

$$+ \sum_{t=1}^{k} \theta^t d^{*t}\{X_s^t(p_s^t) - X^t + p^{*t}[Z_s^t(p_s^t) - Z^t] - \tilde{tb}^t\},$$

where λ is the marginal utility of wealth and $\theta^t d^{*t}$ is the marginal welfare loss associated with tightening the period-t trade balance constraint. It should be noted here that the government can manipulate domestic residents' consumption profiles by setting consumption taxes and taxes on international borrowing appropriately.

In addition to the constraints the first-order conditions that emerge from the government's optimization problem given by (13) are[5]

(14a) $\quad U_Z^t / U_X^t = p^{*t},$ $\hspace{4cm} t = 1, 2, \ldots,$

(14b) $\quad \dfrac{-\partial X_s^t / \partial p_s^t}{\partial Z_s^t / \partial p_s^t} = p^{*t},$ $\hspace{3cm} t = 1, 2, \ldots,$

(14c) $\quad \rho^{t-1} U_X^t / U_X^1 = \begin{cases} d^{*t} \cdot \left[\dfrac{1 + (\theta^t/\lambda)}{1 + (\theta^1/\lambda)} \right], & t = 1, \ldots, k, \\[1.2em] d^{*t} \cdot \left[\dfrac{1}{1 + (\theta^1/\lambda)} \right], & t = k + 1, \ldots, \end{cases}$

where d^{*t} is the world real discount factor for period t.

The first-order conditions (14a) and (14b), in conjunction with the representative agent's first-order conditions (3) and (7), show that the optimal policy calls for setting within-period relative prices confronting consumers and producers equal to world relative prices (i.e., $p^t = p_s^t = p^{*t}$). From (8) and (14c) it is also clear that the optimal policy for attaining a series of trade balance targets entails distorting intertemporal choices. Specifically, in order to induce domestic residents to substitute consumption in the periods after the trade balance targets are lifted for consumption in those periods when they are in effect, international borrowing should be taxed (or equivalent policies introduced) in periods $t = 1, \ldots, k$. Furthermore, taxes on international borrowing should be highest in those periods where the trade balance constraint is most severe (and hence θ' is greatest). This structure of taxes serves to generate the appropriate intertemporal pattern of substitution by domestic residents.[6] It should be noted here that systems of capital controls and dual exchange rates can replicate the optimal tax structure described by (14). (See Adams and Greenwood [1985] on the equivalence of capital controls and dual exchange rates and Greenwood and Kimbrough [1985] for a look at capital controls and fiscal policy.)

The intuition behind these results is straightforward. The goal of achieving a prespecified sequence of trade balances is essentially aimed at attaining a given intertemporal pattern of consumption (and production in a framework that allows for intertemporal production decisions such as investment in physical capital). It is therefore optimal to enact a tax program that strikes directly at intertemporal relative prices while leaving within-period relative prices undistorted. This rules out tariffs, export subsidies, and other trade policies that strike at within-period relative prices as part of the optimal tax package for achieving trade balance targets.

Earlier it was argued that governments may institute policies designed to achieve a target trade balance because consumption smoothing by consumers results in temporary drops in income worsening the trade balance, and policymakers may view causation as running from the trade balance to income rather than the other way around as is actually the case. In fact, if governments institute trade balance targets when income is temporarily low, the burden of adjusting consumption spending will be concentrated in those periods when income shocks occur rather than being spread over consumers' lifetimes. Enacting trade balance targets in response to temporary income fluctuations thus reduces welfare, relative to the no-intervention benchmark, by preventing consumers from engaging in desirable consumption-smoothing behavior. In fact, enacting such targets can result in an intertemporal consumption pattern that, from the perspective of the permanent-income hypothesis, appears to exhibit excess sensitivity to current income.

9.5 Wealth Target

Another reason countries may undertake policies designed to manipulate the trade balance or current account is a preoccupation with their wealth or net foreign asset position. Such concerns may arise because, as in the case of the mercantilists, changes in a country's wealth are erroneously taken to be indicators of changes in welfare or because policymakers desire to shift the intertemporal pattern of utility, $\{U(X^t,Z^t)\}_{t=1}^{\infty}$.

In order to study the optimal tax policy for achieving a target level of wealth, and to examine its connection with trade balance targets, note that by period k, the country's net foreign asset position will be given by

$$b^k = (1/d^{*k}) \cdot \sum_{t=1}^{k} d^{*t}\{X_s^t(p_s^t) - X^t + p^{*t}[Z_s^t(p_s^t) - Z_t]\}.$$

That is, the country's external wealth by period k is simply the sum of principle and interest earned on its past trade balances. If the government adopts a wealth target of $\bar{b}$ for period k, the problem they face is to maximize

$$\sum_{t=1}^{\infty} \rho^{t-1}U(X^t,Z^t) + \lambda \cdot \sum_{t=1}^{\infty} d^{*t}\{X_s^t(p_s^t) - X^t + p^{*t}[Z_s^t(p_s^t) - Z^t]\}$$

$$+ \theta \cdot (\sum_{t=1}^{k} d^{*t}\{X_s^t(p_s^t) - X^t + p^{*t}[Z_s^t(p_s^t) - Z^t]\} - d^{*k}\bar{b})$$

by choosing the time profiles $\{X^t\}_{t=1}^{\infty}$, $\{Z^t\}_{t=1}^{\infty}$, and $\{p_s^t\}_{t=1}^{\infty}$ where θd^{*k} is the marginal welfare cost of raising the period-k wealth target. It is important to note that when policy is directed toward increasing wealth at world prices, as in the problem being studied here, no attention is given to the distribution of foreign asset holdings between private agents, the fiscal authorities, and the central bank but only to the overall level of wealth, b^k. More will be said about this issue in the following section.

It is easily verified that, in addition to the constraints, the first-order conditions for the government's problem are

(15a) $U_Z^t/U_X^t = p^{*t}$, $t = 1, 2, \ldots,$

(15b) $\dfrac{-\partial X_s^t/\partial p_s^t}{\partial Z_s^t/\partial p_s^t} = p^{*t}$, $t = 1, 2, \ldots,$

(15c) $\rho^{t-1}U_X^t/U_X^1 = \begin{cases} d^{*t}, & t = 1, \ldots, k, \\ d^{*t} \cdot \left[\dfrac{1}{1 + (\theta/\lambda)}\right], & t = k + 1, \ldots. \end{cases}$

From (15a) and (15b) it follows immediately that, as was the case with a trade balance target, the optimal attainment of a wealth target does not call for introducing any within-period distortions; the marginal rate of substitution and the marginal rate of transformation between goods at a point in time should both be set equal to world relative prices (i.e., $p^t = p_s^t = p^{*t}$). However, from (15c) it can be seen that, again as was the case with a trade balance target, a wealth target is best attained by taxing international borrowing in periods $t = 1, \ldots$,k. The intuition again is the same: taxing international borrowing in the periods prior to the date when the wealth target is to be met discourages consumption and encourages saving and wealth accumulation. Although the overall character of the optimal tax policies for attaining balance of trade and wealth targets are very similar, there is one key difference: When the government imposes a wealth target, tax rates on international borrowing should be equated in all periods $t = 1, \ldots ,k$. This reflects the optimality, from a welfare standpoint, of spreading the burden of attaining the wealth target evenly across periods $t = 1, \ldots ,k$. However, with balance of trade targets applying to periods $t = 1, \ldots ,k$, taxes on international borrowing will generally differ across periods in a rather complicated way. This means that if policymakers are concerned with increasing wealth, it is inefficient to attempt to do so by imposing a sequence of trade balance targets on the economy. The reason is that by instituting a system of trade balance targets that will produce the target wealth level, the government, generally speaking, imposes an unnecessary constraint on the intertemporal pattern of wealth accumulation that can only reduce welfare. Finally, note that the example of policies aimed at attaining a target wealth level highlights the distinction between wealth and welfare. It is straightforward to show that with a target wealth level of $\bar{b}$ applying to period k, welfare evaluated from period $k + 1$ on is higher than it would have been in the absence of a wealth target. This follows from the fact that the consumer's indirect utility function from period $k + 1$ on is an increasing, concave function in period-k wealth. However, from the perspective of period one, when the wealth target is introduced, agents' lifetime welfare is clearly reduced. That is, the government's policy of enacting taxes to increase wealth, even when optimally carried out, actually reduces welfare. (A related point has been made by Murphy [1985] regarding the impact of tariffs on the time profile of agents' utilities.)

9.6 International Reserve Target

Oftentimes countries that have adopted a fixed exchange rate or a crawling peg find confidence in the exchange rate being undermined by an impending balance of payments crisis. Such crises typically involve a situation in which the central bank's holdings of international reserves have dwindled to so low a level that a speculative attack threatens to deplete the remaining stock. One way to forestall such an attack is to implement a comprehensive package of monetary and fiscal reforms that promises to augment the central bank's reserve holdings through a sustained period of balance of payments surpluses. A key ingredient of such policy reforms is to reduce domestic credit creation, T^t, or to devalue the domestic currency. In the context of the model being used here, these policies would be reflected by a drop in μ^t which would trigger an improvement in the balance of payments, $m_s^t - m_s^{t-1}/(1 + \pi^{t-1}) - \mu^t$, and a buildup of international reserves, b_R^t, by the central bank.

In models similar to the one being used here it has been shown (e.g., Helpman [1981], Lucas [1982], and Stockman [1983]) that exchange rate management policies have no real effects. This result is an open economy implication of Ricardian equivalence. Therefore, under debt neutrality, when policymakers wish to defend the exchange rate by building up the central bank's stock of international reserves to some target level, the first-best policy always involves adjusting the time-path of domestic credit.[7] However, for whatever reasons, countries do not always adjust their domestic credit policies sufficiently, and some of the burden of adjusting the economy to the exchange rate ultimately falls on fiscal policy. This section of the paper examines the optimal tax policy, in the fiscal sense, for achieving a target level of international reserves. The following section takes up the closely related issue of the optimal tax policy for achieving a balance of payments target. It should be borne in mind that in both cases the tax policies being discussed are second-best for the noneconomic objective under consideration; the first-best policy in both instances would be to alter the central bank's real transfer sequence, $\{\mu^t\}_{t=1}^{\infty}$, by changing the time-path of domestic credit. This would directly affect the balance of payments and the central bank's international reserve holdings without creating welfare reducing distortions.

9.6.1 The Government's Optimization Problem

Suppose that the government desires to build the central bank's stock of international reserves up to the target level $\bar{b}_R$ by the end of period k. By repeated substitution using the central bank's budget constraint, (9), it can be shown that period-k reserve holdings will be

$$b_R^k = (1/d^{*k}) \cdot \sum_{t=1}^{k} d^{*t}[m_s^t - m_s^{t-1}/(1 + \pi^{t-1}) - \mu^t]$$

$$= (1/d^{*k}) \cdot \left[d^{*k}(m_s^k - \mu_s^k) + \sum_{t=1}^{k-1} d^{*t}\left(\frac{i^t m_s^t}{1 + i^t} - \mu^t \right) \right],$$

where $(1 + i^t) \equiv (1 + \pi^t)(1 + r^{*t})$ implicitly defines the domestic nominal interest rate, i^t. Recall that arbitrage in the market for good X implies that $1 + \pi^t = (1 + \epsilon^t)(+ \pi^{*t})$, where $\epsilon^t = (e^{t+1} - e^t)/e^t$ is the policy determined rate of depreciation of the domestic currency.

Therefore, it follows that the interest parity condition $1 + i^t = (1 + \epsilon^t)(1 + i^{*t})$ holds, where $i^{*t} \equiv r^{*t} + \pi^{*t} + r^{*t}\pi^{*t}$ is the foreign nominal interest rate. It should be noted here that i^t, which is exogenously determined by world market conditions and domestic policy, is actually the domestic nominal interest rate prior to accounting for any wedge driven between domestic and foreign real interest rates by domestic tax policy. However, this is the nominal interest rate that is relevant for calculating the inflation tax revenues earned by the central bank through the accumulation of interest-bearing international reserves.

Since the international reserve target requires that the central bank's period-k reserves, as given above, meet or exceed $\bar{b}_R$, and since the money supply is demand determined under pegged rates according to (10), the planning problem confronting the government is to choose time profiles for X^t, Z^t, and p_s^t that maximize[8]

(16) $\displaystyle\sum_{t=1}^{\infty} \rho^{t-1} U(X^t, Z^t) + \lambda \cdot \sum_{t=1}^{\infty} d^{*t}\{X_s^t(p_s^t) - X^t + p^{*t}[Z_s^t(p_s^t) - Z^t]\}$

$\displaystyle + \alpha \cdot \left(\sum_{t=1}^{k-1} d^{*t} \left\{ \frac{i^t[X_s^t(p_s^t) + (U_Z^t/U_X^t)Z_s^t(p_s^t)]}{1 + i^t} - \mu^t \right\} \right.$

$\displaystyle \left. + d^{*t}[X_s^k(p_s^k) + (U_Z^k/U_X^k)Z_s^k p_s^k) - \mu^k - \bar{b}_R] \right),$

where use has been made of the fact that optimization on the part of private agent's imposes (7) as an incentive compatibility condition. (It can be seen immediately from [16] that by adjusting $\{\mu^t\}_{t=1}^{k}$ the target can be hit at no cost.)

With some manipulation it can be shown that the first-order conditions for the government's problem yield the following tangency conditions (i^t has been taken to be constant to simplify the notation):

(17a) $U_Z^t/U_X^t = \begin{cases} \dfrac{p^{*t} + \theta^t(i/1 + i)s_X^t}{1 - \theta^t(i/1 + i)s_Z^t}, & t = 1, \ldots, k-1, \\[2ex] \dfrac{p^{*t} + \theta^t s_X^t}{1 - \theta^t s_Z^t}, & t = k, \\[2ex] p^{*t}, & t = k+1, \ldots, \end{cases}$

(17b) $\dfrac{-\partial X_s^t/\partial p_s^t}{\partial Z_s^t/\partial p_s^t} = \begin{cases} \dfrac{\lambda p^{*t} + \alpha(i/1 + i)p^t}{\lambda + \alpha(i/1 + i)}, & t = 1, \ldots, k-1, \\[2ex] \dfrac{\lambda p^{*t} + \alpha p^t}{\lambda + \alpha}, & t = k, \\[2ex] p^{*t}, & t = k+1, \ldots, \end{cases}$

$$(17c) \quad \rho^{t-1} U_X^t/U_X^1 = \begin{cases} d^{*t} \cdot \dfrac{1 - \theta^t(i/1 + i)s_Z^t}{1 - \theta^1(i/1 + i)s_Z^1}, & t = 1, \ldots, k-1, \\[3mm] d^{*t} \cdot \dfrac{1 - \theta^t s_Z^t}{1 - \theta^1(i/1 + i)s_Z^1}, & t = k, \\[3mm] d^{*t} \cdot \dfrac{1}{1 - \theta^1(i/1 + i)s_Z^1}, & t = k+1, \ldots, \end{cases}$$

where

$$\theta^t = \alpha Z_s^t H^t/\lambda U_X^t, \quad H^t = 2p^t U_{XZ}^t - U_{ZZ}^t - (p^t)^2 U_{XX}^t > 0,$$
$$s_X^t = (p^t U_{XZ}^t - U_{ZZ}^t)/H^t > 0,$$

and

$$s_Z^t = (U_{ZX}^t - p^t U_{XX}^t)/H^t > 0.$$

The term s_j^t, $j = X, Z$, is the marginal change in an agent's purchases of good j when the expenditure allocated to period t changes. It follows from the within-period budget constraint that $s_X^t + p^t s_Z^t = 1$.

9.6.2 Interpretation

To begin with, note from the agent's first-order condition (7) and the first-order condition (17a) that given the international reserve target the optimum tax on consumption of good Z can be calculated as

$$\eta^t = \begin{cases} \dfrac{(\theta^t/p^{*t})(i/1 + i)}{1 - \theta^t(i/1 + i)s_Z^t}, & t = 1, \ldots, k-1, \\[3mm] \dfrac{\theta^t/p^{*t}}{1 - \theta^t s_Z^t}, & t = k, \\[3mm] 0, & t = k+1, \ldots, \end{cases}$$

where η^t satisfies $U_Z^t/U_X^t = p^t = (1 + \eta^t)p^{*t}$. The first thing to notice is that the optimal policy calls for no within-period taxes on consumption after the "deadline" period, period k. In interpreting the tax rates for periods $t = 1, \ldots, k$ it is useful to consider as a benchmark the case where the initial distortion-free equilibrium is a steady-state so that p^{*t}, θ^t, s_X^t, and s_Z^t are constant across periods. In this case it is readily seen that the optimal tax structure involves levying a consumption tax on good Z that is constant up until the deadline period and then raising the consumption tax to a higher level in period k when the reserve target must be fulfilled. In fact, the period-k consumption tax rate is somewhat greater than $(1 + i)/i$ times that in the earlier periods. For typical values of the nominal interest rate it follows that the optimal consumption tax in period k may be several times that for periods $t = 1, \ldots, k - 1$.

The intuition behind these results is as follows: As can be seen from (10), enacting a consumption tax raises the demand for money and, given the central bank's domestic credit policy μ^t, improves the balance of payments and leads to an inflow of international reserves. During periods $1, \ldots, k - 1$ the central bank accumulates reserves from increments to money demand at a rate equal to the interest earned on its inflation tax revenues of $i/(1 + i)$. This follows from the fact that while a consumption tax levied in period t improves the balance of payments in period t by $p^{*t}Z_s^t d\eta^t$, it raises agents' initial levels of real balance at the start of period $t + 1$ and thus worsens the balance of payments in period $t + 1$ by $p^{*t}Z_s^t d\eta^t/(1 + \pi^t)$. Therefore, in period t present-value terms, a consumption tax levied then adds $ip^{*t}Z_s^t d\eta^t/(1 + i)$ to the central bank's international reserves. Since the latter influence is not explicitly accounted for during the deadline period, period k, consumption taxes levied then contribute $p^{*k}Z_s^k d\eta^k$ toward the reserve target. It is thus optimal to tax consumption most heavily in period k. Finally, it can be seen that, all else equal, consumption taxes should be relatively low in periods where world relative prices, p^{*t}, are relatively high. This pattern of taxation serves to smooth fluctuations in domestic relative prices facing consumers, $p^t = (1 + \eta^t)p^{*t}$.

Returning to the benchmark steady-state case, it can be seen from (17c) that the intertemporal taxes called for by the optimal plan serve to mitigate the welfare-reducing effects of the within-period consumption taxes that were just discussed. To see this, note first that no intertemporal distortions are introduced between any two periods t and $t + j$ after the deadline period. However, the government's intertemporal taxes act to subsidize international borrowing in periods $1, \ldots, k$.[9] This serves to reallocate consumption from the later periods, where consumers' within-period marginal rates of substitution equal world relative prices, to the earlier periods, where consumption taxes have raised consumers' marginal rates of substitution above world relative prices so that a welfare gain of $\rho^{t-1}U_X^t \eta^t p^{*t}$ attaches to increases in the consumption of good Z. Additionally, given the initial equilibrium was a steady state, it can be seen that agents' intertemporal choices between periods $t = 1, \ldots k - 1$ are left undistorted and hence are all taxed relative to period k. Since all periods $t = 1, \ldots, k$ are subsidized relative to the later periods, it follows that international borrowing is subsidized equally in periods prior to period k (in which consumption taxes are equal) and subsidized at a higher rate in period k (when the consumption tax is the highest).

Equation (17b) characterizes the optimum structure of production taxes. Recalling the competitive profit maximizing condition (3), and using the condition $p^t = (1 + \eta^t)p^{*t}$, it can be demonstrated that the optimal policy calls for the production of good Z to be subsidized at the rate

$$
\eta_s^t = \begin{cases}
\dfrac{\alpha(i/1 + i)\eta^t}{\lambda + \alpha(i/1 + i)}, & t = 1, \ldots, k - 1, \\[2ex]
\dfrac{\alpha\eta^t}{\lambda + \alpha}, & t = k, \\[2ex]
0, & t = k + 1, \ldots,
\end{cases}
$$

where $p_s^t = (1 + \eta_s^t)p^{*t}$. As was the case for consumption decisions, production decisions are left undistorted after period k. Production is subsidized from the current period through period k, with the subsidy remaining constant until period k when it is increased. The explanation for the intertemporal pattern of production subsidies is the same as that outlined earlier for the intertemporal pattern of consumption taxes. The optimal policy calls for subsidies to good Z production because this raises the demand for money and augments the buildup of reserves. Both consumption taxes and production subsidies work in this direction, and it is optimal to distort both decisions until their marginal welfare costs are equal. However, it is readily apparent that this occurs when production subsidies are lower than consumption taxes (i.e., when $\eta_s^t \leq \eta^t$). The reason for this is that since agent's trading opportunities are constrained by the intertemporal budget constraint (11), it is optimal to minimize as much as possible the reduction in the value of domestic output at world prices that is generated by distorting production decisions.

Finally, unlike the optimal policy for a trade balance target, the optimal policy for an international reserve target does, in essence, entail levying tariffs, export subsidies, or equivalent trade distortions that divert within-period domestic relative prices from their world level. This follows from the well-known result that imposing a consumption tax and a production subsidy on importables (exportables) at equal rates is equivalent to imposing a tariff (export subsidy) at that rate. Therefore, from the preceding discussion, it is apparent that the optimal policy for a reserve target can be structured to include tariffs at the rate η_s^t plus additional consumption taxes on good Z at the rate $(\eta^t - \eta_s^t)/(1 + \eta_s^t)$ during those periods when good Z is imported and export subsidies and consumption taxes on good Z at the rates η_s^t and $(\eta^t - \eta_s^t)/(1 + \eta_s^t)$ during those periods when good Z is exported.

At this point it is worth reemphasizing that the first-best policy for building up international reserves is to devalue or reduce the rate of growth of domestic credit. However, neither of these policies have real effects, and they thus alter only the composition of the economy's wealth between private holdings of foreign assets and central bank holdings of international reserves rather than the overall level of wealth. In contrast, the set of taxes outlined above does alter the economy's overall level of wealth. If the policymaker's objective is to attain a target wealth level, it is easy to see by comparing the tax policies implicit in (15) and (17) that international reserve targets are not the welfare maximizing policy.[10] Intuitively, the reason is that instituting international reserve targets imposes a constraint on the distribution of wealth between the private sector, the fiscal authorities, and the central bank that is unnecessary when the goal is simply to accumulate wealth (devaluation or reductions of domestic credit growth can be used to build up international reserves but not wealth). Alternatively, if the distribution of wealth is itself the goal, devaluation or changes in domestic credit are the optimal policy since neither lowers welfare as do the tax policies described by (17). The upshot is that while policymakers worldwide are constantly preoccupied with the level of their central bank's international reserves, tax policies designed with such targets in mind will not generally be optimal from the perspective of wealth accumulation or distribution despite the fact that international reserves held by the central bank do constitute part of a country's wealth.

9.7   Balance of Payments Target

The last section was concerned with a case where the government has a target level of international reserves for period k and allows the balance of payments to adjust optimally to attain this target. An alternative, and generally inferior, policy for building up reserves to support the exchange rate is to impose a sequence of constraints on the balance of payments that assures reserve holdings will reach the target level at the appropriate time. Such balance of payments targets may be imposed either directly by the domestic government or by the domestic government at the behest of international creditors.

9.7.1   The Government's Optimization Problem

To find the optimal tax policy in this instance, note that the sequence of balance of payments targets, $\{\bar{bp}^t\}_{t=1}^k$, requires that

$$m_s^t - m_s^{t-1}/(1 + \pi^{t-1}) - \mu^t \geq \bar{bp}^t, \quad t = 1, \ldots, k .$$

The government's problem is thus to choose $\{X^t\}_{t=1}^\infty$, $\{Z^t\}_{t=1}^\infty$, and $\{p_s^t\}_{t=1}^\infty$ so as to maximize[11]

$$(18) \quad \sum_{t=1}^\infty \rho^{t-1} U(X^t, Z^t) + \lambda \cdot \sum_{t=1}^\infty d^{*t}\{X_s^t(p_s^t) - X^t$$

$$+ p^{*t}[Z_s^t(p_s^t) - Z^t]\}$$

$$+ \sum_{t=1}^{k} \alpha^t d^{*t}[X_s^t(p_s^t) + (U_Z^t/U_X^t)Z_s^t(p_s^t)$$

$$- \frac{X_s^{t-1}(p_s^{t-1}) + (U_Z^{t-1}/U_X^{t-1})Z_s^{t-1}(p_s^{t-1})}{1 + \pi^{t-1}}$$

$$- \mu^t - \bar{b}p^t] \; .$$

In addition to the constraints the first-order conditions for (18) are (again i^t is taken to be constant to simplify the notation)

$$(19a) \quad U_Z^t/U_X^t = \begin{cases} \dfrac{p^{*t} + \delta^t\left(\alpha^t - \dfrac{\alpha^{t+1}}{1+i}\right)s_X^t}{1 - \delta^t\left(\alpha^t - \dfrac{\alpha^{t+1}}{1+i}\right)s_Z^t}, & t = 1, \ldots, k-1, \\[3em] \dfrac{p^{*t} + \delta^t\alpha^t s_X^t}{1 - \delta^t\alpha^t s_Z^t}, & t = k, \\[2em] p^{*t}, & t = k+1, \ldots, \end{cases}$$

$$(19b) \quad \frac{-\partial X_s^t/\partial p_s^t}{\partial Z_s^t/\partial p_s^t} = \begin{cases} \dfrac{\lambda p^{*t} + \left(\alpha^t - \dfrac{\alpha^{t+1}}{1+i}\right)p^t}{\lambda + \left(\alpha^t - \dfrac{\alpha^{t+1}}{1+i}\right)}, & t = 1, \ldots, k-1, \\[3em] \dfrac{\lambda p^{*t} + \alpha^t p^t}{\lambda + \alpha^t}, & t = k, \\[2em] p^{*t}, & t = k+1, \ldots, \end{cases}$$

$$(19c) \quad \rho^{t-1}U_X^t/U_X^1 = \begin{cases} d^{*t}\cdot\dfrac{1 - \delta^t\left(\alpha^t - \dfrac{\alpha^{t+1}}{1+i}\right)s_Z^t}{1 - \delta^1\left(\alpha^1 - \dfrac{\alpha^2}{1+i}\right)s_Z^1}, & t = 1, \ldots, k-1, \\[3em] d^{*t}\cdot\dfrac{1 - \delta^t\alpha^t s_Z^t}{1 - \delta^1\left(\alpha^1 - \dfrac{\alpha^2}{1+i}\right)s_Z^1}, & t = k, \\[3em] d^{*t}\cdot\dfrac{1}{1 - \delta^1\left(\alpha^1 - \dfrac{\alpha^2}{1+i}\right)s_Z^1}, & t = k+1, \ldots, \end{cases}$$

where $\delta^t = Z_s^t H^t/\lambda U_X^t$.

9.7.2 Interpretation

In conjunction with (7) it can be seen from (19a) that the optimal structure of taxes and subsidies on the consumption of good Z satisfies

$$
\eta^t = \begin{cases}
\dfrac{(\delta^t/p^{*t})\left(\alpha^t - \dfrac{\alpha^{t+1}}{1+i}\right)}{1 - \delta^t\left(\alpha^t - \dfrac{\alpha^{t+1}}{1+i}\right)s_Z^t}\,, & t = 1, \ldots, k-1, \\[2em]
\dfrac{(\delta^t/p^{*t})\alpha^t}{1 - \delta^t\alpha^t s_Z^t}\,, & t = k, \\[1em]
0\,, & t = k+1, \ldots.
\end{cases}
$$

Several features of the optimal policy are readily apparent. First, within-period consumption choices should be left undistorted in those periods with no balance of payments objectives ($t = k + 1, \ldots$). Second, during those periods where the government has set balance of payments targets, consumption of good Z in period t should be taxed or subsidized as the shadow value of an exogenous increase in period-t money demand, $\alpha^t - \alpha^{t+1}/(1 + i)$, is positive or negative. Intuitively, when the shadow value of real balances is positive (negative) a tax (subsidy) on the consumption of good Z is called for to raise (lower) the demand for money. To see that $\alpha^t - \alpha^{t+1}/(1 + i)$ can be interpreted as the shadow value of an exogenous increase in the demand for money, note that a one-unit exogenous increase in period t money demand raises current utility by $\alpha^t d^{*t}$, since less reliance on period t distortions is called for to meet the balance of payments target. However, this means greater distortions in period $t + 1$ are called for to meet the balance of payments target then. These added distortions reduce current utility by $\alpha^{t+1}d^{*t+1}/(1 + \pi^t)$. Therefore, in terms of current utility the marginal benefit of an exogenous increase in the period-t demand for money is

$$
\alpha^t d^{*t} - \alpha^{t+1}d^{*t+1}/(1 + \pi^t) = d^{*t}\left[\alpha^t - \frac{\alpha^{t+1}}{1+i}\right].
$$

The term in brackets thus measures the shadow value, as of period t, of exogenous increments to money demand. (Note that period k is a special case of this argument where $\alpha^{k+1} \equiv 0$.)

The exact intertemporal pattern of consumption taxes, η^t, will depend on (i) the sequence of balance of payments targets, $\{\bar{bp}^t\}_{t=1}^{\infty}$, and (ii) the time-path of nominal domestic credit and the exchange rate as reflected in the real transfer sequence, $\{\mu^t\}_{t=1}^{\infty}$. For purposes of illustration, suppose the economy is initially in a steady state with a constant real transfer sequence, $\mu^t = \mu \; \forall \, t$, and a uniform balance of payments target, $\bar{bp}^t = \bar{bp} \; \forall \, t = 1, \ldots, k$.[12] In this case it is easily shown using the balance of payments constraint that the consumption tax on good Z must rise over time. That is, the optimal policy entails $\eta^k > \eta^{k-1} > \ldots > \eta^1 > 0$. The reason for this is that as each successive balance of payments constraint is met, agents' beginning-of-period real balances get higher and higher. In order to generate a constant excess flow demand for money, the demand for money must be pushed higher and higher via increases in consumption taxes. In general, when compared with this benchmark case, those periods with larger (smaller) real transfers and more (less) ambitious balance of payments objectives will have their consumption taxes raised (lowered).

The optimal structure of production subsidies and taxes on good Z can be obtained from (19b). Recalling that $p^t = (1 + \eta^t)p^{*t}$ and using (3) it can be shown that

$$
\eta_s^t = \begin{cases}
\dfrac{\left(\alpha^t - \dfrac{\alpha^{t+1}}{1+i}\right)\eta^t}{\lambda + \left(\alpha^t - \dfrac{\alpha^{t+1}}{1+i}\right)}, & t = 1, \ldots, k-1, \\[2em]
\dfrac{\alpha^t \eta^t}{\lambda + \alpha^t}, & t = k, \\[1em]
0, & t = k+1, \ldots .
\end{cases}
$$

As was the case for consumption, production decisions should be left undistorted in those periods where there is no balance of payments target. In all periods where there is a balance of payments target, the production of good Z should be subsidized. The rationale behind this is that regardless of the shadow value of additional money demand, $\alpha^t - \alpha^{t+1}/(1 + i)$, a production subsidy moves money demand, the value of domestic output at consumer prices, in the appropriate direction. This is illustrated in figure 1 for the case $\alpha^t - \alpha^{t+1}/(1 + i) > 0$ where period-t consumption is taxed because increases in money demand are desirable and in figure 2 for the case $\alpha^t - \alpha^{t+1}/(1 + i) < 0$ where the opposite is true. In both cases the production equilibrium is at A before and at B after the production subsidy is implemented. As can be seen, in both instances the production subsidy moves the value of domestic output at consumer prices in the correct direction as shown by the shift of the p^t line as production shifts from A to B. Third, note that once again the optimal policy calls for production distortions, η_s^t, to be less in absolute terms than consumption distortions, η^t. Finally, in the benchmark case discussed earlier the optimum production subsidy will rise over time (i.e., $\eta_s^k > \eta_s^{k-1} > \ldots > \eta_s^l > 0$).

Turning next to the optimal structure of taxes and subsidies on international borrowing, consider equation (19c). Between periods without balance of payments targets no distortions should be introduced

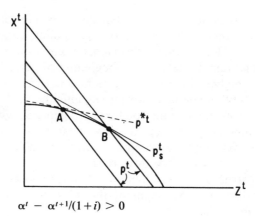

Fig. 9.1 $\alpha^t - \alpha^{t+1}/(1+i) > 0$

into agents' intertemporal consumption pattern. For the periods with balance of payments targets, international borrowing should be subsidized or taxed as the shadow value of money demand, $\alpha^t - \alpha^{t+1}/(1 + i)$, is positive or negative.[13] The intertemporal substitution effects that this pattern of taxes and subsidies generates act to minimize the welfare cost of attaining the balance of payments objectives by shifting agents' consumption profiles towards those periods where consumption of good Z is taxed, and hence $U_Z^t/U_X^t > p^{*t}$, and away from those periods where consumption of good Z is subsidized, and hence $U_Z^t/U_X^t < p^{*t}$. In the benchmark case the optimal policy calls for a rising subsidy to international borrowing throughout the period of balance of payments targets. This reflects the need to mitigate the welfare costs imposed on the economy by the rising consumption tax levied on good Z.

In comparing the case where the government imposes a balance of payments target on the economy for k periods, perhaps with some ultimate reserve target in mind, with that where it has an international reserve target for period k but allows the intertemporal pattern of the balance of payments to adjust optimally, it should be noted that the first-order conditions for the former problem are equivalent to those for the latter when α^t, the marginal cost of tightening the balance of payments constraint, is constant across periods (i.e., when $\alpha^1 = \ldots = \alpha^k$). Therefore, for a given real transfer sequence $\{\eta^t\}_{t=1}^k$, if the sequence of balance of payments targets, $\{\bar{bp}^t\}_{t=1}^k$, is properly chosen the strategy of imposing a sequence of balance of payments constraints can replicate the optimal policy for achieving a target reserve level, $\bar{b}_R$. However, if the ultimate goal is to build the central bank's stock of international reserves up to some desired level, then attempting to accomplish this by instituting some arbitrary sequence of balance of payments targets will not be optimal—the constraint on the time profile

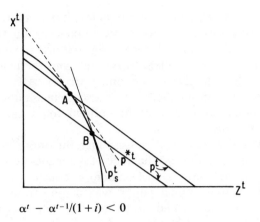

Fig. 9.2 $\alpha^t - \alpha^{t-1}/(1+i) < 0$

of the balance of payments is an extra constraint on the economy and can only reduce welfare more than is necessary in order to attain the reserve target.

9.8 Conclusion

This paper has outlined an extended version of the traditional two-sector model of international trade and public finance that incorporates intertemporal consumption choices and monetary considerations. The resulting framework was used to examine the optimal tax policies associated with various noneconomic objectives relating to the balance of payments accounts. First, the optimal policy for achieving a trade balance objective was considered. This policy was shown to involve levying taxes on international borrowing (or equivalent policies) so as to shift consumption away from those periods where an improved trade balance is deemed desirable. It was also shown that the optimal policy for reaching a trade balance target leaves intact the within-period efficiency conditions $U_Z^t/U_X^t = p^{*t} = (-\partial X_s^t/\partial p_s^t)/(\partial Z_s^t/\partial p_s^t)$. Therefore, trade balance goals do not call for instituting tariffs or export subsidies that drive a wedge between world and domestic relative prices. The optimal policy for a trade balance objective was then compared with the optimal policy for achieving a wealth target. It was demonstrated that the two policies differ, because while a wealth target calls for enacting a time invariant tax rate on international borrowing, the optimal attainment of a trade balance target generally speaking entails a time varying tax rate on international borrowing.

An international reserve target was the next policy for which the optimal structure of taxation was derived. Starting from a distortion-free, steady-state equilibrium, and given a precommitment to certain domestic credit and exchange rate policies, it was shown that the optimal tax structure entails consumption taxes, production subsidies, and subsidies to international borrowing that are constant across periods until the reserve target is to be met, and then raised, perhaps substantially, when the day of reckoning arrives. After this period all distortions should be dismantled. It was also pointed out that the within-period distortions introduced by the optimal policy can be structured to include tariffs and export subsidies.

The fourth, and final, objective for which the optimal tax policy was constructed was a sequence of balance of payments targets. Under the conditions outlined above, and assuming a constant balance of payments objective, the optimal policy was demonstrated to consist of rising consumption taxes and production subsidies as well as rising subsidies to international borrowing throughout the period of balance of payments goals. Again, it was also argued that all distortions should be immediately dismantled after this time. Although not pointed out in the text, it should be apparent that in this instance the optimal policy's within-period distortions can again be replicated by a system of tariffs and export subsidies (accompanied with additional consumption taxes or subsidies as well).

Some interesting results emerge from comparing the optimal tax structures for the four noneconomic objectives that were investigated here. First, while international reserve targets and balance of payments targets are obviously closely related, the optimum tax policies for the two goals differ significantly. This is because the latter policy is aimed at attaining a certain intertemporal behavior for the balance of payments while from the perspective of the former policy such behavior is largely irrelevant. Second, although it is apparent from the balance of payments accounting identities that improving the trade balance is one way to achieve an international reserve target or a balance of payments goal, it is clear that the optimal policies for these objectives differ dramatically. The goals of an improved balance of payments and a reserve target can both be optimally accomplished, given domestic credit and exchange rate policies, via a policy that includes tariffs, export subsidies, and other within-period distortions. However, such distortions and trade impediments are not part of the optimal tax mix for improving the trade balance. An improved trade balance calls for a system of taxes on international borrowing (or equivalent policies). This is in stark contrast to the system of subsidies to international borrowing required by a reserve target and, at least during some periods, by a balance of payments target.[14] Finally, it was argued that international reserve targets cannot be justified (i.e., are not first-best) if the policymaker's goal is to attain a target level of wealth or a given distribution of wealth between the private sector, the fiscal authorities, and the central bank. If the goal is a target wealth level, a constant tax rate on international borrowing should be levied (until the deadline period) and no within-period distortions should be introduced, while if the objective is to alter the composition of net foreign asset holdings, shifts in the time profiles of domestic credit and the exchange rate are appropriate.

A number of extensions and implications of the analysis of optimal policies undertaken here suggest themselves. To the extent that trade barriers are erected and torn down because of noneconomic objectives like the ones considered here, the public-finance-type approach that has been adopted can be used to study the optimal sequencing of economic liberalizations. Capturing important aspects of the liberalization process might entail extending the model to include sector-specific capital or other features giving rise to dynamics on the production side of the economy, but the approach is, in principle, capable of dealing with these and other issues.

Another possible extension concerns the use of the cash-in-advance constraint to model money. It might be useful to model money in a way that allows the velocity of money to vary with nominal interest rates. This could be done by using the transactions technology employed by Adams and Greenwood (1985) or by adopting the variant of the cash-in-advance approach suggested by Svensson (1985). Either extension would give money real effects, essentially through an inflation tax channel, thereby potentially allowing for a more elaborate interaction between monetary and fiscal policies. In the current framework the interaction between monetary and fiscal policies is limited to the impact of domestic inflation on the slopes of the tax rate time profiles. For example, with an international reserve target the slope of the consumption tax profile is adequately summarized by the ratio η^k/η^t, $t = 1, \ldots, k - 1$, in the steady-state case. As can be seen from the results outlined in section 9.6, when the initial equilibrium is a steady state, η^k/η^t is directly related to $(1 + i)/i$. Therefore, the higher the domestic inflation rate, and hence the higher the domestic nominal interest rate, the flatter the time profile of consumption tax rates. Intuitively, as domestic inflation approaches the rate dictated by the optimum quantity of money rule, and hence the domestic nominal interest rate approaches zero, the building up of reserves through the accumulation of inflation tax revenues diminishes. As a consequence, an increasing reliance on consumption taxes to raise money demand during the deadline period is necessitated. Thus as domestic inflation falls toward the optimum quantity of money rate the consumption tax profile gets steeper. Similarly, the production and international borrowing subsidy profiles under a reserve target also get steeper when domestic inflation is reduced.

One final extension would be to allow for intertemporal decisions on the production side of the economy. This could be done along the lines suggested by Aschauer and Greenwood (1983) or by Helpman and Razin (1984). These extensions would also result in money being nonneutral and potentially allow for a richer interaction between monetary and fiscal policies.

Extending the model along the lines suggested above to allow for variable velocity, real effects of inflation, and factor supply decisions can easily be accomplished by introducing leisure into the consumer's utility function and assuming that domestic (foreign) money serves to economize on time spent transacting in domestic (foreign) markets.[15] In this case the optimal policies for trade balance and wealth targets remain the same as outlined in sections 9.4 and 9.5 with the additional proviso that domestic monetary policy should be guided by the optimum quantity of money rule, and interest should be paid on domestic holdings of foreign currency if the optimum quantity of money rule is not being followed abroad. The optimal policies for international reserve and balance of payments targets are more difficult to characterize. At first, such goals seem to call for departing from the optimum quantity of money rule by pursuing policies that generate a real rate of return on domestic money in excess of that on internationally traded bonds (the goal being to stimulate the demand for domestic money). However, equilibria with this characteristic may be problematic. Further research into the link between the monetary mechanism of exchange and the optimal policies for international reserve targets and balance of payments goals thus seems warranted.

Notes

1. For a thorough survey of the literature see Dixit (1985).
2. As will become apparent shortly, since factor supplies are taken to be inelastic in the traditional two-sector model, Helpman's result that the economy's real equilbirium duplicates that of a costless barter economy survives this extension to a production economy. See Aschauer and Greenwood (1983) and Helpman and Razin (1984) for examples in which, because of less than perfectly inelastic factor supplies, the monetary economy's real equilibrium fails to replicate that of a costless barter economy.
3. See Helpman and Razin (1984) for a discussion of alternative monetary mechanisms.
4. As noted by Helpman (1981), by holding interest-bearing reserves the central bank minimizes its operating costs. For a discussion of the implications of interest-bearing versus non-interest-bearing reserves see Persson (1984).
5. This problem has been considered elsewhere by Greenwood and Kimbrough (1987) in a two-period setup similar to the one used here and by Dasgupta and Stiglitz (1974) in a barter economy with public production and non-

traded goods. In both of these papers the constraint (12) holds only for a single period.

6. To see these results a bit more clearly, it may help to rewrite (14c) as

$$\rho^{t-1} U^t_X / \rho^{N-1} U^N_X = (d^{*t}/d^{*N})[1 + (\theta^t/\lambda)] \ ,$$

where $\theta^t \equiv 0$ for $t = k + 1, \ldots$ and N is some arbitrary period after period k. It follows that the optimum tax on international borrowing in period t is θ^t/λ .

7. For a model in which this would not necessarily be the only component of the first-best policy because Ricardian equivalence fails to hold as the result of the uncertain lifetimes of private agents, see Helpman and Razin (1987).

8. From the central bank's budget constraints appearing in (9) it is apparent that the condition $b^k_R \geq \hat{b}^R$ imposes a constraint not only on the behavior of the balance of payments prior to period k but after period k as well. In particular, it is required that

$$(1/d^{*k}) \cdot \left[\sum_{t=k+1}^{\infty} d^{*t} \left(\mu^t - \frac{i^t m^t_s}{1 + i^t} \right) + d^{*k} m^k_s /(1 + \pi^k) \right] \geq \tilde{b}_R \ .$$

The analysis presented in the text assumes that this constraint is met by appropriately setting domestic credit and/or the exchange rate, as captured by μ^t , in some distant future period (i.e., as $t \to \infty$). Alternatively, tax policies like those discussed in the text could be employed. These policies can be derived formally by adding the above as an additional constraint to (16). However, since the policies for periods $t = 1, \ldots , k$ are qualitatively unchanged, this approach has not been adopted in the text. In either case, the important point is that future policies are constrained by today's international reserve objectives.

9. This can be seen by rewriting (17c) as suggested in footnote 6 and noting that the optimal policy calls for subsidizing international borrowing in period t at the rate $\theta^t(i/1 + i)^\gamma s^t_Z$, where $\theta^t \equiv 0$ for $t = k + 1, \ldots$ and $\gamma = 0$ for $t = k$ and $\gamma = 1$ for all other periods.

10. It is possible, in fact, that a country's external wealth, b^k, may actually fall while international reserves are built up to the target level, $\tilde{b}_R$. To see this, note that the policies outlined by (17) reduce income at world prices in periods $t = 1, \ldots , k$. However, consumption smoothing on the part of private agents implies that this burden will be spread over the consumer's entire lifetime so that the trade balance will deteriorate in periods $t = 1, \ldots , k$. Turning to the substitution effects generated by (17), there are two to consider. First, the consumption taxes in periods $t = 1, \ldots , k$ that are instituted to attain the international reserve target raise the relative price of consuming in periods $t = 1, \ldots , k$ versus all future periods. The intertemporal substitution effects generated by the consumption taxes thus work to improve the trade balance in periods $t = 1, \ldots , k$. On the other hand, the international reserve target calls for subsidies to international borrowing in periods $t = 1, \ldots , k,$ and the attendant intertemporal substitution effects should serve to worsen the trade balance in periods $t = 1, \ldots , k$. However, since the subsidies to international borrowing are designed to mitigate the distortions introduced by the consumption taxes, there is some presumption that the latter will dominate so that intertemporal substitution effects will act to improve the trade balance. However, if the wealth effects dominate these substitution effects, the trade balance will, on average, deteriorate in periods $t = 1, \ldots , k,$ and the country's external wealth, b^k, will fall even though international reserves increase to the target level $\tilde{b}_R$.

11. Remarks similar to those in footnote 8 apply here also.

12. For the results that follow, the weaker condition that $\bar{b}p^t + \mu^t$ *be constant for* $t = 1, \ldots, k$ is actually all that is required.

13. Again, following the suggestion made in footnote 6, it can be shown that the optimum subsidy to international borrowing is $\delta^t[\alpha^t - \alpha^{t+1}/(1 + i]s_Z^t$, where $\alpha^t \equiv 0$ for $t = k + 1, \ldots$.

14. If the monetary mechanism of exchange dictates that transactions be carried out in the buyer's currency rather than in the seller's currency as is assumed here, the money market equilibrium condition (10) would be replaced by

$$m_s^t = X^t + p^t Z^t , t = 1, 2, \ldots .$$

As discussed by Helpman and Razin (1984), when the buyer's currency is used for transactions purposes the constraint (11) remains intact so long as foreign nominal interest rates and the rate of depreciation of the home currency, ϵ^t, are constant. In this case it is easy to show that the results for a trade balance target are unaffected while the results for a reserve target and a balance of payments target are modified somewhat. In both instances the qualitative pattern for consumption taxes and taxes on international borrowing is the same as in the body of the paper, but the optimal policy no longer calls for subsidizing domestic production. That is, when the buyer's currency is used for transactions purposes, optimal policies for balance of payments objectives do not involve distorting production decisions. An important corollary of this, of course, is that when the buyer's currency is used for transactions purposes, tariffs, export subsidies, and the like are not a part of the optimal tax policy for balance of payments objectives. The rationale for these results is that when the buyer's currency is used to finance transactions, production distortions do not help to improve the balance of payments. It is, therefore, optimal to leave production decisions undistorted. However, even when the buyer's currency is used to finance transactions it is still true that, unlike a trade balance target, reserve targets and balance of payments targets call for within-period distortions to be introduced.

15. See Kimbrough (1986b, 1986c) for a closed-economy version of the framework that is being suggested here.

References

Adams, Charles, and Jeremy Greenwood. 1985. Dual exchange rate systems and capital controls: An investigation. *Journal of International Economics* 18:43–63.

Aschauer, David, and Jeremy Greenwood. 1983. A further exploration in the theory of exchange rate regimes. *Journal of Political Economy* 91:868–75.

Bhagwati, Jagdish. 1968. *The theory and practice of commercial policy: Departures from unified exchange rates.* Special Papers in International Economics no. 8. Princeton: Princeton University Press.

Boadway, Robin; Shlomo Maital; and Martin Prachowny. 1973. Optimal tariffs, optimal taxes, and public goods. *Journal of Public Economics* 2:391–403.

Dasgupta, Partha, and Stiglitz, Joseph E. 1974. Benefit-cost analysis and trade policies. *Journal of Political Economy* 82:1–33.

Dixit, Avinash. 1983. Tax policy in open economies. In *Handbook of Public Economics,* eds. A. J. Auerbach and M. Feldstein, 313–74. Amsterdam: North-Holland.

Greenwood, Jeremy, and Kent P. Kimbrough. 1985. Capital controls and fiscal policy in the world economy. *Canadian Journal of Economics* 18:743–65.

———. 1987. An investigation in the theory of foreign exchange controls. *Canadian Journal of Economics* 20:271–88.

Helpman, Elhanan. 1981. An exploration in the theory of exchange-rate regimes. *Journal of Political Economy* 89:865–90.

Helpman, Elhanan, and Assaf Razin. 1984. The role of saving and investment in exchange rate determination under alternative monetary mechanisms. *Journal of Monetary Economics* 13:307–25.

———. 1987. Exchange rate managment: Intertemporal tradeoffs. *American Economic Review* 77:107–23.

Johnson, Harry G. 1965. Optimal trade intervention in the presence of domestic distortions. In *Trade, growth, and the balance of payments: Essays in honor of Gottfried Haberler,* ed. R. E. Baldwin et al., 3–34. Chicago: Rand McNally.

Kimbrough, Kent P. 1986a. Foreign aid and optimal fiscal policy. *Canadian Journal of Economics* 19:35–61.

———. 1986b. The optimum quantity of money rule in the theory of public finance. *Journal of Monetary Economics* 18:277–84.

———. 1986c. Inflation, employment, and welfare in the presence of transactions costs. *Journal of Money, Credit and Banking* 18:127–40.

Lucas, Robert E., Jr. 1982. Interest rates and currency prices in a two-country world. *Journal of Monetary Economics* 10:335–60.

Murphy, Robert G. 1985. Trade taxes and economic welfare. *Economics Letters* 18:373–74.

Mussa, Michael. 1974. A monetary approach to balance of payments analysis. *Journal of Money, Credit, and Banking* 6:333–51.

———. 1976. Tariffs and the balance of payments. In *The monetary approach to the balance of payments,* ed. J. A. Frenkel and H. G. Johnson, 187–221. Toronto: University of Toronto Press.

Persson, Torsten. 1984. Real transfers in fixed exchange rate systems and the international adjustment mechanism. *Journal of Monetary Economics* 13:349–69.

Persson, Torsten, and Lars E. O. Svensson. 1986. International borrowing and time-consistent fiscal policy. *Scandinavian Journal of Economics* 88:273–95.

Razin, Assaf, and Lars E. O. Svensson. 1983a. The current account and the optimal government debt. *Journal of International Money and Finance* 2:215–24.

———. 1983b. Trade taxes and the current account. *Economics Letters* 13:55–57.

Stockman, Alan C. 1983. Real exchange rates under alternative nominal exchange-rate systems. *Journal of International Money and Finance* 2:147–66.

Svensson, Lars E. O. 1985. Currency prices, terms of trade, and interest rates: A general equilibrium asset-pricing cash-in-advance approach. *Journal of International Economics* 18:17–41.

Comment   Joshua Aizenman

Introduction

Kimbrough articulates a very useful intertemporal framework for studying optimal policies in an open economy. These policies are applied to achieve exogenous balance of trade and international reserves targets, and they are derived in a welfare framework that recognizes the role of intertemporal budget constraints. The author should be praised for a clear exposition. Kent's methodology is rich. It is, however, applied only to a rather simple economy that includes enough Ricardian features to nullify the role of optimal policies. If we allow for departures from Ricardian assumptions, a richer interpretation of the policies studied in this paper is possible. I will describe such extensions and suggest applications of the methodology for economies in which optimal policies matter, and for which the policy targets can be derived endogenously, rather than postulated exogeneously as in Kimbrough's paper. My comments include three parts. I will start with a brief review of Kimbrough's methodology. Next, I will discuss the monetary framework. Finally, I will suggest possible extensions of the methodology to a non-Ricardian world.

The Methodology

Kimbrough assumes an economy composed of consumers having an infinite horizon, with access to financial markets, and the authorities. Consumer income is generated by producing two goods, transfer payments, and income accruing to the financial portfolio. Money is introduced in a Clower fashion, where domestic money buys domestic goods, and foreign money buys foreign goods. The authorities are composed of two consolidated branches: the fiscal branch, responsible for imposing and collecting the various taxes, and the monetary branch, which manages the exchange rate and the credit policy. The economy is small, and the authorities have the capacity to impose all policies needed to achieve appropriate marginal conditions.

The authorities solve the optimizing problem in two stages. First, the policymaker maximizes an expression of the type

$$(1) \qquad U + \lambda[NPV^*] + \sum_{i=1}^{k} \theta_i H_i ,$$

where U is the utility of a representative consumer: NPV^* is the intertemporal budget constraint, equalizing the net present value of consumption and production evaluated at the *world* prices and interest

Joshua Aizenman is associate professor of business economics at the University of Chicago and faculty research fellow of the National Bureau of Economic Research.

rates. H_i is the constraint imposed by the policy target i. In optimizing equation (1) the policymaker chooses the optimal path of consumption and production. Armed with the resultant optimal path, the policy-maker then moves to the second stage—a design of a menu of taxes to motivate consumers and producers to follow the optimal consumption and production plans. The two-stage methodology simplifies the calculations in such a way that we use the world undistorted prices in stage 1, and we solve for the implied set of taxes only in stage 2.

Kimbrough's article analyzes two distinct sets of issues. First, he examines the design of policies aimed at a balance of trade targets (sections 9.4–9.5). Second, he studies policies aimed at international reserves targets. (sections 9.6–9.7). Trade balance targets are shown to be equivalent to intertemporal consumption targets. To invoke taxes on intertemporal borrowing is thus shown to be optimal. This policy changes the intertemporal prices so that we obtain the desired path of consumption. Optimal policies do not, however, include changes in the within-period relative prices. The second set of targets, related to international reserves, is achieved by using all policy instruments, changing both the within-period and the intertemporal prices.

The Monetary Framework

In developing the monetary sector Kimbrough adopts the cash-in-advance formulation. Accordingly, agents are required to purchase the goods of a country with the money of that country. In this formulation the demand for money does not depend on the interest rate. It is useful to assess the role of the monetary framework in policy-instruments determination. The two sets of issues analyzed by Kimbrough differ sharply from each other in terms of the robustness of the results with respect to changes in the monetary framework. The policy prescriptions relevant for the attainment of the second set of targets (related to reserves and balance of payments objectives) are not robust. Sensible changes in the monetary framework alter the results. As is reported by the author in footnote 14, if the domestic currency is used to finance domestic consumption of both goods, optimal policies aimed at achieving the second set of targets are altered significantly. Furthermore, if one abolishes the Clower constraint in favor of a flexible velocity technology of exchange, the results are affected considerably. Crude empiricism suggests that in most cases the monetary mechanism is indeed of the flexible velocity type, where only domestic money is used in financing consumption of both types of goods.[1] There is, however,

1. Another bothersome feature of the monetary framework applied in the paper is the absence of real balance effects. As is shown by Feenstra (1985), this reflects the specific assumptions regarding the sequence of exchange of goods and money. Note also that a Clower constraint of the type applied in the article implies that inflation tax can be applied to achieve costlessly any revenue target (up to almost all the G.N.P.). These

another difficulty with the proposed policies. As the author rightly points out, the same reserves and balance of payments targets can be achieved at a lowest cost by the appropriate monetary policy, reflecting the comparative advantage of the monetary policy in reaching reserves objectives. Kimbrough offers no economic reason for studying reserves targets in terms of an inferior framework, where only taxes (and subsidies) are instrumental in achieving balance of payments objectives.

Unlike the balance of payments targets, the first set of targets (related to balance of trade objectives) is achieved using policies that are robust with respect to changes in the monetary framework. Kimbrough's analysis of the balance of trade objective provides important insight into this issue.

Extensions and Qualifications

In Kimbrough's analysis, the attainment of all targets reduces welfare, and no clear economic interpretation is provided for the existence of welfare-reducing targets. This is a necessary feature of the Ricardian framework invoked in the paper; in such a framework, any policy is welfare-reducing. Relaxation of the assumptions underlying the Ricardian framework may not be simple but, at the same time, is highly desirable. Specifically, in a non-Ricardian framework the policy targets can be derived endogenously, and the policy instruments have a richer interpretation. In the following comments I would like to propose an alternative interpretation of the results regarding the balance of trade targets and describe non-Ricardian justification for various policies.

An Alternative Ricardian Interpretation of Policies Aimed at Balance of Trade Targets

Kimbrough's results regarding a balance of trade targets have an alternative interpretation, in terms of traditional commercial policies. Equation (13) in the paper can be used to demonstrate that an import level target at time t (IM_t) calls for import tax at time t (I.T.$_t$) . We can summarize this result by

$$(2a) \qquad\qquad IM_t \Rightarrow I.T._t$$

Similarly, an export target at time t (EX_t) calls for an export subsidy at time t (E.S.$_t$) :

$$(2b) \qquad\qquad EX_t \Rightarrow E.S._t$$

As a result, a balance of trade target at time t (B.O.T.$_t$) calls for the simultaneous use of both a tariff and an export subsidy at time t, and optimally calls for equal rates:

considerations suggest that the applicability of a rigid Clower constraint in a public finance context is questionable.

(3)   B.O.T.$_t$ $\Rightarrow$ (E.S.$_t$ & I.T.$_t$)$\Big|$
$\qquad\qquad\qquad\qquad\qquad\qquad\qquad$ equal
$\qquad\qquad\qquad\qquad\qquad\qquad\qquad$ rates

In general, these two policies are equivalent to a uniform consumption tax at time t (C.T.$_t$) *and* a uniform equal production subsidy at time t (P.S.$_t$) . Subject to Ricardian equivalency (R.E.), these policies are equivalent also to a tax on intertemporal borrowing applied at time t (T.B.$_t$) :

(4)   R.E.

$\qquad\qquad\qquad\qquad\qquad\qquad\qquad\qquad\qquad\qquad\qquad\qquad$ $\downarrow$

$\quad$ [(E.S.$_t$ & I.T.$_t$)$\Big|$ $\quad\approx$ (C.T.$_t$ & P.S.$_t$)$\Big|$ $\quad$] $\approx$ T.B.$_t$
$\qquad\qquad\qquad\quad$ equal $\qquad\qquad\qquad\qquad$ equal
$\qquad\qquad\qquad\quad$ rates $\qquad\qquad\qquad\qquad$ rates

In general, however, a segmented capital market will require the simultaneous use of *both* borrowing and consumption/production taxes and subsidies. We turn now to a brief examination of this possibility.

Limited Access to Capital Markets

Suppose that a typical less-developed country faces a balance of trade target. Would intertemporal taxes on borrowing be the optimal policy instrument, as suggested in Kimbrough's article? This seems unlikely, but the methodology applied in the paper is useful in assessing the problem, nevertheless. To take an extreme case, suppose that consumers, in contrast with government, do not have free access to capital markets. The planner problem can still be specified in terms of equation (1). The first-order conditions (equations 14 a–c in the text) are still relevant. The implied policies, however, differ sharply. Notice that the first-order conditions for a balance of trade target (equations 14 a–c) can be written as

$$(5) \qquad \frac{MU_x^t}{MU_x^{t-1}} = k_t\left(\frac{1}{1 + r_{t-1}^*}\right)$$

where MU_x^t is the marginal utility of x at time t, r_{t-1}^* is the world interest rate, and k_t depends on the tightness of the balance of trade target.[2] In the paper, equation (5) has the interpretation that a balance of trade calls for taxes on international borrowing such that the domestic interest rate (r_{t-1}) satisfies

---

2. Equation (2) assumes that the foreign price of X is normalized to 1. Similar equation applies for Y, where P_t^* stands for the external relative prices at $t (P_t^* = P_{y,t}^*/P_{x,t}^*)$:

$$\frac{MU_y^t}{MU_y^{t-1}} = k_t\,\frac{P_t^*}{P_{t-1}^*}\,\frac{1}{1 + r_{t-1}^*}\,.$$

(6)
$$k_t\left(\frac{1}{1 + r^*_{t-1}}\right) = \frac{1}{1 + r_{t-1}}$$

It is noteworthy that there is a broader interpretation of equation (5). In general, a desired change in international prices can also be achieved by a set of time varying uniform consumption taxes, such that:

(6′)
$$k_t\left(\frac{1}{1 + r^*_{t-1}}\right) = \frac{1 + \epsilon_t}{(1 + \epsilon_{t-1})(1 + r_{t-1})}$$

where ϵ_t stands for the consumption tax at time t. In a Ricardian economy the two policies (i.e., a borrowing tax and an intertemporal uniform consumption, and production taxes and subsidies) are equivalent. Notice, however, that once consumers lack access to capital markets, taxes on international borrowing are not an efficient means of reaching the desired intertemporal shadow prices. Equation (5) is still valid. But the appropriate policy will involve imposition of uniform (time varying) consumption and production taxes rather than taxes on borrowing. In the general case, with limited participation of some agents in the financial market, a balance of trade target will require the simultaneous use of both borrowing and uniform (time varying) consumption taxes. Even in this non-Ricardian economy, a major conclusion of Kimbrough's analysis is relevant: balance of trade targets are achieved optimally by leaving within the period relative prices intact.

Costs of Tax Collection and Revenue Targets

Most countries, especially L.D.C.s, are confronted with a tax system in which there are direct collection and enforcement costs associated with various taxes. The presence of collection costs can explain the economics of various distorting policies that lack the appropriate economic justification in a Ricardian world. The problem of the authorities, for example, can be cast in terms of the maximization of a modified version of equation (1), optimizing consumers' welfare subject to a net revenue target:

(1′)   U + λ [NPV*(C + G + C.C. − G.N.P.)]
         + θ[NPV*(G − (T − C.C.))],

where C is private consumption, G is public sector consumption, C.C. is the direct cost of collecting and enforcing taxes, G.N.P. stands for output, G is government consumption, T is the gross tax revenue (including the collection costs C.C.), and NPV* is the net present value obtained using *world* prices.[3] Such a framework can be applied to

3. Thus, C + G + C.C. − G.N.P. = 0 is the economy-wide budget constraint, and G − (T − C.C.) = 0 is the public sector budget constraint.

demonstrate that a weak fiscal system will tend to use both inflation tax and tariffs because both have low collection costs.[4] Furthermore, it can be shown that if the policy target is allocative, we tend to use only one instrument. If the target is the level of imports, only a tariff should be used. If the target is an intertemporal consumption path, only taxes on borrowing should be used. If the target is to raise revenue, then under restrictive conditions on the feasible set of taxes, both tariffs and borrowing taxes will be used.[5] In general, costs of tax collection suffice to explain the application of various policies that otherwise lack an economic justification.

Country Risk

Reserves targets are discussed in sections 9.6–9.7. These targets are welfare reducing in the context of Kimbrough's framework. They can be rationalized for a country facing an upward sloping supply of credit due to country-risk considerations. Such a country will benefit from appropriate build-up of international reserves by the authorities. The authorities will rely on reserves in servicing the debt during a recession where the feasible tax base is small, and will replenish reserves during expansion. Naturally, in a Ricardian world such a task is redundant (or even welfare reducing). In a more realistic world, citizens of a country whose authorities have limited taxing capacity tend to be barred from the international credit market, leaving an important consumption smoothing role for the authorities.[6]

Concluding Remarks

This article presents a very useful methodology for designing optimal policies to achieve exogenous targets. The methodology is even more useful when applied in a non-Ricardian framework. Such an application should modify the analysis in (at least) two ways. First, in a non-Ricardian framework the various policy targets can be derived endogenously. Second, non-Ricardian considerations will affect the optimal policy instruments. For example, in a Ricardian system traditional policies aimed at a balance of trade targets (like a time varying uniform tariffs and uniform equal export subsidies) are equivalent to a tax on intertemporal borrowing. Segmented capital markets break this equivalency, necessitating the use of *both* traditional policies and taxes on intertemporal borrowing. In general, greater segmentation of capital

4. See Aizenman (1985b).
5. See Aizenman (1986).
6. Implications of limited taxing capacity on international borrowing are analyzed by Sachs (1984). On the use of international reserves, see Frenkel and Aizenman (1982). For an analysis of the role of country risk, see Edwards (1985) and Harberger (1976).

markets tend to put a greater weight on tarrifs and export promotions as the efficient means of reaching balance of trade targets. It is noteworthy that even in this non-Ricardian economy, an important insight of Kimbrough's analysis is relevant: balance of trade targets are achieved optimally by leaving within the period relative prices intact.

References

Aizenman, Joshua. 1986. On the complementarity of commercial policy, capital controls and inflation tax. NBER Working Paper no. 1583. *Canadian Journal of Economics* 19; 114–133.

———. 1985b. Inflation, tariffs and tax enforcement costs. NBER Working Paper no. 1712. *Journal of International Economic Integration* (forthcoming).

Edwards, Sebastian. 1985. Country risk, foreign borrowing and the social discount rate in an open developing economy. NBER Working Paper no. 1651.

Feenstra, Robert C. 1985. Anticipated devaluations, currency flight, and direct trade controls in a monetary economy. *American Economic Review,* 75:402–23.

Frenkel, Jacob A., and Joshua Aizenman. 1982. Aspects of the optimal management of exchange rates. *Journal of International Economics,* 13:231–56.

Harberger, Arnold C. 1976. On the determinants of country risk. Unpublished manuscript.

Sachs, Jeffrey. 1984. Theoretical issues in international borrowing. *Princeton Studies in International Finance,* no. 54.

Comment   Robert G. Murphy

Introduction

The article by Kent Kimbrough presents a neatly worked-out solution for the structure of optimal distortionary taxes in an economy facing certain noneconomic constraints on either its trade account or its balance of payments. In particular, for the cases involving balance of payments constraints the author provides very clearly the economic intuition behind what turn out to be rather complicated sets of optimal taxes and subsidies on consumption, production, and borrowing.

The analysis is carried out using a cash-in-advance technology of monetary exchange that implies a unitary velocity of money. In my comments I will consider the extent to which this mechanism of monetary exchange is critical for some of the policy prescriptions presented by Kimbrough, but relatively unimportant for others. In addition, I will raise a few concerns of mainly an expositional nature.

Robert G. Murphy is assistant professor of economics at Boston College.

Monetary Mechanisms and Optimal Taxes

In Kimbrough's article, the particular timing of transactions assumed for the economy along with the cash-in-advance constraint imply a unitary velocity of money. This constant velocity of money assumption links the demand for money directly to the value of domestic production in a rigid fashion. It is this link between domestic production and money demand that determines in part the nature of the policy prescriptions obtained in the paper.

There are two types of noneconomic objectives considered in the paper. One type involves either a cumulative trade balance (wealth) target over a given time interval or a separate trade balance target for each period during a given time interval. The other type involves either a cumulative balance of payments (reserve) target over a given time interval or separate balance of payments targets during a given time interval. The article finds that for objectives related to the trade balance, optimal policy involves only taxes on borrowing during periods when the constraint binds. No within-period distortions on consumption or production are prescribed. It appears that this is a rather general result, one that is *not* dependent on the manner in which money is modeled (although dependent on utility being separable across periods and agents having infinite horizons). The reason the monetary mechanism does not matter here is that trade balance targets to not require any change in the intertemporal pattern of the excess flow demand for money. All that is needed is to alter the intertemporal pattern of consumption.

For objectives relating to the balance of payments, the article shows that optimal policy involves, in general, taxes or subsidies on production, consumption, and borrowing during the periods when the constraint binds. Production and consumption choices are distorted through taxes and subsidies so as to increase the excess flow demand for money and, hence, meet the balance of payments target. Borrowing is subsidized so as to alleviate the welfare loss arising from distortion of within period choices. These results appear to be critically dependent on the manner in which money is modeled. The reason for this is that in order to meet a balance of payments constraint, the government must alter the intertemporal pattern of the excess flow demand for money. The policies that are necessary to achieve these objectives are therefore strongly influenced by the nature of the monetary mechanism.

To illustrate these points, consider an alternative method of modeling money where consumers hold domestic money to reduce the time spent transacting. Furthermore, assume that utility is a function of leisure as well as goods. If labor supply is assumed to be inelastic, as in Kimbrough's paper, then the level of real money balances will directly affect the level of utility but will have *no* direct effect on production. In this framework where the velocity of money is permitted to vary, the government seeks to maximize (notation follows Kimbrough)

(1) $$\sum_{t=1}^{\infty} \rho^{t-1} u(X^t, Z^t, m^t)$$

subject to the constraint that the present value of consumption equal the present value of production and the particular constraint associated with possible noneconomic objectives. For the case of a k-period cumulative trade balance (wealth) target of $\bar{b}$, the LaGrangian expression is

(2) $$\underset{\{X^t,Z^t,m^t,p_s^t\}}{\text{Max}} \sum_{t=1}^{\infty} \rho^{t-1} u(X^t, Z^t, m^t) + \lambda \Sigma d^{*t}\{X_s^t(p_s^t) - X^t + p^{*t}[Z_s^t(p_s^t)$$
$$- Z^t]\} + \theta\{\sum_{t=1}^{k} d^{*t}[X_s^t(p_s^t) - X^t + p^{*t}[Z_s^t(p_s^t) - Z^t]] - d^{*k}\bar{b}\}$$

First-order conditions for this problem are identical to those obtained in Kimbrough's approach except for the additional condition that nominal interest rates be set equal to zero via the optimal rate of inflation. Likewise, results for the case of separate trade balance targets in each period during a given time interval are equivalent for both the money-in-the-utility function approach and Kimbrough's approach.

For the case of a k-period cumulative balance of payments (reserves) target of $\bar{b}_R$, the LaGrangian expression for a money-in-utility function approach is:

(3) $$\underset{\{X^t,Z^t,m^t,p_s^t\}}{\text{Max}} \sum_{t=1}^{\infty} \rho^{t-1} u(X^t, Z^t, m^t) + \lambda \Sigma d^{*t}\{X_s^t(p_s^t) - X^t + p^{*t}[Z_s^t(p_s^t)$$
$$- Z^t]\} + \alpha\{\sum_{t=1}^{k-1} d^{*t}\left[\frac{u_m^t}{u_X^t} m^t - \mu^t\right] + d^{*k}[m^k - \mu^k - \bar{b}_R]\}$$

where the consumer's first-order condition for holdings of real balances, $u_m^t/u_X^t = i^t/(1 + i^t)$ is accounted for in the government's optimization problem. The first-order conditions for the government's policy involve conditions for consumption, production, and borrowing, as well as for real money balances. The first-order conditions for consumption and production are

(4a) $u_Z^t/u_X^t = \begin{cases} \dfrac{p^{*t} - \dfrac{\alpha m^t}{u_X^t \lambda} u_{mZ}^t - \dfrac{i^t}{1 + i^t} u_{XZ}^t}{1 - \dfrac{\alpha m^t}{u_X^t \lambda} u_{mX}^t - \dfrac{i^t}{1 + i^t} u_{XX}^t} \,, & t = 1, \ldots, k-1, \\[2em] u_Z^t/u_X^t = p^{*t} \,, & t = k, k+1, \ldots, . \end{cases}$

(4b)
$$\frac{-\partial X_s^t/\partial p_s^t}{\partial Z_s^t/\partial p_s^t} = p^{*t}, \qquad \text{for all } t.$$

The optimal policy here does not involve *any* production distortion and involves distorting consumption choices only in periods prior to period k. These results differ sharply from Kimbrough's where, production is subsidized in periods one through k and consumption is distorted most heavily during the last period of the constraint. Similar differences in results between the money-in-the-utility function approach and Kimbrough's approach arise for the case of a separate balance of payments target in each period. Thus, the results for optimal tax policy when facing balance of payments targets are extremely sensitive to the manner in which money is modeled.

Expositional Issues

The author does not discuss the production side of the economy in any detail. For instance, the issue of how transactions in factor markets occur is left to the imagination of the reader. In addition, the timing of transactions in goods markets seems somewhat confusing. An agent is described as receiving at the beginning of the period a payment for the goods he sold last period. However, the same agent is described as buying goods at the end of the period. Presumably another agent sells the goods and receives payment? Or is there a "firm" present that pays out "dividends" next period? Clarification of these timing issues would be helpful.

At various points in the article the author notes that the cash-in-advance constraints will be binding when nominal interest rates are positive. This is described as occurring when the nominal interest rate exceeds "the rate dictated by the optimum quantity of money rule." In the context of a model in which inflation has *no* effect on the velocity of money, however, it is not very informative to frame the discussion in terms of the optimal inflation tax.

Conclusion

To summarize briefly, I have strong reservations concerning the particular mechanism of monetary exchange employed by Kimbrough. The unitary velocity of money assumption implied by his monetary framework is of critical importance for the qualitative nature of policies seeking to attain targets related to the overall balance of payments. Future research should attempt to derive optimal policies for achieving balance of payments objectives in settings that permit more plausible mechanisms of monetary exchange. In particular, the role of inflation in distorting consumer behavior should be recognized.

10   Tax Policy and International Competitiveness

Lawrence H. Summers

International considerations are coming to play an increasingly important role in U.S. tax policy debates. Policy discussions of tax provisions bearing on foreign investment in the United States and American investment abroad has long focused on the competitiveness question. Recently, reductions in taxes on business investments have been advocated on the grounds that they will increase American competitiveness. Excessive tax burdens are frequently blamed for the poor international performance of some American industries. Indeed, the President's Commission on International Competitiveness recently urged business tax relief as a major element in a strategy directed at improving the trade position of the United States. Tax increases to reduce looming budget deficits are often defended on the grounds that they will reduce trade deficits.

While economists have long recognized that increased international competitiveness is not necessarily a good thing, because it is the mirror image of a decline in a nation's terms of trade, it is nonetheless an important policy goal. An analysis of the interrelationships between tax policy and competitiveness therefore seems worthwhile. This paper provides such an analysis, stressing the crucial role of capital mobility in determining the impact of tax reforms on an economy's traded-goods sector. I begin by examining theoretically the relationship between tax changes and competitiveness under various assumptions about international capital mobility. Finding the conclusions sensitive to assump-

Lawrence H. Summers is the Nathaniel Ropes Professor of Political Economy at Harvard University and a research associate of the National Bureau of Economic Research.

I have benefited from useful discussions with Richard Cooper, Rudi Dornbusch, and Jeff Sachs. This paper draws in part on earlier joint work with John Earle. I am indebted to Fernando Ramos and Mark Sundberg for valuable research assistance.

tions about capital mobility, I go on to consider empirically the extent of international capital mobility. Drawing on both the theoretical and empirical analysis, I attempt to assess the likely impact of alternative tax reforms on international competitiveness.

The common assumption that capital flows freely internationally leads to striking conclusions regarding the effects of tax policies. Tax measures which stimulate investment but do not affect savings will inevitably lead to declines in international competitiveness as long as capital is freely mobile internationally. The economic mechanism is simple. Measures which promote investment attract funds from abroad leading to an appreciation in the real exchange rate and a reduction in the competitiveness of domestic industry. The accounting identity holding that the current account equals the difference between national savings and national investment, insures that increases in investment *ceteris paribus* will be associated with decreases in the trade balance. Conversely, tax policies which promote savings but do not have a direct impact on investment will improve trade performance.

These results challenge the commonly expressed view that reductions in tax burdens on business will improve competitiveness by enabling them to undertake more productivity-enhancing investment. They also raise an interesting question in political economy. Why do firms in the traded-goods sector, whose competitiveness will be hurt by the capital inflows associated with investment incentives, lobby in favor of them? Consideration of this question leads naturally to an examination of the premise of free international capital mobility that underlies the arguments in the previous paragraph. If capital is not internationally mobile, stimulus to investment will not lead to capital inflows and therefore will not be associated with trade-balance deterioration.

While there certainly is a large pool of internationally mobile capital, Feldstein and Horioka (1980) and Feldstein (1983) have pointed out an important puzzle raised by the hypothesis of perfect international capital mobility. This hypothesis would predict that there should be no systematic relationship between domestic saving and investment rates, since capital can flow freely. Yet across the Organization for Economic Cooperation and Development (OECD) nations there is a very strong positive correlation between savings and investment rates. Over long periods of time, cumulative current-account deficits or surpluses are quite small despite large variations in domestic savings rates. On a very consistent basis, high-savings countries are also high-investment countries, while low-savings countries, like the United States, have relatively low rates of investment.

The observation that domestic savings and investment rates are strongly associated can be interpreted as suggesting that tax policies which raise savings are likely to increase domestic investment significantly. Similarly, policies directed at investment are unlikely to lead to permanent increases in investment unless domestic savings are increased as well. Alternatively, as many international economists argue, the cross-sectional correlation between national savings and investment rates may be a statistical artifact that does not call into question the international mobility of capital. Resolving the issue requires that some interpretation of the close cross-sectional linkages between national savings and investment be provided.

I consider three alternative hypotheses regarding the apparent international immobility of capital. The first is the hypothesis advanced by Feldstein and Horioka that institutional and legal restrictions of a variety of types preclude substantial international capital flows. The second is a possibility advanced by Obstfeld (1985), among others, that the high correlation between domestic savings and investment rates is an artifact of common factors, such as high population growth, that affect both savings and investment. The third hypothesis is that capital is mobile internationally, but that countries systematically utilize economic policy tools in an effort to achieve approximate current-account balance, so that large, sustained capital flows are not observed. My conclusion is that the third hypothesis provides the most satisfactory available explanation for the observed correlations between domestic savings and investment rates. I suggest several reasons why countries might find it desirable to maintain external balance.

This conclusion raises an important question. Given that policies to limit net capital mobility are frequently pursued, how should the effects of tax policy reforms which affect savings or investment be evaluated? If no other policy measures are undertaken, their effects should be analyzed under the assumption that capital is perfectly mobile. But the historical record suggests that current-account imbalances are likely to be offset by other policy actions. Both these issues have obvious relevance to the current American situation, where business tax reductions appear to have stimulated a significant amount of capital formation, and to have drawn capital in from abroad in large quantity, but where the trade deficit is seen as a major problem.

The paper is organized as follows. The first section examines theoretically the effects of alternative tax policies on competitiveness under different assumptions about international capital mobility. It suggests some possible explanations for the paradox that firms in traded-goods industries frequently support tax policies that seem likely to reduce competitiveness. The second section takes up the question of the extent of international capital mobility and documents the very high correlation between domestic savings and investment rates across the OECD nations. The third section considers alternative hypotheses regarding this phenomenon and concludes that it is most likely the result of national economic policies directed at maintaining external balance. Possible reasons why nations might pursue such policies are considered. The fourth and final section considers the implications of the results for tax policy in general and the current American situation in particular.

10.1 Tax Policy in an Open Economy

This section examines theoretically the effects of various tax policies in an open economy where capital is mobile. In considering taxation in an open economy it is crucial to distinguish between taxes on savings and those on investment. As I use the terms here, taxes on savings refer to taxes on capital income received by home-country residents regardless of where the capital is located. The U.S. interest-income tax is an example of such a tax. Conversely, taxes on investment refer to taxes levied on capital within the home country, regardless of its ownership. The tax on corporate income is an example of an investment tax. In closed economies, it is clear that there is no important difference between savings and investment taxes. But in open economies, where capital flows are possible, they will have quite different effects. The model presented below makes it possible to analyze the short- and long-run effects of both pure savings and investment taxes. There are a variety of complexities involved in mapping real-world tax structures with their complex foreign tax credit and deferral provisions into the pure savings and investment taxes treated here. I bypass these problems.

The main conclusions of the formal analysis presented below may be motivated by considering the national income accounting identity $S-I = X-M$. This identity holds that the trade balance $(X-M)$ must equal the excess of domestic savings over investment. Equivalently, as the balance of payments must balance, the current account $(X-M)$ must be just offset by the capital account $(S-I)$. It is apparent from this identity that policies which increase national investment without increasing national savings must necessarily lead to increases in imports or decreases in exports. In either event, the traded-goods sector of the economy will contract. Conversely, policies which increase national savings without affecting national investment will improve the current account and, in a fully employed economy, lead the traded-goods sector to expand.

These results apply in the short and intermediate run. Ultimately, they will be reversed. Consider again the case where investment is increased with no change in savings. Foreigners who finance the excess of investment over savings will accumulate claims on the domestic economy. Ultimately these claims must be paid back, and this will require that the home country run a trade surplus, exporting more than it imports. Similarly, increases in domestic savings without changes in investment will lead ultimately to trade deficits as domestic residents liquidate their claims on foreign economies.

10.1.1 Modelling the Linkages between Tax Policy and Competitiveness

While a number of studies, notably Feldstein and Hartman (1980) and Hartman (1983), have examined the effects of tax policy on capital intensity, they have assumed that there is only one internationally produced good making it impossible to study issues relating to competitiveness. Goulder, Shoven, and Whalley (1983) examine the implications of international capital mobility within the context of a computable general equilibrium model and show that international considerations can have important implications for tax policy. Because the model they consider is not grounded in intertemporal optimization, it is not possible to distinguish the short- and long-run effects of tax policies. Lipton and Sachs (1983) examine a two-country growth model with two sectors producing traded and nontraded goods, and with investment function–based adjustment costs. Their model is sufficiently complex that it must be solved by numerical simulation.

Here I follow very closely Bruno (1982) and less closely Sachs (1981, 1982) in considering a two-period model in which the first period corresponds to the short run and the second period corresponds to the long run. Consideration of a more realistic infinite horizon model would be analytically intractable. I treat the case of a small, open economy that takes both the price of the traded good and the interest rate as given. The analysis could be modified to treat the case of an economy large enough to affect world markets.

Consider a two-commodity, two-period framework. Tradeables Q_f are produced in each period according to the production function $Q_f^t = Q_f(L_f^t, K_f^t)$, which is assumed to have constant returns to scale. The nontradeable domestic good Q_d is produced with the constant returns-to-scale production function $Q_d^t = Q_d(L_d^t, K_d^t)$. The price of tradeables is taken as the numeraire and price of the domestic good is denoted π. Increases in π correspond to real appreciations of the local currency. Production of tradeable goods is allocated between consumption C_f, investment I, and net exports X which may be negative. Production of nontradeable goods is divided between private consumption C_d and public consumption G. It is examined further below. The assumed sectoral specialization of investment and government spending simplifies the analysis and does not alter the basic conclusions.

Total labor supply in each period is fixed at $\bar{L}^t$, ($\bar{L}^t = L_d^t + L_f^t$). Total capital is fixed in the first period and cannot be reallocated between sectors. First-period investment or disinvestment augments the second-period capital stock. ($K_d^2 - \bar{K}_d + K_f^2 - \bar{K}_f = I$). Since for simplicity it is assumed that capital does not depreciate, it is reasonable to allow I to be negative. No new capital goods are produced in the second period, since it represents posterity.

Firms maximize the present value of after-corporate-tax profits:

$$PV = (1 - \tau)[Q_f^1 + \pi^1 Q_d^1 - w^1 L^1 + R^{-1}(Q_f^2 + \pi^2 Q_d^2 - w^2 L^2)] - I^1$$

where $R = (1 + r)$. Note that since capital does not depreciate, the firm is allowed no tax depreciation allowances. Maximization subject to the production functions and factor accumulation constraints yields standard first-order conditions:

(1) $\pi^t \partial Q_d^t / \partial L_d^t = \partial Q_f^t / \partial L_f^t = w^t$ $t = 1,2$

(2) $R = (1 - \tau)\pi^2 \partial Q^2 / \partial K_d^2 = (1 - \tau)\partial Q_f^2 / K_f^2$

where equality of first-period marginal products at the point K_d, K_f has been assumed.[1]

At this point, we are ready to examine the implications of a corporate tax change for factor and product prices in the long run. Figure 10.1 depicts the factor-price frontiers in the two sectors under the assumption that the traded-goods sector is more capital intensive. Production occurs at the intersection of the two frontiers. The relative price of the

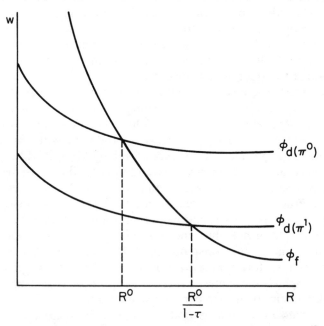

Fig. 10.1   The long-run effects of corporate tax increase

nontraded good, π, shifts until the factor-price frontiers intersect at the world interest rate. Now consider a corporate tax increase. The factor-price frontier for the tradeable good does not shift, but the required pre-tax return on capital is increased from R^0 to $R^0/1 - \tau$. This necessitates a change in π to shift the domestic-goods factor price frontier. It is clear from figure 10.1 that under our assumption that the traded-good sector is more capital intensive than the nontraded-goods sector, a corporate tax will lower capital intensity in both sectors and reduce the relative price of domestic goods, thereby causing the traded-goods sector to contract. The last result would be reversed if the opposite factor intensity assumption was maintained.

Leamer (1980) presents some rather dated evidence on the relative capital intensities of U.S. traded and nontraded goods in the context of a study of the Leontief paradox. His data, drawn from Leontief's original work, indicate that the traded-goods sector is much more capital intensive than the nontraded-goods sector. However, he notes that the more recent data provided in Baldwin (1971) suggests the opposite conclusion. At present, I am unaware of more satisfactory evidence on this question for the United States. It seems appropriate to be agnostic in the relative capital intensity question and to conclude that capital intensity effects will not lead to large effects of tax policies on the long-run composition of national output.

As just demonstrated, it is possible to examine the impact of a corporate tax change on factor and product prices in the long run without specifying anything about product demands. In order to address the sectoral composition of output and employment and to consider short-run issues, it is necessary to specify how demand is determined. For simplicity, I assume that consumers maximize a Cobb-Douglas utility function:

(3) $U = \alpha ln C_f^1 + (1 - \alpha) ln C_d^1 + D[\alpha ln C_f^2 + (1 - \alpha) ln C_d^2]$

where D is a discount factor, and α is the share of consumption-expenditure devoted to the foreign good.

Households maximize utility subject to their budget constraint which holds that:

(4) $C_f^1 + \pi^1 C_d^1 + [(1 - \theta)R]^{-1} (C_f^2 + \pi^2 C_d^2) = \Omega$

where Ω represents the present value of their endowment in terms of the foreign good, and θ is the tax rate levied on savings. Net household wealth Ω is given by:

(5) $\Omega = (Q_f^1 + \pi^1 Q_d^1) + [(1 - \theta)R]^{-1}(Q_f^2 + \pi^2 Q_d^2) - T - I$

where $T = T^1 + R^{-1}T^2 = \pi^1 G^1 + R^{-1}\pi^2 G^2$ is the total cumulative revenue of the government. Since $C_d^t + G^t = Q_d^t$, it follows that:

(6) $\Omega = Q_f^1(\pi^1) + \pi^1 C_d^1 + \{[(1 - \theta)R]^{-1}w^2L^2$

$$- [(1 - \theta)R]^{-1}\pi^2G^2 + \bar{K}_d + \bar{K}_f\}$$

where it can be assumed that Q_f is a negative function of π^1.

At this point we are ready to solve the model using the very ingenious graphical technique developed in Bruno (1982). Equation (6) and the assumption of Cobb-Douglas utility imply that:

(7) $\pi^1 C_d^1 = b\Omega[\pi^1, R(1 - \theta) G^2]$

The $b\Omega$ function is negatively related to all three of its arguments. It is plotted as the line marked $b\Omega$ in figure 10.2. In order to characterize first-period equilibrium we add a supply function for the total value of C_d:

(8) $\pi^1 C_d^1 = \pi^1 Q_d^1(\pi^1) - \pi^1 G^1.$

This curve is also depicted in quadrant 1 of figure 10.2.

Together these two schedules already permit us to characterize the determination of first-period equilibrium. Note that any policy which reduces first-period consumption, such as a reduction in the individual tax rate θ, will lead to a reduction in π^1 and an increase in the size of

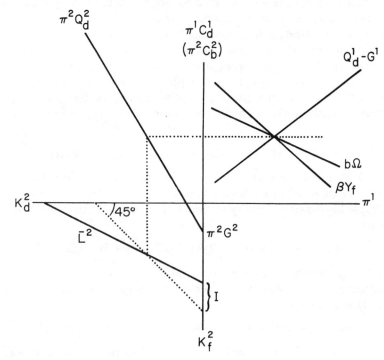

Fig. 10.2   The determination of long-run equilibrium

the tradeable-goods sector. Likewise a decrease in public consumption will lead to a reduction in π, and an increase in competitiveness.

In what follows it will be useful to examine the behavior of domestic savings S. Note that $S_1 = Y_f - C_f^1$. Given our assumption of Cobb-Douglas utility, C_f^1 is proportional to πC_d^1. Drawing in the schedule $\beta Y_f(\pi_1)$ where $\beta = (1 - \alpha)/(\alpha)$, we can see that savings is proportional to the vertical distance between this schedule and the $b\Omega$ schedule. Note that the βY^f schedule is steeper than the $b\Omega$ schedule because $b < \beta$.

We are now ready to consider second-period equilibrium and the determination of investment. The determination of second-period factor and product prices has already been discussed. These serve to uniquely determine capital-labor and capital-output ratios in both sectors. In quadrant 2 of figure 10.2, the relationship between $\pi^2 C^2 d$ and K^2 is depicted. The slope of this schedule increases with the period-2 capital output ratio and the intercept is $\pi^2 G^2$. It is possible to put $\pi^1 C_d^1$ and $\pi^2 C_d^2$ on the same axis because they are proportional by the Cobb-Douglas assumption.

The requirement of full employment in period 2 is expressed as the $\bar{L}^2$ schedule in quadrant 3. It will be less (more) steep than the 45° line as the nontraded-goods sector is more (less) capital intensive than the traded-goods sector. The equation of this schedule is $\gamma_d^2 K_d^2 + \gamma_f^2 K_f^2 = \bar{L}^2$, where γ_i represents the labor-capital ratio in sector i, which is determined by factor prices. The level of investment can be read as the vertical distance between the $\bar{L}^2$ schedules and the 45° line's K_f^2 intercept.

The schedules in figure 10.2, along with the factor-price frontiers in figure 10.1, serve to fully characterize equilibrium. Notice, finally, that the current account, CA, is given by $S - I$, which can be read from figure 10.2.

10.1.2 Savings Incentives

At this point, we are ready to consider the effects of policy changes. The effect of a decrease in period-1 public consumption is depicted in figure 10.3. As already noted, the relative price of nontradeables, π, declines. Employment in the traded-goods sector increases, while decreasing in the nontraded sector. National savings increases. None of the schedules in the other quadrants shifts. It is apparent that in the long run K_d^2 increases and K_f^2 decreases. Since capital-labor ratios are unchanged, it follows that employment in the traded-goods sector will decline in the long run after its initial increase. Investment will increase (decrease) as the traded-goods sector is less (more) capital intensive than the nontraded goods sector. As long as the nontraded-goods sector is not "far" more capital intensive than the traded-goods sector, savings

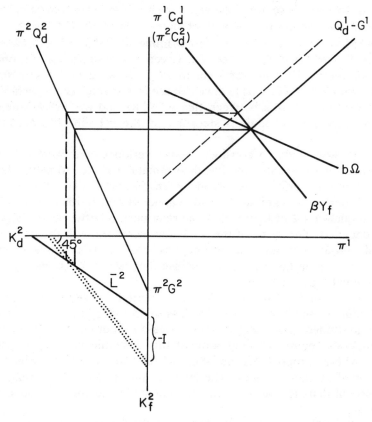

Fig. 10.3   The effect of a saving incentive

will increase more than investment, and a current-account surplus will result.

The effects of a decrease in θ, which reduces private consumption, parallel those of a reduction in public consumption. They cannot be neatly analyzed diagrammatically because a change in θ breaks the proportionality between $\pi^1 C_d^1$ and $\pi^2 C_d^2$. Note however that the effect of a savings incentive will be to raise $\pi^2 C_d^2$, and give rise to second-period effects very similar to those of a change in government spending. The traded-goods sector will expand in the short run and contract in the long run. Investment may rise or fall but it is unlikely to change a great deal.

10.1.3   Investment Incentives

The effects of an investment incentive, treated here as a decline in τ, are depicted in figure 10.4. The solution is most easily achieved working backwards. It is clear that, with capital mobile, the long-run

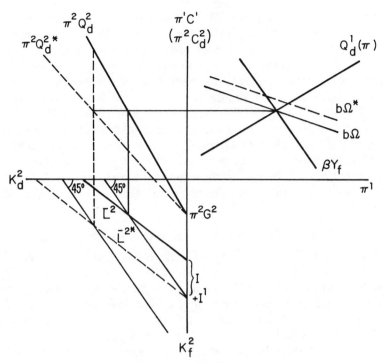

Fig. 10.4   The effect of an investment incentive

effect of an investment incentive will be to raise capital intensity in both production sectors and to raise real wages. Thus the $\bar{L}^2$ schedule in the third quadrant shifts downwards. The shift will be parallel in the special case depicted here where the elasticities of substitution in the two sectors are equal. The capital output ratio in the domestic goods sector must increase, shifting the $\pi^2 C_d^2$ schedule down and to the left. Finally, the increase in second-period real wages increases human wealth and shifts the $b\Omega$ schedule in the first quadrant upwards.

The effect of an investment incentive is to reduce short-run competitiveness and to reduce domestic savings. Long-run capital intensity is increased, so the current account declines unambiguously. An investment incentive has an ambiguous effect on π^2, the relative price of nontradeables, depending on the relative capital intensities of the two sectors. In the special case of the two sectors with equal capital intensity, an investment subsidy will increase long-run employment in the traded-goods sector. More generally, however, the result is ambiguous.

In assessing the implications of this theoretical analysis, a crucial question arises. How much real time corresponds to the short and long run in the stylized two-period model considered here? The issue is difficult to judge, but it seems likely that the model's short-run predictions are applicable over fairly long horizons. Policies directed at increasing the domestic capital stock are likely to lead to increased net investment for many years as new capital is accumulated. The available evidence, while weak, suggests that capital adjusts relatively slowly to its desired level. Likewise simulations of the type presented by Summers (1979) and Chamley (1981) suggest that households will take periods of up to a decade to fully adjust their wealth holding following a change in the available rate of return. These considerations suggest that, with a horizon of a decade or less, it is probably appropriate to use the short-run predictions of the economy to tax reforms. The simulation results of Lipton and Sachs (1983) are consistent with this suggestion.

10.1.4   The Political Economy of International Competitiveness

The arguments in this section raise an obvious question. Why is business-tax relief so frequently advocated as a vehicle for increasing international competitiveness? The analysis here suggests that tax reduction measures, which encourage investment, inevitably reduce competitiveness and hurt firms in the traded-goods sector as long as capital is mobile internationally. In part, advocacy of tax relief must result from a failure to consider its general equilibrium ramifications. With fixed real exchange rates, tax relief does help the traded-goods sector. Its advocates may fail to take account of the increase in real exchange rates that necessarily accompanies capital inflows. But economists should be reluctant to assume that self-interested parties are advocating positions contrary to their interests. It is therefore worthwhile to consider other reasons why those in the traded-goods sector might advocate tax relief.

A first possibility is that they are motivated by long-run considerations. Accumulating debt to foreigners will eventually require that we run a trade surplus. But it seems unlikely that such a long-run consideration plays an important role in current policy debates. A second explanation starts with the recognition that the traded-goods sector is not monolithic. Tax reforms which benefit firms in some, but not all, of the traded-goods sector may cause their competitiveness to increase even as the total traded-goods sector is shrinking. It might, for example, be argued that incentives to invest in plant and equipment benefit American manufacturers at the expense of farmers. The corporate sector is so large a fraction of the traded-goods sector that it seems unlikely that this is the whole story.

A third explanation for the advocacy of investment incentives to increase competitiveness is that advocates suspect that investment incentives will not, in fact, lead to prolonged capital inflows. This may be because capital mobility is limited, and so investment incentives will lead to only small capital inflows. Alternatively, it may be because governments are perceived as unlikely to permit large trade deficits to continue for long periods of time. In either of these cases, tax incentives will raise the after-tax profits of firms in the traded-goods sector and will not lead to significant declines in competitiveness. I explore the question of the extent of international capital mobility in the remainder of the paper.

10.2   National Savings and National Investment

The preceding section demonstrated that the assumption of perfect international capital mobility has important implications for the analysis of competitiveness. It also is important for other fiscal questions. With internationally mobile capital, taxes on investment will all be borne by labor. Government budget deficits will not affect national levels of investment, but will instead reduce investment around the world. More generally, policies which increase national savings will have no effect on national investment.

In provocative recent papers, Feldstein and Horioka (1980) and Feldstein (1983) point out that if national savings do not affect national investment as the capital mobility hypothesis implies, one would not expect to see any strong relationship between national savings and investment rates. Yet, as table 10.1 demonstrates, there is a very close association between levels of national savings and national investment. While the long-run average net savings rate varied across countries between 6.5 and 19.6%, the largest average current account deficit was 8.3%, and the largest surplus was only 2.3%. The correlation between domestic savings and investment rates was .92.

Table 10.2 presents regressions of the national investment rates on national savings rates for a number of different intervals. Using both net and gross measures, the data suggest a strong relationship between investment and savings.[2] In all cases, the savings variable is highly significant. It is noteworthy that there is no evidence that the impact of national savings on national investment has declined through time, even though institutional barriers to international capital mobility have been broken down over the past 25 years. There is some evidence, however, that the correlation between savings and investment rates has declined through time.

Comparisons of the size of actual capital flows with those that might be expected highlight the apparent immobility of capital. Consider a policy which raises the return on domestic investment by 20%. This is about the right order of magnitude for the 1981 and 1982 U.S. tax reforms. Assuming a Cobb-Douglas production function with a capital

Table 10.1   **Net Savings and Investment, 1960–1983**

Country	Net Savings GDP	Net Investment GDP	I-S GDP
U.S.A.	.065	.066	.001
Iceland	.071	.113	.042
U.K.	.074	.070	−.004
Sweden	.008	.102	.013
Ireland	.091	.174	.083
Canada	.098	.110	.012
Denmark	.098	.128	.030
Belgium	.105	.115	.010
Spain	.108	.122	.014
Finland	.110	.124	.014
Italy	.112	.115	.003
France	.112	.121	.009
Turkey	.118	.153	.035
Norway	.126	.144	.018
Germany	.129	.124	−.005
Netherlands	.142	.129	−.013
Austria	.145	.152	.007
Australia	.146	.165	.019
New Zealand	.150	.188	.038
Greece	.155	.179	.024
Switzerland	.182	.159	−.023
Portugal	.191	.265	−.074
Japan	.196	.191	−.003

Source: OECD.

share of .25, an increase of about 20% in the capital stock would be required to equalize the return on domestic and international investment. With a capital output ratio of 1.5, this would mean a capital inflow of close to 30% of GNP. Only one OECD nation, Portugal, experienced a capital inflow of this magnitude over the 1975–81 period. Stating the point differently—the capital flows that are observed do not seem to be large enough to have very large effects on rates of return.

A number of papers including Sachs (1981, 1982), Feldstein (1983), and Caprio and Howard (1984) have examined the relationships between changes in domestic savings and investment rates. While the approaches taken in these papers differ somewhat, several conclusions emerge. There is a positive relationship between changes in domestic savings and changes in domestic investment that is weaker than the relationship between savings and investment levels. Also, it appears that shocks both to domestic savings and to domestic investment have significant effects on the current account, although their relative importance is a subject of debate. Finally, there is very weak evidence that the degree of international capital mobility has increased somewhat

Table 10.2   **The Correlation Between National Investment and National Savings**

Period	Intercept	S_i	R^2
		Net	
1960–1964	.015	.962	.821
	(.013)	(.095)	
1965–1969	.043	.750	.687
	(.016)	(.106)	
1970–1974	.042	.777	.733
	(.017)	(.099)	
1975–1979	.025	.941	.528
	(.024)	(.185)	
1980–1983	.024	.960	.586
	(.018)	(.164)	
		Gross	
1960–1964	.029	.920	.879
	(.017)	(.073)	
1965–1969	.047	.834	.783
	(.023)	(.093)	
1970–1974	.049	.835	.755
	(.026)	(.106)	
1975–1979	.065	.789	.439
	(.042)	(.185)	
1980–1983	.086	.679	.464
	(.032)	(.152)	

in recent years. But, none of the time-series analysis calls into question the proposition that domestic savings and investment rates are closely linked.

One consideration that could account for some degree of association between domestic savings and investment rates is the fact that countries are not perfectly "small" on the world capital market. A share of each country's savings would be invested in it, even if capital were perfectly mobile. It seems unlikely that this can account for a large part of the correlation between savings and investment rates. Even for the United States, a dollar of savings would be expected to produce only about 25 or 30 cents of domestic investment, if capital were really perfectly mobile. Moreover, this point has no force in considering the cross-sectional association between domestic savings and investment rates.

Another possible source of association between domestic savings and investment is Keynesian effects. Increases in investment which raise domestic income temporarily would be expected to increase domestic savings as well. The fact that savings and investment rates are about equally highly correlated over short and long periods of time suggests that this is not likely to be too important a factor.

It is not clear how to interpret the observation that savings and investment rates are highly correlated across countries. The questions of policy interest concern the allocation of the marginal dollar of domestic savings, or the financing of a marginal dollar of domestic investment. It is conceivable that incremental savings are invested in a very different way than the average dollar of savings. The fact that the linkages between changes in savings and changes in investment are weaker than those between levels suggests this view. An argument of this kind must explain, however, why ongoing capital flows are not observed between countries with stable high and low savings rates. In the next section we consider alternative explanations for the close association between savings and investment rates across nations. These explanations have differing implications for the hypothesis of marginal capital mobility and for the effects of fiscal policies.

10.3   Explaining Apparent Capital Mobility

The previous section documented the very high correlation between national savings and investment rates. This section considers three possible explanations for this phenomenon. These explanations assume in turn that capital mobility is greatly limited by institutional factors, that the correlation between national savings and investment rates is a spurious reflection of third factors, and that apparent capital immobility reflects the endogenous adjustment of savings and investment rates. While there is some element of truth in each of these explanations, we are led to accept the third one as the primary reason for the close association of domestic savings and investment rates.

10.3.1   Capital Immobility

A first natural explanation for the observed savings and investment patterns is that most capital is immobile. While some capital can flow freely, restrictions in financial institutions, capital controls, and the perceived risks of foreign investment greatly reduce the flow of capital. As Feldstein and Horioka (1980) suggest, "official restrictions impede the export of capital. Moreover the fear of future capital export controls by potential host countries . . . deters investors. . . . Important institutional rigidities also tend to keep a large segment of domestic savings at home. The most obvious of these in the United States is the savings institutions that are required by law to be invested in mortgages on local real estate."

There is, of course, a large pool of very liquid international capital. The argument, however, is that only this money is freely mobile with other savings being immobile. This raises an immediate problem. If only a small pool of "hot money" were available to arbitrage large international return differentials, one would expect that it would all end up in one place. As long as some mobile funds are located almost everywhere there is a presumption that rates of return must be equalized.

The related argument of Feldstein and Horioka, that returns on short-term financial assets are arbitraged while returns on longer-term investments are not equalized, is also difficult to accept. Arbitrage, like equality, is transitive. As long as there are institutions in each country (e.g., Citibank) which hold different types of domestic assets, and also hold some foreign asset, we can be sure that the returns on domestic and foreign assets are arbitraged. Equalization of returns does not require that there be any agent who makes long-term investments both at home and abroad. As long as the standard assumption of marginal domestic capital mobility is maintained, the existence of investors at interior solutions holding any domestic and any foreign assets is sufficient to insure marginal capital mobility on an international basis.[3]

A clear piece of evidence suggesting the mobility of capital internationally is the fact that the relatively small net flows of capital that are observed reflect large offsetting gross flows. If capital were immobile, one would expect to see small gross as well as net flows. Unfortunately data on foreign investment by domestic firms and domestic investment by foreign firms are not available on a consistent international basis. Therefore, table 10.3 presents some information on gross and net flows of investment for the United States. In 1982, both capital inflows and outflows for the U.S. were more than ten times the

Table 10.3   **Net and Gross Flows in the U.S.**

	1981	1982
	(Billions of $)	
Current-account balance[a]	4.5	−8.1
Net foreign investment	4.1	−4.6
Increase in U.S. assets abroad[b] (capital outflows)	109.3	118.3
Increase in foreign assets in the U.S.[b] (capital inflows)	77.9	84.5

Source: Survey of Current Business, March 1983, pp. 13 and 51.

Note: The reason that the difference of the gross flows is not equal to the reported net flows is a sizable statistical discrepancy.

[a]The current-account balance and net foreign investment are conceptually the same, differing only by the allocations of SDRs ("capital grants" in the NIPA) and some small definitional differences.

[b]The net increase over the year; that is, conceptually, the difference between the value of assets at the end of the year and the value at the year's beginning.

net flow of capital. Even these figures underestimate the true flows, because they fail to take account of replacement investment by Americans abroad and foreigners here.

Large reciprocal gross investment flows also call into question Feldstein's (1983) argument that subjective uncertainties inhibit capital flows. Feldstein and Horioka argue that foreign investment is typically directed at exploiting specialized opportunities rather than the general pursuit of higher returns. This claim is difficult to reconcile with the large volume of portfolio investment and with Hartman's (1983) demonstration that foreign direct investment is very sensitive to tax considerations. Recall that no foreign direct investment is necessary for international arbitrage to equalize returns. Even granting that direct foreign investments represent special situations, it is still reasonable to expect that increased domestic savings that reduce domestic rates of return would lead to more specialized foreign investments.

This discussion suggests that there exist capital flows which seem to have the potential to equalize rates of return around the world. A more subtle explanation for capital immobility, which accommodates this observation, might suggest that *total* net capital mobility is limited by fears of expropriation. This is the essential idea lying behind the burgeoning literature on international debt. It was first treated formally by Eaton and Gersovitz (1981). While capital can be freely moved, investors are aware that, if a country has imported too much capital, the gains from expropriating it will exceed the costs that can be imposed. In this case, marginal investors will not invest abroad even if foreign assets are yielding higher returns. At the margin, capital will be immobile. Changes in domestic saving will affect international capital flows only insofar as they affect countries' debt capacity by affecting the size of the "punishment" that can be inflicted on them for defaulting.

It would seem likely that arguments of this type would be more applicable to less-developed countries (LDCs) than to the OECD nations where expropriations seem implausible. One way of testing this explanation for apparent capital immobility is to examine the association between savings and investment across a broad range of countries. If expropriation fears were a major cause of capital immobility, one would expect to see savings and investment rates even more closely associated among LDCs than among the OECD nations. This hypothesis was tested by examining data on national savings and investment rates for 115 countries using data provided by the World Bank.

A regression of investment rates on savings rates using data arranged over the 1973–80 period yields:

$$I/Y = 18 + .311(S/Y) \qquad R^2 = .24$$
$$(1.1)\ (.051)$$

These results were almost unchanged when the OECD countries were excluded from the sample. As a further check, the equation was reestimated dropping observations with large residuals from the sample. Observations with residuals with absolute value greater than two and three times the standard error of the regression were omitted. This did not have a significant impact on the results. One possible explanation for the low correlation between savings and investment is that aid flows drive a wedge between investment and savings even though capital is immobile. However, subtracting aid flows from investment had little impact on the results. It might be argued that the low correlation between domestic savings and investment is the result of measurement error. This seems unlikely. In most cases, domestic savings is estimated as a residual. When this method is used, measurement error may result in a spurious positive correlation between measured savings and investment.

The results suggest a much greater degree of apparent capital mobility when a large sample of countries is considered. Similar results are reported by Fieleke (1982) and Frankel (1985). This provides evidence against the hypothesis of capital immobility, which offers exactly the wrong predictions—that capital should be most mobile against politically allied developed countries with well-functioning capital markets.

It does not seem reasonable to conclude that capital immobility is the right way to explain the close association between national savings and investment rates. I therefore turn to other explanations.

10.3.2 Common Factor Explanations

Another possible explanation for the close association between national savings and investment rates is the fallacy of the common cause. Perhaps there is some third factor which determines both savings and investment, leading them to be highly correlated, even though exogenous changes in savings would have only very small effects on investment. Two such factors suggest themselves. Countries with high rates of population- or productivity-growth would be expected to have high investment rates because of the opportunities created by a rapidly growing labor pool. Lifecycle savings considerations suggest that such countries should also have high savings rates, as young savers are more numerous and have more lifetime income than older dissavers. Thus, growth could be a common factor accounting for associations between savings and investment. Obstfeld (1985) provides a rather elaborate example illustrating this point.

A second factor that could lead to a positive association of savings and investment is initial wealth. A clear example is provided by a nation ravaged by war. Such a country would be expected to have a high investment rate because of the destruction of its capital stock, and a high savings rate because of households' desire to rebuild their wealth holdings. Any source of initial differences in national wealth income ratios would tend to work the same way.

The growth explanation for the strong association between savings and investment rates is easily tested. It is only necessary to add measures of the rate of growth to a regression of the investment rate on the savings rate.

A regression of the net investment rate on the net savings rate and the rates of population growth and productivity growth using the data in table 10.1 yields:

$$I/Y = -.015 + 1.02\ S/Y - .002n + .0026g \qquad R^2 = .703$$
$$\quad\ \ (.023)\quad (1.39)\qquad\ \ (.01)\quad\ \ (.001)$$

Similar results are obtained reversing the equation, using gross rather than net concepts and varying the sample period. Adding growth variables actually increases the coefficient on S/Y. This implies that variations in savings that are uncorrelated with variations in growth actually have more relation to investment than variations explained by the growth variables. Growth is not the spurious factor accounting for the strong correlations between national savings and investment rates.

There is no single variable which can capture the possible effects of initial conditions on both savings and investment. Therefore it is necessary to take a more indirect approach. Estimating the basic investment-savings relationship with instrumental variables, using as instruments any variable expected to affect savings but not investment, will yield a consistent estimate of the "pure" correlation between savings and investment. Feldstein and Horioka report a number of estimates of this type using social security variables as instruments. They find that this has little effect on the estimated savings coefficient. Indeed, in several cases it actually increases. Frankel (1985) presents some corroborating evidence.

In order to further examine this issue, the basic savings investment relationship was reestimated using the government budget deficit as an instrument. Because of data limitations, a smaller sample (14 countries) and a shorter time period (1973–80) were used in the estimation. For this sample the net result of an OLS regression was:

$$I/Y = .02 + .97\ (S/Y)$$
$$\quad\ \ (.03)\quad (.13)$$

Using the government deficit as a share of GDP as an instrument, the result was:

$$I/Y = -.10 + 1.45\ (S/Y)$$
$$\qquad\qquad\quad (1.10)$$

This result is surprising. The coefficient on the savings variable rises substantially rather than declining. It attains an implausible value exceeding one. On the "spurious factor" explanation, one would have expected the savings coefficient to decline.

There is no evidence here to support the "spurious factor" explanation for the close association of national savings and investment rates. But the last equation does raise a puzzle. Why should purging the savings and investment variables of the effects of their common causes cause their estimated association to increase? Clearly the answer must have something to do with the properties of the deficit variable. This issue is explored in the next subsection.

10.3.3 The Maintained External Balance Hypothesis

The assumption has been made so far that national savings and investment rates are exogenously determined. Feldstein and Horioka treat differences in national savings rates as a consequence of "basic structural differences among countries." In their formal model (1980, p. 324), the level of public savings is an exogenous variable affecting the national savings rate.

An alternative view is that countries consistently manipulate the levels of economic policy with a view to maintaining external balance. Such an argument has been made by Fieleke (1982) and Tobin (1983) among others. In this case, capital appears immobile only because countries pursue policies that bring savings and investment into balance. Possible rationales for this behavior are discussed below.

The endogeneity of budget policy can easily explain the empirical results in the preceding section. Consider the special case where capital is completely mobile on world markets, and countries set budget deficits according to:

$$(9) \qquad D_i = \alpha(PS_i - I_i) + u_i, \quad \text{with } 0 \leq \alpha \leq 1$$

where D_i is the deficit, PS_i is private saving, and u_i represents the effect of other factors on the deficit of country i. The assumption that deficits are exogenous corresponds to $\alpha = 0$ in this formulation. Standard calculations suggest that the coefficient on saving in our basic equation will equal:

$$(10) \qquad \hat{\delta}_{\text{OLS}} = \frac{(1 - \alpha)\sigma_{PS,I} + \alpha\sigma_I^2}{(1 - \alpha)^2\sigma_{PS}^2 + \alpha^2\sigma_I^2 + 2\alpha(1 - \alpha)\sigma_{PS,I} + \sigma_u^2}$$

Notice that in the special case where $\alpha = 1$ and $\sigma_u^2 = 0$, $\hat{\delta} = 1$, and that with Feldstein and Horioka's implicit assumptions that $\alpha = 0$ and $\sigma_{PS,I} = 0$ in a perfect capital market, $\hat{\delta} = 0$. As these polar cases suggest, increases in α and reductions in σ_u^2 will tend to raise the value of $\hat{\delta}$. Direct estimation of (9) yields:

(11) $D_i = -.01 + .715 \, (PS_i - I_i)$ $R_2^2 = .77$

         $(.004)$ $(.107)$ $\sigma_u^2 = .00024$

Using this estimated value of α and the observed sample moments tautologically yields the *OLS* estimate for δ. If we reevaluate (10) assuming that $\alpha = 0$ and that $\sigma_u^2 = \sigma_d^2$, the implied value of δ is .597. This confirms that some of the strength of the Feldstein and Horioka results arises from deficit policy actions directed at maintaining external balance. Note that Feldstein (1983) admits that some positive association between PS_i and I_i is to be expected, arising from factors such as growth rates that simultaneously affect both PS_i and I_i. And other policy levers besides deficits may be used to bring savings and investment into balance. Hence, the remaining correlation of .6 should not be treated as evidence of the immobility of capital.

The maintained external balance hypothesis also explains the paradoxical results obtained when D_i is used as an instrument. In this case, the probability limit of the coefficient of interest is given by:

$$\hat{\delta}_{IV} = \frac{\sigma_{D.I}}{\sigma_{D.S}} = \frac{\alpha\sigma_I^2 - \alpha\sigma_{PS.I}}{\alpha^2\sigma_I^2 - \alpha(1 - \alpha)\sigma_{PS}^2 + \alpha(1 - 2\alpha)\sigma_{PS.I} + \sigma_u^2}$$

which will be greater than unity as long as:

$$\alpha(1 - \alpha) \, \text{var} \, (I\text{-}PS), > \sigma_u^2$$

The estimates of δ_{IV} and σ_u^2 reported above imply that this condition is satisfied in practice.

This section has shown that the maintained external balance hypothesis can explain how the observed high correlation of national savings and investment rates could occur in a world with perfect capital mobility. It also explains an additional finding (the high degree of capital mobility among less-developed countries) that is anomalous given the view that capital is internationally immobile. In these nations, the pressure to maintain external balance is much weaker, and so fiscal policy actions are not taken to prevent capital flows. As a consequence, greater current-account imbalances and capital mobility are observed.

The maintained external balance hypothesis seems on the basis of the evidence considered here to be the most plausible explanation for the high cross-sectional correlation between domestic savings and investment rates. By its nature it is difficult to test, since levels of national savings and investment are affected by a wide variety of policy levers, and so the stance of policy towards saving and investment in any given country is difficult to evaluate. Below, I discuss a number of plausible reasons why nations might seek to maintain external balance. The fact that countries so frequently resort to capital controls that force savings and investment into balance makes it very plausible that they also use other policy levers to achieve the same purpose.

Capital will be effectively immobile internationally if nations act so as to avoid either capital outflows or capital inflows. Either would be sufficient to preclude capital flows. Consider first the incentives nations might have to avoid capital outflows. The fundamental reason why nations might prefer to do this is that the social return to domestic investment exceeds that of foreign investment, even when their private returns are equated. Most obviously, this will be the case where there are taxes on domestic investment. More subtly and more importantly, there is the risk associated with capital expropriation by government action or by labor.[4] Keynes (1924) puts the argument well: "Consider two investments, the one at home and the other abroad, with equal risks of repudiation or confiscation or legislation restricting profit. It is a matter of indifference to the individual investor which he selects. But the nation as a whole retains in the one case the object of the investment and fruits of it; whilst in the other case both are lost. If a loan to improve South American capital is repudiated we have nothing. If a Poplar housing loan is repudiated, we as a nation still have the houses."

Note that the phrase "legislation restricting profit" covers a host of possibilities far short of outright nationalization. There is also the possibility that capital expropriation will take the form of actions by workers to raise wages and capture the rents that can be earned from irreversible capital investments. Together these possibilities seem likely to be of substantial importance. They provide a motivation for countries which find themselves exporting capital on a substantial scale to pursue measures directed at spurring domestic investment. Insofar as they suggest that the social return to foreign investment may be rather low, they also suggest the possible desirability of reducing savings when they are primarily flowing abroad. Certainly this was Keynes's view regarding the huge British capital outflows in the early part of this century.

It is noteworthy in this regard that capital-exporting nations tend to be large countries with substantial international power. The British in the Victorian era and the United States during the post–World War II period are obvious examples. The current Japanese situation is less clear. Where capital outflows are made by dominant international powers they may confer external benefits which raise their social return by increasing international influence. Large countries may also regard themselves as relatively immune from expropriation risks. The striking feature of table 10.2 is that almost all of the small countries are capital importers. With large countries unwilling to export capital in large quantities, however, the scope for international capital mobility is relatively limited.

Keynes went on to provide an additional reason why a nation might want to limit its capital exports.[5] He wrote that "Foreign investment does not automatically expand our exports by a corresponding amount. It so affects the foreign exchanges that we are compelled to export more in order to maintain our solvency. It may be the case—I fancy that it now is the case—that we can only do this by lowering the price of our products in terms of the products of other nations, that is by allowing the ratio of real interchange to move to our disadvantage."

This consideration, which is important only for countries with some market power, may also help to explain why large capital outflows are so rare. A possible example is provided by the efforts of the United States to limit capital outflows in the early 1960s in an effort to maintain the value of the dollar. Whether the motivation for maintaining the value of the dollar was enjoying favorable terms of trade is not clear.

There are also reasons why countries would be reluctant to accept large capital inflows. Where these are associated with large movements in real exchange rates, they are likely to damage severely an economy's traded-goods sector. This may generate political pressures to increase domestic savings or to reduce the rate of investment. These pressures are likely to be particularly serious in situations where the real exchange rate changes quickly or where the traded-goods sector is not benefiting from the capital inflows. It should not be surprising that capital inflows into Canada to finance development of its natural resources have proved more politically acceptable than recent inflows into the United States to finance budget deficits.

These arguments are suggestive as to why we see such a small volume of net international capital mobility. Evaluating their relative importance is left for future research. In the next section, we tentatively accept their validity and explore their implications for economic policy.

10.4 Conclusions

Our analysis of the historical experience of the last twenty years suggests that capital was internationally mobile but that governments acted so as to permit only relatively small capital flows. This makes it difficult to analyze the effects of tax policy changes. Such changes, if not accommodated by other policies, would lead to significant capital flows with associated implications for competitiveness. But the historic record suggests that policy changes are adopted to maintain external balance. If such changes are always adopted, capital is effectively immobile. National investment cannot be increased without increasing national savings. The effect of any policy depends on the policies it engenders. Consider, for example, an investment tax credit. The resulting capital inflow would lead to a trade deficit. If this created pressures leading to an increase in public savings, the ultimate result would be more domestic investment, with only a small effect on the traded-goods sector. If, on the other hand, other countries responded to their capital outflows by strengthening capital controls, the result would be increased domestic interest rates and only relatively small investment increases. In this case short-run competitiveness might actually be improved by investment tax incentives.

Clearly there are no general principles which can be used to assess the effects of different policies in all situations. Neither the analytic benchmark of perfect capital mobility nor the polar opposite assumption that capital is immobile seems appropriate in assessing the effects of tax reforms.

These points are well illustrated by considering the current American situation. The dollar is extremely strong, having risen by about 60% in the last four years. This has led to the large trade and current-account deficits, which are regarded by many observers as a cause for grave concern. Beyond the direct effects on industries producing traded goods, concerns are expressed about the United States becoming a debtor nation, and about a weakening in our national commitment to free trade. Following the Reagan tax incentives, an increase of close to 25% in the capital stock would be necessary to bring the after-tax return to capital back to its former level. Since the United States is not a small country on the world capital market, not all of these funds would come from abroad even if capital were perfectly mobile. But with mobile capital, one would have to predict a cumulative current-account deficit in excess of 15% of GNP in response to the 1981 tax cuts. This is on top of any current-account deficit attributable to federal budget deficits. It seems unlikely that such large, sustained capital inflows will be allowed to materialize. Some combination of increased savings through reduced budget deficits and expansionary monetary policy is likely to be used to restore external balance. Thus, the recent U.S. experience is in a sense the exception that proves the validity of the maintained external balance hypothesis.

Note, finally, that the maintained external balance hypothesis resolves the riddle of why firms producing traded goods favor investment incentives. If they expect these incentives to be coupled with other policies directed at stabilizing the current account, they are rational in advocating investment incentives. This is true if investment incentives are accommodated by increased public savings, expansionary monetary policies, or even protectionist policies. This point may well be illustrated by the evolution of the U.S. economy over the next few years.

Notes

1. Note that the formulation here requires that capital invested in either sector earn the world rate of return R in period 2. As Frankel (1985) has stressed, there is no reason to expect that real interest rates measured relative to a domestic price index that includes both tradeable and nontradeable goods will be equalized across countries. Indeed, as long as purchasing power parity fails as a description of exchange rate behavior, real interest rates cannot be equalized, measured both relative to price changes in tradeable goods and the domestic consumption basket. In the model considered here, despite capital mobility, there is no real interest rate equalization measured in the standard way using general domestic price indices.

2. There is no obvious reason for regressing investment on savings rather than running the reverse regression. The interested reader can compute the coefficient that would be obtained from the reverse regression by dividing the reported coefficient into the regression's R^2. The reverse regression coefficients tend to be a little smaller than the reported coefficients.

3. Zeira (1986), in a very perceptive analysis, notes that this conclusion is only correct if assets are perfect substitutes in individual portfolios. The empirical importance of this qualification is, however, open to question, given the findings of Frankel (1985) that the standard CAPM along with reasonable assumptions regarding risk aversion implies that assets are in fact very close substitutes.

4. I am indebted to Jeff Sachs for bringing Keynes's discussion of this issue to my attention.

5. This argument in many ways parallels the one developed by Roger Gordon in his discussion of this paper.

References

Baldwin, Robert E. 1971. Determinants of the commodity structure of U.S. trade. *American Economic Review* 61 (March): 126–46.

Blanchard, O., and L. Summers. 1984. Perspectives on high world real interest rates. *Brookings Papers on Economic Activity* 2:273–334.

Bruno, M. Adjustment and structural change under supply shocks. NBER Working Paper no. 814.

Caprio, G., and D. Howard. Domestic saving, current accounts, and international capital mobility. International Finance Discussion Paper-244.

Chamley, C. 1981. The welfare costs of capital taxation in a growing economy. *Journal of Political Economy* (June): 468–96.

Eaton, J., and M. Gersovitz. 1981. Debt with potential repudiation: theoretical and empirical analysis. *Review of Economic Studies*.

Feldstein, M. 1983. Domestic savings and international capital movements in the long run and the short run. *European Economic Review* (March): 129–51.

Feldstein, M., and D. Hartman. 1979. The optimal taxation of foreign source investment income. *Quarterly Journal of Economics*.

Feldstein, M., and C. Horioka. 1980. Domestic savings and international capital flows. *The Economic Journal* 90:314–29.

Fieleke, N. 1982. National saving and international investment. In *Saving and government policy*. Conference series no. 25. Boston Federal Reserve Bank.

Frankel, J. 1986. International capital mobility and crowding out in the U.S. economy: imperfect integration of financial markets or of goods markets. In *How open is the U.S. economy?* St. Louis Federal Reserve conference volume.

———. 1985. The implications of mean-variance optimization for four questions in international macroeconomics. *Journal of International Money and Finance.*

Goulder, L., J. Shoven, and J. Whalley, 1983. Domestic tax policy and the foreign sector. In *Behavioral Methods in Tax Simulation Analysis,* ed. M. Feldstein.

Hartman, D. Domestic tax policy and foreign investment: some evidence. NBER Working Paper no. 784.

Keynes, J. M. 1924. Foreign investment and national advantage. *The Nation and Athenaeum* (August 9).

Leamer, Edward E. 1980. The Leontief Paradox reconsidered. *Journal of Political Economy* 88 (June): 495–503.

Lipton, D., and J. Sachs. 1983. Accumulation and growth in a two country model: a simulation approach. *Journal of International Economics.*

Obstfeld, M. 1985. Capital mobility in the world economy: theory and measurement. Carnegie Rochester Public Policy Conference.

Sachs, J. 1981. The current account and macroeconomic adjustment in the 1970s. *Brookings Papers on Economic Activity* 201–82.

———. 1982. The current account in the macroeconomic adjustment process. *Scandinavian Journal of Economics.*

Summers, L. 1979. Tax Policy in a Life Cycle Model. NBER Working Paper no. 302.

Zeira, J. 1986. Risk and the current account. Mimeographed.

Comment   Jeffrey A. Frankel

This paper is a much-needed attempt to interpret the businessman's view that taxation which raises the cost of capital is "bad for international competitiveness," and specifically that cutting corporate income taxes would help the national trade balance. This view needs interpreting, because we would expect, from the identity that the current-account balance is equal to national savings minus investment, that any incentives that succeed in stimulating investment would in general *worsen* the trade balance. At least we would expect this in the short run. In the longer run, intertemporal considerations suggest that the current-account balance will be zero. Summers proposes the size of the tradable-goods sector as the definition of "competitiveness," in place of the size of the trade balance, thus leaving the question open.

The paper is divided into two, very different, parts. The first part is theoretical. Its conclusion is that, if tradable goods are capital intensive, then subsidies to investment will increase the size of the tradable sector,

Jeffrey A. Frankel is a professor of economics at the University of California, Berkeley, and a research associate of the National Bureau of Economic Research.

under the condition of imperfect international capital mobility. The latter qualifying condition is a controversial one. The second half of the paper attempts to measure the degree of capital mobility, along the lines of the Feldstein-Horioka tests of saving-investment correlation. Presumably the aim is to see whether investment incentives do increase the size of the tradable-goods sector; but the capital mobility testing is an entirely self-contained discussion. I will allocate most of my comments to that part of the paper.

There have been many econometric critiques of the Feldstein-Horioka literature, and Summers mentions most of them. The critiques are correct on the econometrics (though Feldstein and Horioka themselves made a better attempt to address problems of econometric endogeneity, through the use of instrumental variables, than many of the critics who followed in their footsteps). But in my view the critiques are beside the point, if the point is to estimate the degree of capital mobility in the sense of the degree of international integration of financial markets. Let us begin by reviewing the statistical facts. They have been found puzzling to many who interpret them in terms of the degree of capital mobility, and in any case are considered striking by all parties.

First, the correlation of national investment with national saving (defined as private savings minus the government budget deficit) is greater than zero, and in fact is relatively close to unity. If one accepts a causal interpretation, the finding says that changes in national saving are offset by net capital inflows only to a relatively minor degree, and are reflected primarily as changes in national investment; fiscal crowding out of investment, for example, does take place. This was the original result of Feldstein and Horioka, interpreted by them as evidencing a low degree of international capital mobility.

Summers adds a second statistical fact by including less-developed countries (LDCs) in the sample: the saving-investment correlation is no lower for industrial countries than for LDCs. This finding, noted earlier by Fieleke (1982, pp. 154–55), seems puzzling. In light of the default risk, the greater government use of capital controls, and the less advanced state of financial markets in LDCs, one would expect to find lower capital mobility for this group.

A third statistical fact is analogous to the preceding one, but in the time dimension rather than the cross-section dimension: the saving-investment correlation is no lower after 1974 than it was before 1974. Again, in light of the greater use of capital controls and the less advanced state of financial markets before 1974 than after, one would expect a higher degree of capital mobility in the later period. The Summers paper—both the results reported in table 10.2 and the discussion of them—is ambiguous on the question of how the saving-investment correlation has changed over time. But Feldstein (1983) and Penati and Dooley (1984) found no sign of a decline in the correlation.[1]

Most economists seem inclined to conclude from the statistical finding that the saving-investment correlation is stubbornly high, that there must be something wrong methodologically with this way of estimating the degree of capital mobility. Hence the many econometric critiques. Most can be subsumed in the general complaint that the righthand-side variable is correlated with the error term, that is, that national saving is endogenous. Though this econometric problem is an ever-present danger in macroeconomics, it is particularly likely to arise when the lefthand-side and righthand-side variables are linked by an identity (via the current account, in this case). There are four common varieties of the critique: the procyclicality of both saving and investment rates, the large-country problem, the government policy reaction problem (which Summers calls the "maintained external balance hypothesis"), and the influence of population growth, or other third factors, on both saving and investment rates. All are potentially serious problems, but in my view all can be handled with some degree of success. A cross-section study largely avoids the procyclicality and large-country problems from the beginning.[2] To deal with the possible endogeneity with respect to the growth rate, Summers adds it as a separate variable, and finds no effect. As a cure for the endogeneity of national saving, he also tries instrumental variables. But his choice of instrumental variable, the government deficit, guarantees a bad outcome because it is also endogenous. This Summers himself concludes, precisely on the grounds of the maintained external balance hypothesis: governments tend to react to current-account imbalances by varying fiscal (among other) policies so as to minimize such imbalances. Feldstein and Horioka used instrumental variables that can more plausibly be argued to be exogenous, such as the ratio of the retirement-age population to the working-age population. But it turns out that such regressions do little or nothing to reduce the coefficient on national savings.[3]

1. I also have found coefficients that are, if anything, higher later in the twentieth century than earlier (Frankel 1986), and, if anything, higher for industrial countries than for LDCs (Dooley, Frankel, and Mathieson 1986).
2. The latter is the problem in a time series study that when a country that is large in world financial markets experiences a fall in savings, there may be an increase in the rate of return to capital and a consequent fall in domestic investment, not because of imperfect capital mobility but because there are (equal) effects on the rate of return and investment everywhere in the world. Obstfeld (1986), for example, attributes the finding of a high saving-investment correlation for the United States to the large-country effect.
3. I consider the level of military expenditure, an important determinant of government expenditure that is driven primarily by political events, to be another good instrumental variable. But using military expenditure and the retirement ratio as instrumental variables does little to reduce the saving coefficient (Frankel 1986).

After the best possible fix-ups are applied, econometric problems undoubtedly still remain. But it seems likely that even genuinely exogenous shifts in national savings do not in fact provoke a sufficiently large capital inflow to keep the domestic rate of return and investment from changing. It is in this sense that the econometric critiques are beside the point.

The condition that we are really interested in testing is that capital is sufficiently mobile to equalize expected real rates of return internationally. After all, the only reason one might have for thinking that national investment rates would be insulated from domestic disturbances would be that investment depends on a rate of return that is in turn tied to an exogenous world rate of return. Subject only to the quality of the data on expected rates of return, equalization of the returns is a condition that can better be tested directly. Tests of real interest rate parity abound; Mishkin (1984) is one example. They all tend to find large and sustained deviations. The observed failure of capital movements to equalize rates of return is itself sufficient to negate the hypothesis that savings should have no effect on investment, econometric problems aside.

Why are real rates of return not equalized? Imperfect integration of financial markets, attributable in the case of LDCs to political risk in particular, is certainly one explanation. But even if political risk and exchange risk were unimportant enough that uncovered interest parity were to hold well, i.e., even if financial markets were perfectly integrated internationally, there would be no reason to expect real interest parity to hold. Let us label the domestic real interest rate $r = i - \pi$, and the foreign real interest rate $r^* = i^* - \pi^*$, where i and i^* are the domestic and foreign nominal interest rates, respectively, and π and π^* are the domestic and foreign expected inflation rates, respectively. Then the real interest differential can be broken into two components:

$$r - r^* = (i - i^* - \Delta s^e) + (\Delta s^e - \pi + \pi^*),$$

where Δs^e, is the expected rate of change of the spot exchange rate. It is clear that even if arbitrage in financial markets were to eliminate the first term, i.e., even if uncovered, or "open," interest parity were to hold, real interest parity would not hold unless the second term, representing expected real depreciation of the currency, were also to equal zero. Expected real depreciation is zero if purchasing power parity holds, but it is well known by now that purchasing power parity empirically does not hold, even approximately and even in the relatively long run. Thus there is good reason to expect real interest parity to fail, and there is in turn no reason to expect savings and investment rates to be uncorrelated, problems of econometric endogeneity aside. International portfolio investors may have reason to arbitrage away gaps in countries' nominal rates of return when expressed in a common numeraire; but they have no reason to arbitrage away a gap between the domestic rate of return expressed in terms of domestic goods and the foreign rate of return expressed in terms of foreign goods. Put differently, crowding out of investment occurs, but the failure of international capital mobility to prevent it may have more to do with the imperfect integration of goods markets than with the imperfect integration of financial markets.

Two qualifications to the purchasing power parity argument can be made. First, statements about tax policy such as Summers has in mind are often made in a context of comparative-statics public finance. In such a context, very long-run measures of expected rates of return, which might show purchasing power parity holding, are relevant. But if this is the argument, then a decade, which is the approximate span of time over which the cross-section studies typically average the savings and investment rates, may not be a long enough run. Expected real depreciation of the U.S. dollar has by a variety of measures been positive throughout the 1980s. (Furthermore, American businessmen's concerns with competitiveness and the trade balance are not primarily concerned with the longer run.)

Second, it should be noted that proponents of the saving-investment approach to measuring capital mobility over the rate of return approach often argue that what matters is the less measurable return on real capital, not the more measurable real return on bonds, and that the two are not necessarily equal even within a country. But foreign investors who purchase equities or undertake direct investment are no more likely to evaluate returns in terms of local purchasing power than are investors who purchase bonds. On the other hand, it is true that political risk, especially in LDCs, has usually been considered a more serious barrier to the equalization of returns on direct investment than on bonds, with the implication that the imperfect integration of financial markets becomes relatively more important for LDCs. In short, all three factors—expected real depreciation, political risk, and exchange risk—can be relevant in explaining international differences in real rates of return.

The position of the Summers paper is that barriers to international capital mobility, such as the three obstacles to real interest rate equalization just named, are not particularly important. The high observed effects of national saving on investment are instead attributed to government behavior under the maintained external balance hypothesis. He ties this conclusion back to the original question of why businessmen claim that they need tax advantages in order to compete internationally. The concluding paragraph offers the novel argument that businessmen expect enhanced investment incentives to lead to a worsening of the current account, which in turn will prompt the government to adopt other measures to move the current account back toward balance (not, presumably, including a rollback of the investment incentives!), and that the businessmen who are in tradable-goods industries will benefit from these other measures. It seems to me that a much less convoluted way of getting the same result is that a reduction in corporate taxes is directly in the interest of corporations, and that they find it useful to cite international competition as their justification. It may be rational for businessmen to try to argue to the public that investment incentives improve the trade balance, just as it is our role as economists to point out that investment incentives, whatever their other advantages, in fact have no such effect.

References

Dooley, Michael, Jeffrey Frankel, and Donald Mathieson. 1986. International capital mobility among industrialized countries vs. LDCs: What do saving-investment correlations tell us? NBER Working Paper no. 2043. Forthcoming in International Monetary Fund *Staff Papers* 34 (Sept. 1987): 503–30.

Feldstein, Martin. 1983. Domestic saving and international capital movements in the long run and the short run. *European Economic Review* 21:129–51.

Feldstein, Martin and Charles Horioka. 1980. Domestic saving and international capital flows. *Economic Journal* 90:314–29.

Fieleke, Norman. 1982. National saving and international investment. In *Saving and Government Policy*. Federal Reserve Bank of Boston Conference Series no. 25.

Frankel, Jeffrey. 1986. International capital mobility and crowding out in the U.S. economy: Imperfect integration of financial markets or of good markets? NBER Working Paper no. 1773. In *How open is the U.S. economy?* R. Hafer, ed. Federal Reserve Bank of St. Louis. Lexington: Lexington Books.

Mishkin, Frederick. 1984. Are real interest rates equal across countries? An investigation of international parity conditions. *Journal of Finance* 39:1345–58.

Obstfeld, Maurice. 1986. Capital mobility in the world economy: Theory and measurement. Eds., Karl Brunner and Allan Meltzer. Carnegie-Rochester Conference Series on Public Policy (supplementary series to the *Journal of Monetary Economics*). Amsterdam: North-Holland.

Penati, Alessandro and Michael Dooley. 1984. Current account imbalances and capital formation in industrial countries, 1949–1981. International Monetary Fund *Staff Papers* 31:1–24.

Comment   Roger H. Gordon

The declining international competitiveness of the United States has been of much concern to policy makers. Summers, by analyzing the

Roger H. Gordon is a professor of economics at the University of Michigan in Ann Arbor and a research associate of the National Bureau of Economic Research.

short- and long-run effects of various policies on international competitiveness, provides an important public service by making this policy debate more informed.[1]

The key question in his analysis is the degree to which the U.S. economy approximates a small, open economy, where there is no direct link between domestic savings and investment. Summers reexamines the evidence presented originally by Feldstein and Horioka (1980) that domestic savings and investment rates are closely linked statistically, and argues that this close link is the result of policy decisions to keep them closely linked.

This argument seems quite plausible. Concern with the current account deficit or surplus certainly affects policy decisions both here and abroad. The recent pressure in the United States to cut the deficit in order to alleviate this trade deficit is only a recent example. How much importance to assign to this factor is a more difficult question, however. Summers's statistical evidence must be interpreted with some care given the large differences between the deficit as actually measured and the size of public savings as it ought to be measured.[2] There is no reason to expect that the measurement errors will be uncorrelated with savings or investment rates.

Several questions remain, however, even if we accept Summers's argument. First, why have governments chosen so consistently to restrict any current account deficit or surplus? Since, given the normal vagaries of policy-making, it seems difficult to attribute the close association between savings and investment across many countries and over an extended period of time entirely to the use of policy, what else may be going on?

The model that Summers develops in the first part of the paper does not really help in answering these questions. As Summers argues, if saving increases in a country, "investment may rise or fall but it is unlikely to change a great deal." In the next section, he argues that if investment increases, then domestic savings should fall.[3] This model therefore cannot help in explaining the close association between saving and investment. In addition, within the model, since the country is a price taker in the international markets, it is easily shown that the government cannot improve welfare by distorting decisions made by

1. However, why policy should be concerned with the size of the traded-goods sector of the economy per se on efficiency or welfare grounds is not clear.

2. Probably the two largest problems in the measure of the deficit are first the omission of the change in the implicit debt of the Social Security and other transfer programs, and second the lack of correction for the effects of inflation on the real value of outstanding debt. See Kotlikoff (1984) for further discussion.

3. This argument ignores any tax increase necessary to finance the investment incentives. It is not clear what happens to savings due to this tax change if a balanced budget is required.

the private market, so would have no clear reason to seek to restrict current account deficits and surpluses—private decisions are Pareto optimal, given internationally set prices.

However, a simple alternative to this model, which I would like to present next, can imply not only a close association between savings and investment if there is no government intervention, even though goods flow freely across borders, but also the desirability on welfare grounds of government intervention to further restrict the current account deficit or surplus.

To keep the story simple, let there be two countries each of which produces a single commodity. The two commodities are not perfect substitutes, and consumers in each country consume both commodities. Each consumer has a relative preference for the locally produced good.

In order to explore savings and investment decisions in the home country, assume that the world lasts for two periods. Output in the foreign country in period i is assumed to be exogenous and to be denoted by Y_i. Domestic output in the first period is also assumed to be exogenous and denoted by X_1. This output can be consumed at home, consumed abroad, or invested at home. Only the locally produced good is suitable for investment. If S denotes first-period investment in the home country, then second-period resources are assumed to equal $S + f(S)$, where $f'(.) > 0$ and $f''(.) < 0$.

Let H_{ij} (F_{ij}) represent the amount of the domestic (foreign) good produced in period i which is consumed that period in country j. The government is assumed not to use any resources, so that the first-period resource constraint implies that $S = H - H_{11} - H_{12}$.

Let $U(H_{11}, F_{11}, H_{21}, F_{21})$ represent the utility of the representative domestic consumer, where $U(.)$ satisfies the normal properties of a utility function. Let the market prices for these four goods be denoted by $(1 + d)$, $P_1(1 + d)$, 1, and P_2 respectively. If this individual maximizes utility subject to the given market prices for the four goods, then among other conditions it must be the case that:

(1a) $U_1/U_3 = 1 + d$, and

(1b) $f' = d$.

Therefore, investment occurs until the marginal product of capital equals the market determined interest factor d, and the marginal time preference rate with respect to the domestic good must also reflect this interest factor.

Similarly, let $V^1(H_{12}, F_{12}) + \beta V^2(H_{22}, F_{22})$ represent the utility of the foreign consumer, where $V^i(.)$ also satisfies normal properties of a utility function.[4] This consumer is subject to the trade balance constraint, which requires that

$$(2) \qquad (1 + d)H_{12} + H_{22} = P_1(1 + d)F_{11} + P_2 F_{21}.$$

Given that $F_{12} = Y_1 - F_{11}$ and $F_{22} = Y_2 - F_{21}$, we can solve for utility maximizing behavior of the foreign consumer subject to the above budget constraint, and find for example that

$$(3a) \qquad V_2^1/V_1^1 = P_1,$$

$$(3b) \qquad V_2^2/V_1^2 = P_2, \text{ and}$$

$$(3c) \qquad V_2^1/V_2^2 = (1 + d) P_1/P_2.$$

It follows from equation (3a) that $P_1 = p^1 (H_{12}, F_{11})$, and from (3b) that $P_2 = p^2(H_{22}, F_{21})$ for some functions $p^1(.)$ and $p^2(.)$. Given standard assumptions about the utility function, all the first derivatives of these functions p^i will be positive.

One interesting case to explore is when the home country is sufficiently small relative to the foreign country that the foreign interest rate can be taken to be exogenous. Denote this rate by r. It then follows from equation (3c) that $(1 + d)P_1/P_2 = 1 + r$, implying that $1 + d = P_2(1 + r)/P_1$. Since d represents the home interest rate, this result tells us how the amounts traded affect the home interest rate.

For example, in the context of Summers's argument, given currently high U.S. deficits, current demand for U.S. goods should be relatively high and the model, for plausible parameter values, would imply a low value of P_1.[5] Conversely, in the second period, when the U.S. debt is repaid, demand for U.S. goods is low and so P_2 should be high. Together these imply that the U.S. interest rate will exceed the foreign interest rate r. Since investors will invest in any project at home earning at least the domestic interest rate, we find that the deficit should cause a drop in domestic investment, and also, given equation (1a), an increased incentive to save. Therefore, this model describes how market forces can push domestic savings and domestic investment together.

Assume now that through its tax policy the government can determine the consumer's consumption bundle. What government policy will maximize the consumer's utility, taking account of the effect of the policy on market prices?

The objective of the government is to maximize $U(H_{11}, F_{11}, H_{21}, F_{21})$ subject to the domestic resource and the trade balance constraints:

---

4. The superscripts are used primarily to make clear what the arguments of V are in any given context and not necessarily to describe differences in tastes between the periods.

5. Examples certainly exist, however, with the opposite implication, e.g., when the deficit results primarily from an increased demand for the foreign good.

(4a) $\quad H_{22} + H_{21} = f(X - H_{11} - H_{12}) + X - H_{11} - H_{12}$, and

(4b) $\qquad P_2(1 + r) H_{12}/P_1 + H_{22} = P_2[(1 + r)F_{11} + F_{21}]$.

The first-order conditions with respect to H_{12} and H_{22} together imply that

(5) $\qquad 1 + f' = (1 + d)[\dfrac{1 - (H_{12}/P_1)(\partial P_1/\partial H_{12})}{1 - (H_{22}/P_2)(\partial P_2/\partial H_{22})}]$, and

(6) $\qquad U_1/U_3 = 1 + f'$.

Recall that without government intervention, $f' = d$. The extra expression in equation (5), to the extent it differs from one, represents the desired intervention by the government. The numerator and denominator each take the form of $(1 - 1/\epsilon)$, where ϵ is a price elasticity of demand abroad for the domestic output. But this is just the standard form for the ratio of the marginal revenue to the price when a monopolist sells in a given market. To the extent that the price elasticities differ in the two periods, the government should push sales towards that period where the price elasticity is greater.[6]

To explore the implications of equation (5) let us examine two examples. Consider first the situation where the foreign consumer's utility function can be expressed as

(7) $\qquad V(H_{i2}, F_{i2}) = (H_{i2} + A)^\alpha F_{i2}^{(1-\alpha)}$.

One way to rationalize the extra term A is to argue that there are really fewer goods than countries, so that the home country is not the only supplier of its particular output. The home country takes as given the supply of its good produced elsewhere, denoted by A, when making its own decisions.[7] The smaller the home country's share of the market for its output, the larger is A relative to H_{i2}.

Given this utility function, equation (5) can be reexpressed as

(5a) $\qquad 1 + f' = (1 + d)\dfrac{1 - H_{12}/(H_{12} + A)}{1 - H_{22}/(H_{22} + A)}$.

If current deficits cause current exports of the domestic good to be a relatively small share of the foreign supply of this good, then equation (5a) indicates that the marginal product of capital should be raised above what would occur without intervention. In other words, given the low current rate of savings, there is an incentive for the government to raise the domestic interest rate so as to restrict investment and

6. For a related argument on the use of government policy to exploit monopoly power in the international securities market, see Gordon and Varian (1986).

7. It would be interesting but more complicated to explore more sophisticated interactions of the policies in different countries.

encourage savings, pushing the savings and investment rates together.[8] This is just the type of government behavior that Summers argues does occur.

Note in equation ($5a$) that if A equals zero, so that the foreign utility function is Cobb-Douglas, the equation breaks down. In this case, the optimal policy is to sell virtually nothing abroad in each period—given the Cobb-Douglas specification, foreigners will spend a fixed fraction of their income buying the domestic good, regardless of the available supply, so that the optimal supply from the home country's viewpoint is zero. Assuming the foreign consumer's utility function to be Cobb-Douglas is *not* an innocuous assumption.

Equation ($5a$) also implies that when A is larger, perhaps due to the home country being smaller, there is less incentive for government intervention. This is consistent with the evidence in Summers which shows that savings and investment are less closely related in a sample of smaller countries than they are in the OECD countries.[9] Even if there were no important government intervention, if A is larger then the behavior of the home country should have less effect on the size of P_1 relative to P_2 given this utility function, implying that the home country's domestic interest rate would be less affected by the time pattern of its trade balance. This further helps explain the above evidence.

As a second example, assume that the empirical evidence indicates that $\ln H_{i2} = aP_i + Z\beta$ for some set of coefficients a and β, and for some set of other explanatory variables Z. Given this empirical evidence, equation (5) can be reexpressed as

$$
(5c) \qquad 1 + f' = (1 + d)\frac{(1 - 1/aP_1)}{(1 - 1/aP_2)}.
$$

In this example, a current deficit should lead to a strong dollar, so a relatively small value of P_1. Therefore, equation ($5c$) implies that the government should lower the domestic interest rate, stimulating investment and discouraging savings. This specification implies government behavior contrary to Summers's argument.

At least with the first example, this model helps explain why governments may in fact have acted so as to restrict the trade deficit or surplus. Given the large budget and trade deficit currently in the United States, the model can be used to argue for increased savings incentives and perhaps for a cut in the budget deficit. These policies, by raising the price of goods produced abroad, would improve the competitive

8. Given equation (6) however, we see that there is no incentive to cause the value of the marginal product of capital to differ from the marginal time preference rate.

9. Similar evidence on a weaker association between savings and investment in smaller countries is found in Obstfeld (1985).

position of domestic firms. However, the model would argue against enacting investment incentives, given the budget deficit, and in fact would support raising the required rate of return on domestic investment in line with the increase in the return to savings, contrary to what is advocated by those concerned with international competitiveness. The motivation behind these policies in the model is to prevent the price of U.S.–produced goods from being driven down too far when the debt is eventually repaid and the market is flooded with U.S. goods. Policies which reduce the build-up in the debt, by increasing savings and reducing investment, look attractive within the model.

This model therefore seems to provide a framework that can rationalize not only the evidence in Feldstein and Horioka (1980) that current account deficits and surpluses never become very large but also the argument by Summers that governments seem to set policy to further restrict these deficits and surpluses. How important government policy is relative to market forces in pushing savings and investment rates in a country together remains an open question, however.

References

Feldstein, Martin S., and Charles Horioka. 1980. Domestic savings and international capital flows. *The Economic Journal* 90:314–29.
Gordon, Roger H., and Hal R. Varian. 1986. Taxation of asset income in the presence of a world securities market. NBER Working Paper no. 1994.
Kotlikoff, Laurence J. 1984. Taxation and savings: a neoclassical perspective. *Journal of Economic Literature* 22:1576–1629.
Obstfeld, Maurice. 1985. Capital mobility in the world economy: theory and measurement. NBER Working Paper no. 1692 (August).

Contributors

Andrew Abel
Department of Finance
The Wharton School
University of Pennsylvania
2319 Steinberg-Dietrich Hall
Philadelphia, PA 19104

Joshua Aizenman
Graduate School of Business
University of Chicago
1101 East 58th Street
Chicago, IL 60637

David Backus
Department of Economics
Queen's University
Kingston, Ontario K7L 3N6
Canada

Olivier Jean Blanchard
Department of Economics
Massachusetts Institute of
   Technology
E52-252A
Cambridge, MA 02139

William H. Branson
Woodrow Wilson School
Princeton University
Princeton, NJ 08544

Willem H. Buiter
Department of Economics
Economic Growth Center
Yale University
27 Hillhouse Avenue
P.O. Box 1987—Yale Station
New Haven, CT 06520

Guillermo A. Calvo
Department of Economics
University of Pennsylvania
3718 Locust Walk
Philadelphia, PA 19104

John T. Cuddington
Department of Economics
Walsh School of Foreign Service
Georgetown University
Washington, DC 20057

Michael Devereux
Department of Economics
University of Toronto
150 St. George Street
Toronto, Ontario M5S 1A1
Canada

Rudiger Dornbusch
Department of Economics
Massachusetts Institute of
   Technology
E52-357
Cambridge, MA 02139

Stanley Fischer
Department of Economics
Massachusetts Institute of
  Technology
E52-280A
Cambridge, MA 02139

Robert P. Flood
Department of Economics
Room I-320
Northwestern University
2003 Sheridan Road
Evanston, IL 60201

Jeffrey A. Frankel
Department of Economics
University of California
250 Barrows Hall
Berkeley, CA 94720

Jacob A. Frenkel
Department of Economics
University of Chicago
1126 East 59th Street
Chicago, IL 60637

Roger H. Gordon
Department of Economics
University of Michigan
Ann Arbor, MI 48109

Robert J. Hodrick
Department of Finance
Kellogg Graduate School of
  Management
Northwestern University
2003 Sheridan Road
Evanston, IL 60201

Patrick J. Kehoe
Department of Economics
University of Minnesota
1035 Management and Economics
271 Nineteenth Avenue South
Minneapolis, MN 55455

Kent P. Kimbrough
Department of Economics
Duke University
Durham, NC 27706

Malcolm D. Knight
Centre for Labour Economics
The London School of Economics
  and Political Science
Houghton Street
London WC2A 2AE
United Kingdom

Linda S. Kole
Department of Economics
University of Maryland
College Park, MD 20742

Paul R. Masson
External Adjustment Division
Research Department
International Monetary Fund
700 Nineteenth Street, NW
Washington, DC 20431

Warwick J. McKibbin
National Bureau of Economic
  Research
1050 Massachusetts Avenue
Cambridge, MA 02138

Robert G. Murphy
Department of Economics
Boston College
Chestnut Hill, MA 02167

Maurice Obstfeld
Department of Economics
University of Pennsylvania
3718 Locust Walk
Philadelphia, PA 19104

Alessandro Penati
Department of Finance
Wharton School of Management
3402 Steinberg-Dietrich Hall
University of Pennsylvania
Philadelphia, PA 19104

Douglas Purvis
Department of Economics
Queen's University
Kingston, Ontario K7L 3N6
Canada

Kenneth Rogoff
Department of Economics
University of Wisconsin
1180 Observatory Drive
Madison, WI 53706

Jeffrey D. Sachs
Department of Economics
Littauer M-14
Harvard University
Cambridge, MA 02138

Alan C. Stockman
Department of Economics
University of Rochester
Rochester, NY 14627

Lawrence H. Summers
Department of Economics
Littauer Center 229
Harvard University
Cambridge, MA 02138

Stephen J. Turnovsky
Department of Economics
University of Illinois
330 Commerce West
1206 South Sixth Street
Champaign, IL 61820

Sweder van Wijnbergen
Country Policy Department
The World Bank
1818 H Street, NW
Washington, DC 20433

Author Index

Subject Index